Interpretive Guide
to the
Millon
Clinical
Multiaxial
Inventory

2ND EDITION

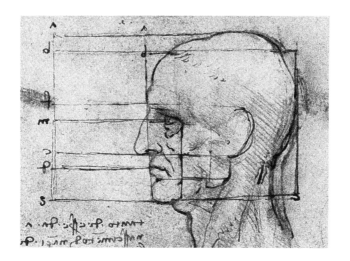

Interpretive Guide
to the
Millon
Clinical
Multiaxial
Inventory

2ND EDITION

JAMES P. CHOCA
ERIC VAN DENBURG

AMERICAN PSYCHOLOGICAL ASSOCIATION

WASHINGTON, DC

Published by
American Psychological Association
750 First Street, NE
Washington, DC 20002

Copies may be ordered from
APA Order Department
P.O. Box 92984
Washington, DC 20090-2984

In the UK and Europe, copies may be ordered from
American Psychological Association
3 Henrietta Street
Covent Garden, London
WC2E 8LU England

Typeset in Futura and New Baskerville by EPS Group Inc., Easton, MD

Printer: Braun-Brumfield, Inc., Ann Arbor, MI
Cover Designer: Minker Design, Bethesda, MD
Technical/Production Editors: Mollie R. McCormick and Ida Audeh

Library of Congress Cataloging-in-Publication Data
Choca, James. 1945–
    Interpretive guide to the Millon Clinical Multiaxial Inventory / James P. Choca and Eric J. Van Denburg.—2nd ed.
        p.   cm.
    Includes bibliographical references and index.
    ISBN 1-55798-383-6 (acid-free paper)
    1. Millon Clinical Multiaxial Inventory.   2. Personality disorders—Diagnosis.
I. Van Denburg, Eric J. (Eric James)   II. Title.
    [DNLM: 1. Personality Disorders—diagnosis.]
RC473.M47C48   1996
616.89'075—dc20   96-28271
                                                                      CIP

British Library Cataloguing-in-Publication Data
A CIP record is available from the British Library

Printed in the United States of America
First edition

Contents

Foreword to the First Edition

Professor Choca has begun his preface to this exemplary book by offering a brief glimpse into the origins of his professional career. Perhaps I can be permitted to sketch the early events that gave rise to the professional career of the Millon Clinical Multiaxial Inventory (MCMI).

A year or two after the publication in 1969 of my *Modern Psychopathology* text, I began, with some regularity, to receive letters and phone calls from graduate students who read the book and thought it provided ideas that could aid them in formulating their dissertations. Most inquired about the availability of an "operational" measure they could use to assess or diagnose the pathologies of personality that were generated by the text's theoretical model. Regretfully, I said that there was no such tool available. Nevertheless, I encouraged them to pursue whatever lines of interest they may have had in the subject. Some were sufficiently motivated to state that they would attempt to develop their own "Millon" instrument as part of the dissertation enterprise. At first, I was pleased to see the appeal of my work and considered such aspirations to be not only ambitious but highly commendable.

As the number of these potential Millon progenies grew into the teens, however, my concern grew proportionately regarding both the diversity and adequacy of these representations of the theory. To establish a measure of instrumental uniformity for future investigators, as well as to assure at least a modicum of psychometric quality among tools that ostensibly reflected the theory's constructs, I was prompted (perhaps "driven" is a more accurate word) to consider undertaking the test-construction task myself. At that time, in early 1971, I fortunately was directing a research supervision group composed of psychologists-and psychiatrists-in-training during their internship and residency periods. All of them had read *Modern Psychopathology* and found my proposal of working together to develop instruments to identify and quantify the test's personality constructs to be both worthy and challenging.

I set as our initial task that of exploring alternate methods for gathering relevant clinical data. About 11 or 12 of us were involved in that early phase. Some were asked to analyze the possibilities of identifying new indexes from well-established projective tests, such as the Rorschach and the Thematic Apperception Test; others were to investigate whether we could compose relevant scales from existing objective inventories, such as the Sixteen Factor Personality Questionnaire (16PF) and the Minnesota Multiphasic Personality Inventory (MMPI). Another group examined the potential inherent in developing a new and original structured interview. After 4 or 5 months of weekly discussions, the group concluded that an entirely new instrument would be required if we were to represent the full scope of the theory, especially its diverse and then-novel pathological personality patterns (our work, it should be recalled, preceded by several years that undertaken by the DSM–III Task Force). It was judged further that we would attempt to construct both a self-report inventory and a semistructured interview schedule.

Naively, we assumed that both construction tasks could be completed in about 18 months, a time period that would allow several members of the research group to participate on a continuing basis. Despite the fact that we "postponed" developing the interview schedule after a brief initial period, the "more limited" task of the inventory took almost 7 years to complete. The framework and preliminary item selections of the inventory were well underway, however, by the end of the first full year of our work and was described briefly in a book I coauthored in 1972: *Research Methods in Psychopathology*. The initial forms of the clinical instrument were entitled the *Millon-Illinois Self-Report Inventory*; it was at this early phase that Jim Choca became acquainted with the test-construction project, although he was by then quite knowledgeable about the theory and its personality derivations. Since then, he has remained one among a small group of very early adherents who has not only followed the development of the test but has continued to contribute to its further progress. For his diligence and creative efforts, he, and his younger colleagues, have both my respect and admiration.

In this book, Choca, Shanley, and Van Denburg join that growing list of psychologists and psychiatrists who demonstrate that valid personality assessments are neither impertinent nor grandiose fantasies of an arrogant and inchoate science. As I have written elsewhere, psychodiagnostic procedures in the past contained more than their share of mystique. Not only were assessments often an exercise in oracular craft and intuitive artistry, but they typically were clothed in obscure and esoteric jargon. A change in the character of personality theory and assessment began to brew in the late 1960s. Slow though these advances might have been, there were clear signs that new ideas would soon emerge. Projective techniques such as the Rorschach began to be analyzed quantitatively and were increasingly anchored to the empirical domain. The so-called objective inventories, such as the 16PF and MMPI, were being interpreted increasingly in terms of configural profiles. No longer approached as sets of separate scales, these formerly segmented instruments were now being analyzed as holistic integrations that possessed clinical significance only as gestalt composites. In addition, the former insistence that diagnostic interpretation be "objective," that is, anchored solely to empirical correlates, gave way to clinical syntheses, including the "dynamics" of the previously maligned projectives. Although part-function instruments, oriented toward one expressive form of pathology or another (e.g., anxiety or depression), are still popular, the newest tools moved increasingly toward composite structures, (i.e., "whole" personalities). These personality formulations were not conceived of as random sets or discrete attributes (i.e., scales) that must be individually deduced and then pieced together but as integrated configurations from the start. Hence, we have seen the development of various tools explicitly designed to diagnose, for example, the "borderline" personality. The MCMI represents the most recent trend in holistic personality scales, going one step beyond most techniques by including all of the *Diagnostic and Statistical Manual* (*DSM*) personality disorders in a single inventory. Holism is not limited to inventories alone. New structured interview schedules and clinical rating scales have been developed to provide another rich source of data. Not to be overlooked is the sound psychometric manner in which most of these newer tools have been constructed, thereby wedding the empirical and quantitative features that were the major strength of the structured objective inventories with the dynamic and integrative qualities that characterized the more intuitive projective techniques. It is in bridging the quantitative and integrative that Choca, Shanley, and Van Denburg make their special contribution in this book.

We should also not overlook the very special status assigned the personality syndromes in the *DSM*. With the advent of the third edition of this official classification, personality disorders not only gained a place of consequence among syndromal categories but became central to its multiaxial schema. The logic for assigning personality its own special status is more than a matter of differentiating syndromes of a more acute and dramatic form from those of a longstanding and prosaic character. More relevant to this partitioning decision was the assertion that personality can serve usefully as a dynamic substrate from which clinicians can better grasp the significance and meaning of their patients' transient and florid disorders. In the *DSM*, then, personality disorders not only attained a nosological status of prominence in their own right but were assigned a contextual role that made them fundamental to the understanding and interpretation of all other psychopathologies. Here, again, Choca, Shanley, and Van Denburg have provided readers with an opportunity to examine the various ways in which the MCMI demonstrates the interrelationships between Axis I and Axis II.

As Choca notes in his preface, the approach he and his colleagues have taken in the text differs in certain respects from my most recent formulations; they remain truer to my early notions than I have. Hence, I am hesitant to endorse their entire thesis; for example, I do not share the confidence they show in drawing certain distinctions among their profile interpretations, nor do I believe that the MCMI personality "disorder" scales are best conceived of as personality "styles." This latter point reflects matters of a pragmatic rather than of a conceptual nature. Although the issue deserves a full explication on my part, the foreword to a book is not the place to expand on contentions of this sort. To be brief, I have judged it best to opt in favor of focusing an inventory on target rather than broad-based populations; hence, the MCMI is oriented toward matters of import among adult mental health patients, the MAPI centers attention on adolescent clinical populations, the MBHI focuses on those whose primary ailments are of a medical or physical nature, and the forthcoming MPSI (Millon Personality Style Inventory) addresses traits among nonclinical or so-called normal adults (as can be seen, I, too, have chosen the "style" terminology, but only for people who do not evince discernable psychic pathology).

Despite differences such as these, I consider this book to be the product of research clinicians of the highest order, and I am delighted by the thoroughness and balance they have shown in presenting the strengths and limitations of the MCMI. I continue to learn much from them, as no doubt will readers of this book.

Perhaps the text's greatest value to its readers is an implicit one, namely, that the growing appeal of the MCMI lies in its heuristic fertility.

The inventory is more than another "objective" tool in the diagnostician's assessment kit. It provides clinicians with a theoretical schema for mastering the realm of personality pathology, a means for understanding the processes that underlie their patient's overtly dysfunctional behaviors, thoughts, and feelings. Moreover, the openness of the theory not only illuminates the patient's personal life but encourages the clinician to uncover insights beyond those on which the MCMI's interpretative model has been grounded.

Finally, let me congratulate the authors on being the first to provide the profession with a full text on the instrument. Although several other MCMI volumes are "in the pipeline," few will be as informed and as carefully reasoned as theirs.

Theodore Millon

Acknowledgments

We would like to thank all of those who have theorized about or researched the fields of personology and psychometrics. High on that list, of course, is Theodore Millon. In our opinion, Dr. Millon's well-conceptualized personality prototypes have given the field of personology a new and exciting beginning. His personal encouragement, and the support that our work has always received from him, have given further impetus to our enthusiasm about personology.

This book contains the contributions of many other individuals. Until his death in 1991, Dr. Robert B. Meagher was often the person we consulted about our ideas for the MCMI. His friendship and opinions have been painfully missed.

We are indebted to our research associates and past or present members of the staff at Lakeside. The list of such people includes Mary Ellen Bratu, Linda Bresolin, Ann Buckinham, Dan Garside, Eve Gordon, Alexander Kristevski, Terrill Loane, Elie Mangoubi, Sarah Meagher, Kevin Miller, Jeri Morris, Andrew Mouton, Ann Newman, Paul Retzlaff, Luke Shanley, and Steven Strack. The input of professionals at other hospitals where we work, especially Dr. Rose Gomez, also has been greatly appreciated.

We are indebted for the support that our professional projects have always received from the hospital administration, especially our chief of staff, Dr. C. Raymond Zeiss, and our director, Mr. Joseph L. Moore.

The help of Diana Kristufek, who typed much of the manuscript and helped with the preparatory work, was invaluable. We are indebted to Beata Plaza for the administration and processing of many inventories. Our librarian, Linda Schmidt, consistently provided us with the many necessary references in a competent and effective manner.

This edition of the book benefited from the comments and recommendations of reviewers of the first edition, such as the work of Jon Allen (1993), Richard Lanyon (1993), and Kaser-Boyd (1993).

Finally, we would like to thank the staff of the Books Department of the American Psychological Association (APA), particularly APA Books Director Julia Frank-McNeil, Acquisitions and Development Manager Mary Lynn Skutley, Development Editor Ted Baroody, and Technical/Production Editors Mollie R. McCormick and Ida Audeh.

James P. Choca
Eric Van Denburg

Introduction

This book was written to help professionals in the mental health fields, particularly psychologists, understand and interpret any of the three versions of the Millon Clinical Multiaxial Inventory (MCMI). To appreciate all sections of this book, readers will need to be acquainted with the basic concepts in the field of psychological testing and statistics. Knowledge of psychopathology and the fourth edition of the *Diagnostic and Statistical Manual of Mental Disorders* (*DSM–IV*; American Psychiatric Association, 1994), the psychiatric classification system, also will be necessary.

The MCMI is available in three versions: the original (MCMI-I), the second edition (MCMI-II), and the most current edition, the MCMI-III. This second edition of our *Interpretive Guide* was written to include the third version of the MCMI and to update our discussions with the multitude of studies that became available after the publication of our first edition in 1992. We also tried to take into consideration the criticisms and many suggestions for improvements we received about the first edition. Following one of those suggestions from a reviewer, and Craig's (1993b) book of narratives, we have included literature references in the personality narratives (chap. 6), so that the book can be used as a more actuarial guide. This edition of the *Interpretive Guide* also includes enhancements in the statistical discussions that were part of the first edition and compares the MCMI with many more personality instruments than the previous edition.

Throughout this work, we use the label *MCMI* when the issue being discussed applies to any version of the test. Otherwise, we note whether we are referring to the MCMI-I, MCMI-II, or the MCMI-III.

The book is divided into 10 chapters. We begin with an overview of how the test was designed and organized (chap. 1). A brief description of the kinds of items used for each of the clinical scales also is included in that chapter. In chapter 2, we discuss the basics of personality style theory and the model that provides the theoretical underpinning for the MCMI. Chapter 3 reviews the processes used to standardize the three versions of the test and the statistical properties of those instruments. In chapters four and five, we explore extraneous variables that may affect the validity of the instrument, both in terms of individual variables (chap. 4) and the response sets used by the person taking the test (chap. 5).

We then share our ideas about how the MCMI can be used in the assessment of personality styles (chap. 6) and provide our own narratives. The use of the test in the assessment of personality disorders and clinical syndromes is discussed in chapter 7. In chapter 8 we explore the use of the MCMI with other psychological tests. To further aid in the clinical use of the test, we provide five case reports from our own practice in chapter 9. We conclude with a discussion of how the MCMI may be useful in treatment planning and psychotherapy.

Part I

Design, Development, and Operating Characteristics of the MCMI

Overview of the MCMI

The Millon Clinical Multiaxial Inventory (MCMI) is a 175-item, true–false self-report psychological inventory intended to be used with psychiatric patients. The MCMI is now one of the most popular instruments of its kind (Piotrowski & Keller, 1989; Piotrowski & Lubin, 1989, 1990). The inventory is being used in other countries and has been translated into several other languages (Luteijn, 1990; Montag & Comrey, 1987; Mortensen & Simonsen, 1990; Simonsen & Mortensen, 1990). During the past 5 years, only two personality tests (the Minnesota Multiphasic Personality Inventory [MMPI] and the Rorschach) have been the subject of more published studies than the MCMI (Butcher & Rouse, 1996; Ritzler, 1996).

In contrast to the empirical-keying method used for the MMPI (Hathaway & McKinley, 1967), the MCMI items were chosen on a theoretical basis, following the concepts and ideas developed by Millon before the creation of the inventory.

In keeping with the current psychiatric nosology, the MCMI is partly categorical in nature: It has different scales to measure different prototypes (e.g., the dependent personality) that are conceptually different from other entities (e.g., the narcissistic personality). It avoids some of the drawbacks of a categorical system (see Widiger, 1992) by offering dimensional scores for each of the prototypes. In other words, cutoff scores and different scales allow the classification of the examinee as having or not having a particular attribute, and the inventory still permits measurement of the level of strength of any of the attributes.

The MCMI-I has 20 clinical scales, the MCMI-II has 22, and the MCMI-III has 24. The scales are clustered into four groups: personality scales, severe personality patterns, clinical syndromes, and severe clinical syndromes. All versions of the test also have an adjustment factor and a Validity scale. The MCMI-II and the MCMI-III have two other scales measuring examinee response tendencies.

In this chapter, we discuss the use of the MCMI, the type of individual who may be an appropriate examinee, and the advantages of this test over similar instruments. How the test is administered and scored is covered next; throughout those two sections, we focus on the literature about the test rather than on the actual scoring details (for which the reader is referred to the test manual). A review of the scales, and the types of items that the different scales contain, then is presented. We conclude by presenting the logic that is followed in interpreting MCMI results.

Uses of the MCMI

One way in which the MCMI can be used is for clinical decision making, or the identification of individuals who have or do not have a particular disorder or psychological attribute. For instance, the MCMI-I has performed well in predicting which individuals would be recommended for discharge from the air force (Butters, Retzlaff, & Gibertini, 1986; Retzlaff & Deatherage, 1993). Although it also proved capable of significantly discriminating between the incarcerated felons who dropped out of school and those who completed the program, the means obtained for the two groups were so similar that the test may not be easily used for this purpose (Ahrens, Evans, & Barnett, 1990).

The fact that the MCMI weighted scores are tied to the base rate (BR) of a particular attribute potentially makes this instrument highly useful in a selection type of situation. In an article that has become a classic in the psychometric literature, Meehl and Rosen (1955) highlighted the importance of examining local prevalences when a test is used to place examinees into diagnostic groups. Consider, for instance, a psychiatric ward in an upper-middle-class neighborhood in which 95% of the patients carry the diagnosis of major depression. If a depression scale were to be used for diagnosing depression in such a setting, the clinician would have a difficult time obtaining results that were much better than chance. Clinicians can calculate the gain the scale would offer by determining the positive predictive power of the scale in their specific situation.[1] If the gain is not sufficient, it may be possible to improve the test performance using the bootstrap methodology (see the section on operating characteristics in chap. 3). Although in some settings the gain may still not be enough to warrant the use of the test, the MCMI can usually improve diagnostic accuracy enough to make the testing worthwhile.

The MCMI has been used to describe the psychological characteristics of a sample (e.g., Bryer, 1990). When the sample is made up of individuals with a common psychological attribute or clinical diagnosis (e.g., alcohol abusers), the findings can be generalized to speak for that particular group of people. The many studies that exemplify this use are covered throughout this book.

Even more commonly, the MCMI is used to obtain information about a particular individual. In the chapters that follow, we also review many such attempts, as well as how the information thus obtained can be used in therapy.

Wakefield and Underwager (1993) warned against the uninformed use of the MCMI in a forensic setting. When used properly, however, the test also can be helpful in the courts. For readers interested in this use, we recommend consulting McCann and Dyer (1996).

The MCMI was designed to measure personality traits and psychopathology. If the question of interest does not involve directly one of these two areas, the use of this test probably is inappropriate. Consider, for instance, a situation in which one desires to learn about an individual's marital stability. Because neither personality traits nor psychopathology address directly the issue of marital longevity, a diagnostician in this situation would be better off using other instruments.

---

[1] The positive predictive power (PPP) can be calculated using the following equation: PPP $= (P \times Sn)/(P \times Sn) + (1 - P)(1 - Sp)$, where P is the local prevalence, Sn is the sensitivity of the scale from the test manual, and Sp is the specificity of the scale (Gibertini, Brandenburg, & Retzlaff, 1986). Applying this equation to the example given earlier and using the values for the Depression scale of the MCMI-III, we would obtain a PPP of .98: PPP = $(.95 \times .57)/(.95 \times .57) + (1 - .95)(1 - .73)$ = .98. Because we would be able to guess correctly 95% of the time by assuming that all patients in the ward were depressed, the scale would help us improve our decision effectiveness by only 3% ([.98 − .95] × 100) and may not be worth the bother. In a more heterogeneous setting, where the prevalence of depression is 30%, the PPP would be .48 and the gain we would achieve by using the Major Depression scale would be a more enticing 18%. More generally, the higher the prevalence of an attribute in a particular population, the less the statistical gain one would achieve by using any instrument.

The Appropriate Examinee

Some minimal requirements have to be met before the test can be administered meaningfully. The examinee has to be old enough to fit the norms of the test and has to be intellectually and emotionally intact enough to make sense of the test items. Although most of the items, at least in the case of the MCMI-II, require only fourth- or fifth-grade reading skills (Schinka & Borum, 1993), special caution is recommended for those who have fewer than 8 years of education.

As a self-report questionnaire, the MCMI is likely to be most productive and revealing when the examinee is reasonably intelligent, has no difficulty understanding the items, knows himself or herself well enough to answer the questions accurately, and is willing to share what he or she knows openly and nondefensively. In other words, the ideal examinee is one who can become an active collaborator in the diagnostic process and has the necessary skills to be an effective contributor in this enterprise. Unfortunately, clinicians often are called on to test people who are not optimal examinees and who, for whatever reason, do not meet all of these requirements. The less ideal the examinee is, of course, the less meaningful the results are bound to be. In extreme cases, such results should be seen as invalid and should be disregarded. In any case, the limitations of having a self-report inventory should be kept in mind.

Millon (e.g., 1982, 1983, 1987, 1994) repeatedly has warned against the use of the inventory with individuals who are not psychiatric patients. His argument has been that the test was designed for, and standardized with, a psychiatric population and that the test norms may not be valid if the examinee does not fit the standardizing group. Moreland (1992), going a step farther, suggested that the clinical group with which the test is used must be similar to that used to standardize the test.

We have taken issue with that viewpoint (Choca, Shanley, et al., 1992). The major argument in favor of the restriction is the principle that psychological tests should be used only with individuals who resemble the norming population. On a test of manual dexterity, for instance, it is obviously inappropriate to compute the standard score of an 80-year-old individual using norms from adolescents. However, the principle can and should be disregarded when there is a good reason to do so. Neuropsychologists routinely use the Wechsler Adult Intelligence Scale, a test standardized with individuals who had not suffered brain damage, to measure the effects of brain damage. In this case, the whole purpose of the testing is to be able to compare the examinee with a population who may be different, at least in terms of brain functioning, from him or her.

We do not think that there is anything intrinsically wrong with using the MCMI with individuals who are not psychiatric patients as long as the clinician keeps in mind the group with which the examinee is being compared. In spite of our viewpoint, we do not take Millon's (1982, 1983, 1987, 1994) concerns lightly. Several of the properties of the inventory make the scores obtained by the nonpsychiatric examinee difficult to interpret.

One problem in interpreting the scores of a nonpsychiatric examinee is that the weighted score used by the test, the BR score, is anchored on the prevalence of particular attributes in the psychiatric population (see chap. 3). From a purely statistical standpoint, the test would be expected to overdiagnose problems with the nonpsychiatric examinee. The reason for this is that the cutoff score for the different scales is set to diagnose a proportion of the population consistent with the prevalence of the characteristic in the psychiatric sample. Choosing the same proportion in a nonpsychiatric sample, in whom the prevalence of the trait is much lower, would lead to having too many individuals scoring above the cutoff point.

Looking at the issue from an item content point of view, on the other hand, would lead to the opposite expectation. In our response to Wetzler (1990), we argued that the severity of the items, tailored as it is for individuals having emotional problems, may mean that these items would not be endorsed by less disturbed individuals (Choca, Shanley, et al., 1992). The lack of endorsement then would result in an underdiagnosis of psychological attributes. Thus, from this vantage point, scores below the cutoff may still be revealing meaningful information in the case of a nonpsychiatric individual. A BR score of 35 or below clearly would be indicative of an absence of the attribute being measured because that score was used as the anchor point for the average in the nonpsychiatric sample. However, the clinician would have no scientific way of determining what to interpret among the scores that fall above a BR score of 35.

Users of the MCMI often have disregarded Millon's instruction to use the test only with psychiatric patients, and there are several published studies involving a nonpsychiatric sample (e.g., Repko & Cooper, 1985). An additional problem with Millon's stance is the issue of what constitutes a psychiatric patient. The chronically psychotic individual who has multiple admissions to psychiatric wards obviously is a psychiatric patient, but what about a college student who uses the counseling service at the university when he is feeling depressed because his girl-friend left him? Is he a psychiatric patient? What about the high-functioning woman who has become anxious and uncomfortable while having to compete in a male-dominated law firm? In spite of the specific criteria used in the fourth edition of the *Diagnostic and Statistical Manual of Mental Disorders* (*DSM–IV;* American Psychiatric Association, 1994), the current nosology still largely avoids where the boundary is between normality and psychopathology (Kendall, 1983; Sabshin, 1989). Moreover, clinicians occasionally are asked to test individuals to decide precisely on whether the individual has a diagnosable psychiatric disorder; if it is inappropriate to use an instrument designed for psychiatric patients, we may be creating an unsolvable dilemma.

After consideration of all of these issues, we continue to use the MCMI with people who are not emotionally disturbed, but we do so cautiously. In our experience, almost all examinees will have an elevated score on at least one of the basic personality scales, and such a finding should not be taken to mean that they have a personality disorder (see chap. 6 for further discussion). On the other hand, we expect nonpsychiatric examinees to have no elevations on any of the severe personality scales or on the clinical syndrome scales. If such elevations do occur, we would search for further evidence of psychopathology in the history or in other test results before making a diagnosis. The user also will have to make other appropriate adjustments. For one thing, the narratives often have to be altered: Instead of talking about "obsessions" and "compulsions," one may discuss the examinee's orderly nature and preference for well-established behavior patterns.

Advantages of the MCMI

The choice of the MCMI over another self-report inventory is partly a matter of personal preference and partly dependent on the professional's competence in interpreting the test protocol. There are, however, good arguments for encouraging clinicians to choose this instrument instead of others.

In our opinion, the main advantage the MCMI has over its main competitor, the MMPI, is that it is especially designed to measure personality traits (Axis II of the *DSM–IV*). That the MCMI has an underlying theory, is much shorter, and is just as valid and reliable as the MMPI, also may be considered. Some practitioners have used both the MCMI and the MMPI and have discussed how the two tests complement each other (see chap. 9). More commonly, however, these tests are considered to be so similar that one is chosen over the other.

Compared with other instruments designed to measure personality traits (e.g., the NEO Personality Inventory), the MCMI is a clinical inventory. It conceptualizes personality in the way clinicians think, using prototypes that have been part of the clinical literature for years. We have no doubt that a dependent personality disorder can be partially described in terms of primary traits such as conscientiousness or lack of openness to experience. However, to the clinician, the dependent personality prototype involves more than the sum of such primary traits. The same way that the term *water* is much more meaningful to the average person than *two molecules of hydrogen and an oxygen molecule*, the five-factor model description of the dependent personality seems too convoluted and unduly complicated to us. Again, this may be a question of what the clinician understands best or is most comfortable with.

The MCMI is routinely used by itself, as a screening instrument, or as part of a test battery. When used as part of a battery, the referral question and history can be used to determine what other tests should be included. A typical battery to evaluate emotional problems may include more specialized self-report questionnaires (e.g., the Eating Disorders Inventory) and projective tests such as the Rorschach and the Thematic Apperception Test. We routinely have used the MCMI as part of a neuropsychological battery to evaluate brain dysfunction (see chap. 7).

Administration

The MCMI typically is administered using a well-designed form sold by National Computer Systems (NCS). Examinees answer the items on the same paper on which the items are presented. Examinees should complete the inventory alone in a comfortable setting; the room should be well lit and quiet. The procedure should be explained well, and the examinee should be checked using the first few items to ensure that the instructions have been understood. An audio recording and computer presentations of the items also are possible.

Although the test was designed to be a self-report inventory, it has been used successfully having one person describe another person he or she knows well. In that case, the agreement between the scores obtained by the person and those generated by the other tends to be higher on scales measuring overt traits (e.g., Schizoid, Narcissistic, Compulsive, Hypomanic, Drug Abuse) and lower on scales that include many items dealing with personal feelings (Wheeler & Schwarz, 1989).

One issue that comes up repeatedly during the administration of the MCMI is the examinee's difficulty in deciding whether the item is mostly true or false. Some examinees object to statements that have the word *always* or *never* in them, pointing out that such statements are invariably an exaggeration and, strictly speaking, could never be true or false. In such cases, we are likely to agree with the examinee but encourage him or her to decide whether it is "mostly" true or false and to mark the form accordingly.

Some of the substance abuse items raise questions among non-substance abusers who feel that certain items imply they have a problem, regardless of their answer. In those cases, we reassure the examinee that, for instance, admitting "success" in drinking a minimal amount of alcohol does not imply that drinking was a problem at one time. With any other question, the examiner should encourage the examinee to complete the inventory in the most accurate way possible without ever suggesting what the answer should be. Examinees should be encouraged to answer all items, and, if some are blank at the end, the examiner should have the examinee read the items again and try to arrive at a decision.

Scoring

Once a completed MCMI protocol has been obtained, the test must be scored. For the MCMI-I, the raw scores are obtained by simply counting the number of items for a given scale that were marked in a given direction. In the case of the MCMI-II, an item may add 1, 2, or 3 points toward the raw score of a particular scale depending on how central to the concept of that particular clinical entity the item is theoretically thought to be.

Although the practice of differential raw score weights makes sense from a theoretical viewpoint, it has been criticized by several investigators. It has been argued that the weights add to the complexity of scoring the inventory without improving the performance of the test (Retzlaff, Sheehan, & Lorr, 1990; Streiner, Goldberg, & Miller, 1993). Streiner and Miller (1989) demonstrated through mathematical logic that the differential weighting could not be expected to have a significant effect. In fact, Retzlaff (1991) showed that the scores obtained with and without the weighting correlated at .97 and above on almost all scales and that the practice does not reduce the item overlap matrix enough to warrant its continued use. In response to these issues, the item weights were reduced to adding 2 points for the prototypical items and the rest of the items counting only 1 point for the MCMI-III (Millon, 1994).

The MCMI-II and the MCMI-III have been keyed so that most of the items have to be endorsed as true to count on the scale for which they were designed. This dependence on the "true"-keyed items for the calculation of raw scale scores has been noted as a potential problem. In a series of studies, Strack and his colleagues showed that the examinee's tendency to endorse items as true is a response bias, akin to what is measured by the Disclosure index, and that it strongly affects scale scores (Strack, 1991a; Strack, Lorr, & Campbell, 1990; Strack, Lorr, Campbell, & Lamnin, 1992).

In any event, the raw score for any of the three versions can be computed manually using the scoring templates sold by NCS. The user can process the data through one of the systems offered by NCS: The test blank can be mailed to the company in Minneapolis for scoring, or it can be processed on an IBM-compatible PC using NCS software and decoding equipment. In all cases, the user must purchase the appropriate materials or services from NCS before administering the test.

Once the raw scores are computed, they have to be converted into a standardized score. The MCMI-I uses different conversion tables for gender and ethnic or race. Although similar ethnic or racial tables are offered in the MCMI-II manual, only the general tables for men and women are used by NCS to convert the raw scores into standardized scores. This practice was adopted because of concerns that the tables for minorities were based on samples that were too small. The MCMI-III has no norms for minorities.

The standard score used by the MCMI is the BR score. The BR score was developed in lieu of the *T* score often used by previous tests, such as the MMPI, and has been praised as a significant psychometric advance (Wetzler, 1990).

One problem with the T score is that it assumes a normal distribution of the characteristics being measured, an assumption that obviously does not hold because psychiatric disorders are not distributed normally. The end result is that the same T elevation defines different percentiles of the population for the different scales; in other words, a T score of 80 on the Depression scale of the original MMPI is associated with a different percentile rank than the same T value on the Schizophrenic scale. This effect is undesirable because it takes away the meaning for the relative elevations of the different scales.

Another problem with the T score is that it does not take into account the prevalence of the attribute being measured. The T score basically reflects how the examinee compares with the members of the standardizing population. On the original MMPI, the mean was 50 and the standard deviation was 10; therefore, the usual cutoff score of 70 is 2 SDs above the mean and defines 2% of the population. This 2% almost never corresponds to the prevalence rate of a particular disorder and introduces an automatic error. For instance, one third of the psychiatric patients are thought to have a dependent personality (style or disorder); using a T score cutoff of 70 when testing for a dependent personality can be expected to return 2% of the sample and to miss the great majority of the true-positive cases.

Both of the aforementioned problems led to the use of standardized scores for the MCMI that anchor cutoff scores to the prevalence of a particular disorder or trait in the psychiatric population (the BR score). The BR score is designed to indicate the probability that a particular examinee is similar to the group of psychiatric patients who were thought to have a particular trait or disorder. This measure obviously is different from one that indicates how far away from the mean of the nonpsychiatric population an examinee is on a particular trait (the T score of the MMPI). Thus, the standardized scores of these two tests (the MMPI and the MCMI) were specifically designed to give different information.

Millon anchored the BR scores on four different points: A BR score of 35 was defined as the median score for the normal or nonpsychiatric population; a BR score of 60 was set as the median for psychiatric patients; a BR score of 75 served as the anchor point for the definite presence of the particular characteristic being measured; and a BR score of 85 was defined as the point at which the characteristic in question is the most predominant characteristic for the individual.

In addition to placing the individual in the same position relative to the standardizing population, the BR score takes into account the prevalence of the particular characteristic in the population. Following Meehl and Rosen's (1955) suggestion, the BR score involves an adjustment to the cutoff point to maximize correct classification by considering the effect of the BR on the frequency of true-positives and false-positives. Thus, psychiatric disorders with high base rates will need lower cutoff points and psychiatric disorders with low base rates will need relatively higher cutoff points (Millon, 1977). It has been argued that using standard scores that take into account prevalence improves the effectiveness of the diagnostic system (Finn, 1982; Meehl & Rosen, 1955; Widiger, Hurt, Frances, Clarkin, & Gilmore, 1984; Widiger & Kelso, 1983). In fact, Duthie and Vincent (1986) demonstrated that the hit rate of the Diagnostic Inventory of Personality and Symptoms jumped from 44% to 70% when BRs were used instead of T scores.

One can think of the BR score as indicating the probability that the examinee has the particular characteristics being measured rather than the simple position that he or she occupies in the normal distribution. As a result, a low BR score does not indicate anything about the examinee, as opposed to a low T score, which implies an absence of the characteristic being measured. That aspect of the BR score simplifies the process of interpreting the scores because the user needs only to attend to the elevations obtained, and the low scores can be mostly disregarded.

Some critics of the MCMI have noted that, in spite of its advantages, the BR score poses substantial problems. It is likely, for instance, that many practitioners will want to use the MCMI with hospitalized patients and others may want to use it for outpatient screening (Hess, 1985). There is the possibility that two such different patient samples with potentially different BRs, when subjected to the same cutoff scores, would produce classification accuracy rates that are substantially different from those in the test manual. In such cases, the cutoff scores included in the test manual will not result in optimally accurate diagnoses (Butcher & Owen, 1978). Meehl and Rosen (1955) cautioned against the use of "inflexible cutting scores" for any psychometric device. Widiger (1985) suggested that "the MCMI would be improved by employing alternative cutoff points that varied according to the local base rate" (p. 987). Clinicians have long been urged to systematically collect local clinic prevalence data that then could be used in estimating pretest probabilities (Meehl & Rosen, 1955). To determine adequately whether the MCMI and other instruments contribute to or take away from the accuracy of clinical decision making, the long-standing pleas for the collection of local prevalence or BR data appear to be as relevant today as they were 35 years ago (Gibertini, Brandenburg, & Retzlaff, 1986).

After the BR score is computed for each scale of the MCMI, these scores are adjusted to take into consideration the examinee's response set or answering biases. The MCMI-I adjusted the BR score of some of the scales in accordance to a "weight factor" designed to indicate whether the examinee was likely to deny emotional traits or inflate them. Some scores also were adjusted when particular personality scales were predominantly elevated; this adjustment was based on the assumption that some personality styles include a tendency to exaggerate or minimize the presence of emotional problems.

In addition to both of these adjustments, the MCMI-II introduced adjustments for examinees appearing to be depressed or anxious, adjustments that were based on the results obtained on the Desirability and Debasement scales of the inventory, and adjustments for examinees who were in an inpatient psychiatric unit at the time they completed the test. Similar adjustments have been made for the MCMI-III. (For more information on how the adjustments are made, see the manual of the version that is being used.)

The adjustment of the BR scores of the MCMI has been controversial. Strack (1991b), for instance, noted that the system is "elaborate" and "confusing" (p. 3) and worried about scales that are corrected "up to four or five times" (p. 4). The fact that "one cannot ascertain how the specific correction weights were derived, nor evaluate their clinical utility" also concerned him (Strack, 1991b, p. 4). The adjustments obscure the issue of where the respondent actually falls with regard to the norms on any of the adjusted scales (Choca, Shanley, et al., 1992).

Using the MCMI-II results of 141 patients, H. R. Miller, Goldberg, and Streiner (1993) demonstrated that the profiles generated by the initial and the corrected BR scores were virtually identical. It also was apparent that the 3-point code types (i.e., the highest three scale elevations) usually were the same regardless of whether the corrections were applied. H. R. Miller et al. argued that the modification of the BR scores complicated the scoring and interpretation of the inventory without adding to its usefulness.

Test Scales

In the sections that follow, the scales of the MCMI-III are clustered into six groups: the Validity scale; the modifying or response set indexes assessing the manner in which the examinee responded to the test; scales that measure personality styles; scales measuring severe personality patterns; and the scales designed to tap the Axis I disorders, which are grouped into clinical syndrome scales and severe clinical syndrome scales.

Because our own approach is to depathologize the personality scales and discuss them as measuring styles that are found in the normal population, we group the two new scales of the MCMI-II (the Self-Defeating and the Aggressive scales) and the Depressive Personality scale of the MCMI-III with the severe personality patterns.

In the rest of this section, we offer our own characterization of the kinds of items that are included in the different scales. We describe only the MCMI-III because it is the most current version of the test.

Through the years, the labels used for the different scales have changed for the Millon instruments, a fact that occasionally creates some confusion. We note the different names that scales might have had in this chapter, but subsequently we use only the name used for the MCMI-III (written in italics in the ensuing sections). Although we restrict ourselves to one name for simplicity and consistency, the reader should be aware that the original sources cited in this book might have referred to particular scales by a different name.

The Validity Scale

The *Validity scale* (Scale V) contains three or four items (depending on the version of the test) that are so absurd that all of them should be marked false by any examinee able to appropriately read and understand the items.

Response Set Scales

Millon (1987) noted that some examinees approach a self-report inventory with a response set that alters the clinical picture that will emerge from the test. For conscious or unconscious reasons, certain individuals are inclined to put their best foot forward and to deny characteristics that are not socially desirable. On the opposite side are people invested in portraying themselves as being more severely dysfunctional than they actually are. The next three scales were designed to assess such response sets and to flag those individuals who are unwilling or unable to appropriately read, understand, and complete the inventory. Millon called these scales "modifying indices" because they are used to adjust the weighted scores of some of the clinical scales.

The first modifying index, the *Disclosure Index* (Scale X), is not a scale in the usual sense of the word but is a composite score computed from the personality scales. Theoretically, this scale contains traits that are, to some degree, neutral in terms of their desirability, providing a measure of how readily the individual is to "own" any psychological attribute. Although the notion that the items used are neutral has been questioned (Piersma, 1989a), the index is still thought to provide a measure of the openness with which the test is taken.

The *Desirability Index* (Scale Y) measures the tendency to portray oneself in a good light. Items that make the examinee look confident or gregarious and allege a regard for authority and a respect for the rules of society are the most prominent. Other items would indicate that the examinee is efficient and organized, avoids confrontation, has a moralistic but fun-loving attitude, experiences elevated moods, and denies the presence of alcohol abuse.

The *Debasement Index* (Scale Z), on the other hand, was designed to tap an attempt to look bad on the inventory. The most prominent items speak of feeling physically and emotionally empty, having low self-esteem, and becoming angry or tearful at the slightest provocation. Feelings of being unwanted and disliked may be present, along with possible self-destructive behaviors, feeling tense, being uncomfortable around others, or feeling guilty and depressed. Slightly less important are erratic moods, a desire to hurt people, a suspicious attitude, and mental confusion.

Personality Style Scales

The first of the personality scales is the *Schizoid*, Asocial, Introversive, or Passive-Detached scale (Scale 1). The main factor measured by this scale on the MCMI-II was that of social isolation (Choca, Retzlaff, Strack, Mouton, & Van Denburg, in press; Stewart, Hyer, Retzlaff, & Ofman, 1995). Another important aspect may be passivity and lack of energy (Stewart et al., 1995).

The *Avoidant*, Inhibited, or Active-Detached scale (Scale 2A) measures a style that, like the Schizoid scale, is marked by social detachment.

Avoidant individuals, however, face an approach–avoidance conflict: They would like to relate to others but feel such apprehension in social settings that they avoid interpersonal situations to decrease their anxiety. The items of this scale loaded onto two factors on the MCMI-II. The first of these factors reflects introversion and social isolation, and the second seems to tap an aimless and empty feeling (Choca et al., in press; Stewart et al., 1995).

The next two scales represent personality styles characterized by a need for strong relationships with people who are supportive and reassuring. The items of the *Dependent,* Submissive, Cooperative, or Passive-Dependent scale (Scale 3) underscore submissiveness, agreeableness, sociability (Choca et al., in press; Stewart et al., 1995), and self-depreciation (Stewart et al., 1995).

The most obvious features found in the *Histrionic,* Sociable, Gregarious, Dramatic, or Active-Dependent scale (Scale 4) for the MCMI-II were extraversion (Choca et al., in press; Stewart et al., 1995), agreeableness, and behavioral acting-out (Choca et al., in press). Predominant elevations on this scale are associated with an inclination to assess life events positively (Leaf, Ellis, DiGiuseppe, Mass, & Alington, 1991).

A positive view of life events also characterizes the next two scales (Leaf et al., 1991), the styles that Millon referred to as the "independent" styles. The personality styles that these scales were designed to measure are characterized by self-sufficiency in the person's relationships with others. Extroversion, a feeling of being special or unique (Choca et al., in press; Stewart et al., 1995), and interpersonal arrogance (Choca et al., in press) are the highlights of the *Narcissistic,* Confident, or Passive-Independent scale (Scale 5) of the MCMI-II.

The underlying theme of the antisocial style in Millon's system is the view of the world as a competitive place. The items of the *Antisocial,* Forceful, Competitive, or Active-Independent scale (Scale 6A) load onto factors reflecting behavioral acting-out, social mistrust (Choca et al., in press; Stewart et al., 1995), and social independence (Choca et al., in press).

The last two personality styles describe people who relate in a way that is neither dependent nor independent. Factors found for the MCMI-II *Compulsive,* Respectful, Conforming, Disciplined, or Passive-Ambivalent scale have included conscientiousness, restraint, affective stability, interpersonal ambivalence, closeness to experience, irritable intolerance, and a sense of virtuosity (Choca et al., in press; McCann, 1992; Stewart et al., 1995). Predominant elevations on this scale have been found to be associated to fewer negative reactions to life events and have been taken, as a result, as a psychological asset (Leaf et al., 1991).

Finally, the *Negativistic*, Passive-Aggressive/Explosive, Sensitive, Impulsive, or Active-Ambivalent scale (Scale 8A) demonstrates an intense dislike of being controlled and a resentful attitude toward authority. Factors found with the MCMI-II have included neurotic moodiness (Choca et al., in press), disagreeableness (Choca et al., in press; Stewart et al., 1995), and emotional impulsiveness (Stewart et al., 1995). At least in the case of the MCMI-I, this scale appears to be related to perfectionism (Broday, 1988).

Severe Personality Scales

The two personality scales that were added for the MCMI-II (the Aggressive and the Self-Defeating scales), and the Depressive personality scale that was added to the MCMI-III, are grouped in this book with three other scales designed to measure severe personality patterns. We do not think that the eight scales already discussed measure a personality "disorder" but a personality "style," which may or may not constitute a personality disorder. By contrast, the five scales to be considered at this time are more clearly associated with a pathological way of functioning. Consistent with this view, four of these five scales have been found to yield higher scores with psychiatric patients than they do with nonpsychiatric people (Strack, Lorr, & Campbell, 1989).

The *Depressive* Personality scale (2B) involves a tendency to have a pessimistic outlook in life. Individuals with elevations on this scale exhibit a melancholic mood and are unlikely to experience much pleasure in life. Similar individuals often harbor a chronic sense of loss and feel hopeless about the prospect of experiencing much pleasure in life. They typically have a low opinion of themselves.

The *Aggressive* or Sadistic scale (Scale 6B) is probably a more pathological variant of the antisocial personality style. This scale was designed to measure a tendency for an individual to be at least aggressive if not hostile in his or her interactions with others. An elevation on this scale describes an individual who tends to emphasize the ability to remain independent and who is not inclined to do what others tell him or her to do. Competitive by nature, such an individual may be seen as behaving in a callous manner in the struggle to get ahead of everyone else. He or she is likely to be distrusting, to question the motives that others may have for their actions, and to assume that a person has to be vigilant and on guard to protect oneself. Projection is typically used as a defense so that individuals obtaining elevations on this scale would be inclined to blame others for anything that goes wrong. Such a person is likely to be interpersonally "touchy": Excitable and irritable, he or she may have a history of treating others in a rough or mean manner and of angrily "flying off the handle" whenever he or she is confronted or opposed. Factorial studies with the MCMI-II characterize the scale as tapping emotional acting-out (Choca et al., in press), strong-willed determination and social independence (Choca et al., in press; Stewart et al., 1995), and defensive aggression (Stewart et al., 1995).

The *Self-Defeating scale* (Scale 8B), on the other hand, is considered to be a more pathological variant of the negativistic personality style. Judging from the items contained on this scale, individuals obtaining elevated scores usually have a poor self-image and believe that they need the help of others to make ends meet. Their self-images typically are so poor that they are uncomfortable when they are treated nicely and seem to seek out situations in which they will be hurt or rejected. It is as if they have come to expect mistreatment and routinely have, almost by design, the type of interpersonal interactions that would be expected to bring about the abuse. The resentment that these people harbor typically plays a role in bringing about negative interpersonal interactions. Even though such individuals are inclined to put themselves down, some of the items deal with the likelihood that they will also devalue others. Other items relate to demonstrations of resentment in an insulting or even hostile way and the derivation of some pleasure from humiliating others. This tendency can be expected to create ill-will from others, which then activates their own resentment in an angry, frustrating vicious cycle. Three factors have been found for the MCMI-II items: Dysthymia, Self-Abasement, and Agreeableness (Choca et al., in press; Stewart et al., 1995). Hyer, Davis, Woods, Albrecht, and Boudewyns (1992) reported an association between elevations on this scale and a history of suicidal gestures, premature termination of treatment, a tendency to endorse more psychopathology, and a lower adjustment potential.

Considered possibly a pathological variant of the schizoid and avoidant personality styles, the *Schizotypal scale* (Scale S) was designed to measure a fear of human contact, suspicion and mistrust of others, and a preference for a life of passive isolation with few real relationships. Predominant among the items are those dealing with being somewhat eccentric and having habits that others may find peculiar. Judging from other items, individuals having elevations on this scale may have a rich fantasy life and mix their own personal idiosyncrasies with other material in their conversations. They may appear anxious and apprehensive or may demonstrate a flattening of affect. Finally, they may have feelings of depersonalization, feelings of emptiness, or ideas of reference. Paranoia, Introversion, and Aimless Lassitude have been found to be factors of the MCMI-II version of this scale (Choca et al., in press).

The *Borderline scale* (Scale C), originally labeled the Cycloid or Cyclothymic scale, was designed to measure a pervasive pattern of instability in terms of moods, interpersonal relationships, and self-image. Elevations on this scale indicate that examinees typically respond in an impulsive and overemotional way and that their affective responses tend to be labile, at times showing apathy and numbness and demonstrating an excessive amount of intensity or involvement at other times. Sadness, hopelessness, and aimlessness may be underlying a more obvious emotional response. Such individuals may have significant problems with authority and resent any control placed on them. They can be aggressive, angry, or even cruel and are plagued by destructive ideas, which may be directed at themselves or others. The anger may be displaced temporarily by bothersome feelings of guilt or remorse. Their self-image also may be problematic because there also are items relating to feeling worthless, being encumbered by self-doubt, and feeling used by others. For the MCMI-II, the items of this scale have been grouped into four factors: Depression, Behavioral Acting-Out, Submissive Dependency, and Hostile Dominance (Choca et al., in press). There are indications that this scale, at least with the MCMI-I, tends to be elevated for any individual who has a personality disorder regardless of the type (Divac-Jovanovic, Svrakic, & Lecic-Tosevski, 1993). If so, elevations of this scale could indicate the presence of a personality disorder.

Because the conceptualization of the borderline syndrome in the literature is a "booming confusion" (Blatt & Auerbach, 1988, p. 199), it requires a few additional comments. Blatt and Auerbach provided a framework for making sense of the many ways in which borderline patients have been characterized. They argued that there are three types of syndromes for which this label has been used. When used in the sense of borderline schizophrenia, the term describes an "unstable" condition marked by "social role dysfunction, eccentricity, social withdrawal, attenuated psychotic symptoms, and multiple, bizarre, neurotic symptoms" (Blatt & Auerbach, 1988, p. 199). Under stressful conditions, these patients may develop a temporary psychotic state. It would seem that this type of "borderline schizophrenia" does not fit the *DSM–IV* conceptualization of the borderline patient and may be better labeled a schizotypal personality disorder. On the MCMI, perhaps an elevation of the Schizotypal scale should be expected. Accompanying that elevation, one may find elevations on the scales that measure social detachment—the Schizoid and the Avoidant—and possibly in the psychotic scales if the patient takes the test during a period of regression.

Blatt and Auerbach (1988) also discussed two other definitions of the borderline patient that refer to a "relatively stable character pathology" (p. 199). The first of these personality disorders, which they called the "anaclitic" type, is characterized by "profound feelings of dependence and loneliness, fears of abandonment, and great affective lability in response to rejection or object loss" (Blatt & Auerbach, 1988, p. 199). This is the type of borderline patient that is described by the *DSM–IV* criteria. Although the Borderline scale of the MCMI-I was not originally designed to measure the borderline syndrome as it is known today, the MCMI-II and MCMI-III versions were substantially revised; the latter appears to be much more consistent with the *DSM–IV* criteria.

Basically, the *DSM–IV* borderline patient is an impulsive and emotionally labile person. Because these attributes also are an important aspect of several personality styles, an elevation on at least one of the basic personality scales is to be expected. In fact, many of the theoreticians who have written on the topic of the borderline disorder (e.g., Kernberg, 1975) have distinguished between different styles of borderline patients, such as the hysterical or the narcissistic borderline patient. Stone (1980) offered a three-dimensional diagnostic cube that allows the categorization of several of the Millon personality styles at the borderline "psychostructural level" (p. 36). In our experience, individuals meeting criteria for the *DSM–IV* borderline personality disorder are likely to have elevated scores on either the Histrionic or the Negativistic scale of the MCMI-III.

As always, distinguishing between the different personality styles can add much to the understanding of patients' basic inclinations. For instance, much of the mood fluctuations and instability exhibited by histrionic borderline patients is likely to be designed to get attention. Therefore, helping the patients understand and deal with the attentional needs can be expected to be therapeutic. By contrast, negativistic borderline patients can be expected to benefit from exploring how they deal with their anger; the impulsive acting-out in that case often can be best understood as angry disappointments in relating to others.

Returning to our review of the scales, a suspicious and mistrustful attitude and a feeling of superiority are the most pronounced features measured by the *Paranoid scale* (Scale P). Other important factors deal with resenting authority and criticism, being insensitive to other people, and feeling emotionally and physically unconnected. Individuals with elevations on this scale may express a fear of losing autonomy and may be highly resistant to attempts by others to control their lives. A tendency to be perfectionistic and well organized, to be moralistic, to have little patience, and to be short-tempered may be present, along with a somewhat competitive attitude. The three factors that seem to make up most of this scale in the MCMI-II include Paranoia, Resentful Irritability, and Hostile Brashness (Choca et al., in press).

Clinical Syndrome Scales

The last two groups of scales were designed to measure symptoms that are superimposed on the personality style. Typically, these symptoms are more closely associated with the patient's presenting complaints than are the personality scales and lead to Axis I *DSM–IV* diagnoses. The MCMI sets aside a group of three scales to represent the severe clinical syndromes (discussed in the next section).

An elevation on the *Anxiety Disorder scale* (Scale A) is related to apprehension, phobic reactions, indecisiveness, tension, restlessness, and physical discomforts associated with tension. Other items deal with feeling confused, having a perceived inability to "do things right," and a diminished self-confidence. Adding in a lesser way to this scale are feelings of being unwanted and unappreciated, having a tendency to break into tears or become angry for no apparent reason, being dependent on someone else, and feeling depressed. This scale has been praised as "the most sensitive of the MCMI scales as a measure of psychological distress and disturbance" (Smith, Carroll, & Fuller, 1988, p. 172).

The *Somatoform Disorder scale* (Scale H) is characterized by complaints of fatigue, weakness, tension, jumpiness, inordinate sweating, aches, pains, and physical discomforts. To a lesser degree, the scale contains items dealing with a lack of self-confidence, being dependent on others, feeling mentally confused and unable to sort out one's thoughts, being easily provoked to the point of tears, having difficulty sleeping, and needing to be the center of attention.

The *Bipolar Manic scale* or Hypomania scale (Scale N) was designed to measure restlessness, overactivity, elevated moods, pressured speech, impulsiveness, and irritability. Other contributing items deal with being gregarious and seeking attention, experiencing intense emotions, demonstrating jumpy and erratic behavior and moods, feeling superior to others, and being psychologically insensitive. A few items referring to a heightened sensitivity to sounds and a tendency toward alcohol abuse also are present.

An apathetic and dejected mood; feelings of discouragement, guilt, or hopelessness; and a lack of personal initiative are the cardinal issues reflected by the items of the *Dysthymic Disorder scale* (Scale D). Physical and emotional exhaustion, difficulty sleeping, low self-confidence, and self-destructive thoughts or actions also may be present, along with a tendency to break into tears or become angry at the slightest provocation. Judging by the items included, a distrust of others and a somewhat perfectionistic attitude also may be present.

The *Alcohol Dependence scale* (Scale B) is characterized by a history of excessive drinking that has produced problems in both the home and the work situations. Items dealing with diminished self-confidence and impulsivity also are evident, as is an aversion to being controlled and feeling tense, tired, sweaty, lonely, empty, and hopeless. A wish to be sociable and the experience of guilt feelings or mood swings affect this scale in a lesser way, as does respect for authority and lack of trust.

Similarly, the *Drug Dependence scale* (Scale T) is characterized by a history of drug use pronounced enough to cause difficulties in either the home or the work situation. Items highlight impulsivity, a tendency to hurt oneself or others, a propensity to use others, a resentment of authority, and an aversion to being controlled. Other contributing issues include suspiciousness, unexplained mood swings, feelings of guilt and remorse, professing to having no clear-cut goals and feeling aimless, being angry, feeling jumpy or tense, having low self-esteem, and behaving competitively.

The *Post Traumatic Stress* scale (Scale R) is new to the MCMI-III. This scale assesses the experience of a traumatic life situation and symptoms resulting from that experience, such as anxieties and nightmares.

Severe Clinical Syndrome Scales

The last three clinical syndrome scales are segregated by Millon into another group, this one of psychotic disorders. We think that such a distinction is not consistent with the *DSM–IV*. Moreover, the traditional contention that "psychotic" disorders are more dysfunctional regardless of severity is widely disputed, so there may be no wisdom in viewing these scales as being drastically different from the rest. Nevertheless, these scales are treated as a separate group by the MCMI, and there is no reason not to be consistent in this book.

The first of these scales is the *Thought Disorder scale* (Scale SS). This scale was designed to select individuals suffering from confusion and disorganization of their thought processes, inappropriate affect, and unsystematized delusions or hallucinations. Contributing items also question the examinee about being suspicious and mistrustful, desiring isolation, concern about being used by others, and experiencing sensations of physical or mental imbalance. Low self-esteem, a desire to hurt oneself and others, feeling unwanted and disliked, emotional constriction, and ideas of reference also are factors affecting this scale. Finally, a tendency to be rigid in one's thinking may be present.

In addition to the Mania and the Dysthymia scales described earlier, the MCMI contains a *Major Depression scale* (CC) that measures a more severe affective disorder. Such a disorder would be characterized by a depressed mood of such magnitude that it prevents the individual from functioning. This depressed mood may be accompanied by difficulty sleeping, feelings of hopelessness, a fear of the future, agitation, and psychomotor retardation. Other features include feeling physically drained, becoming angry or tearful with little provocation, feeling unworthy or undeserving, engaging in self-destructive behaviors, being socially withdrawn or too sexually inhibited, feeling tense, and experiencing diminished self-confidence or confusion.

Finally, the *Delusional Disorder scale* (Scale PP) assesses the presence of irrational ideas, particularly persecutory or grandiose ones. Feelings of superiority and fears of being used by others are markedly noticeable. Minor items that add to this particular scale include being moralistic, believing that some unknown entity is able to interfere with one's life, feeling emotionally detached, being rigid, feeling confused, and being somewhat perfectionistic.

Special Scales

Retzlaff and Gibertini (1990) developed eight factor-based special scales for the MCMI-I. This contribution was built on two of their earlier factor-analytic studies (Gibertini & Retzlaff, 1988a; Retzlaff & Gibertini,

1987b). The three personality scales derived in that manner were labeled *Aloof/Social, Submissive/Aggressive,* and *Labile/Restrained.* These scales were said to reflect the dimensions that Widiger, Frances, Spitzer, & Williams (1988) proposed as underlying the *DSM–III* personality disorders.

The factor analyses of the clinical syndrome scales of the MCMI-I led to five factor-analytic scales: Detached, Submissive, Suspicious, High Social Energy, and Generalized Distress. Retzlaff and Gibertini (1990) included a table with the items that load on the different scales as well as the means and standard deviations for each of the scales. The reader therefore has all the information that would be needed to score and interpret these scales.

Those five MCMI-I scales are still considered experimental. Only one study that we are aware of has used these scales (Adams & Clopton, 1990). The scales, however, are partially supported by our own work with this test (Choca, Greenblatt, Tobin, Shanley, & Van Denburg, 1989). Using a sample of more than 2,000 psychiatric inpatients, we uncovered 17 factors, some of which resemble the eight scales offered by Retzlaff and Gibertini (1987b, 1990).

Using the clients of a Vietnam veterans' center connected with our facility, we tried to develop an MCMI-I scale to measure posttraumatic stress disorder (PTSD). Through empirical keying, we were able to pick 17 items that significantly differentiated between the clients who were diagnosed with PTSD and those who were not. When this scale was tested on a second sample for cross-validation, however, the means and standard deviations of the PTSD and non-PTSD groups were so close that they were practically indistinguishable. Unfortunately, this was the case even though the differences were statistically significant (Choca, Shanley, Peterson, & Hong, 1987).

State Versus Trait

The MCMI theoretically measures fairly permanent attributes or traits as well as temporary states, such as a depressed mood. Some support for such theoretical expectations can be found in that the test–retest reliability tends to be higher for the personality scales than for the scales measuring clinical syndromes (see chap. 3). However, the test results are so colored by the feelings and perceptions of the examinee at the time of testing that they should be seen only as a reflection of the person at that time. Especially when the individual is acutely disturbed, or feeling much different from his or her usual, the results are likely to be much different from the results obtained on other occasions. As Piersma (1989a) warned, the possibility of such changes has to be constantly borne in mind.

Logic and Steps in MCMI Interpretation

Several logical sequential steps in interpreting an MCMI profile typically are followed (Craig, 1993b; Millon, 1994; E. Van Denburg & Choca, in press). The steps we use are to (a) examine the issue of the validity and defensiveness; (b) characterize the individual's basic personality style; (c) evaluate, with both MCMI and historical data, the level of functionality of the personality style; (d) describe the clinical syndrome or Axis I symptoms that the person appears to be experiencing; and (e) integrate all of the information in a holistic formulation of the individual. To accomplish this, we take into account both the theory and the research that is available about the instrument. In our own clinical work, we emphasize the value of data from other sources, including historical information about the examinee and the results obtained through other psychological instruments.

Much of this book can be seen as an elaboration of these five steps. Information about the examination of invalidity and defensiveness, for instance, is discussed in chapter 5. Chapter 6 covers the descriptions of personality styles (Step 2). The issue of how to distinguish between personality styles and personality disorders (Step 3) is discussed in chapter 2 in our review of personality theory; other materials that are relevant to that issue are included in discussions of personality styles (chap. 6) and personality disorders (chap. 7). The evaluation of clinical syndromes (Step 4) is covered in chapter 7. Help with the integration of results from other instruments can be obtained in chapter 8. The culmination of the diagnostic process (Step 5) is illustrated through the cases offered in chapter 9 and the treatment recommendations in chapter 10.

2 Personality Theory

The MCMI is not intrinsically tied to any of the traditional schools of psychology and can be used by clinicians having highly different views. The reasons for this eclecticism are that the test itself was designed to measure fairly covert traits or symptoms and that it does not have items dealing with etiology. Because the different schools of psychology are distinguished mostly by the causative factors they propose, a clinical tool that does not measure etiology will tend to be acceptable to a wider range of professionals.

This is not to say that the MCMI does not have a theoretical basis. Millon's theoretical writings have covered the entire gamut: He has hypothesized how personality traits may relate to one another (Millon, 1969, 1973, 1981, 1995; Millon & Millon, 1974), what the etiology of particular personality styles may be (Millon, 1969, 1973, 1990, 1995), and even how the adaptive potential of the personality style may fit into evolutionary theory (Millon, 1990). As opposed to the empirically derived Minnesota Multiphasic Personality Inventory (MMPI), the structure of the test obviously is tied to a way of viewing the individual.

In this chapter, we discuss personality style theory and the prototypes that Millon (1969) proposed. We believe that the MCMI's strength is that it provides a measure of the personality style; as a result, it is important for the reader to develop some appreciation for the importance of this concept in understanding an individual.

As Endler and Edwards (1988) suggested, personality issues are best understood from a systemic, or interactional, view. From this perspective, as the individual relates to his or her environment, a certain amount of conflict often occurs. Dohrendwend and Dohrendwend (1981) showed that stressful life situations typically have significant effects on any individual's well-being. Different individuals, however, react differently to a particular life stressor depending on the psychological meaning that the specific event may have for them (Endler & Magnusson, 1976). A threshold can be postulated, a threshold that varies from one person to the next, below which the friction is tolerated and causes no further difficulties even if it is experienced as tension or discomfort.

To avoid the discomfort resulting from friction between a person and his or her environment, the individual uses defense mechanisms. To the extent that these defenses lower the level of tension and do not cause additional problems, they are adaptive and allow the person to function better than he or she would without such mechanisms. When excessive, however, either the tension or the defenses can become a problem that the individual has to face, in addition to whatever difficulty was originally causing the friction. By then, either the friction or the defensive structure has become maladaptive and can be thought to be psychopathological.

Much of the friction that is generated between an individual and the environment is attributable to incompatibility. Consider, for instance, a person who has a great need to please others and has a tendency to be uncomfortable in situations in which decisions have to be made without consultation with others. As an entry-level employee, he or she may be placed under the tutelage of an older, more knowledgeable individual who is willing to teach the "tricks of the trade." Under this supervisor's mentorship, the employee performs well: The situation represents a good fit, and this good fit benefits this hypothetical worker, his or her supervisor, and the company.

Such a treasured employee eventually probably will be promoted to head a particular section of the company. Depending on the circumstances, the compatibility may drastically decrease. If this individual is not given much guidance in the new position and is expected to exert authority over disgruntled or problematic employees, he or she may be poorly equipped to do the job and may start experiencing a great deal of tension, unhappiness, or even psychopathology.

Although it may occur often enough, the good-fit scenario is not the most typical situation that can be discussed with regard to the compatibility between an individual and the environment. Most people are not lucky enough to have such a perfect fit with their surroundings that there is no friction. On the other hand, when the goodness of fit is awful, most individuals escape the situation altogether. As a result, in the great majority of the cases that one comes upon, the fit between the individual and the environment includes complementary areas as well as difficulties.

To understand the relationship between an individual and the environment, many elements have to be considered. Aspects of the environment, for instance, have to be understood, including the social and occupational situations in which the person may be involved. There also are many aspects that the individual brings into this equation, including his or her stage in life and abilities, expectations, and goals. Throughout this book we hope to make the reader more aware of the contribution of yet another factor: the individual's personality style.

Personality Style Theory

By the term *personality style*, we mean the psychological essence of the person regardless of pathology or ability to cope. The definition offered by the *DSM–III–R*[1] was that of an "enduring" pattern of "perceiving, relating to, and thinking about the environment and oneself" that is "exhibited in a wide range of important social and personal contexts" (American Psychiatric Association, 1987, p. 335). In other words, a personality style is the set of lifelong assumptions that the person holds about the self and the world, along with the typical ways of thinking and feeling, and the behavioral patterns associated with those assumptions. Although personality traits were traditionally thought to be more egosyntonic and stable than the symptoms of a clinical syndrome, the fact that such distinctions do not appear to hold in many cases has been ·well documented (Bronisch & Klerman, 1991).

The area to be emphasized in our definition is that the personality style involves lifelong *assumptions* about oneself and others. This particular quality is what best sets the personality style apart from most other clinical constructs. From the basic assumptions people have about themselves and the world typically emanate patterns of thinking, ways of feeling, and patterns of behaviors that are compatible with those assumptions. For example, people who see themselves as being less ca-

---

[1]We offer the wording in the revised third edition of the *Diagnostic and Statistical Manual of Mental Disorders* because the definition used in the fourth edition of the manual makes the Axis II sound more pathological and is, as a result, less helpful in our discussion of personality *styles.*

pable than other people usually feel inadequate and behave in a co-operative and submissive manner.

The personality style also can be seen as a conglomerate of personality traits that tend to cluster together (Buss, 1989). As is the case with most human attributes, personality traits are not always distributed in a way that makes logical sense or that is internally consistent. One may encounter a disorganized, overemotional, and easily distractible individual who nevertheless keeps an impeccable office in which every file is labeled and every piece of paper is in the right place. There may be an inadequate-dependent man who becomes a tyrant at home after he has had a few drinks. These are, however, the exceptions rather than the rule. The majority of the theorists would hold that most individuals who are orderly also are careful, clean, meticulous, disciplined, and punctual. It is the clusters of traits that tend to go together that we refer to as a personality style.

There are personality theorists who hold to a "situation-specific" rather than "trait" conceptualization of the personality (e.g., Mischel, 1968, 1973). As Buss (1989) argued, however, the debate over the relative power of the situation (or experimental manipulation) and the traits is unproductive; what needs to be studied is the way that traits and situations interact to produce a particular feeling or behavior.

Personality styles include the defenses that are typically used in coping with objectionable aspects of reality. However, the concept of personality styles goes beyond the definition of a defense mechanism. Thus, although some relationship exists between personality styles and defenses, the correlations are not high (Whyne-Berman & McCann, 1995).

As conceived here, personality styles are nonpathological entities. As Benjamin (1993) suggested, it is the song we sing through life that may have many different renditions while retaining the same melody. Personality styles involve assumptions about life that are intrinsically neutral and that invariably have more than a grain of truth in their depiction of reality. For instance, an individual who comes to assume that he or she is more capable or appealing than others can obviously validate that assumption by emphasizing his or her positive attributes and the deficiencies or limitations that others may present. In other words, the fact that people have some positive attributes and that other people are less fortunate in some ways is true of absolutely every human being, but it is emphasized only by those who have come to view themselves as superior.

Generally, we assume in this book that no personality style is necessarily better than any other. We hold this assumption in spite of the fact that it is not totally true. Both Millon (1981) and the fourth edition of the *Diagnostic and Statistical Manual of Mental Disorders* (*DSM–IV*; American Psychiatric Association, 1994) discussed personality styles that are presumed to be more adaptive. Moreover, there is some evidence that supports the contention that some characterological tendencies may be more impairing. Strack et al. (1989), for instance, showed that psychiatric patients as a group tend to score higher than normal individuals on the Schizoid, Avoidant, and Negativistic scales of the MCMI-I and of the Personality Adjective Checklist. Normal individuals, on the other hand, were inclined to score higher on the Histrionic and Narcissistic scales of the MCMI-I. Their findings suggest an association between personality traits involving internalized and inhibited behaviors and maladjustment. Other researchers similarly have shown "healthy correlates" of histrionic, narcissistic, antisocial, and compulsive personality inclinations (Butters et al., 1986; Leaf, Alington, Ellis, DiGiuseppe, & Mass, 1992; Leaf, Alington, Mass, DiGiuseppe, & Ellis, 1991; Leaf, DiGiuseppe, et al., 1990; Leaf, Ellis, DiGiuseppe, Mass, & Alington, 1991; Nakao et al., 1992; Retzlaff & Deatherage, 1993). Elevations of the Negativistic scale of the MCMI-I have been associated with poor performance (Retzlaff & Deatherage, 1993) and are accompanied by more elevations of other scales than expected (Chick, Martin, Nevels, & Cotton, 1994). Finally, there even is evidence that the treatment response of patients with the "healthier" personality disorders was considerably better than the response of patients with the more dysfunctional personality types (Vaglum et al., 1990).

The research design issues raised by those investigations are so complex that it makes the question difficult to research.[2] Moreover, even if there is some advantage to particular personality styles, it is un-

---

[2]The attempt to show that different personality styles may be associated with different types of clinical syndromes (Axis I psychopathology) or with the severity of those syndromes does not really answer whether different personality styles are more or less functional in and of themselves. It also is of little value to compare individuals with different personality styles without taking into account the severity of their particular style, because extreme and inflexible styles, regardless of the type, can be expected to be less functional than those that are less extreme or more flexible. To answer the question one would have to, for instance, match individuals with different personality styles on the basis of the severity of their style, without taking into account their level of adjustment. One then would have to find a way to measure success or adjustment that is not biased against one or more of the personality styles. Self-report measures would not be acceptable because, for example, narcissists may see themselves as being more successful than dependent individuals. Similarly, many markers of success in American society can be expected to be related to traits such as self-confidence; another element a researcher would like to avoid in such a project is a circular definition of success or adjustment and narcissism. Further complicating the task is the fact that most personality styles represent a combination of more than one of the "pure" styles, so that the number of different groups necessary to do the work with accuracy becomes astronomical.

deniable that well-functioning people can be found with any one of the trait clusters that we refer to as *personality styles*. Conversely, groups of very dysfunctional psychiatric patients have been found to have personality styles that are thought to be healthier (e.g., Craig & Olson, 1990).

We assume, therefore, that every personality style will give its bearer advantages and disadvantages. The orderly and disciplined individual, for example, will tend to perform better when the task demands meticulousness and careful attention to detail. Alternatively, this individual may have difficulty with change, or with situations in which a particular way of behaving cannot be rehearsed beforehand. In other words, the same character traits that can help a person become a good accountant may be a liability if the person wanted to become a stunt car driver.

Unfortunately, none of the ways of defining a personality style will allow a clear and unequivocal differentiation of this construct from other clinical entities (Hirschfeld, 1993). One must be aware that these definitions represent human attempts to conceive reality, not reality itself (Schwartz, Wiggins, & Norko, 1989). There is actually no clear-cut distinction between the personality style and the other psychological aspects of the individual. Widiger (1989) pointed out that the boundaries between personality and clinical syndromes are often unclear. The borderline personality disorder, for instance, is characterized partly by mood instability resembling affective disorders; the schizoid, avoidant, and schizotypal personalities have much in common with schizophrenia. When all is said and done, a clinician needs to develop an intuitive feeling for where to draw the line in what will be considered a personality style and what may be better conceived as abilities, psychopathology, motivated behavior, or other human attributes. The idea of personality styles is, at best, a conceptual framework that can be used to understand the vicissitudes of human nature rather than a tangible entity that one may be able to see in an indisputable manner.

The conceptualization of personality styles is further complicated by two facts. First, the relative dominance of the personality traits that make up the personality style cluster changes from one individual to another. As Widiger (1992) pointed out, there are different ways in which individuals may accumulate enough characterizing traits (or *DSM–IV* criteria) to be considered to have a particular personality. The fact that one histrionic individual may be uncomfortable when he or she is not the center of attention could make that person appear different from another histrionic individual who may not be uncomfortable in such circumstances. Second, most individuals have a mixture of elements in their personality, a fact that further complicates the clinical picture. A histrionic-narcissistic person may appear much different from a histrionic-dependent or a histrionic-negativistic individual.

Historical Perspective

Primitive descriptions of personality styles can be traced back to the Greeks. In his book *The Sacred Disease*, Hippocrates (460–357 B.C./1950) proposed that there were four "humors" in the human body and that the balance of these humors led to the person being either "quiet, depressed, and oblivious" or "excited, noisy, and mischievous." It is of interest that even Hippocrates's etiological concepts have survived the passage of time: Researchers are still trying to find some chemical explanation for personality characteristics (e.g., Choca, Okonek, Ferm, & Ostrow, 1982; Shaughnessy, Dorus, Pandey, & Davis, 1980).

Several of the founding fathers in the field of psychopathology wrote about particular personality styles. Freud and Abraham, for example, described the "oral-receptive character," which was the precursor of the dependent personality style (Abraham, 1927). W. Reich (1949), another early psychoanalyst, also addressed the vicissitudes of character formation and the consistent patterning of defenses within a given personality. Perhaps the first person to emphasize the role of the underlying personality as a general aspect of all human beings was Adler (1956). The Adlerian approach is to describe the client's *lifestyle* on the basis of his or her history, attempting to conceptualize what makes that person "tick." After a thorough evaluation of a client, a man may be described as being angry at his mother for abandoning him when he was 1 year old and dedicating his life to finding women who have problems with commitments so that they can be punished for their disloyalty. Done in this manner, the person's lifestyle has the potential for being true to the uniqueness and individuality of the human being because such a description would not apply to many other individuals.

The Adlerian approach, however, can be problematic in several ways. The issue of the validity and reliability in such a diagnostic system seems paramount: The odds that another clinician would arrive at the same statement regarding a person's lifestyle are extremely low. In fact, it is possible that the same clinician, on seeing the patient on a different occasion, may arrive at a somewhat different conceptualization of the person's psychological essence. There also is the issue of how much of the conceptualized lifestyle is a product of what the client actually is presenting, as opposed to being an imaginative fabrication on the clinician's part or a countertransference of the clinician's psychological issues.

Thus, in spite of the appeal of the Adlerian system, to use the concept of personality style productively, a model or system would appear to be needed. In allowing the clinician to classify or group individuals, such a model would offer great advantages: One then can compare or contrast one person with another or apply data collected from a group of individuals (e.g., histrionics) to a single person who is thought to be a member of that group.

Any time a system of classification is developed, one must accept that individuals need to be bent to fit the model and that the sense of uniqueness that the individual presents must be forfeited to some degree. If clinicians were unwilling to do so, they would have to resign themselves to having little say about the individual in addition to what the person says about himself or herself or to have the same set of psychodynamics for everyone.

One method that has been followed in developing a valid and reliable system for assessing personality styles is seemingly empirical and nontheoretical. Cattell (1946, 1965) factor analyzed all of the words pertaining to the personality that could be found in the English language. This search for the basic personality traits culminated in the creation of the Sixteen Personality Factor Questionnaire (16PF) and its recent revision (Cattell, 1986), the 16PF.

Cattell's approach obviously enjoys a scientific purity and psychometric simplicity that is difficult to match. More recently, McCrae and Costa (1985, 1986) revived the factorial approach and used it to develop their own questionnaire (Costa & McCrae, 1985). Although Costa and McCrae's five-factor model has received wide recognition and support (e.g., Wiggins & Pincus, 1989), it may never have wide appeal for practicing clinicians. One problem is that most of the research was based on normal samples, and the question has been raised about the appropriateness of using the five-factor model with emotionally disturbed individuals (Ben-Porath & Waller, 1992a, 1992b; see also Costa & McCrae, 1992a, 1992b).

The other problem we see is inherent in the factorial approach. Even if these factors are the building blocks of any personality system, and even if they can be systematically integrated into a personality style, they do not have the same meaning to the clinician. It may be more scientific to describe a person as being high in extraversion and low in conscientiousness, but somehow the characterization becomes clinically meaningful only when one is told that the patient is histrionic. We contend that, in breaking personality into components, the five-factor model makes the description less recognizable and practical. The same criticism can be raised about the Edwards Personal Preference Schedule (Edwards, 1959), a measure of needs and motives.

In the 1950s, Timothy Leary proposed a circumplex model of personality style theory. Leary's model defined interpersonal personality styles on the basis of a circle in which the two axes represent the continua of control and affiliation (Leary, 1957; Leary & Coffey, 1955). The circle is divided to yield eight basic personality styles: managerial-autocratic, responsible-hypernormal, cooperative-conventional, docile-independent, self-effacing-masochistic, rebellious-distrustful, aggressive-sadistic, and competitive-narcissistic. Benjamin (1974, 1984, 1993, 1995) expanded the model into the three dimensions—focus, affiliation, and interdependence—that allow consideration of intrapsychic phenomena.

Kiesler (1983) also conducted a great deal of research on his circumplex model of personality functioning, devising what he called the *interpersonal circle*. He posited two central relationship issues for all people: how friendly or hostile they will be with each other and how much in charge or control each will be in their relationships.

Leary's (1957) circumplex continues to have a following and has been shown to have commonalities with the third edition of the *Diagnostic and Statistical Manual of Mental Disorders (DSM–III;* American Psychiatric Association, 1980) and the Millon system (DeJong, van den Brink, Jansen, & Schippers, 1989; Morey, 1985; Widiger & Kelso, 1983; Wiggins, 1982). Nevertheless, the model has not been accepted widely. The problem may lie in that the intricacies of the model are more than most people can master easily. The lack of acceptance also may be related to the fact that psychiatric nosology is based on prototypes rather than on the kind of continua that Leary proposed (Schwartz et al., 1989). In other words, none of the different editions of the *DSM* have allowed for an individual to be *a little* schizophrenic or have ever recognized that psychological traits are a matter of degree. Because clinicians are accustomed to thinking that an individual is either schizophrenic or not schizophrenic, in an all-or-none fashion, a system that calls for continua seems foreign and unduly complex. Finally, and perhaps most importantly, Leary's circumplex did not lead to labels such as "schizoid" or "dependent" that are easily recognized by the majority of the professionals in the field.

Millon's Typology

Like Leary, Millon (1969) proposed a system based on personality prototypes rather than on single traits. He described what in theory would be the prototypes of particular personality styles and left the job of determining how close that prototype matches a particular individual to the diagnosing clinician or the psychometric instrument. Millon arrived at his original eight basic styles (schizoid, avoidant, dependent, histrionic, narcissistic, antisocial, compulsive, and negativistic) by borrowing from the descriptions that had been previously used for personality disorders. In so doing, he generated a system that benefited from the wisdom of many years of clinical practice. Moreover, Millon's typology seemed familiar to the practitioners in the field because it retained trait clusters that were well-known to clinicians.

By molding his personality styles in the image of the personality disorders, Millon (1969) was postulating that there were similarities between the way "normal" individuals function and the kind of pathology characterized by the personality disorders. Supporting this hypothesis is the work of Strack et al. (1989), who showed that the factorial structure of two personality instruments—the MCMI and the Personality Adjective Check List—were virtually identical for normal individuals and psychiatric patients.

Even though the Millon styles are single prototypes that have no intrinsic logical relation to one another, Millon suggested schemas that can be used to organize these personality styles. One such model fits all the personality styles in a circle in which the vertical axis represents affiliation, with the poles of autonomy versus enmeshment, and the horizontal axis, which deals with the level of emotionality, with the poles being expressiveness and impassiveness. This circular representation of the personality disorders, which obviously resembles the Leary circumplex, has been shown to have an empirical basis (Sim & Romney, 1990; Soldz, Budman, Demby, & Merry, 1993b; Strack et al., 1990). As might have been expected, the Millon prototypes that can be defined clearly by the two axes of the circumplex (avoidant, schizoid, dependent, histrionic, and narcissistic) are placed consistently in the same quadrant by different investigations, whereas the other prototypes (e.g., compulsive, negativistic) have not been placed in the circumplex in a reliable manner (Matano & Locke, 1995).

In more recent theoretical work, Millon (1990, 1995) proposed the use of three polarities (pleasure–pain, active–passive, and self–other) that he viewed as having roots in the evolution of humanity and from which the personality prototypes were derived. The usefulness of these three polarities in the understanding of personality patterns was supported by the data gathered on undergraduates by Pincus and Wiggins (1990). Partial support also was offered by the factor analysis that Strack, Lorr, Campbell, and Lamnin (1992) performed on the personality scales of the MCMI-II. The factor they labeled Introversion-Extraversion, for instance, reflects well Millon's idea of the self–other polarity; two other factors extracted, Aggressive-Assertive and Dependent-Acquiescent, could be seen as mapping into the active–passive polarity. That leaves only the Restrained-Emotional factor, which did not appear to resemble as well the remaining pleasure–pain polarity.

Attempts to fit the Millon personality styles into the five-factor model also have been made (Costa & McCrae, 1990; Dyer, 1994). The five factors that can be used to explain all important personality aspects according to this model are Extraversion, Agreeableness, Neuroticism, Openness to Experience, and Conscientiousness. The contention that the MCMI may be reflecting these five factors can be supported partly by the factor analyses of the MCMI-II items. All the available factor analyses of single items have produced factors that reflect some of the personality aspects included in the five-factor model (Choca et al., in press; Retzlaff, Lorr, Hyer, & Ofman, 1991; Stewart et al., 1995). Nevertheless, Millon's model obviously includes attributes that go beyond the five-factor model (Dyer, 1994).

Basically, Millon's model first examines whether the person is inclined to form strong relationships with others. For those who do not form strong relationships, the model then distinguishes between individuals who are loners by design, having little interest in interpersonal relationships (schizoids), and individuals who isolate themselves as a defensive maneuver against the possibility of rejection (avoidants). If the person ordinarily forms strong interpersonal relationships, the model then examines the type of relationship formed in terms of the assumptions the individual makes about the self and the other people in the environment.

Some of the people who form strong relationships with others recognize their need for others to feel safe and comfortable. Of these, the dependent style characterizes a person who believes that others know best. Such people typically establish submissive relationships in which the other person takes responsibility for any decision that is made. By contrast, the histrionic style is not as clearly submissive but frequently needs the attention of others.

Some individuals form relationships with others in which they play the stronger or more dominant role. The first of these two styles is the inverse of the dependent, in that it typifies a person who believes himself or herself to be more capable, gifted, or appealing than other people. Instead of behaving submissively, the narcissistic individual is inclined to tell other people what to do. The second independent personality style defines a person who sees the world as a competitive situation in which those who do well achieve their goals by being dominant and strong, even if at the cost of being unkind or hurtful toward others (antisocial).

Millon acknowledged that there are two other personality styles that have been recognized widely and proposed a way of fitting them into the general scheme. In the model, these two other personality styles are conceived as people who relate in a way that is neither dependent nor independent, a way that Millon labeled *ambivalent.* The first of these two styles is not ambivalent in the usual sense of the word, but it does relate to other people in a way that is not consistently dependent or independent. For the compulsive individual, the world is a hierarchical structure in which a person either has a higher or a lower rank than another. Using this hierarchical view, compulsive individuals relate in a dependent or compliant manner toward those perceived to have higher status and in an independent or authoritative way with those having a lesser rank.

The last style is characterized by individuals who see themselves as being inadequate and in need of support but who are highly cynical about the abilities of others and are not inclined to put others on a pedestal. As a result, they behave in a fairly conflictual way toward others in terms of the dependence–independence parameter. A prevalent substyle of relating for these negativistic individuals is the passive–aggressive substyle, in which the person is able to be overtly compliant while venting his or her conflictual feelings covertly. An explosive substyle involving a cycle of hostile eruptions followed by periods of contrition also can be found.

In our view, not all of the recognized personality disorders can be depathologized easily into describing a personality style. For example, the borderline personality disorder involves a pattern of unstable relationships accompanied by an identity disturbance, impulsive acting-out, self-damaging acts, mood instability, a chronic sense of boredom or emptiness, inappropriate intense anger, and possible paranoid ideation or dissociative symptoms (American Psychiatric Association, 1994). In contrast to the personality styles described already, it is difficult to conceive the core of this disorder as resulting from a basic assumption of life (Clarkin, Widiger, Frances, Hurt, & Gilmore, 1983). Moreover, this disorder has been seen theoretically as resulting from a failure of integration in the basic personality (Dorr, Barley, Gard, & Webb, 1983; Kernberg, 1975). Thus, in contrast to the personality styles in which some advantages can be seen for individuals having that particular style, the borderline pattern seems intrinsically problematic and disadvantageous.

If the premise is accepted that some of the personality disorder prototypes cannot be applied to define normal individuals, then it becomes a matter of judgment whether a recognized personality pattern has enough good qualities that it should be considered a personality style. In his original writings, Millon (1969) recognized the eight personality styles that we recognize in this book. We accept the borderline, paranoid, and schizotypal personality disorders as personality disorders, but we think that these three patterns of behavior are not found in individuals who do not have an emotional disorder.

In the MCMI-II (Millon, 1987), two additional personality styles were added: the sadistic and the self-defeating. In this book, we also treat those two additional entities as pathological patterns, not as basic personality styles.

The sadistic and self-defeating prototypes were being discussed as additional personality disorders by the work group revising the *DSM–III* when the MCMI-I was being revised. These discussions were surrounded by much controversy because the inclusion of those two categories was opposed vehemently by certain segments of the population. In the end, those disorders were relegated to the appendix of the *DSM–III–R* as proposed categories "needing further study" (American Psychiatric Association, 1987, p. 367) and were dropped altogether from the *DSM–IV* (American Psychiatric Association, 1994). Unfortunately, this turn of events left the MCMI-II and, later, the MCMI-III, with two categories that may never become part of the official nomenclature.

In addition to the historical issues, we have trouble visualizing how either the sadistic or the self-defeating disorders can be conceptualized as a personality style that offers some advantage to individuals who bear those traits. Moreover, both of these styles appear to include one of the basic eight personality styles: The sadistic personality probably is a variant of the negativistic or antisocial styles, whereas the self-defeating personality probably involves dependent or avoidant elements.

The eight prototypes that we are referring to as personality styles are not mutually exclusive. In fact, most individuals we encounter fit more than one prototype. The interpretive system we use considers the three highest personality style elevations in describing the personality style of one individual. This approach adds considerable complexity to the interpretations but has the advantage of returning some of the uniqueness that a particular individual presents, as well as describing with greater fidelity the way the individual is prone to think, feel, and behave.

Personality Styles and Personality Disorders

It seems clear that personality traits or styles distribute themselves in a continuum and can be seen to have normal or pathological variants in different individuals. Wiggins and Pincus (1989), for instance, examined personality dimensions from different inventories and concluded that "conceptions of personality disorders were strongly and clearly related to dimensions of normal personality traits" (p. 305).

Personality disorders are defined by the *DSM–IV* as "enduring pattern of inner experience and behavior that deviates markedly from the expectations of the individual's culture" (American Psychiatric Association, 1994, p. 629). The *DSM–IV* adds that the pattern has to be "pervasive and inflexible," "stable over time," and lead to "distress or impairment" (American Psychiatric Association, 1994, p. 629). In other words, the clinician has to contend with the kind of personality that his or her subject may have and the diagnosis of the character structure being further complicated by the issue of the functionality of the personality pattern.

After looking at Charlie Brown, one could decide that he typifies the dependent personality style. The figure that emerges from Charles Schultz's famous cartoon is one of an individual who tends to feel less capable than others and blames his lack of leadership for the frequent loss of baseball games. A cooperative person, he never gets angry and is inclined to try to follow the advice or recommendations of others.

The fact that this fictitious figure fits nicely the dependent prototype, however, does not mean that Charlie Brown suffers from a personality disorder. Even though he has dependent traits, Charlie Brown does not meet criteria for the dependent personality disorder of the *DSM–IV* because he is able to function well in spite (or because) of his dependency. In fact, in many ways the success of the Charlie Brown portrayal may be due to his being a typical "normal" neighborhood kid, with whom everyone can identify.

By contrast, the figure of Oblomov characterized by Ivan Goncharov in the story by the same name is one of an individual who is constantly comparing himself unfavorably with others. Oblomov feels so inadequate that his life is restricted to the mere essentials, with his ability to function leaving much to be desired. Accordingly, we would see Charlie Brown as having a dependent personality style and Oblomov as suffering from a dependent personality disorder.

What makes a personality style dysfunctional? At a concrete level, the issue can be answered for a particular individual by determining whether the person meets the *DSM–IV* criteria for any of the specific personality disorders. In some ways, however, this approach evades the real question by relying on what the *DSM–IV* experts could agree on as signs of pathology.

Using a statistical notion of normality, it could be argued that the extremity of the traits that make up the personality structure can lead to maladjustment (Kiesler, 1983; Leary, 1957; Sim & Romney, 1990). From this viewpoint, the difference between Charlie Brown and Oblomov is that the feelings of inadequacy that Charlie Brown harbors are mild, whereas Oblomov feels so inadequate that he cannot get himself to do any of the things that "others" can do.

More typically, the concept clinicians use to differentiate between functional and dysfunctional personality structures is that of adaptive flexibility (Kiesler, 1986a; Leary, 1957; Sim & Romney, 1990). Niccolo Machiavelli already had very definite ideas about this issue in the 16th century. In his book *The Prince*, Machiavelli (1532/1931) explained that a person "may be seen happy today and ruined tomorrow" (pp. 204–205) without having changed his or her disposition or behavior. This early political scientist believed that the person who adapts to the environment tends to prosper, whereas those who "clash with the times" do not.

Machiavelli also conceded that adaptability is especially difficult when people always have prospered by acting in a particular way. Nevertheless, using our terminology, histrionic individuals who are by nature spontaneous and disorganized could make good pilots only if they learned to check the aircraft compulsively before flying. Individuals with antisocial tendencies will need to drop their guarded competitiveness to some degree if they are to establish intimate relationships in life. Philosopher Jan Patocka claimed that the real test in life is not how well people can play the role they invented for themselves but how well they play the role that destiny brings them (cited in Terry, 1990). If individuals are able to be flexible and use personality traits that are not part of their nature in response to specific situations, the results are likely to be more positive than in the case of people who can behave only in the manner that is most egosyntonic.

Inflexibility also could be postulated to lead to the kind of vicious cycles that Millon (1981) talked about as leading to psychopathology. When compulsive individuals inappropriately persist in using compulsive defenses to deal with the difficulties they are facing, the maladaptive persistence is likely to intensify their problems, which, in turn, could lead to using the compulsive mechanisms even more.

In addition to the elements of extremeness and inflexibility, Leary (1957) postulated that maladjustment also could result from a discrepancy between the person's self-perception and the way he or she is perceived by others. Sim and Romney (1990) supported that contention by showing that such discrepancies were significantly larger for a group with personality disorders than they were for a nonpsychiatric control group.

Finally, maladjustment also could result from a poor fit between the individual and the environment. If, in the view of the clinician, the maladjustment is attributable mostly to incompatibility, then the person should not be seen as having a personality disorder because the symptoms would be expected to be temporary. Because the issue of the goodness of fit is present with everyone, and because the environment could possibly be accommodated so that even people with obvious personality disorders would be able to function, this issue constitutes a gray area that often is a matter of clinical judgment. To decide, however, the clinician needs to look at the life of the client longitudinally and to determine whether the person continually has had characterological difficulties regardless of the situation he or she was facing.

Personality Styles in Social Context

As we have already noted, the complexities of defining and understanding an individual's personality style are complicated further because personality styles do not exist in a vacuum. People partly define themselves through their social relationships: They are more inclined to feel adequate or even grandiose when they are relating to people who feel inadequate: an old Spanish proverb tells us that "in the land of the blind, the one-eyed is king."

Ibsen's (1879) play, *A Doll's House*, illustrates the depth of understanding that the concept of personality styles can bring into the assessment of interpersonal relationships. At the beginning of the play, Ibsen portrays an overadequate–underadequate marital relationship. Torvald Helmer is a compulsive-narcissist who carries himself with an air of self-importance and who sets all of the rules for the family. By contrast, the histrionic Nora is a submissive social butterfly. They were seemingly happy until someone attempted to blackmail them. We then learn that when Torvald was seriously ill (in other words, at a time when Nora did not have the kind of support she needed to be able to cope well with her environment), she forged her father's signature on a document. On hearing about the forgery, Torvald decided not to take the blame for this crime and was not willing to shelter his wife in that particular situation; he did not assume the protecting role that Nora expected him to take.

The decision not to take the blame is consistent with Torvald's own personality style: the perfectionistic attitude of the obsessive–compulsive person and the emphasis on an unblemished status of the narcissistic person made it particularly difficult for him to be generous at the time. For Nora, however, her husband's decision meant that he was undependable and that when the chips were down, she might be left to fend for herself. This realization made her so uncomfortable that even after the threat had miraculously disappeared, she was not able to regain her composure or return to the kind of marital relationship she once had. The play ends with Nora leaving the home to "find herself." It is clear at that point that the trauma catalyzed changes in Nora so that she was bound to be a less trusting and more self-sufficient woman in the future.

One could fantasize about the kind of relationship the marriage of Torvald and Nora could become if a more assertive Nora were to return to the marriage. Faced with the positive changes that might have taken place in Nora's personality, Torvald also could become a higher functioning individual by giving up some of his obsessive controls and his narcissistic need to place others at a level lower than himself. The marriage then may eventually become less of an overadequate–underadequate relationship and more of an equal relationship. Realistically, before such a development is finalized, one would have to expect a period of unrest. We could envision the marriage turning, at least for a period of time, into a conflictual relationship in which Torvald attempts to reestablish the kind of dominance he once had while dismissing the fact that the changes in Nora will not permit the relationship to return to its origin.

Ibsen's play illustrates how personality styles complement or clash with each other and how the changes in one personality style affect the entire relationship. We think that this kind of analysis can be helpful not only in looking at the kinds of relationships that patients establish in their lives but also at the kind of relationship they will establish with clinicians in the therapeutic setting.

Our interpretation of Ibsen's play was based entirely on his descriptions of the protagonists and on the way they behaved as the drama unfolded. Possibly someone else could read the same work and conceptualize the main characters in a completely different way. Moreover, in our clinical work, we encounter many individuals who would have difficulty describing themselves with the clarity and insight that Ibsen offered in his work. As a result, it is extremely helpful to have an instrument that allows individuals to reveal themselves in a way that permits a formulation of their particular personality style. In the chapters that follow, we describe how the MCMI is organized and how well it performs that function.

3   Psychometric Characteristics

In this chapter we summarize the procedures that were followed in the development of the MCMIs, as well as the standardization data offered in the test manuals (Millon, 1977, 1987, 1994). We also review investigations by other authors who examined the validity, reliability, or factorial structure of the test. (Studies dealing with the concurrent validity of the MCMI, that is, the relationship of the MCMI to other tests, are discussed in chap. 9.)

The change of the MCMI into the second and third versions has been more of an evolution than the birth of an entirely new test. Considering the criticisms and shortcomings of one version, as well as developments in psychiatric nosology and his own theory, Millon built one version on the foundations of the preceding version. Because the second and third editions were, in a way, refinements of the first, many of the original developmental exercises and studies were not repeated. The end result is that one has to understand the development and functioning of previous versions to fully appreciate the current version. To achieve that full appreciation, we present the topics of this chapter as a progression from the original MCMI to the present form of the test.

In spite of the changes that have been made for the two revisions, the MCMI has maintained the same view of psychopathology and scale organization. To those who were accustomed to one version, the next version seemed like an old friend because it had the same "clinical feel." Clinicians must fight the tendency to assume that, because one test looks similar to another, they must have the same psychometric properties. The number of items that the MCMI-III has in common with the original MCMI is minimal, and a study done with the MCMI-I cannot be considered to be true for the MCMI-III. In this chapter and the chapters that follow, we attempt to make clear which version of the test was used in any study cited so that the reader can judge what is known about which version.

Item Development

MCMI-I

Three successive steps were used for the initial (theoretical) test construction of the MCMI-I. In the first step, more than 3,500 items were written on the basis of Millon's ideas (as expounded by Millon, 1969). These items then were grouped into a set of 20 scales. In the second step, the item pool was edited to reduce redundancy and increase relevance and simplicity (Millon, 1982, 1983). Empirical procedures were used to reduce further the item pool. Such procedures included asking patients to judge the clarity and difficulty level of the items and having clinicians group the items into the scales of the inventory (Millon, 1982, 1983).

Two provisional research forms, each containing 556 items, were administered to a diverse clinical sample of more than 200 patients. Item analyses then were carried out using item–scale intercorrelations and item endorsement frequencies. Such item analyses allowed further reduction of the item pool.

The Research Form, containing 289 items, was developed. This inventory was subsequently validated by 167 mental health clinicians from various locations in the United States and Great Britain who rated 682 patients on the 20 clinical entities represented by the MCMI-I scales.

Comparisons of endorsement frequencies for the 20 clinical criterion groups were used to eliminate items and to make decisions on scale overlap. The 289 items of the MCMI-I Research Form were reduced to 150, 4 of which were correction items.

Analysis of the first external validation study resulted in the decision to drop three clinical syndrome scales—Sociopathy, Hypochondriasis, and Obsession-Compulsion—because they were deemed to lack clinical utility. In their place, three new clinical scales were developed: Drug Abuse, Alcohol Abuse, and Hypomania. These scales were developed following the same procedures described earlier, and the new items were added to the 150 items for the MCMI-I Research Form.

The newly expanded form was administered to criterion groups such as patients in alcohol and drug treatment programs and patients with a history of manic episodes. Comparison groups were 64 "general psychiatric" patients and a group of 33 nonpsychiatric respondents.

The task at this point was to identify scale configurations that would be externally valid or empirically based. Modifications of the configurations were made to bring them closer to the internal structure, dynamic relationships, and substantive hypotheses of Millon's (1969) theory of personality. To keep the number of profiles manageable, it was decided initially to construct profile patterns only from the subsection with the eight personality styles and to limit profiles to two scale high-point pairs. Once the basic 2-point configuration had been established, high scores from pathological personality scales (S, C, P) and from symptom disorder sections (A through PP) were added only as separate elaborations or as modifiers of the basic 2-point configural pattern. Homologous or equivalent configurations were selected when the theoretical considerations were combined with data showing that clinicians assessed differing high-point pairs as representing similar or identical diagnostic entities. The external criteria against which valid profile configurations were assessed were the profiles that clinicians had constructed when asked to make multiple diagnoses and to quantify assessments of their patients' basic personality and pathological patterns (Millon, 1982).

One problem that frequently has been cited with regard to the MCMI is the high interscale correlation (Choca, Bresolin, Okonek, & Ostrow, 1988; Choca, Peterson, & Shanley, 1986a; Wiggins, 1982). Using Guilford's (1936) formula, the covariation ranged from −.46 (for the Antisocial-Aggressive and Dependent-Submissive scales) to .65 (for the Borderline and Dysthymia scales). Millon (1982) believed that the intercorrelations and clustering of the scales mirrored his theoretical position and clinical realities. However, as Wiggins (1982) noted, "when 20 scales averaging 37 items per scale are scored from a common pool of only 171 items, the psychometric consequences of such a high degree of scale redundancy will almost certainly be unfavorable" (p. 211).

Standardization work also was done with the correction scores (Weight Factor, Adjustment Score, and Validity Index) of the MCMI-I to ensure that these measures would detect tendencies in response distortion. Data were collected from 75 nonclinical respondents who were instructed to "fake good," "fake bad," and respond randomly in the inventory; the results are in the manual.

Finally, the issue of how accurate the individual cutoff scores were in making diagnostic decisions with the MCMI-I was examined. A cross-validation sample of 256 patients closely matching the construction sample was used. For "presence of syndrome" (base rates [BRs] = 75), the percentage of correct classifications ranged from 77 to 95. For "most prominent syndrome in category" (BR = 85), the percentage of correct classifications ranged from 82 to 98.

MCMI-II

The revision of the MCMI-I was stimulated by several factors. The proposal of two new personality disorders—the sadistic or aggressive personality and the masochistic or self-defeating personality—encouraged the plan to expand the MCMI-I to include those personalities. Additional theoretical developments pointed to the need to modify descriptions of the borderline and antisocial personalities and to revise the characterization of the clinical syndrome of major depression. A third factor involved the desire to bring the inventory's scales into closer coordination with the psychiatric nosology of the time, the third edition of the *Diagnostic and Statistical Manual of Mental Disorders* (*DSM–III*; American Psychiatric Association, 1980) and the preliminary work that was being done for its successor, the revised *DSM–III* (*DSM–III–R*; American Psychiatric Association, 1987). Enhancement of individual scale validity and the reduction of spurious scale overlap were additional goals that stimulated revision.

Studies undertaken after the original standardization of the MCMI-I led to the finding that 40–50 items were expendable. MCMI-II item replacement studies were aimed at generating items for two new personality scales. MCMI-I Scale 8 (Negativistic) was divided into separate scales: 8A (Negativistic) and 8B (Self-Defeating). MCMI-I Scale 6 (Antisocial-Aggressive) was divided into separate scales: 6A (Antisocial) and 6B (Aggressive/Sadistic). A pool of 364 new items was reduced to 193 in a series of editing stages and after a consensus study of best fit for the two new scales done by eight clinician judges. These 193 new items were added to the set of 175 MCMI-I items to constitute the new and "substantively valid" MCMI-II Provisional Form of 368 items, coordinated with preliminary *DSM–III–R* criteria as well as theoretically based attributes (Millon, 1987).

A sample of 108 patients was given the MCMI-II Provisional Form. New items were reduced to 111 using a variety of criteria. A population of 184 patients was then given the MCMI-II Research Form by clinicians who diagnosed the patients on both axes of the *DSM–III–R* in accordance with the published drafts of diagnostic criteria then in development (American Psychiatric Association, 1985). Correspondence between items and their criterion groups were evaluated using the same procedures used in the external validation studies for the original MCMI-I. The extent to which an item differentiated relevant criterion groups from the population of "general psychiatric patients" was the most important issue in determining selection of final items. The decision to retain or drop an item was not based on any particular cutoff score or fixed level of diagnostic efficiency. The new 111 items were reduced to a final group of 45 items on the basis of the data obtained. These 45 new items replaced 45 of the original MCMI-I items that had been found in previous item-evaluation studies to be expendable. Thus, the final MCMI-II consisted of 175 items, the same number of items contained in MCMI-I (Millon, 1987).

MCMI-III

The revision of the MCMI-II was prompted by the wish to add two more scales and to align the instrument, even more than before, with the criteria that were being developed for the fourth edition of the *DSM* (*DSM–IV*; American Psychiatric Association, 1994). The work began with the selection of 150 new items. Some of these items were designed to measure the depressive personality, a new personality prototype that was being proposed for the *DSM–IV*, and posttraumatic stress disorder. The rest of the items were derived from the criteria sets in the draft for the *DSM–IV* (American Psychiatric Association, 1993).

Reacting to the criticism (see below) that the previous versions of the MCMI were not designed to measure the categories of the *DSM*, Millon (1994) made every effort to produce statements that reflected the diagnostic criteria of the available draft for the *DSM–IV*. The test manual offers two examples for each of the scales of the parallel items that were included. One is told, for instance, that "the second *DSM–IV* schizoid criterion is 'almost always chooses solitary activities'" and that the comparable test item is "When I have a choice, I prefer to do things alone" (Millon, 1994, p. 17) or that "the first DSM-IV criterion for the histrionic personality is 'is uncomfortable in situations in which he or she is not the center of attention'" which translates into an MCMI item reading "I never sit on the sidelines when I'm at a party" (Millon, 1994, p. 18).

All items that met theoretical goals were added to the 175 items of the MCMI-II. The resulting 325-item form was called the MCMI-II Research Form (MCMI-IIR). This research form then was distributed to several hundred clinicians who regularly used the MCMI-II, and completed tests were collected on about 1,000 examinees. Examination of these data led to the elimination of items with an unexpectedly high or low endorsement rate, items that had a high correlation with another item, or items that appeared to be prototypic on more than one scale.

Standardization

MCMI-I

MCMI-I norms are based on numerous clinical groups and nonclinical samples. Drawn from industrial plants, colleges, and personnel offices, the 297 nonclinical respondents served to anchor BR scores: The median scores for this group were arbitrarily assigned a BR score of 35 on all scales except for the Hypomania scale (Millon, 1982). Patient populations whose test data provided the basis for MCMI-I norms included 1,591 clinical respondents from the construction phases of test development (see the manual for more information about the samples).

Raw scores were converted to BR scores on the basis of known prevalence data. Cutoff scores, determined by calculating the optimal ratio of true-positives to false-positives, were designed to ensure the maximum degree of correct diagnostic classifications (Millon, 1982). A BR score of 74 was selected as the cutoff or the point on all MCMI-I scales beyond which scale percentages would correspond to the clinically judged prevalence rate for the presence of a personality feature or symptom. A BR score of 84 was selected as the cutoff for all scales beyond which scale percentages would correspond to the clinically judged prevalence rate for the most prominent personality or symptom syndrome. Except for the Hypomania scale, all MCMI-I scales were assigned the BR score of 60 to designate the raw score median for all patients in the test construction studies. Because there were differences in prevalence rates and median raw scores between male and female respondents on several MCMI-I scales, cutoffs for BR scores of 35, 60,

75, and 85 did differ slightly for men and women on those scales. The manual indicated that the percentile of correct classifications ranged from 77 to 98 using a BR score of 85 and the cross-validation sample (Millon, 1982, p. 59).

A review of the data on the percentage of true- and false-positives and correct classifications for the validation samples indicated that most false-positive cases were found among "overlapping" clinical syndromes or personality patterns. For example, both the Narcissistic and the Histrionic scales tapped personality features that often were clinically demonstrated in the same patient. Such personality features often came up high on their respective MCMI-I scales even when they were not judged by clinicians to be concurrently present. Consequently, one of these would be scored as a false-positive. On the other hand, scales measuring traits or syndromes that are viewed as theoretically and clinically disparate seemed to produce far fewer false-positives. For example, there were almost no false-positive cases between the Histrionic scale and the Schizoid scale. Because these two scales do not measure theoretically overlapping traits or syndromes, patients who scored highest on one of them rarely scored high on the other.

Further review of the true- and false-positive data revealed problems with or weaknesses of the usefulness of certain aspects of the MCMI-I in differential diagnosis. First, the Compulsive scale (Scale 7) appears to be the least effective of the MCMI-I scales in terms of the ratio of true-positives to false-positives and in terms of the correct classification percentage. Thus, clinicians should be cautious about the significance of the results of Scale 7, especially if this is not corroborated by clinical observation or other test data. Second, there is a problem within the subsection of the three pathological personality disorder scales (Schizotypal, Borderline, and Paranoid). The majority of false-positives on this subsection of the scales appeared to represent cases in which clinician judges did not rate a concurrent presence of personality disorders but in which the patient produced overlapping high MCMI-I scores. It appears that when a patient has a marked degree of severity in a personality area measured by any one of these three scales, that "dimension of severity may occasionally overpower and blur the differential diagnostic efficiency of the scales" (Millon, 1982, p. 17).

Although the data just discussed on raw score–BR score conversions and cutoff scores on the MCMI-I were contained in the original manual (Millon, 1977), notable revisions soon followed. In 1981, the data for 43,218 patients on the MCMI-I were reviewed, resulting in the recalculation and adjustment of the transformation of raw score to BR scores. This patient population included 23,296 (54%) women and 19,922 (46%) men, of whom 16% were inpatients and 84% were outpatients. On the basis of numerous selected subsamples, BR scores between the major cutoff scores of 85, 75, 60, and 35 were smoothed proportionately to represent each scale's raw score patient-frequency distribution. To determine the BR-20 point, the 10th percentile for patients on each basic personality scale was used. The 30th percentile among patients on each basic personality scale was used to determine the BR-40 point (Millon, 1982).

MCMI-II

The standardization of the MCMI-II was done with a sample of 1,292 patients (for more information about the sample, see Millon, 1987). The same anchoring procedures detailed earlier were followed for the standardization of this version.

MCMI-III

The standardization of the MCMI-II was done with a sample of 1,079 patients (for more information about the sample, see Millon, 1994). The same anchoring procedures detailed earlier were followed for the standardization of this version.

Validity

Operating Characteristics of a Test

Three different types of test validity commonly are recognized. The issue of face validity was discussed previously in the descriptions of how the items were developed. The term *concurrent validity* refers to correlations of one test with other tests measuring similar constructs when taken by the same individuals at approximately the same time. Although such correlations can be used to ascertain that the test is measuring what it is supposed to measure, the correlations also reveal the relation between the two tests in question. In this book, we discuss most of the concurrent validity studies in chapter 5, emphasizing what the data disclose about the relationship among the instruments involved. In this chapter, we discuss only data showing the validity of the MCMI against

Table 1

Hit Rates Possible When a Diagnostic Scale Is Administered to a Heterogeneous Group

| Test result | Patient diagnosis | |
	Positive (patient depressed)	Negative (patient not depressed)
Positive	Cell a: True-positives	Cell b: False-positives
Negative	Cell c: False-negatives	Cell d: True-negatives

external nontest criteria. These types of data are referred to as the operating characteristics of a test; a brief discussion of operating characteristics is offered before the presentation of the MCMI studies.

When a diagnostic scale, for instance a scale designed to measure depression, is administered to a heterogeneous group of individuals, the possible "hit rates" are shown in Table 1. In this context, the *prevalence*, or the base rate, of the disorder is defined as the total number of positive occurrences of the disorder (a + c) divided by the total number of patients (a + b + c + d). *Sensitivity*, the proportion of true-positives, is the probability that the test score will be elevated when the disorder is actually present (a/[a + c]). *Specificity*, the proportion of true-negatives, is the probability that the test score will not be elevated when the disorder is absent ([d/(b + d]). The *positive predictive power* (PPP) is probably the most clinically relevant measure because it represents the likelihood that the disorder is present when the test score is elevated. The PPP is calculated as the proportion of true-positive cases across all cases in which the test was positive ([a/(a + b]). *Negative predictive power* (NPP) is the probability that the disorder is absent when the test is negative (d/[c + d]). Finally, *overall diagnostic power* represents the proportion of correct classifications ([a + d]/(a + b + c + d]).

The PPP and the NPP are influenced by the magnitude of the sensitivity and specificity of the test and the prevalence of the disorder in the population. When the sensitivity and specificity of the test are high (e.g., 90%), the PPP and the NPP indexes are optimal. However, as prevalence decreases, so does PPP. In populations that have few cases with a particular diagnosis, even tests with high specificity and sensitivity can have low PPP for that diagnosis. The overall diagnostic power also varies in its usefulness because disorder prevalence rates vary (Baldessarini, Finklestein, & Arana, 1983).

Test users are encouraged to consider carefully how a test will perform with their particular population (see chap. 1). In cases in which the prevalence of particular disorders differs considerably from the prevalence found in the standardizing sample, the bootstrapping method may be useful. When enough data for an instrument are available, the bootstrap method can be used to adjust the cutoff score (e.g., the BR score of 75 or 85 in the MCMI) in accordance with the estimated local base rate of the attribute (Rorer & Dawes, 1982).

The external nontest criteria typically used to validate a test are clinician ratings. The gold standard is the rating of experienced clinicians using a structured interview. When several such clinicians offer a rating on the same individual, agreement can be established by calculating the kappa value. Unfortunately, clinicians are not too reliable. *DSM* field trials found kappa values to be as low as .26 for the personality disorders. The unreliability of the external criteria creates a ceiling for the validity of any scale using that criteria. Retzlaff (1995a) noted, for instance, that if the kappa value for the compulsive personality disorder is .26 and the disorder has a prevalence of .05, a scale attempting to measure this construct could not have a PPP of more than .30 and therefore would accurately identify only 30% of those who scored above the cutoff. The impressive part of this calculation is that it has considered only the reliability of the external criteria and the prevalence of the disorder; any imperfection of the scale, of course, would lower its PPP and usefulness even further.

MCMI-I

Millon (1983) presented data on the generally high sensitivity and specificity of the MCMI-I scales. Gibertini et al. (1986) found that the MCMI-I scales varied widely in their usefulness for assigning diagnostic labels to individual patients. PPPs ranged from 19% to 84%. Defining a good scale as one with a PPP of 70% or higher, a fair scale as having a PPP of 50–69%, and a poor scale as having a PPP below 50%, they rated each scale for its ability to predict the "presence of a syndrome": Eight were good (Avoidant, Dependent, Histrionic, Negativistic, Borderline, Anxiety, Dysthymia, and Drug Abuse); 9 were fair (Schizoid, Narcissistic, Antisocial, Compulsive, Schizotypal, Paranoid, Somatoform, Hypomania, and Alcohol Abuse); and 3 were poor (Psychotic Thinking, Psychotic Depression, and Psychotic Delusions). They also rated each scale for its ability to predict the "most prominent syndrome": Five were good (Avoidant, Schizotypal, Paranoid, Anxiety, and Dysthymia); 11 were fair (Schizoid, Dependent, Histrionic, Narcissistic, Antisocial, Compulsive, Negativistic, Borderline, Hypomania, Alcohol Abuse, and Drug Abuse); and 4 were poor (Somatoform, Psychotic Thinking, Psychotic Depression, and Psychotic Delusions).

The MCMI-I scales also were found to have generally high NPPs. Thus, negative test scores rarely will be false-negatives, and patients who are actually free of a given disorder will tend not to score in the clinical range for the presence of that disorder.

A third finding discussed by Gibertini et al. (1986) concerns the generally high overall diagnostic power of the MCMI-I and the factors that one must consider in interpreting the value of this global index. Figures for the overall diagnostic power of the inventory for correctly classifying patients on the presence or absence of a trait or disorder range from 82% to 94% for the presence of a syndrome and from 86% to 97% for the most prominent syndrome (Millon, 1983). Crucial to understanding the meaning of the overall diagnostic power index is an awareness that, especially when prevalence is low, the index can be misleading because it is possible to have high overall diagnostic power even when the actual number of false-positives and false-negatives is greater than the number of true-positives.

Streiner and Miller (1990) compared the sensitivities and specificities of four diagnostic procedures. They used clinical discharge diagnosis, the MCMI-I, and diagnoses made on the basis of structured interviews (the Diagnostic Interview Schedule and the Personality Disorder Interview). The research participants ($N = 239$) were taken from a variety of settings, primarily inpatient facilities. A relatively new statistical technique, the maximum-likelihood estimation approach, was used to estimate sensitivities and specificities of each approach. No one technique was definitively better, although the structured interviews seemed better for making diagnoses. Psychometric properties of the various methods differed depending on the diagnosis of the patient. The MCMI tended to have higher specificity than sensitivity.

When the test is used in an inpatient psychiatric setting, it may not perform as well as would have been predicted from the operating characteristics of the standardizing population. The prevalence of the different disorders will differ enough in such a setting from the prevalence found in the standardization sample that too few or too many examinees would score beyond the cutoff BR scores of 75 or 85. Greenblatt, Mozdzierz, Murphy, and Trimakas (1992) used the bootstrap method (discussed earlier) to adjust the cutoff scores to reflect better the local prevalence rates. The adjustments improved the PPP of 10 of the MCMI-I scales in their inpatient setting, with no loss of NPP.

One area of controversy with the MCMI has been over how validly the instrument measures the psychiatric disorders and syndromes of the *DSM–III*. The NCS printout for the MCMI-I was identified as a *"DSM–III* report" and provided Axis I and Axis II diagnoses (Millon, 1983, p. 25; Widiger, Williams, Spitzer, & Frances, 1985). All 11 personality scales of the MCMI-I were given titles of an Axis II diagnosis from the *DSM–III*. The remaining syndrome or symptom scales of the MCMI-I were named to closely resemble the *DSM–III* diagnoses on Axis I. Instructions in the manuals for the MCMI-I (Millon, 1977, 1982, 1983) explained that elevations on the scales were to be interpreted as indicating the presence of *DSM–III* disorders. The test author had described a variety of efforts to coordinate the MCMI-I as closely as possible to the *DSM–III*, writing that "no other diagnostic instrument currently available, other than the MCMI, is fully consonant with the nosological format and conceptual terminology of this official system" (Millon, 1983, p. 1).

Critics objected to the contention that the MCMI-I was a measure of *DSM–III* disorders (J. Reich, 1985; Widiger & Frances, 1987; Widiger & Sanderson, 1987; Widiger, Williams, Spitzer, & Frances, 1985, 1986). They argued that there had been no published research to support the alleged correspondence between the MCMI-I and the *DSM–III*. Furthermore, they noted that the derivation and cross-validation research for the MCMI-I scales had used Millon's (1969) taxonomy, not that of the *DSM–III*. After detailing differences between the *DSM–III* diagnostic criteria for numerous personality disorders and the criteria that Millon had written as initial drafts for these personality disorders, Widiger et al. (1985) supported their contention with an evaluation of content validity, which was conducted by eight graduate student judges, of the Aggressive and Gregarious scales of the MCMI-I. These critics did acknowledge that an analysis of the content validity of the MCMI-I was not necessarily relevant to its predictive validity and observed that Millon's personality types represented, in many cases, marked improvements over the *DSM–III* categories. Moreover, some scales were observed to be highly similar to *DSM–III* categories, and one was even essentially synonymous with a psychiatric disorder described in Axis II of the *DSM–III*.

Millon (1985, 1986) answered his critics by noting that the original MCMI was altered in the later stages of its development to improve its usefulness to clinicians. Millon (1985) argued that the real issue was whether the MCMI's conceptual and trait-oriented criteria were at least as good as the biographical and behavioral criteria of the *DSM–III* in "achieving high concordance with independently derived clinical assessments" (p. 380).

The controversy continued with an article by Widiger and Sanderson (1987), who examined the effectiveness of four of the personality scales against the findings of the Personality Interview Questions, a semistructured interview that was administered by a college senior. The findings demonstrated good convergent validity for the Avoidant and Dependent scales; the Antisocial and Negativistic scales, on the other hand, were judged to be much less successful. These findings were thought to be consistent with Widiger and Sanderson's contention that the MCMI-I is more congruent with the *DSM–III* for the disorders for which Millon's typology coincides with the *DSM–III* prototype.

Similarly, Torgersen and Alnæs (1990) reported a good correspondence between the *DSM–III* personality disorders, as measured by the Structured Clinical Interview for the DSM–III, and the Avoidant and Dependent scales of the MCMI-I. A fair correspondence was found for the Schizotypal, Histrionic, Borderline, Narcissistic, and Paranoid scales, whereas the Schizoid, Negativistic, and Compulsive scales showed poor correspondence.

In other studies, however, the MCMI-I has not fared well. Piersma (1986a, 1987a) compared MCMI findings with the *DSM–III* diagnoses at the time of discharge. He noted that an elevation of a personality scale was obtained in 98% of the patients, whereas only 40% of the sample had received the diagnosis of a personality disorder from the clinician. Moreover, the MCMI diagnosis was consistent with the clinician only 20% of the time regarding the particular type of personality disorder (1987a).

Wetzler and Dubro (1990) compared the results on the MCMI-I with the admitting diagnoses of experienced psychiatrists. They found the test to have a high sensitivity, such that almost 75% of the patients with a personality disorder were identified, but the test tended to err by classifying many patients judged not to have a personality disorder as having one (false-positives). The PPP of the test in this study was .49;

because the base rate for the presence of a personality disorder was .51, the effectiveness of the test was considered to be poor. Wetzler and Dubro pointed out that the poor concordance with the MCMI-I has been obtained in studies using diagnoses generated in standard clinical practice as the criterion measure; they noted that the MCMI-I has performed better when a semistructured interview was used. This observation opens to question whether it is the MCMI-I that is deficient or the clinical diagnosis used as criterion measure.

We now discuss validity studies considering specific scales rather than the entire MCMI-I. An investigation of 82 psychiatric inpatients, classified by means of the Structured Interview for the DSM-III Personality (SIDP), showed poor concordance between the MCMI-I personality scales and the *DSM-III* diagnosis. The sensitivity and PPP were generally low and were down to zero on the Compulsive scale (H. J. Jackson, Gazis, Rudd, & Edwards, 1991). Similar findings have been documented by other researchers (Hogg, Jackson, Rudd, & Edwards, 1990; Nazikian, Rudd, Edwards, & Jackson, 1990).

There is one more investigation of this type that we know about. The report was published in 1993, 6 years after the MCMI-II became available. The 1979 edition of the MCMI-I was compared with the outcome of a checklist taken from the 1987 *DSM-III-R*. Needless to say, the test did not do well. The authors reported that only the Schizotypal scale of the MCMI-I was related to its respective *DSM-III-R* personality disorder and that the test showed low sensitivity, poor specificity, and low predictive and diagnostic power (Chick, Sheaffer, Goggin, & Sison, 1993). Although this investigation seemed to stack all cards against the MCMI-I, the results still warn us that the MCMI-I scores do not translate into *DSM-III-R* categories.

In fact, and as noted in the previous section, a significant problem in applying the classic method for concurrent validation to measures of personality trait is that the method assumes that the criterion measure is error-free and that clinicians have some way of knowing who has a particular personality style. Even more than the Axis I clinical syndromes, personality disorders lack clinical consensus (Tyrer, 1988). As a result, instruments that attempt to measure the personality structure are attempting to hit an unclear and ambiguous target. Taking that issue into account, H. R. Miller, Streiner, and Parkinson (1992) used maximum-likelihood estimates in their study of personality measures. This procedure statistically computes what combinations of data from different instruments best define the construct to be evaluated (e.g., the dependent personality). After the construct has been defined through this concordance of multiple measures, that definition then becomes the criterion against which the individual measures are compared. Their data showed that none of the instruments (i.e., the Minnesota Multiphasic Personality Inventory [MMPI], the MCMI-I, and the SIDP) were in consistent agreement either with each other or with the maximum-likelihood estimate definition of the disorder.

Of the personality scales of the MCMI-I, the Narcissistic scale has been shown to be a valid measure of narcissism, making the MCMI "more useful than the MMPI" in the measurement of this construct (Chatham, Tibbals, & Harrington, 1993, p. 248).

The Borderline scale of the MCMI-I, on the other hand, has been shown to have a modest (.37) correlation with the *DSM–III–R* clinician diagnosis of borderline personality (Lewis & Harder, 1991) and is not thought to be useful as a screening measurement for that disorder (Patrick, 1993).

The validity of the symptom formation scales of the MCMI-I also has come to the attention of researchers. Sexton, McIlwraith, Barnes, and Dunn (1987) used discriminant analysis and the MCMI-I to predict the discharge diagnosis of patients with affective disorders and schizophrenia with 48% accuracy. Greenblatt and Davis (1993) calculated a modest PPP of .40 and an NPP of .86 on the basis of the data by Sexton et al. Greenblatt and Davis also noted that the scales that appear to be most relevant to schizophrenia (e.g., Psychotic Thinking or Schizotypal) lacked influence in the discriminant equation. Helmes and Barilko (1988) found the MCMI-I to be "marginally inferior" (p. 80) to the MMPI in predicting symptoms taken from the chart even though the MCMI-I is substantially shorter.

In our work with people with affective disorders, the Dysthymia and Hypomania scales seemed useful diagnostically because they correctly classified 65% and 56% of the patients in a depressed and manic state, respectively (Choca et al., 1988). Similar support for the Dysthymia scale has been cited by other researchers (J. O. Goldberg, Shaw, & Segal, 1987; O'Callaghan, Bates, Jackson, Rudd, & Edwards, 1990; Wetzler, Kahn, Strauman, & Dubro, 1989), although Flynn and McMahon (1983a) found only modest correlations between the scale and three items dealing with depression and suicidality from an unstandardized survey. The Dysthymia scale has been shown to perform as well as two other depression scales in the diagnosis of depression among individuals with alcoholism (Tamkin, Carson, Nixon, & Hyer, 1987).

With our patients with affective disorders, the Cycloid scale seemed to be affected by a depressed mood but appeared to be fairly insensitive to mood elevations. As a result, we thought that the Cycloid scale was somewhat redundant with the Dysthymia scale (Choca et al., 1988). It is noteworthy that this scale was changed to the Borderline scale for the MCMI-II.

The Psychotic Depression scale was so seldom elevated in any of the samples available that it was thought to be of little clinical utility (Choca et al., 1988; J. O. Goldberg et al., 1987; O'Callaghan et al., 1990; Wetzler et al., 1989). Flynn and McMahon (1983a) also reported a modest correlation between this scale and their three items dealing with depression and suicidality. J. O. Goldberg et al. (1987) factor-analyzed the items of the Major Depression scale and discovered three factors: Mood Disturbance, Suicide Ideation, and Dependency Conflicts. They thought that the problem with this scale was that it neglected the vegetative symptoms of depression.

The substance abuse scales also have received the attention of researchers. Jaffe and Archer (1987) compared five scales on their ability to predict drug use among college students. The two MCMI-I substance abuse scales performed well: The discriminant functions used one or both of the scales to predict each of the 12 different categories of substance use except tobacco. The intercorrelation between the two MCMI substance abuse scales was reported to be .65, and the authors noted that the scales had 15 items in common. Accordingly, they questioned whether both of the scales were needed. In their own work, Jaffe and Archer found that the Alcohol Abuse scale was more useful than the Drug Abuse scale, even when the drug use being predicted was not alcohol.

Using a psychiatric population, Bryer, Martines, and Dignan (1990) investigated the effectiveness of the MCMI-I substance abuse scales in distinguishing between substance abusers and the rest of the patients. Using the cutoff BR score of 75, both of the scales were found to correctly classify 79% of the sample. The Alcohol scale had 43% true-positives and 52% false-positives, whereas the Drug Abuse scale yielded 49% true-positives and 64% false-positives.[1] Bryer et al. (1990) questioned

---

[1]Kessel and Zimmerman (1993) pointed out that Bryer, Martines, and Dignan (1990) defined the false-positive rate unconventionally. They calculated the false-positives by dividing the number of cases in which the scale was elevated and the diagnosis was absent by the total number of cases in which the scale was elevated. According to the conventional definition, the number of cases in which the scale is elevated and the diagnosis is absent is divided by the total number of cases in which the diagnosis is absent.

the utility of the scales as screening instruments in a psychiatric population because, with their data, "subjects scoring above [the] cutoff, more often than not, did not have the substance abuse history that the particular scale had predicted" (p. 440).

The performance of the MCMI-I substance abuse scales also may leave something to be desired when they are used with a substance-abusing population. Gibertini and Retzlaff (1988b) found that only 17% of their sample from an inpatient alcohol rehabilitation program had elevated scores on the Alcohol Abuse scale. The same problem was found by H. R. Miller and Streiner (1990), who reported that the Alcohol scale identified only 33–43% of the alcoholic patients. Gibertini and Retzlaff (1988b) complained that the scale tends to measure only severe and prolonged substance abuse, so that there are few false-positives, but that it tends to miss many of the problem drinkers. Similarly, more than half of the former opiate addicts studied by Marsh, Stile, Stoughton, and Trout-Landen (1988) or the opioid and cocaine addicts studied by Calsyn, Saxon, and Daisy (1990, 1991) failed to have elevated scores on the MCMI-I Drug Abuse scale. Moreover, few of the items that make up these substance abuse scales actually address substance abuse. Because there is little evidence for a generic addictive personality, it has been argued that the MCMI-I substance abuse scales can be expected to perform fairly poorly (Bryer et al., 1990; Marsh et al., 1988). In fact, Calsyn et al. (1990) concluded that the true-positive rate was so low that the Drug Abuse scale of the MCMI-I was useless.

We now review studies comparing the performance of the MCMI-I to that of similar instruments against nontest criteria. To some extent, the practical question to ask is how effective the MCMI-I scales are compared with other available assessment instruments. This is the most important question to ask because clinicans will have to choose one fallible instrument over another fallible instrument. Even the MMPI, the traditional standard in this area, has significant limitations in its ability to predict clinical diagnoses (e.g., Pancoast, Archer, & Gordon, 1988).

Several investigations have compared the general diagnostic value of these two inventories. Libb et al. (1992), for instance, studied the concordance of the MCMI-II, the MMPI-I, and the clinical syndrome (Axis I) discharge diagnosis of 166 psychiatric patients. Although both tests performed reasonably well in the discriminant function analyses, the MCMI-II achieved a higher hit rate (79% vs. 68% for the MMPI). The superior performance was shown to have resulted from the greater accuracy of the MCMI-II in identifying the group with affective disorders.

Dubro, Wetzler, and Kahn (1988) compared the efficiency of the MCMI-I, the MMPI Psychopathic Deviate (*Pd*) scale, and the Personality Diagnostic Questionnaire (PDQ). The SIDP was used as the measure against which the other instruments were examined. Dubro et al. found the MCMI-I to have "excellent sensitivity" when used as a screening instrument, to be a "fair" predictor of the cluster of personality disorders in which the patient would fall, and to be "fairly successful" at identifying the four personality disorders that enjoyed enough representation in the sample to make statistics meaningful (p. 261). Of the three instruments, only the PDQ was occasionally more effective than the MCMI-I. Because the PDQ consists of items taken directly from the *DSM–III* personality disorder criteria (from where the SIDP also is taken), the finding that the MCMI-I was generally as successful as this instrument provided strong support for the test's validity. Another study that compared different assessment techniques showed the MCMI-I scales to be more closely related to diagnostician ratings than the personality scales developed by Morey, Waugh, and Blashfield (1985) from the MMPI (Morey, 1986).

Three studies compared the usefulness of the MCMI-I and the MMPI with two highly different patient populations. Patrick (1988) administered both tests to 103 psychiatric inpatients and found that two MCMI-I clinical syndrome scales (i.e., Psychotic Thinking and Psychotic Depression) were "grossly inaccurate" according to the criterion of concordance with final chart diagnosis, a finding also supported by O'Callaghan et al. (1990). A third clinical syndrome scale, Psychotic Delusions, did identify one of two paranoid disorders in the sample, but this was offset by its relatively high false-positive rate. The true-positive rate was found to be lower than that reported by Millon (1983) for psychotic disorders despite a high prevalence of schizophrenia in the sample. The MMPI was found to be more accurate than the MCMI-I in the identification of both schizophrenia and major depression. Using a similar psychiatric population, Helmes and Barilko (1988) reported that the MCMI-I could diagnose only 1 of 10 symptoms recovered from the patient's chart; the MMPI was not much more effective because it was able to discriminate only 2 of the 10 symptoms.

Generally, the MCMI-I has not performed well in the diagnosis of schizophrenia. The Thought Disorder scale (Scale SS) has been shown repeatedly to perform poorly, as already noted. Because that scale was the only scale designed to measure schizophrenic symptoms, analysis of the score pattern is the only valid alternative. Such analyses have failed to confirm Millon's expectations (see Table 7 in chap. 7), but they actually have led to unanticipated findings. McCann and associates (del Rosario, McCann, & Navarra, 1994), for instance, obtained fewer scale elevations with the schizophrenic group than with a presumably less disturbed inpatient control group. The work of J. J. Jackson, Greenblatt, Davis, Murphy, and Trimakas (1991) suggested that the problem may be that many schizophrenics are not inclined to report their symptoms in self-report inventories.

Uomoto, Turner, and Herron (1988) compared the MCMI-I and the MMPI in predictions of surgical outcome in patients who underwent lumbar laminectomy. Neither instrument was found to be markedly superior to the other for this purpose. If a clinician must choose only one personality measure, Uomoto et al. suggested the MMPI because only three MMPI scales (*Hs*, *L*, and *K*) and two demographic variables (age and financial compensation) were needed to obtain a reasonably good hit rate for predicting outcome of lumbar laminectomy. Uomoto et al. noted that they used the MCMI-I with a normal (nonpsychiatric) population even though the test author advised against doing that. They also noted another methodological limitation in that both patient and surgeon bias might have influenced results because outcome ratings were made by the surgeons. Finally, they noted that although psychological factors are important, physiological variables such as the presence versus absence of disk herniation play a crucial role in deciding surgical outcome.

MCMI-II

In developing the MCMI-II, clinician judges made the diagnostic assignments on the basis of the criteria from the draft of the *DSM–III–R*. For the external validity of the MCMI-II, Millon (1987) reported that the sensitivity of the scales ranged from 50% to 79%, the specificity ranged from 91% to 99%, the PPP ranged from 58% to 80%, the NPP ranged from 93% to 98%, and the overall diagnostic power ranged from 88% to 97%. Reexamination of the standardization data by others also is available in the literature (e.g., McCann, 1990a).

In spite of those outstanding figures, the MCMI-II has had difficulty demonstrating the diagnostic efficiency of its personality scales when pitted against the outcome of the *DSM–III–R* semistructured interviews.

Overall kappa coefficients for the presence or absence of a personality disorder have been reported in the range of .26 to .28 using a BR score of 84 or higher. Some of the individual kappa coefficients have been so low as to indicate no relationship between the MCMI-II elevation and the outcome of the semistructured interview (Hart, Dutton, & Newlove, 1993; Renneberg, Chambless, Dowdall, Fauerbach, & Gracely, 1992; Soldz, Budman, Demby, & Merry, 1993a; Turley, Bates, Edwards, & Jackson, 1992).

As far as we can tell, none of the other personality instruments have fared much better in clinical trials against the *DSM–III* or its successors. Hunt and Andrews (1992), for instance, obtained disappointing results with the revision of the PDQ. Problems also have been reported with the Wisconsin Personality Disorders Inventory (Klein, Benjamin, et al., 1993). Greater convergence in the personality area has been reported between the MCMI-II and the MMPI-2 than between either one of these instruments and results of a structured interview (Butler, Gaulier, & Haller, 1991; Hills, 1995). As a result, it has been impossible to determine whether the problem lies with the tests (MCMIs included), with the semistructured interview used, or with the *DSM* itself, which may have its own validity and stability difficulties.

The convergence between the MCMI-II personality scales and the personality scales of the MMPI—revised for the MMPI-II by Colligan, Morey, and Offord (1994)—has also left something to be desired. According to Wise (1996), the average correlation between scales designed to measure the same personality prototype is very modest (.54) and accounts for only 29% of the variance. Regarding the clinical syndrome scales, Libb, Murray, Thurstin, and Alarcon (1992) obtained a better hit rate with the MCMI-II than with the MMPI-1 in a sample of hospitalized psychiatric patients. Libb et al. found the MCMI-II affective disorder scales to be particularly proficient. McCann (1990b) found support for the convergent validity of the MCMI-II using a multitrait-multimethod factor analysis and the MMPI. Poor discriminant validity, however, was found for the Alcohol Abuse, Drug Abuse, and Paranoid scales. The sample included only 85 psychiatric inpatients, so caution must be used in accepting the findings. The fact that a psychoticism factor has been notably missing from the factor analyses of the MCMI-II items (Retzlaff, Lorr, et al., 1991), however, also may be used to question the effectiveness of the Thought and Delusional Disorder scales of this test.

Some investigators have analyzed the performance of specific scales. Hart, Forth, and Hare (1991) examined the effectiveness of the Antisocial scale using a sample of 119 male convicts. The sensitivity of this scale proved to be acceptable at .88, as was the NPP of .92. The specificity of .38 and the PPP of .26, however, were disappointingly lower than what Millon had reported. The findings suggest that the scale overpathologizes patients on the antisocial personality and further support our contention that elevations of the personality scales do not indicate the presence of a personality *disorder* as much as a personality *style*.

Hart et al. (1991) distinguished between two factors of psychopathy. Their first factor reflects affective and interpersonal characteristics (e.g., callousness, manipulativeness, lack of anxiety), whereas the second factor measures aspects of the chronically unstable antisocial lifestyle (e.g., impulsivity, criminality, substance abuse). The MCMI-II Antisocial scale was found to be measuring mostly attributes of the second factor. (Factor 1 characteristics were found to be only weakly related to the Aggressive scale [6B] of the MCMI-II.) Like the diagnostic criteria of the *DSM–III–R*, the MCMI-II was thought to emphasize the antisocial lifestyle at the expense of affective and interpersonal characteristics.

Piersma (1991) examined the degree to which the Dysthymia and Major Depression scales of the MCMI-II would distinguish between a major depression and another type of depression. Using a cutoff BR score of 75, he reported that the Major Depression scale missed 39% of the individuals in his sample. Another study similarly showed the Dysthymia scale to have good specificity and overall diagnostic value, whereas the Major Depression scale seems to be insensitive to depression (Wetzler & Marlowe, 1993). Wetzler and Marlowe also concluded that the Hypomania scale did not diagnose adequately the manic individuals in their study.

The low hit rate previously reported for the substance abuse scales of the MCMI-I does not appear to have been improved by the MCMI-II. Fals-Stewart (1995) reported that the Drug Abuse scale missed almost half, and the Alcohol Abuse scale missed 30%, of honestly responding patients involved in a treatment program for substance abuse.

Finally, McCann and associates (see del Rosario et al., 1994) studied the effectiveness of the Thought Disorder scale in diagnosing schizophrenic patients. Their data showed that neither this scale nor the Delusional Disorder scale led to higher scores when the schizophrenics were compared with a mixed inpatient control group. In spite of the poor overall performance of the scales, the Thought Disorder scale did have adequate specificity even if it proved to be highly insensitive. For the clinician, the finding means that a lack of elevation on this scale has no diagnostic relevance but that when the scale is elevated, the possibility that the patient does suffer from a thought disorder should be considered seriously.

MCMI-III

The prevalence, sensitivity, and specificity of the MCMI-III scales are provided in the manual (Millon, 1994). Using those data, Retzlaff (1996) calculated the predictive powers. He noted that the PPP was uniformly poor, ranging from 0 to .32 for the personality scales and from .15 to .58 for the Axis I disorder scales. Millon (personal communication, September 24, 1994) believed the low PPP was attributable to the poor quality of the external validity study. However, further studies are needed before the diagnostic value of the test can be determined.

Reliability

MCMI-I

Test–retest studies for the MCMI-I involved more than 140 patients and yielded reliability coefficients ranging from the low .60s to the low .90s. Most of the basic personality scales were in the .80s, the pathological personality scales were in the high .70s, and the clinical syndrome scales were in the mid-.60s (Millon, 1982).

Because the MCMI is designed to differentiate among enduring personality characteristics and more transient clinical symptoms, the scales would be expected to perform differently in test–retest studies. The findings reported are consistent with the theoretical expectation in that the basic and pathological personality scales showed a higher stability than the symptoms scales.

Millon's (1982) findings have been supported by other investigations examining the stability of the scores (McMahon, Flynn, & Davidson, 1985b; T. J. Murphy, Greenblatt, Mozdzierz, & Trimakas, 1990; Overholser, 1989; Piersma, 1986d; J. Reich, 1989; Wheeler & Schwarz, 1989), even though the coefficients have typically been lower than those reported by Millon. Higher stability estimates for basic personality scales when compared with stability estimates for symptom scales generally are reported.

Data are available on the stability of the MCMI-I Drug Abuse scale. Flynn and McMahon (1983b, 1984b) reported a reasonable coefficient (.74) when the score obtained a month after admission to a treatment program was compared with the score obtained 3 months later. The low coefficients (.45 and .55) obtained when the scores at intake were compared with those obtained a month later, however, should be a warning about possible inaccuracies when the MCMI is used with drug abusers who are in the process of drug withdrawal. Similar changes have been documented with depressed individuals (Libb, Stankovic, Sokol, et al., 1990).

Internal consistency data for the MCMI-I scales are presented in the manual for the test (Millon, 1982). Kuder-Richardson coefficients ranged from a low of .58 for the Psychotic Delusion scale to a high of .95 for the Borderline scale. Except for the Psychotic Delusion scale, all scales had coefficients at or above .70.

The retest stability of high-point scale profiles is important because of the increasing use of such configurations in clinical interpretation. The data Millon (1987) presented were based on results from 421 psychiatric patients who had been tested at a variety of points in their treatment. Millon reported that patients had the same first or second highest scale on two administrations in about 70% of the MCMI-I cases. In addition, approximately 50% of the patients had the same highest 2-point code in either the same or reverse order.

Piersma (1987a) examined changes in the MCMI-I personality diagnosis that a psychiatric inpatient would receive on admission as opposed to that received at the time of discharge. He reported that only 27% of the sample would have received the same diagnosis in terms of the patient's elevations on the MCMI. T. J. Murphy et al. (1990), who also looked at the number of examinees with a similar personality profile on the second testing, found similarly disappointing results. The stability of score profiles admittedly is much more difficult to accomplish than having test–retest scores that are highly correlated. Nevertheless, the findings should be seen as a warning to clinicians that the configuration of the scores may change for many individuals from time to time.

In summary, studies on the test–retest stability of the MCMI-I provide support for the assertion that the instrument reliably assesses the presence of both enduring personality traits and transient symptom states. Reliability figures, of course, vary depending on the population studied, the length of interval between the first and second testings, and the timing of testing sessions at the first or second admission, midphase, or discharge points. Test–retest stability is higher for personality style scales as a group than it is for clinical symptoms scales as a group; this situation is entirely consistent with the underlying theory and intent of these instruments. The highest stability results for the personality scales and symptoms scales were found for nonpatient participants who received no clinical interventions. The theoretically expected pattern of relatively high reliability for personality scales and relatively low reliability for symptoms scales was most obvious in the studies in which both inpatients and outpatients were tested shortly after entering treatment and shortly before leaving treatment.

MCMI-II

Stability coefficients for the MCMI-II scales for a variety of populations are reported in the manual (Millon, 1987). Test–retest intervals ranged from 3 to 5 weeks. Coefficients for 91 nonclinical participants were both high and fairly consistent; as one might expect with this population, personality scales were not significantly more stable than clinical symptom scales. The basic personality scales had stability coefficients ranging from .80 to .89; for the severe personality scales, the range was .79–.89, and for the nine clinical syndrome scales the range was .78–.91. The high stability coefficients attained for this nonclinical control group represent solid evidence for the test–retest reliability of the MCMI-II scales and also provide a basic frame of reference against which data from other groups can be compared. That the nonclinical group obtained the highest stability coefficients among all samples studied was interpreted to be a function of the fact that they had not been subjected to any intervention aimed at changing their psychic state as well as being a function of the ease with which nonclinical participants can respond consistently to test items that represent extremes in emotionality and social behaviors.

The lowest stability coefficients were found in a group of 47 heterogeneous psychiatric inpatients who were tested at intake and again at discharge. The stability coefficients ranged from .59 to .75 for basic personality scales, from .49 to .72 for the severe personality scales, and from .43 to .66 for the clinical symptoms scales (Millon, 1987). These findings were supported by Piersma (1989b), except that his coefficients were somewhat lower than Millon's. Piersma also was able to demonstrate that the MCMI-II yielded higher stability coefficients than the original test version.

Stability data for the two-scale, high-point profiles of the MCMI-II also are presented in the manual (Millon, 1987). On the basis of 168 heterogeneous psychiatric inpatients and outpatients who were retested at intervals of 3–5 weeks, almost 65% had the same first or second highest MCMI-II scale on both administrations. Forty-five percent of patients had the same highest two-scale profiles, either in the same or the reverse order. These are impressive reliability figures, especially because the number of scales involved has increased from the MCMI-I to the MCMI-II. In addition, the latest stability data for the 2-point profiles on the M MI-II include more cases that were tested at intake and at discharge, an arrangement that is considered to be the most stringent gauge of reliability (Millon, 1987).

MCMI-III

The alpha coefficients for internal consistency are provided in the test manual (Millon, 1994, p. 31). The reported coefficients seemed acceptable, ranging from .66 for the Compulsive scale to .90 for the Major Depression scale. Similarly, the test–retest correlations show good stability, ranging from .82 for the Debasement scale to .90 for the Somatoform scale.

Psychometric Structure

MCMI-I

Factor-analytic techniques have been used with the Millon instruments even though the application of such techniques to the MCMI-I and the MCMI-II is fraught with difficulties and limitations. Perhaps the most basic problem is that the Millon instruments are, by design, essentially nonfactorial: The underlying structural model calls for built-in scale overlaps and considerable item redundancy (Millon, 1982). An illustration of the difficulties that such overlap presents for the execution and interpretation of factorial solutions by scales can be found in the first of two analyses reported in the manual (Millon, 1982). "Scales 8, C, A,

H, D, and CC load .892 or better on Factor 1,'' Hess (1985) observed, ''yet all but 4 of Scale A's 37 items appear on at least one of the other five scales'' (p. 985). Certainly, the real meanings of such loadings by scales are highly questionable when 89% of Scale A's items are shared. The impact of item overlap and the resultant high interscale correlation on an overdetermined factor structure has been cited repeatedly in the literature (Choca et al., 1986a; Gibertini & Retzlaff, 1988a; Hess, 1985; Montag & Comrey, 1987; Widiger, 1985).

As Guilford (1952) noted, factor-analyzing a group of scales that share items may be inappropriate. The reason for this was explained by Gibertini and Retzlaff (1988a) in the following manner:

> When two or more scales share items they become linearly dependent to an extent proportional to the percentile of the item-overlap. This essentially guarantees that the correlation matrix to be factored has some degree of structure not provided by the subject response patterns. Some part of the resulting factor pattern, in other words, will be artificial. This artificial structure will be constant across populations. If this effect is large relative to that of the subject response patterns, then the artificial structure will ''drive'' the factor analysis and create very stable factors which have little to do with subject responses. (p. 66)

Note that the same problem has been cited with regard to the MMPI (Shure & Rogers, 1965).

Beyond the essentially nonfactorial structure of the Millon tests, there are important additional conceptual and methodological difficulties. For instance, the selection of a factor method and choosing a solution to summarize the covariation matrix involve complex methodological questions. There also are the issues of weighing, for various sample populations, the influence of differences in demographic features and clinical homogeneity (Millon, 1982).

Many factor-analytic studies have been reported for the Millon instruments. Researchers have examined populations of general psychiatric patients (Choca et al., 1986a, 1989; Choca, Shanley, Peterson, & Van Denburg, 1990; Greenblatt, Mozdzierz, Murphy, & Trimakas, 1986; Lorr, Retzlaff, & Tarr, 1989; Millon, 1982, 1987; Piersma, 1986b; Strauman & Wetzler, 1992), women with eating disorders (Head & Williamson, 1990), alcohol abusers (Gibertini & Retzlaff, 1988a; Lorr et al., 1989; McMahon & Davidson, 1988; McMahon, Gersh, & Davidson, 1989b), drug abusers (Flynn & McMahon, 1984a), substance abusers (Millon, 1982), and air force trainees (Gibertini & Retzlaff, 1988a; Retzlaff & Gibertini, 1987b). Retzlaff, Lorr, et al. (1991) obtained data for male and female college students and reported on a sample of male veterans in posttraumatic stress disorder, alcohol, and psychiatry programs.

Despite differences in the subject population used, the studies just mentioned have reported a strong similarity among the available factorial solutions. The factor for paranoia, for example, was found in 10 of the applicable studies, lability and schizoid detachment were labeled in 9, passive-submission-aggression was noted in 7, and both psychoticism and general maladjustment were found in at least 5 of the investigations. Table 2 shows a sample of the different studies available in the literature and the factors that emerged from those studies.

Researchers have reported that results of their factor-analytic studies lend support to the Millon instruments in terms of the underlying theory, a fairly stable factorial structure, the arrangement of and relations among component personality and symptoms scales, and their clinical usefulness with patient populations. Piersma (1986b), for instance, concluded that his results give further support to Millon's goal of constructing "an instrument that is capable of assessing both presenting symptomatology and more enduring, long-term personality traits and characteristics" (p. 584). McMahon and Davidson (1988) contended that their results suggest that the original MCMI-I may provide a "more differentiated classification" of substance abusers than has been found in various MMPI studies.

McMahon, Applegate, Kouzekanani, and Davidson (1990) examined the factor structure of the MCMI-I in a well-defined alcoholic population using the stringent standards of confirmatory factor analysis. Results were inconclusive for an initial analysis based on all 20 scales of the test. However, a second analysis, which was based on only the first 8 personality scales of the test, produced a good fit between a two-factor model and the test data. Retzlaff, Lorr, et al. (1991) reported that the factors they found were highly consistent with the scale keyings of the MCMI-II scales.

Most factor-analytic studies of the Millon instruments have been based on the scores respondents obtained on the 20 clinical scales; as already noted, item overlap and interscale correlation can produce an artificially stable factor structure. Some investigators have attempted to deal with the overlap problem by using correlations of shared and unshared scale items (Lumsden, 1986, 1988). Others have performed a factor analysis on the matrix of the item-overlap coefficients (Gibertini & Retzlaff, 1988a). Finally, attempts also have been made to use the

Table 2

Sample of the Available Factor Analyses of the MCMI Using All Scales

First author	Year	Participants	No. of factors	Names given to factors
Choca	1986a	Psychiatric	3	Maladjustment Labile Acting-Out Psychoticism
Flynn	1984a	Drug abusers	4	Negativism Detachment Passive-Submissiveness Paranoid
Gibertini	1988a	Air Force trainees	4	Distress Social Acting-Out Suspiciousness Submissive-Aggressiveness
Gibertini	1988a	Alcohol abusers	4	Distress Social Acting-Out Suspiciousness Submissive-Aggressiveness
Greenblatt	1986	Psychiatric	3[a]	Detachment Impulsiveness Psychoticism
Lewis	1990	Psychiatric	3	General Maladjustment Acting-Out Avoidant-Schizoid
McMahon	1988	Alcohol abusers (two samples)	4	Schizoid-Avoidant Anxious-Depressed Lability of Mood Paranoid-Delusional
McMahon	1989	Alcohol abusers	4	Schizoid-Avoidant Somatoform Drug Abuse-Hypomania Paranoid-Delusional
Millon	1977	Psychiatric	4	Lability Paranoia Schizoid Social Restraint
Millon	1977	Substance abusers	4	Lability Paranoia General Pathology Lability-Schizoid
Piersma	1986b	Psychiatric	5	Interpersonal withdrawal Emotional Distress Impulsivity-Negativism Paranoid Distrust Dependency-Submission
Strauman	1992	Psychiatric	3	Anxious Depression Emotionality Paranoid Manic Thinking Schizoid Thinking

[a]Using nonmetric multidimensional scaling.

Bashaw and Anderson statistical correction to change the correlation matrix (Helmes, 1989). None of these attempts have been successful in reducing the problem to any significant degree.

Perhaps the only way to avoid the issue of scale overlap is to work with the respondents' answers to the individual items of the inventory rather than the overlapping scales. We collected 2,129 MCMI-I protocols from male patients hospitalized on acute care psychiatric units at two different Veterans Administration medical centers. The patients' responses then were subjected to a principal-components analysis and a varimax rotation. Seventeen interpretable factors emerged from that analysis, accounting for 41% of the total variance: Depression, Schizoid, Hypomania, Dependent, Narcissistic, Alcohol, Conflictual, Compulsive, Histrionic, Drug Abuse, Suicidal, Paranoid, Tearfulness, Validity, Somaticism, Tiredness, and Changeability (Choca et al., 1989).

This item-based analysis, then, yielded considerably more factors than scale-based factor analyses. Of the 17 interpretable factors that emerged, 14 contained loadings that made them resemble scales from the MCMI-I. Support was found for 6 of Millon's basic personality scales, 1 of his pathological personality disorder scales, and 5 of his clinical symptom syndrome scales. Three factors (Suicidality, Tearfulness, and Tiredness) appeared to be part of a depression cluster but emerged as separate factors. There was one factor—Changeability—that loaded on items dealing with changing one's opinion or feelings and that could be seen as being associated with the MCMI-I Borderline scale. The Avoidant and the Antisocial scales were not represented in this factorial solution. The MCMI-I scales most poorly represented in the factor structure were those assessing psychoticism and severely maladaptive personality scales, a surprising finding in a sample of acute-care psychiatric inpatients. Also, in contrast to scale-based factor analyses, no general maladjustment factor emerged.

In a second item-based factorial study, Lorr et al. (1989) analyzed MCMI-I data from a sample of 253 psychiatric outpatients and 185 alcoholic inpatients. Although the findings have to be interpreted with caution because of the small sample used, we include the results here because they seem to support some of our own findings. Six personality factors emerged that were interpreted as follows: Social Introversion-Extraversion, Dependency on Others, Verbal Hostility, Need to Please Others, Self-Dramatization, and Orderliness. The five symptom factors that emerged were named Depression, Manic Excitement, Drug Abuse, Alcoholic Misuse, and Suicidal Ideation. Of the six interpretable personality factors, five could be seen to correspond well to Millon's (1969) personality disorders. The Social Introversion-Extraversion factor is similar at one pole to the Avoidant and Schizoid scales; at the opposite pole it is similar to the Histrionic scale. The factors Dependency on Others and Need to Please Others appear to be similar to Millon's Dependent scale. The factor for Self-Dramatization appears to represent aspects of Millon's Histrionic scale. The Orderliness factor corresponds well with Millon's Compulsive scale. The Verbal Hostility factor represents much of Millon's Antisocial scale. In this analysis, no dimensions separated out that would correspond closely to Millon's Narcissistic or Negativistic scales.

Factor-analytic studies of the MCMI-I at the item level represent an important methodological refinement in that they avoid the problem of item overlap. Such studies allow for the ascertainment, without influence by the scale keys, of latent variables that underlie the individual items. In marked contrast to scale-based factor analyses that typically have yielded three to five factors for the MCMI-I, these studies have demonstrated a factor structure for Millon's test that is at once more diverse, more differentiated, and well defined and lends support to the stability of the underlying personality theory's structural model. The authors (Choca et al., 1989; Lorr et al., 1989) of the two item-based factor analyses have obtained highly similar results: They also, interestingly enough, offered similar recommendations: Develop nonredundant scales, add missing scales, and enlarge the scales that need a greater number of items for their definition.

MCMI-II

For the MCMI-II, the scale-based factor analysis produced a broader range of factors than did the previous scale-based studies for the MCMI-I (Millon, 1987). On the basis of 769 cases from the normative psychiatric population, the results of the varimax-rotated factor matrix for the MCMI-II were reported in that test's manual and are summarized briefly here.

Factor 1, which might be called "Maladjustment," accounted for 31% of the variance. Dominant themes included low self-esteem, limited and poor interpersonal relationships, peculiarities of cognition and behavior, and depressed affect. High positive loadings were found on the Avoidant, Self-Defeating, Schizotypal, Thought Disorder, and Major Depression scales. Moderately high positive loadings were found on the

Negativistic, Schizoid, and Borderline scales. Factor 2, which might be called "Acting-Out/Self-Indulgent," accounted for 29% of the variance. Dominant themes included stimulus-seeking, self-indulgent and acting-out pathologies associated with interpersonal hostility, abrasive self-confidence, and manic temperament. High positive loadings were found on the Histrionic, Narcissistic, Hypomania, and Drug Dependent scales. Relatively high positive loadings were found on the Antisocial, Aggressive-Sadistic, and Paranoid scales. Factor 3, which might be called "Anxious and Depressed Somatization," accounted for 13% of the variance. Dominant themes included covarying symptomatology of the classic triad with moderate severity. High positive loadings were found on the Anxiety, Dysthymia, and Somatoform scales. Factor 4, which might be called "Compulsively Defended/Delusional-Paranoid," accounted for 8% of the variance. Dominant themes included pervasive suspicions defended by rigid emotional controls with periodic explosive outbursts. High positive loadings were found on the Compulsive, Paranoid, and Delusional Disorder scales. Relatively high positive loadings were found on the Aggressive/Sadistic and Schizoid scales. Negative loadings were found on the Histrionic, Bipolar, Manic, and Negativistic scales.

Factor 5, which might be called "Submissive/Aggressive-Sadistic," accounted for 7% of the variance. This is a bipolar factor with one end represented by low self-esteem, self-abnegation, and submissiveness and the opposite extreme reflecting interpersonal hostility, exploitation, and intimidation with associated high self-confidence. Positive loadings were found on the Dependent and Self-Defeating scales and negative loadings were found on the Aggressive-Sadistic, Antisocial, and Narcissistic scales. Factor 6, which might be called "Addictive Disorders," accounted for 5% of the variance. Dominant themes included both alcohol and other drug addiction as well as antisocial personality features. Positive loadings were found on the Alcohol, Drug, and Antisocial scales. Factor 7, which might be called "Psychoticism," accounted for 4% of the variance. Dominant themes included the psychotic realm of frankly thought-disordered and delusional experiences as well as chimerical or confused thinking. Positive loadings were found on the Delusional Disorder, Thought Disorder, and Paranoid Personality scales. Factor 8, which might be called "Self and Other Conflictual/Erratic Emotionality," accounted for 3% of the variance. Dominant themes included internal conflict, interpersonal ambivalence, and erratic and unstable emotionality. High positive loadings were found on the Borderline, Negativistic, and Self-Defeating scales.

Strack et al. (1992) conducted separate factor analyses on the 13 personality scales and the 9 clinical syndrome scales of the MCMI-II. They also examined both the BR scores and the "residual scores." Analyses using BR scores yielded four factors for the personality scales. Analyses using "residual scores" yielded what Strack et al. regarded as a more meaningful set of three bipolar factors for both the personality scales and for the clinical syndrome scales. They also stated that their findings are generally supportive of Millon's (1969) contention that personality disorders are associated reliably with clinical syndromes. For example, Strack et al. found that social introversion was strongly associated with disordered thinking and that traits of emotionality were strongly associated with substance abuse, depression, and anxiety.

McMahon, Kouzekanani, and Bustillo (1991) investigated the factor structure of the MCMI-II in 278 male inpatient cocaine abusers selected from four treatment facilities in Florida. Their results indicated that the MCMI-II factor structure is highly similar to that found by McMahon and Davidson (1988) with the original MCMI and a sample of alcohol abusers. In addition, three of the four factors found in this analysis revealed clear similarities to Millon's (1987) factor analysis of the MCMI-II based on a psychiatric population. McMahon, Kouzekanani, and Bustillo described the first factor as reflecting a pattern of aggressive acting-out; the second factor was characterized as involving a detached interpersonal style accompanied by anxious-depressed emotionality; a dependent interpersonal style with anxiety and somatic complaints was reflected on the third factor, whereas the last factor revolved around compulsive personality features.

A factor analysis of the MCMI-II items showed 8 personality and 9 symptom factors for a patient sample as well as 7 personality and 7 symptom factors for a college student population (Retzlaff, Lorr, et al., 1991). Because the sample consisted of only 207 male Veterans Administration patients and 278 college students, the results have to be interpreted with caution. Nevertheless, Retzlaff, Lorr, et al. thought that their data generally supported the scale keyings on the new MCMI-II.

Of the 13 personality scales of the MCMI-II, for example, 9 are represented by factors in one or both of their samples. Only the Paranoid, Schizotypal, Negativistic, and Avoidant scales lack clear identification. Of the 9 clinical symptom scales on the MCMI-II, 5 are represented by the following factors in the samples: Somatoform, Mania,

Dysthymia, Alcohol Abuse, and Drug Abuse. However, only nonsignificant aspects of the three psychotic scales were seen, and no factor for the Anxiety scale was found. The psychometric convergence of so many of the MCMI-II scales at the item level is particularly noteworthy, as Retzlaff, Lorr, et al. (1991) observed, because factor-analytic methods were not used in the construction of the MCMI-II, a test developed with techniques of domain theory, with items deliberately composed for a priori psychopathology constructs.

In summary, scale-based factor analyses of the MCMI generally have produced solutions within a range of three to eight factors. Such solutions have been interpreted with some consistency. Millon (1982) described his own findings as reflecting the classical tripartite distinctions for affective, paranoid, and schizophrenic disorders: moving toward, moving against, and moving away. Certain solutions have recalled Eysenck's (1976) triad of neuroticism, extraversion, and psychoticism. Evidence is available for factors that correspond closely to Millon's detached, dependent, and independent typology (McMahon, Gersh, & Davidson, 1989a). Among the factors that have emerged most consistently from scale-based studies, despite differences in naming or labeling as well as differences in order of emergence or percentage of variance accounted for, paranoia, emotional lability, schizoid detachment, passive-aggressive, psychoticism, and general maladjustment appear to have been the most prominent across a variety of population samples.

Regrettably, researchers continue to use questionably small samples for factor analysis or to neglect the role of important patient variables (e.g., sex, race, age, socioeconomic status, diagnostic assignment). The former practice ignores Comrey's (1978) comments on the most common methodological problems in factor-analytic studies. Beyond being sufficiently representative to allow generalization of results, the sample should be large enough to give stable correlation coefficients.

All of the MCMI-II factor-analytic studies discussed thus far used scale scores. Unfortunately, the high interscale correlations may be dictating the stability of the test structure found in those studies. Lorr and his associates (Lorr, Strack, Campbell, & Lamnin, 1990; Retzlaff, Lorr, et al., 1991), however, conducted item factor analyses with the MCMI-II that overcome this problem. They found six or seven factors using the personality scale items that seem to reflect hostility, social introversion, conformity, submissiveness, antisocial attitudes, and suspiciousness. The items keyed to clinical syndrome scales led to five, six or eight factors depending on the sample. These factors generally reflected depression, suicidal ideation, substance abuse, a tendency to cry, mania, and somatic preoccupation. The clustering of the items contributing to the different factors usually supported Millon's (1987) keying of the items. Because no hierarchical analyses were done, the factors reflect the structure of the test at the scale level rather than the more global factors obtained from an analysis of the scale scores.

The *DSM–IV* proposes that the 11 personality disorders can be grouped into three clusters. Cluster A is associated with odd, eccentric, or asocial inclinations; Cluster B is characterized as flamboyant and dramatic; and Cluster C describes anxious or fearful tendencies (American Psychiatric Association, 1994). Bagby, Joffe, Parker, and Schuller (1993) questioned whether data collected with the MCMI-II supports the *DSM* theoretical clusters. Using MCMI-II standardization data, the authors generally answered their own question in the affirmative. Thus, the Schizoid, Paranoid, and Schizotypal scales have a reasonable loading on Cluster A, even though this loading was the smallest one obtained (.56); the Histrionic, Narcissistic, Antisocial, and Borderline scales loaded clearly only on Cluster B, and the Avoidant, Dependent, Compulsive, and Negativistic scales had a significant loading on Cluster C. The only problem found was that the Schizoid, Paranoid, and Schizotypal scales loaded almost as highly on anxious and fearful tendencies (Cluster C) as they did on the cluster to which they are assigned.

MCMI-III

Given the issue of the interscale correlations, no factor analysis was done as part of the standardization of this version of the MCMI. Issues dealing with the structure of this version will have to wait the availability of other studies.

Validity of the NCS Automated Report for the MCMI-I

The diagnostic accuracy of the computer-generated MCMI-I diagnoses has been found deficient every time it has been examined. For example, DeWolfe, Larson, and Ryan (1985) studied 48 patients suffering from a bipolar affective disorder. Only 13 of the 48 reports accurately classified the patients. Similar findings were obtained by Piersma (1987b) with 151 consecutively admitted psychiatric inpatients at a large private hospital. His results indicated that the computer-generated diagnoses underestimated the number of depressive disorders and overdiagnosed anxiety disorders judging from the diagnoses of admitting psychiatrists.

Finally, Bonato, Cyr, Kalpin, Prendergast, and Sanhueza (1988) compared diagnoses derived from the MCMI-I with those generated independently by both structured and unstructured interviews for 31 consecutive referrals to an outpatient clinic. Bonato et al. reported extremely low (15%) agreement between the MCMI-I and the criterion diagnoses.

The validity of the NCS report as a whole has been the subject of additional studies. C. J. Green (1982) reported that 23 clinicians rated the information provided by these interpretive reports for 100 of their patients as adequate or better 89% of the time. The clinicians compared MCMI-I and MMPI-I interpretive programs on the basis of adequacy of report information, descriptive accuracy, and utility of the report format. They rated MCMI-I reports as valid, useful, and more accurate than MMPI-I programs in assessing interpersonal relations, personality traits, and coping styles. Green's accuracy figures were dismissed by Lanyon (1984) on the basis that there had been no standard against which to compare the reports. Lanyon also expressed a concern about the "Barnum effect," namely, that a report may be rated as highly accurate because it is filled with generalizations that apply to almost anyone rather than because it is a pointed description of the individual patient.

One way to deal with the Barnum effect is to have experienced clinicians rate the accuracy of two reports for each patient, with one report having been prepared in the usual manner and the other chosen at random (Webb, Miller, & Fowler, 1970). One then can take the difference between the two types of reports as a measure of the incremental validity of the reports prepared in the usual fashion over the BR. Moreland and Onstad (1987) implemented this strategy and had eight doctoral-level clinical psychologists in six settings rate 99 pairs of reports on their own patients. Seven report sections were rated separately. The researchers formed a composite rating of overall report accuracy by giving each report 1 point for each of the seven report sections rated as "accurate." Case reports obtained a median accuracy rating of 5 (M = 4.16, SD = 2.20, mode = 6), whereas the control reports chosen at random obtained a median accuracy rating of 2 (M = 2.66, SD = 2.23, mode = 1). The difference between the case and control ratings was highly significant ($p < .0001$). The researchers regarded this as a conservative estimate of the accuracy of the MCMI-I interpretive reports because, for purposes of analysis, report sections that were rated as "unclear" or "don't know" were considered inaccurate. Evaluated singly, five of the report's seven sections exceeded chance accuracy. The researchers noted that the sections of the report that demonstrated the greatest incremental validity (i.e., those dealing with Axis I and Axis II diagnoses and narratives) also are those for which there is the best empirical support (Millon, 1983). Moreland and Onstad (1987) concluded that the NCS system "for the MCMI can be much more accurate than the ascription of symptoms, traits, and so on, at random" (p. 114). This work, however, was criticized as possibly having methodological problems, such as using a sample of clinicians that might not have represented the field at large (Cash, Mikulka, & Brown, 1989). Although Moreland and Onstad recognized some limitations of their data, they were able to defend their "cautious" conclusions in a follow-up article (Moreland & Onstad, 1989) and continue to feel that the report is of good quality (Moreland, 1992).

Finally, interpretive reports produced by different instruments for the same patients can be compared. When the automated reports of substance abusers were rated by chemical dependency counselors, Siddall and Keogh (1993) obtained more favorable ratings for the Diagnostic Inventory of Personality and Symptoms than for the MCMI-I.

4 Effect of Individual Variables

In this chapter we review studies in which individual attributes, such as gender, race, age, socioeconomic status, birth order, and education, have been shown to influence the results obtained on the MCMI. Traditionally, this effect has been called *test bias* and has been seen as an unwanted error of the measurement, an element that lowers the validity of an instrument.

Regarding the effect of the examinee's race, the outcome of recent litigation has demanded that evaluations not lead to a disproportionate number of individuals being chosen from one race over another, even if the difference in test performance could be explained in terms of the characteristics of the minority groups involved (e.g., *Larry P. v. Wilson Riles* [Lambert, 1981]; the "Golden Rule" settlement [Anrig, 1987]; *Watson v. Fort Worth Bank & Trust* [Bersoff, 1988]). This particular interpretation continues to be controversial (Denton, 1988) because it is just as logical to argue that the test is measuring what it is supposed to measure and that different groups have different qualities or attributes.

Regardless of our viewpoint on the cause of group differences, it seems imperative for clinicians to be aware of the effect that particular examinee variables may have on the test results. For example, if women were much more prone than men to score higher on the Self-Defeating scale of the MCMI-III, then an elevation on this scale by female respondents would be seen as less pathological than the same elevation by male respondents. Such knowledge then could be used to modulate our interpretations. A marginally elevated score may be dismissed in some cases, whereas more significant elevations may be seen as partly constituting a socioculturally determined defense. In the review that follows, we examine the literature from that perspective, not necessarily seeing any differences found between groups as a flaw of the test but as data with which clinicians must be familiar.

Gender

Wierzbicki and Goldade (1993) asked college students to rate the items of the MCMI-I on whether they were more likely to be endorsed by men or women. Their data showed that items on 10 of the 11 personality scales of this inventory were perceived to be more associated with one gender than the other. The standardizing data for all versions of the MCMI have shown that men and women do respond differently on this test. As a result, Millon (1982, 1987, 1994) thought it necessary to use different tables for the conversion of raw scores to a base-rate (BR) score for men and women. It is important to examine how effectively the use of different conversion tables equalizes the test results if one is going to offer the same interpretation to similar elevations regardless of the person's gender.

Although still inadequate, the information available on sexual differences on the MCMI-I suggests that the test may pathologize stereotypically feminine traits. Piersma (1986c), for instance, discovered that women scored significantly higher than men on 5 of the MCMI-I scales at the time of admission and on 5 scales at the time of discharge. However, the 5 scales at the time of admission were not the same ones at the time of discharge. The 3 scales on which women scored significantly higher than men at both times were Dependent, Psychotic Depression, and Psychotic Delusion.

Similarly, Cantrell and Dana (1987) reported significant sex differences using the MCMI-I in their sample of psychiatric outpatients. Women obtained significantly higher scores on 6 scales—Dependent, Borderline, Anxiety, Somatoform, Dysthymia, and Psychotic Depression—and tended to have a greater number of scales elevated above a BR score of 74. Although men also scored higher than women on some scales in both studies, the incidence of such occurrences was less frequent and the mean differences were less pronounced.

That scores on the same scales were not consistently found to be

Table 3

Millon Clinical Multiaxial Inventory Scales Showing Gender Differences

Scale	Women		Men	
	M	*SD*	*M*	*SD*
Dependent	82	23	58	24
Psychotic depression	65	12	57	14

Note. Data are from Cantrell and Dana (1987).

more elevated when one gender was compared with the other suggests using the findings with caution. Nevertheless, both studies showed that women scored higher on the Dependent and Psychotic Depression scales. Table 3 shows the means and standard deviations of these scales taken from Cantrell and Dana (1987). The difference found with the Psychotic Depression scale seemed less critical, but, as can be seen, the average female score on the Dependent scale was above the usual clinical cutoff of 74.

A meta-analysis of available studies using the Dependent scale of the MCMI-I showed that women obtained higher scores than men (Bornstein, 1995). The same study, however, indicated that all scales designed to measure dependency behave in the same manner, a finding suggesting that women generally may acquire higher dependency traits as part of the sex role socialization experiences in American culture.

The obvious concern would be that, using the MCMI-I, women would be diagnosed erroneously as suffering from a dependent personality disorder. As a result, readers are strongly encouraged to interpret elevations of the Dependent scale with caution in the case of women, making sure that the patient clearly meets criteria from the revised fourth edition of the *Diagnostic and Statistical Manual of Mental Disorders* (*DSM–IV*; American Psychiatric Association, 1994) before this diagnosis is given.

Lindsay and Widiger (1995) examined possible sex and gender bias of the items of the MCMI-II, the MMPI, and the Personality Diagnostic Questionnaire–Revised. From 6 to 31 of the 175 items of the MCMI-II test showed sex bias, depending on which of the four criteria for bias was used. From this point of view, the test performed slightly better than the MMPI but worse than the revised Personality Diagnostic Questionnaire.

Race

Public and scientific debate over the adequacy of psychological instruments in evaluating members of minority groups have been around for more than six decades (Cronbach, 1975). Although the original conversion tables for the MCMI did not distinguish between individuals of different races, a 1984 manual supplement included separate conversion tables for Black, White, and Hispanic examinees.

In spite of Millon's efforts, racial differences have been noted with the MCMI-I. Pochyly, Greenblatt, and Davis (1989; Davis, Greenblatt, & Pochyly, 1990) examined the effect of race and level of education on the Asocial, Avoidant, Schizotypal, Psychotic Thinking, and Psychotic Delusions scales. Their sample consisted of patients diagnosed as schizophrenic and those having nonpsychotic diagnoses. Those particular scales were chosen because they are purported to show maximal differences between the two diagnostic groups in question. A multivariate analysis of variance showed that race was the only main effect that reached significance. Subsequent univariate tests showed that White patients scored significantly lower than Black patients on the Asocial, Avoidant, and Psychotic Thinking scales. Later work by this group indicated that Black schizophrenics scored higher than White schizophrenics on the Paranoid and Psychotic Delusions scales (J. J. Jackson et al., 1991).

Using a similar sample from another Veterans Administration hospital, we also have examined the issue of racial differences with the MCMI-I (Choca, Peterson, & Shanley, 1986b; Choca et al., 1990). We used the *DSM–III* discharge diagnoses to examine the predictive power of the test for Black and White patients. Data analysis showed that there were differences in the way that the MCMI-I predicted the *DSM–III* diagnoses for anxiety disorders, affective disorders, substance abuse disorders, and psychotic disorders, but not for personality disorders.

We then matched examinees according to diagnostic groups to conduct an item analysis. Differences between Black and White examinees were found in 45 of the 175 items of the MCMI-I. At the scale level, an analysis of variance indicated a significant overall effect for race. Scores obtained by the Black and White groups were significantly different on 9 of the 20 scales. White patients scored higher on the Dysthymia scale, whereas Black patients scored higher on the Histrionic, Narcissistic, Antisocial, Paranoid, Hypomania, Alcohol Abuse, Drug Abuse, and Psychotic Delusion scales. Partial replication of our results was obtained by Hamberger and Hastings (1992), who found a tendency for Black men who abused their wives to score higher on all of the aforementioned scales except the Histrionic, Antisocial, and Alcohol Abuse scales. Finally, we also conducted two separate factor analyses on each of the racial groups. We obtained identical solutions for both.

In other words, the available data indicated that there are MCMI-I items that tend to be answered differently by White and Black patients. Similarly, some of the scales tend to lead to higher scores by one racial group over another. However, the fact that the structure of the instrument remains the same suggests that the instrument measures the same global attributes regardless of race.

One possible explanation for the differences we obtained at both the item and the scale levels is that the two racial groups were not similar psychopathologically. For example, it could be argued that the symptoms of one of the groups were more severe than the other. It also could be argued that the categories used to match the two groups were too general and therefore did not adequately equalize the groups in terms of the characteristics measured by the MCMI-I. For example, matching examinees on the presence or absence of a personality disorder does not mean that the resulting groups are going to be similar in their histrionic tendencies. Greenblatt and Davis (1992) examined whether the MCMI-I could predict accurately the self-reported anger and psychosis of White and Black examinees. The MCMI-I correctly identified patients of both races who were concerned about their anger or psychosis, with the two racial groups showing the same pattern of scale elevations.

On the other hand, in reporting the diagnostic inaccuracies of the MCMI-I Drug Abuse scale (see chap. 3), Calsyn et al. (1991) noted that the insensitivity of the scale is considerably worse for White respondents than it is for Black respondents. In other words, when testing addicts, the Drug Abuse scale is more likely to be elevated if the examinee is Black than if the examinee is White.

When the MCMI-I items were being evaluated for the construction of the MCMI-II, item-endorsement frequencies for Black, White, and Hispanic examinees were studied to reduce potential minority biases. Millon (1987) randomly selected 200 patients from each of these three groups and performed a full replication study. When the endorsement frequencies were calculated on all 171 clinical items for the first 100 patients in each ethnic-racial group, significant differences among the groups were found for 36 items. When the endorsement frequencies were calculated on all clinical items for the second 100 patients in each ethnic-racial group, significant differences among the groups again were found for 13 of those 36 items. Those 13 items were then set for replacement in the MCMI-II.

Unfortunately, 39 of the 45 items that we found to be problematic in our study were included in the MCMI-II. As a result, we would expect that the newer test also would contain differences in the way items are endorsed by White and Black examinees. Although the MCMI-II manual includes "preliminary norms" for Black and Hispanic patients, these conversion tables are not used because the sample size was considered inadequate (Millon, 1987). As a result, it is possible that the scale differences that have been found with the MCMI-I would be even more pronounced with the newer versions because no allowance is made for cultural differences. Indeed, the preliminary data that are available with the MCMI-II suggest a general trend for nonpsychotic Black psychiatric patients to score higher on the MCMI-II Schizophrenia and Paranoid scales (Davis, Greenblatt, & Choca, 1990).

So as not to mislead readers, we note that the kind of racial differences found with the MCMI are typical of psychological tests in general. As the reviews by Reynolds (1982, 1983) and Jensen (1980) indicated, this problem plagues most of the measures of intellectual ability. The Minnesota Multiphasic Personality Inventory (MMPI) has been defended by those who feel that documented racial differences were attributable to methodological problems (Dahlstrom, Lachar, & Dahlstrom, 1986; Pritchard & Rosenblatt, 1980). Nevertheless, most MMPI studies on the topic have shown differences between minority-group members and White Americans (Butcher, Braswell, & Raney, 1983; Costello, Fine, & Blau, 1973; Costello, Tiffany, & Gier, 1972: Davis, Beck, & Ryan, 1973; Genther & Graham, 1976; S. B. Green & Kelley, 1988; Gynther, 1972, 1981; Gynther & Green, 1980; Hibbs, Kobos, & Gonzalez, 1979; Holcomb & Adams, 1982; Marsella, Sanaborn, Kameoka, Shizuru, & Brennan, 1975; McCreary & Padilla, 1977; McGill, 1980; C. Miller, Knapp, & Daniels, 1968; C. Miller, Wertz, & Counts, 1961; Page & Bozlee, 1982; Plemons, 1977; Pollack & Shore, 1980).

Gynther (1989) reviewed six summaries of Black–White MMPI studies that were published between 1960 and 1987. Some of his comments about bias issues in the MMPI appear to be relevant to racial bias issues in the MCMI. He noted a surprising lack of response to the joint recommendations of Pritchard and Rosenblatt (1980) and Gynther and Green (1980) that studies be done to generate data to which the accuracy test can be applied to assess test fairness. He concluded by favoring a strategy of "underinterpretation" that involves a conservative approach in evaluating the profiles of Black people. In this approach, moderate elevations, for blue-collar job applicants especially, would not be viewed as indicating the same degree of deviant behavior as they would for White people.

Age

A number of theorists have discussed adult developmental trends. Contemporary theorists have expanded on Jung's (1933) notions of male midlife as a time for the development of contrasexual characteristics (for a review, see Neugarten, 1975). Most notably, Gutmann (1980, 1987) contended that men typically move from deriving pleasure through active mastery of the social and physical environment to discovering sensual pleasures and warm human relationships. Similar themes are echoed in Levinson's (1978, 1980) theory of adult development.

In other words, the theory posits that men become less assertive or competitive and more dependent and affectively involved as they age. Following these ideas, we studied the scores generated by 277 Black and 761 White male psychiatric inpatients (Hoffman, Choca, Gutmann, Shanley, & Van Denburg, 1989). We expected that Dependent scale scores would show increases with age and that Histrionic, Narcissistic, and Antisocial scale scores would show decreases. Although women are theoretically supposed to experience the opposite trend, our population came from a Veterans Administration facility and the sample did not include enough women to study trends among women.

Our results using the MCMI-I showed that the two races behave differently as they age. For White examinees, age was correlated positively with Dependent scale scores and correlated negatively with Histrionic and Narcissistic scale scores, as expected, but no changes were found on Antisocial scale scores. For Black examinees, the Antisocial scale scores were correlated negatively with age.

We also examined the relative frequencies with which the different

Table 4

Frequencies for Which a Personality Scale Constituted the Highest Elevation Among the Millon Clinical Multiaxial Inventory Personality Scales

MCMI-I scale	Percentiles		Aging change (%)
	20–44	45–99	
No scale elevated	1.9	5.4	−3.5
Schizoid	7.4	6.7	.7
Avoidant	18.0	14.5	3.5
Dependent	18.8	29.1	−10.3
Histrionic	7.1	4.2	2.9
Narcissistic	13.4	6.4	7.0
Aggressive	8.0	6.2	1.8
Compulsive	5.2	10.8	−5.6
Negativistic	20.2	16.7	3.5

Note. We used the usual base-rate cutoff score of 75 for determining the records in which no scale score was elevated. The aging change was computed by subtracting the percentile of the older group from that of the younger group.

personality scales constituted the highest elevation for the older and younger groups. As can be seen in Table 4, the biggest change between the younger and the older examinees was the frequency with which the Dependent scale received the highest elevation: This scale constituted the highest elevation for only 18.8% of the younger group but was the highest scale for 29.1% of the older group. Next was the difference in the frequency with which the Narcissistic scale was the highest elevation. The trend with this scale was in the opposite direction, with the scale constituting the highest elevation for the younger and older groups in 13.4% and 6.4% of the younger cases, respectively.

Our results supported the current theories of adult development. The findings also addressed the issue of interpreting elevated scores on the MCMI. Of the 922 male patients in the normative sample of the MCMI-I, 15% were aged 18–25 years, 27% were aged 26–35 years, 27% were aged 36–45 years, 23% were aged 46–55 years, and 8% were aged 56+ years (Millon, 1982); the age distribution for the MCMI-II was even more skewed toward the younger examinees (Millon, 1987). Because the great majority of the standardizing populations were younger than 56 years of age, the norms are going to be much more reflective of the way younger people fill out the inventory, and clinicians may not have to be concerned about the aging trends at that end of the continuum.

Our data would suggest, however, that clinicians have to be more careful with older men who have elevated scores on the Dependent scale. Such an elevation has to be interpreted in light of the aging trends, and caution has to be exercised before making statements that make an older man appear pathologically dependent.

Davis and Greenblatt (1990) also conducted a study of veterans. They found main effects for age and race and an overall trend for older patients to obtain lower scale scores. Several design differences, however, prevent one from determining whether there are personality changes in adulthood. And the fact is that the issue of personality changes as the result of aging is clearly controversial. In a recent review of their studies on adult personality changes, McCrae and Costa (1990) offered convincing support for the contention that there are no major changes actually taking place as one ages. They summarized many studies with cross-sectional as well as longitudinal designs so that their evidence cannot be disregarded easily. Perhaps the best way of integrating the available information is to note that all of their studies were done using their own inventory (the NEO Personality Inventory), which was designed to reflect the five-factor model of personality (Costa & McCrae, 1985), and it may be that this inventory is not a sensitive measure of the traits that change with aging.

Preliminary MCMI-II data with 1,400 psychiatric patients show a tendency for the Dependent scale to be more elevated with the older individuals, whereas the elevation of the Compulsive and Borderline scales diminishes. No significant differences were found in this pattern between men and women or between White and Black individuals (Choca, Van Denburg, Bratu, & Meagher, 1995).

Birth Order

One small-scale study was done by Curtis and Cowell (1993) using the MCMI-I. They investigated correlations of birth order and scores on the Narcissism scale of the test. They found that firstborn and only-born children tended to score higher than middle-born and lastborn children on both the MCMI-I and Narcissistic Personality Inventory. The study was limited by the small sample size and modest robustness of the data. There were no reports of the intercorrelations of the two tests.

Culture

There have been little MCMI data comparing individuals of different cultures. A study by Glass, Bieber, and Tkachuk (1996) contrasted the MCMI-II scores of 46 Alaska Native incarcerated men with scores of 21 nonnative incarcerated men. Natives obtained a higher Debasement Index than the nonnative group. They scored significantly higher on the Compulsive, Avoidant, and Schizoid personality scales as well as on the Alcohol and Thought Disorder scales. These findings were used to characterize the Alaska Native inmates as more deprecating, self-restrained, and detached than nonnatives and more inclined to abuse alcohol. Glass et al. warned against generalizing the findings because of the small size of the sample they used.

5 Invalidity and Defensiveness

In this chapter we discuss the use of Millon's Modifying Indices in assessing the usefulness of the scores obtained with a particular individual and in the adjustment of the base-rate (BR) scores.

The MCMI-I had only one scale for evaluating the response set of the examinee. This scale, the Validity scale, consists of four items that are blatantly implausible. The MCMI-I also computed an index from the raw score of the 8 personality scales (Millon, 1977).

The assessment of the examinee's response set becomes more involved in the second and third versions of the MCMI. The latter versions used the Validity scale of the MCMI-I and formalized the computation of an index from the raw scores of the personality scales under the name of the Disclosure Index. Two additional scales were introduced with the MCMI-II to assess whether the examinee is trying to create a positive or a negative image. These scales are the Desirability and Debasement scales. The Disclosure, Desirability, and Debasement scales, as well as other internal calculations, then are used to adjust the BR scores of certain scales.

In spite of the fact that the adjustments to the BR scores have been criticized as being excessive (see chap. 3), these adjustments are not strong enough to correct for response sets in many cases (McNiel & Meyer, 1990). It would seem that when the primary intent of the examinee is to draw a biased picture of himself or herself, no amount of score adjustment will correct the profile so that it can be interpreted without taking the response set into consideration. Because of the complexities involved, it is important for MCMI users to be particularly knowledgeable of the data available for the Modifying Indices. In this chapter we first note what is known about these measures and then discuss the kind of score profiles that may be expected with examinees who are attempting, consciously or unconsciously, to portray a particular image on the test.

Interpreting the Validity Scale

The first score one looks at when interpreting the MCMI is the score obtained on the Validity scale. Simulation studies have shown this scale to be remarkably effective in identifying more than 90% of the randomly answered protocols (Bagby, Gillis, & Rogers, 1991; Retzlaff, Sheehan, & Fiel, 1991).

Validity scores of 1 or more most probably mean that all other results are uninterpretable. Such a score indicates that the examinee was not reading and understanding the inventory for some reason, so that the answers are likely to be random choices. Because the items are keyed such that they elevate only the scale score if they are answered "true," the scale is highly sensitive to random responding as long as the response set was not that of answering all of the items "false" (Retzlaff, Sheehan, & Fiel, 1991).

Using the MCMI-II, Bishop (1993) showed that a high proportion of substance abusers (16%) obtain an invalid protocol, possibly because of subtle intellectual impairment present during the withdrawal phase. The Validity score was correlated negatively with the Vocabulary score of the Shipley Institute of Living Scale. This finding seems to indicate that examinees who are unable to understand the meaning of words or unwilling to take the time and effort necessary to read and comprehend what is being read will not respond to the MCMI adequately.

Although Millon accepts protocols containing a Validity score of 1 as valid, much caution should be used with such protocols. After all, a score of 1 on the Validity scale means that the examinee claimed that one blatantly absurd item was true about himself or herself. (For example, the examinee may claim never to have had any hair on any part of his or her body.) The reason a Validity score of 1 is acceptable is that, unfortunately, many examinees used in the standardization studies scored some points on this scale; as a result, a score of 1 was not statistically out of the acceptable range. Even if statistically acceptable, clinicians have to consider whether the same person who would make some outlandish claim on the MCMI can evaluate accurately, for example, the connotations of believing that the world would be a better place if people's morals were improved.

Thus, users should look carefully at protocols that have a Validity score of 1. If it is possible to explain such a score in a way that still allows the thinking that the rest of the items were answered accurately, the rest of the scores may be examined. If no such explanation is obvious, the user is encouraged to disregard all the other findings. In our own practice, we typically tell the examinee that the test was invalid and suggest that he or she may not have been paying close attention to all the items. In most cases, one can have the examinee fill out the inventory again, this time making certain to read the items carefully.

In cases in which the bad Validity scale item is explainable in some way, we then are inclined to examine the rest of the scores to see whether they make clinical sense. If the rest of the scores are in any way surprising for the particular patient, we see the protocol as invalid and disregard the findings. For our research work, we have used only those protocols with a Validity score of 0.

Interpreting the Disclosure Index

The Disclosure Index is a composite score derived from the raw scores obtained on the personality scales. For the MCMI-I, this index is a simple addition of the applicable raw scores (Millon, 1982). The MCMI-II and the MCMI-III use an equation to weigh the raw scores of the different personality scales in a way that makes theoretical sense (Millon, 1987, 1994). The Disclosure Index was found to accurately identify more than 90% of the simulated "fake bad" protocols with the MCMI-II (Retzlaff, Sheehan, & Fiel, 1991).

If the Disclosure Index obtained is outside of the acceptable range, the acceptability of the profile is in question. An unacceptably low Disclosure Index score is obtained by individuals who mark most of the items false. One possibility is that the individual did not read or understand the inventory. If all items are answered false, the Validity scale score would be 0 because the items were written in a way that they indicate an invalid protocol only if they are answered true. If this possibility seems to have been the case, refer to the comments in the previous section on invalid protocols.

Another possibility that may lead to an unacceptably low Disclosure Index score would be that the examinee is highly defensive. In that case, the individual might have read and understood all of the items but claimed that few of the traits or psychological attributes included in the inventory applied to him or her. Unfortunately, this index tended to remain in the acceptable range when examinees were asked to "fake good" in the inventory (Retzlaff, Sheehan, & Fiel, 1991; Van Gorp & Meyer, 1986). In cases in which the unacceptably low Disclosure Index score is attributable to defensiveness, the thinking would be that the defensiveness is so profound that little can be learned from looking at any other score and that the protocol should be seen as invalid. In such cases it may be possible to coach the individual into completing the inventory again, this time in a less defensive manner.

When accompanied by a Validity scale score of 1 or above, an unacceptably high Disclosure Index score usually is associated with an invalid protocol. For such cases, refer to the discussion in the first part of this chapter. Otherwise, an unacceptably elevated Disclosure Index score may be an indication of faking bad on the examinee's part. Such an individual usually claims to have so many symptoms and psychological traits that it does not seem possible, even when the person is compared with the most incapacitated of psychiatric patients. The validity of the Disclosure Index in the case of fake bad conditions was supported by both of the studies available (Retzlaff, Sheehan, & Fiel, 1991; Van Gorp & Meyer, 1986).

Disclosure Index scores within the acceptable range may be outside the average range. Even though the protocol is then seen as valid, the index betrays a particular response set that the individual is using. In that case, Millon would use the score to adjust the weighted scores of the clinical scales so that they may better represent the actual clinical picture. In addition, however, the fact that the Disclosure Index is outside the normal range is interpretable. When the index score is elevated, the indication would be that the individual has a tendency to think that he or she has more traits or symptoms than the average patient in the standardizing population. Elevations of this scale have been shown to indicate a tendency to exaggerate one's psychopathology (Grossman & Craig, 1994). In the case of a low (but acceptable) Disclosure Index score, the implication would be one of defensiveness (see the next section for a further discussion of defensive personality styles).

Interpreting the Desirability and Debasement Index

The Desirability and Debasement scales were first introduced with the MCMI-II and were kept for the MCMI-III. Desirability measures the tendency to portray oneself in a good light. Items included make the examinee look confident, gregarious, cooperative, efficient, well organized, and allege a regard for authority and a respect for the rules of society. Elevations indicate a tendency to minimize psychological problems (Grossman & Craig, 1994).

The Debasement scale, on the other hand, was designed to tap an attempt to look bad in the inventory. Prominent items deal with feeling physically and emotionally empty, having low self-esteem, becoming angry or tearful at the slightest provocation, feeling unwanted or disliked, feeling tense, being uncomfortable in the presence of others, or feeling guilty and depressed. Erratic moods, a desire to hurt people, a suspicious attitude, and mental confusion also may be present. This scale typically becomes elevated when the examinee responds to the instrument in a way that exaggerates psychopathology (Grossman & Craig, 1994). The Debasement scale was found to identify accurately more than 90% of the simulated fake bad protocols (Retzlaff, Sheehan, & Fiel, 1991).

Millon (1987) used the difference between the scores obtained on these two scales to modify some of the clinical scales so that they better reflect the picture that others may see looking at the individual. Elevations of these two scales, however, are obviously interpretable using the descriptions provided previously.

The effectiveness of the Desirability and Debasement scales in detecting dissimulation or malingering has been the subject of several studies. Retzlaff, Sheehan, and Fiel (1991) found these two scales to have only modest effectiveness in detecting malingering. In their study, only 52% of their fake good groups were screened by the scales; the scales detected 48% of the examinees in one of their fake bad groups and 92% in the other. Bagby, Gillis, and Dickens (1990) used a discriminant function to discover which participants had been asked to fake good or fake bad; they were able to classify correctly only 67% of their sample during the cross-validation phase of the study.

Wetzler and Marlowe (1990), on the other hand, reported that 17% of their psychiatric inpatients scored higher than a BR score of 84 on the Debasement scale. Their finding suggested that this index may reflect a "cry for help" and be an expression of distress rather than intentional dissimulation in the case of severely disturbed examinees.

Defensive Personality Styles and Fake Good Response Sets

We have argued that elevations among the 8 basic personality scales are associated only with a particular personality style and are not necessarily suggestive of psychopathology. Nevertheless, an MCMI protocol containing no elevations is theoretically indicative of a healthy personality. It is possible to obtain such a personality profile, referred to as *Profile 000*, in a nondefensive manner, a manner that leads to acceptable Disclosure Index levels and average scores on the other Modifying Indices. Respondents fitting such a profile typically admit having some dependent traits, some narcissistic traits, some competitive traits, and so on, but they would not have enough of an inclination in any one of these areas to cause an elevation on the particular personality scale score.

Such people may be described as not having a characteristic style, a ready-made routine, or typical way in which they react to environmental events. Being this way may have the advantage of allowing individuals to readily vary their response according to the situation. It may have the disadvantage of preventing individuals from having an automatic response, a pattern of behavior that comes out naturally and predictably regardless of the situation at hand.

Clinicians must remember, however, that most individuals taking the MCMI will have at least one elevation in one of the personality scale scores. In Repko and Cooper's (1985) sample of nonpsychiatric workers' compensation patients, for instance, only 4% did not have any elevated scores. Thus, when no elevations are obtained, one possibility to be considered is that of defensiveness on the examinee's part. In our own work, we have come to recognize two defensive "no-elevation" profiles.

In the first such profile, the Compulsive scale is the highest elevation of the protocol and is more elevated than the rest of the personality scales. We refer to this style as *Profile 070* and describe it as being indicative of individuals who have an air of perfectionism and a tendency to deny faults or limitations. Typically, this profile describes individuals who are guarded, private, and uncommunicative. Interpersonally, they seem distant and unavailable and have difficulty expressing emotions. In spite of appearing somewhat uncomfortable, they may speak of themselves in an overly superficial manner and try to project the image of someone who is doing well after having solved most of his or her problems. Behind this façade one may find an individual who is feeling vulnerable and insecure, at least about the outcome of the psychological testing.

The other profile we have come to recognize is similar to the first, but, instead of having only the Compulsive scale score elevated above the rest, the Compulsive and the Narcissistic scale scores both are prominent. We refer to this profile as *Profile 075* and describe it as follows: The compulsive aspects shown by the MCMI suggest that such individuals place an emphasis on perfectionism and maintaining good control of their environment. Similar individuals are somewhat defensive and unlikely to admit failures or mistakes. At times, they may be seen as being too inflexible, formal, or proper and may relate to others somewhat distantly. Together with these compulsive elements, these individuals may have a tendency to feel that they are special and have few faults. Similar individuals believe that they are more capable or worth more than almost everyone else. People with this profile attempt to tell others what to do and are most comfortable when placed in a position of leadership, but they usually share little of their own private affairs with those around them.

In support of the aforementioned contentions, it has been shown repeatedly that fake good groups tend to yield a narcissistic-compulsive profile (Craig, Kuncel, & Olson, 1994; Retzlaff, Sheehan, & Fiel, 1991). There also is a general trend to reduce scores in all of the scales (Fals-Stewart, 1995). The fact that it is difficult to distinguish between fake good malingering and a valid profile also has been demonstrated repeatedly (Craig et al., 1994; Retzlaff, Sheehan, & Fiel, 1991; Van Gorp & Meyer, 1986). This would be especially true in the case of people who have mild emotional problems because, for them, the lack of significant elevations among the symptom scales cannot be used as further evidence that the inventory was not completed meaningfully. Additionally, investigators have shown that the fake good condition tends to elevate the Desirability Index and may depress both the Debasement and the Disclosure scale scores of the MCMI-II (Bagby, Gillis, Toner, & Goldberg, 1991; Fals-Stewart, 1995; Grossman & Craig, 1994).

One group of patients especially prone to minimize their pathology is substance abusers. Because recreational use of alcohol and drugs is widely accepted in American society, the boundary between pathological and nonpathological use is blurred and easily permits a denial of problem abuse. Results of several studies have shown that the majority of substance abusers are able to avoid detection of their substance abuse problem on the MCMI-II (Craig et al., 1994; Fals-Stewart, 1995). It seems that patients whose substance abuse is milder in severity are more able to avoid detection than those who have a more chronic and severe problem (Craig et al., 1994). Clinicians should examine the prototypical items for the substance abuse scales because many of the patients avoiding detection still endorsed one or more of the prototypical items in the scorable direction. Additionally, diagnosticians may want to investigate further an MCMI showing the modal substance abuse denial profile. This profile is characterized by elevations on the Narcissistic, Antisocial, and Aggressive scales, no elevations on the clinical syndrome scales, and low Disclosure and Debasement scores (Craig et al., 1994).

Fake Bad Response Sets

Fake bad profiles are easily discernible on the MCMI-I. Typically, such profiles have many scales with a BR score above 85. In terms of the Modifying or Validity indices of the MCMI-II, the fake bad condition may lower the Desirability score while causing elevations on the Debasement and the Disclosure scores (Bagby, Gillis, Toner, et al., 1991; Grossman & Craig, 1994). The clinical scales that tend to be elevated include the Schizoid, Avoidant, and Negativistic personality scales; the severe personality scales; and the Anxiety and Dysthymia scales (McNiel & Meyer, 1990; Retzlaff, Sheehan, & Fiel, 1991; Van Gorp & Meyer, 1986).

Lees-Haley (1992) studied MCMI-II scores of personal injury claimants who fraudulently claimed to have a posttraumatic stress disorder after a relatively minor incident at work. Using a BR cutoff score of 60, Lees-Haley classified correctly 73% of the fraudulent claims using the Disclosure scale, 87% using the Debasement scale, and 97% of the real-injury control group using either scale. These findings should be viewed with caution, however, because our nonfraudulent clinical population routinely scores above a BR of 60 on those scales.

Subtle and Obvious Subscales

Peterson, Clark, and Bennet (1989) found little difference between MCMI-I profiles under instructions to fake good and those obtained when examinees were asked to answer the items honestly. That finding led them to suggest that the subtle–obvious distinction that has been used so often with the MMPI is not important for the MCMI-I.

Michael Wierzbicki, however, repeatedly has investigated the use of the subtlety of the MCMI-I items and obviously holds a different opinion. In a 1992 study, Wierzbicki and Howard were able to distinguish Subtle and Obvious subscales for both the personality and the symptom scales of the MCMI-I using college students to judge the subtlety of the items. The authors then showed that their Subtle and Obvious subscales behaved in the expected manner when the test was given to convicts undergoing a presentencing psychological evaluation. Differential responding to the Subtle and Obvious subscales also has been reported with college students (Wierzbicki & Daleiden, 1993). Moreover, it is possible to distinguish between college students who were given fake good or fake bad instructions through their differential response to the Subtle and Obvious subscales (Wierzbicki, 1993b). Although there is a significant correlation between subtlety and the level of severity of the items, the correlation ($r = -.48$) is lower than what has been reported for the MMPI. As a result, the problem of contaminating the measurement of obviousness with symptom severity may be less of an issue with the MCMI (Wierzbicki, 1993a). An additional problem is that the Wierzbicki scales are available only for the MCMI-I.

Part II

Interpreting the MCMI

6 Interpreting Personality Styles

From our perspective, the original 8 personality scales measure personality *styles* rather than *disorders* (Choca, Shanley, et al., 1992). We agree with Birtchnell's (1991) warning against interpreting high scores on these personality scales as indicators of psychopathology. Instead, we view the scales as measuring basic assumptions, predominant attitudes, and typical ways of interacting, and we do not consider an elevation in these scale scores as being necessarily pathological. We believe that our approach makes the results of the MCMI more valid because, when these scales are interpreted as measuring personality disorders, both the MCMI-I (Brown, 1992; Calsyn & Saxon, 1990; Cantrell & Dana, 1987; Chambless, Renneberg, Goldstein, & Gracely, 1992; Chick et al., 1993; Craig, 1988; Hart et al., 1991; Holliman & Guthrie, 1989; Inch & Crossley, 1993; King, 1994; Piersma, 1987c; Repko & Cooper, 1985; Wetzler, Kahn, Cahn, van Praag, & Asnis, 1990) and the MCMI-II (Chambless et al., 1992; Hart et al., 1993; Inch & Crossley, 1993; Renneberg et al., 1992; Turley et al., 1992) have been shown to overpathologize respondents. Results of the aforementioned investigations typically show that almost everyone who takes the MCMI will have at least an elevation on one of the personality scales. From our viewpoint, a serious, unfortunate mistake that is commonly made with the MCMI is to interpret personality scale elevations as evidence of a personality *disorder*. Because this is the area in which we differ the most from the automated interpretations generated by the National Computer Systems program for the MCMI, we share the methodology and narratives that we use for our own discussions of test profile patterns.

The least sophisticated way of interpreting the results of psychological inventories such as the MCMI is to take one elevated scale score at a time and describe what that particular elevation indicates about the examinee. Such a simplistic method forfeits the more finely detailed information that would be derived from an integrative view of the elevated scales. Consider, for instance, two people for whom the Negativistic scale (Scale 8A) constitutes the highest elevation. One such individual may have as a second elevation the Dependent scale (Scale 3); in that case, one may talk about a person who feels inadequate but does not typically behave cooperatively because he or she does not feel that other people are going to adequately meet his or her dependency needs. By contrast, if the second elevation is found on the Antisocial scale (Scale 6A), the negativistic tendencies may be discussed more accurately in terms of the juxtaposition of feelings of inadequacy and the view of life as a tournament in which every person has to fend for himself or herself. Therefore, the ideal would be a system that allows any one finding to be adjusted and expanded by any other finding.

Although this is a goal worth striving for, those who work with the MCMI typically operate in a way that represents a compromise between the simplistic interpretations based on "1-point" elevations and the ideal report that takes into account every scale elevation at the same time. For one thing, at times one may not have a clear idea of how the cluster of traits that are described by one elevation are altered by the presence of another elevation. Moreover, those who routinely administer this test have ready-made interpretations, and the number of narratives needed would be prohibitive if every scale were to be considered in combination with every other scale.

We recommend first looking at the personality style by separating the original 8 personality style scales from the rest. Therefore, our first interpretive step includes the Schizoid (1), Avoidant (2A), Dependent (3), Histrionic (4), Narcissistic (5), Antisocial (6A), Compulsive (7), and Negativistic (8A) scales. In taking this step, we temporarily disregard the new personality scales that were added to the MCMI-II and MCMI-III to measure depressive (2B), aggressive (6B), and self-defeating (8B) personalities, as well as the three severe personality scales. These 6 scales, which inherently denote the presence of psychopathology, would be considered for interpretation later on. We also recommend interpreting only the three highest elevations among the 8 scales. Taking all possible permutations of the 8 different scales results in 336 interpretive narratives, which still is an unwieldy number.

In theory, although all 336 of these permutations would constitute discrete personality profiles, we narrow our range of narratives to approximately 70 because empirical data indicate that many of these possible permutations are seldom encountered. For example, Lorr and Strack (1990) conducted a cluster analysis of the personality scales of the MCMI-II using 166 male psychiatric patients. Four clusters were found with two types of analyses: the antisocial-sadistic-negativistic cluster, the avoidant-schizoid cluster, the schizoid-dependent-compulsive cluster, and a cluster with a relatively flat profile. Donat and colleagues (Donat, 1991; Donat, Geczy, Helmrich, & LeMay, 1992) found five clusters that resembled some of Lorr and Strack's clusters. A study using a larger number of participants found 20 common 2-point profiles that accounted for 82% of the examinees (Retzlaff, Ofman, Hyer, & Matheson, 1994). The clusters found in the various studies appeared to be fairly large groupings into which many of the different personality profiles could be subsumed. Even though the knowledge of those clusters may help to describe specific individuals who fit the cluster profile, it would not seem reasonable to limit our interpretive statements to describing only those broad categories.

Our system involves giving an individual a narrative that approximates his or her particular profile, even if it does not exactly fit the elevations that the respondent obtained. Table 5 shows a mapping of all possible profiles among the personality styles onto the available narratives. The coding of the profiles is performed in the following manner: The first number represents the highest elevation above the cutoff base-rate (BR) score of 75, the second number represents the second such elevation, and the third number represents the third such elevation. A 0 denotes that no scale is elevated above the cutoff, so that 12A0 means that the Schizoid and Avoidant scales were the only two scales having significant elevations. When fewer than three numbers are given, it does not matter which other scale is elevated; in other words, 51 means that the Narcissistic scale is the most elevated, followed by an elevation on the Schizoid scale, which may be followed by an elevation of any other scale or no other elevations. Having decided which narrative may constitute the best fit using the table, the reader then can go on to find the narrative later in the chapter.

The narratives provided were generated from our clinical work. Each of them was originally written for one examinee. Repeated use of the narratives led to further refining of the descriptions, often involving the omission of statements that did not apply to subsequent examinees

Table 5

Mapping of Personality Profiles Into Narrative Clusters

0	→	000	2A0	→	2A00	30	→	300	40	→	400	50	→	500	6A0	→	6A00	70	→	700	8A0	→	8A00
070	→	070	2A10	→	12A0	312A	→	32A0	41	→	400	51	→	500	6A10	→	612A	71	→	72A0	8A10	→	8A12A
075	→	075	2A13	→	32A1	314	→	32A1	42A	→	400	52A	→	52A0	6A12A	→	612A	72A	→	72A0	8A12A	→	8A12A
10	→	100	2A14	→	2A00	315	→	32A0	430	→	340	53	→	530	6A13	→	6A12A	730	→	370	8A13	→	8A00
12A0	→	12A0	2A15	→	2A00	316A	→	32A0	431	→	340	540	→	540	6A14	→	6A00	731	→	370	8A14	→	8A00
12A3	→	2A31	2A16A	→	2A00	317	→	32A0	432A	→	340	541	→	540	6A15	→	6A12A	732A	→	370	8A15	→	8A00
12A4	→	12A0	2A17	→	2A00	318A	→	32A0	435	→	340	542A	→	540	6A17	→	6A12A	734	→	370	8A16A	→	8A00
12A5	→	12A0	2A18A	→	18A2A	32A0	→	32A0	436A	→	340	543	→	540	6A18A	→	2A6A0	735	→	370	8A17	→	8A00
12A6A	→	12A0	2A30	→	2A30	32A1	→	32A0	437	→	438A	546A	→	546A	6A2A	→	6A00	736A	→	736A	8A2A0	→	8A2A0
12A7	→	12A0	2A31	→	2A31	32A4	→	32A1	438A	→	450	547	→	540	6A3	→	46A8A	738A	→	738A	8A2A1	→	8A2A0
12A8A	→	12A8A	2A37	→	32A7	32A5	→	32A0	450	→	450	548A	→	548A	6A40	→	46A8A	74	→	740	8A2A5	→	8A2A0
130	→	132A	2A34	→	2A38A	32A6A	→	32A0	451	→	450	56A	→	56A4	6A41	→	46A8A	75	→	750	8A2A6A	→	8A2A6A
132A	→	132A	2A35	→	2A38A	32A7	→	32A0	452A	→	450	57	→	750	6A42A	→	46A8A	76A	→	6A70	8A2A7	→	8A2A0
132A	→	138A	2A36A	→	2A38A	32A8A	→	32A7	453	→	450	58A	→	58A0	6A43	→	46A8A	78A	→	8A70	8A2A3	→	8A2A3
134	→	138A	2A38A	→	2A38A	340	→	32A8A	456A	→	456A				6A45	→	456A				8A2A4	→	8A2A3
135	→	138A	2A4	→	2A4	341	→	340	457	→	450				6A47	→	46A8A				8A30	→	38A0
136A	→	137	2A5	→	2A50	342A	→	340	458A	→	458A				6A48A	→	46A8A				8A31	→	38A0
137	→	138A	2A6A	→	2A6A0	345	→	340	46A	→	46A8A				6A50	→	6A50				8A32A	→	38A2A
138A	→	100	2A7	→	72A0	346A	→	354	470	→	470				6A51	→	6A50				8A34	→	38A0
14	→	100	2A8A0	→	2A8A0	347	→	340	471	→	470				6A52A	→	6A50				8A35	→	38A0
15	→	100	2A8A1	→	2A8A0	348A	→	348A	472A	→	472A				6A53	→	6A53				8A36A	→	38A0
16A	→	100	2A8A3	→	2A38A				473	→	473				6A54	→	6A50				8A37	→	8A37
17	→	170																					

18A0 → 18A2A	2A8A4 → 2A8A0	350 → 530	475 → 46A8A	6A57 → 6A50	8A4 → 8A40
18A2A → 18A2A	2A8A5 → 2A8A0	351 → 530	476A → 470	6A58A → 6A58A	8A50 → 58A0
18A3 → 138A	2A8A6A → 8A2A6A	352A → 530	478A → 6A8A	6A7 → 6A70	8A51 → 58A0
18A4 → 138A	2A8A7 → 2A8A0	354 → 354	48A0 → 48A0	6A8A0 → 6A8A0	8A52A → 58A0
18A5 → 138A		356A → 356A	48A1 → 48A0	6A8A1 → 6A8A0	8A53 → 58A0
18A6A → 138A		357 → 357	48A2A → 48A0	6A8A2A → 6A8A0	8A54 → 548A
18A7 → 138A		358A → 356A	48A3 → 48A0	6A8A3 → 6A8A0	8A56A → 8A56A
		36A → 36A0	48A5 → 458A	6A8A4 → 6A8A0	8A57 → 8A57
		370 → 370	48A6A → 46A8A	6A8A5 → 6A58A	8A6A0 → 8A6A0
		371 → 370	48A7 → 48A0	6A8A7 → 6A8A0	8A6A1 → 8A6A0
		372A → 32A7			8A6A2A → 8A2A6A
		374 → 370			8A6A3 → 8A6A0
		375 → 370			8A6A4 → 8A6A4
		376A → 370			8A6A5 → 8A56A
		378A → 370			8A6A7 → 8A6A0
		38A0 → 38A0			8A70 → 8A00
		38A1 → 38A0			8A71 → 8A70
		38A2A → 38A2A			8A72A → 8A70
		38A4 → 38A0			8A73 → 8A37
		38A5 → 38A0			8A74 → 8A70
		38A6A → 38A0			8A75 → 8A57
		38A7 → 38A0			8A76A → 8A70

Note. Profile clusters (first number) and the narrative prototype that may be appropriate (after the arrow) are shown. A zero among the profile clusters means that no other scale is elevated above the base-rate score of 75. When only two numbers are given, the third elevation is unimportant (e.g., 14 means that the Schizoid scale [Scale 1] is the highest elevation, the Histrionic scale [Scale 4] is the second elevation, and it does not matter what else is elevated).

obtaining the same test profile. Nevertheless, the narratives have not been validated systematically and experimentally; they are offered as an aid to diagnosticians who would still be expected to decide what part of the narrative, if any, applies to the individual being evaluated.

In spite of our attempt to make the narratives as benign as possible, we still use many negative terms. There are two reasons for this. First, negative terms unfortunately tend to be more meaningfully descriptive: Most people would claim to be cooperative, but only a few would admit being submissive or compliant, even though all three of those terms mean the same thing. Second, because the MCMI is designed to be used with a psychiatric population, clinicians often are in the position of having to highlight problem areas without giving equal emphasis to psychological strengths.

We attempted to cite, within the narrative, empirical studies that offer information about that personality style. The mapping given in Table 5 also was used with these citations. For instance, we cited a study by Hamberger and Hastings (1986), who investigated the 6A54 profile, in the 6A50 narrative because that is the narrative we would use for that particular personality style. A second caveat: We made no effort to distinguish between the different versions of the MCMI in this section. In the majority of the citations, the MCMI-I was used; we had hoped that the findings also would apply to the MCMI-II and the MCMI-III, but that expectation remained largely untested at the time this book was written. Finally, many of these citations note the prevalence of the personality style in question among individuals' other characteristics, such as alcoholism or posttraumatic stress disorder. Needless to say, such data cannot be used in isolation to infer the presence of the other characteristic.

If read in sequence, these narratives are highly repetitive because they often describe traits that already were described in a previous narrative. We intend for the reader to use them in a cookbook fashion, examining only the one that applies for the particular respondent in question.

Profile 100: Schizoid

The Schizoid scale of the MCMI contains items that deal with a lack of close relationships with others and a lack of interest or ability in expressing feelings or emotions. Individuals who obtain elevated scores on this scale are probably private and prefer to be alone rather than with others.

Similarly scoring people, labeled "affectless schizoids" by Millon (1995), tend to be uninsightful and are not interested in exploring their personal feelings. Their detachment may result from relating better to inanimate objects and not caring about interpersonal rewards. They lead unemotional lives and are not inclined to get too disturbed when things do not go their way, but they also do not experience much excitement when good things happen. This tendency to remain on an even keel can be a real asset because emotions will seldom interfere with the decision-making process. These people may be seen, however, as being emotionally bland and lacking an effective rapport with the people around them. In terms of coping strategies, higher scores on this scale are associated with lower levels of seeking social support, higher levels of acceptance of the status quo, and a greater tendency to use alcohol or drugs (Vollrath, Alnæs, & Torgersen, 1995).

Given this personality style, these individuals may be reluctant to engage in therapy. Because they are not likely to value the explorations and insights that are often seen as being an important part of therapy, establishing a therapeutic alliance is likely to be problematic. Modes of treatment that deemphasize emotional rapport or the understanding of psychodynamics may be more in tune with the individuals' approaches to life. In addition, the therapist must be comfortable with a distant relationship and must accept that, although cooperative, the clients may never be active collaborators in the therapeutic process.

Profile 12A0: Schizoid-Avoidant

High scores on these scales of the MCMI characterize people who keep a significant emotional distance from others. Such individuals are most comfortable when they are alone and are referred to as the "remote schizoids" (Millon, 1995). They tend to like jobs or hobbies that involve objects and that have minimal human contact. In extreme cases, these individuals may be single, and their history may show signs of an inability or unwillingness to establish a meaningful relationship outside of the nuclear family. Otherwise, these individuals restrict the number of relationships that they form and tend to have superficial friendships when they do exist.

For these individuals, the inclination to be loners seems to be the result of two different dynamics. First, they appear to be uninterested in interpersonal relations. They are not too adept at understanding and enjoying the subtleties and nuances of interpersonal emotions and communications, a situation that might then have led to their being apathetic about the relationship itself. They typically do not have strong emotions and live fairly bland affective lives.

A second dynamic that seems to be operating in their lives is that they seem to be sensitive and afraid of being rejected by others. As a result, social situations are a source of significant tension, leaving them feeling nervous and not looking forward to this type of activity. They would like to be accepted and appreciated and realize that they have to take part in social events to obtain that kind of satisfaction. Relating to others, however, is so uncomfortable that they avoid the situation in spite of the positive effects that it could have.

On the positive side, avoidant-schizoid individuals are self-sufficient people who do not depend on others for the fulfillment of their own needs. They often lead lives that are fairly free of overemotionality and in which psychological issues tend not to interfere with their behavior. On the other hand, they may be perceived by others as isolated loners who lead somewhat empty and unproductive lives.

Research indicates that this profile prevails among schizophrenics (Josiassen, Shagass, & Roemer, 1988); this profile also has been found among forensic inpatients

(McNiel & Meyer, 1990), alcoholics (Retzlaff & Bromley, 1991), and drug addicts treated in a therapeutic community (Fals-Stewart, 1992). In the latter study, avoidant-schizoid addicts were found to be likely to become self-critical, discouraged, and drop out of treatment; they also had worse outcomes, were less able to maintain abstinence, and relapsed faster than the rest of the group. Concomitant Minnesota Multiphasic Personality Inventory (MMPI) codes have been reported as either 28/82 (Antoni, Tischer, Levine, Green, & Millon, 1985a) or 78/87 (Antoni, Levine, Tischer, Green, & Millon, 1987).

Individuals with this personality style may have difficulty establishing therapeutic alliances. The discomfort that they experience in interpersonal relationships will probably make the sessions unenjoyable. In addition, a therapist also would have to be concerned about them feeling rejected any time that an uncomplimentary interpretation is made. When the treatment plan involves giving negative feedback or is intended to confront objectionable aspects of the personality or behavior, the therapeutic situation will be experienced as threatening or stressful. To maintain the alliance but still contribute to the client's growth, the therapist must achieve a careful balance between uncritical support and the threatening therapeutic work. The therapist also must be ready to allow the emotional distance that such patients may need, as well as tolerate their inability to talk about their lives and feelings nondefensively. These individuals will feel most enhanced with a therapist who treats them with admiration and respect.

Profile 12A8A: Schizoid-Avoidant-Negativistic

This MCMI profile characterizes people with introversive, avoidant, and negativistic elements in their personality styles. Such individuals have little interest in experiencing the subtle aspects of interpersonal relationships. Because of their lack of interest in interpersonal matters, these clients are likely to have turned their attention to areas that do not involve direct contact with people, such as reading or art. At worst, such individuals may be perceived as being emotionally insensitive in a distant and apathetic way. Such people probably have few friends and little real interpersonal involvement.

High scores on these three scales also suggest a general unresponsiveness to stimuli. Similar individuals are not particularly energetic or enthusiastic and their thinking is usually vague, unclear, and somewhat impoverished. They are not prone to understanding or interpreting past events or to planning for their own future. At times, they may appear evasive and overly defended, but most typically they just seem somewhat apathetic, dull, and uninteresting.

The detachment from others is accompanied by conflicts these clients experience when they are in social situations. They typically feel somewhat inadequate and often wish that someone would provide nurturance, shelter, and guidance. They fear rejection, however, and often seem nervous, moody, and resentful. At times, they may be friendly and cooperative, but anger and dissatisfaction soon color most of their relationships. Results of one study showed this profile to be the modal code for depressed patients who responded to tricyclic antidepressants (Joffe & Regan, 1989a).

Given their personality styles, these clients may have some difficulty establishing therapeutic alliances. The discomfort experienced in interpersonal relationships probably will make the sessions unenjoyable. In addition, a therapist would have to be concerned about clients feeling rejected any time that an uncomplimentary interpretation is made. Finally, the clients' dependency conflicts will mean that they are likely to respond negatively to the therapist's leadership. Thus, it may be difficult to get them to be motivated collaborators in the treatment process. The therapist must be ready to allow the emotional distance that these clients may need and to tolerate their inability to talk about their own lives and feelings nondefensively. If care is taken not to issue many directives or much advice, the resentment that such clients usually develop when they feel dependent on a relationship may be minimized.

Profile 132A: Schizoid-Dependent-Avoidant

Labeled "ineffectual dependent" by Millon (1995), this MCMI personality style emphasizes introversive aspects accompanied by dependent and avoidant traits. These individuals lack interest in other people. They do not seem happy when things come out well, nor are they too upset by unfortunate events. They are not interested in interpersonal situations. They are quiet and often stay by themselves, typically taking the role of passive observers, seldom taking sides or verbalizing a strong opinion. Rarely the center of attention, these individuals typically fade into the background. They have few friends; when relationships do exist, they tend to be superficial. They are socially indifferent and have little apparent need to communicate or to obtain support from others.

Together with the emotional indifference, such clients tend to feel less important or capable than other people. Similar individuals are easily led by others and are submissive and dependent. They are uncomfortable with highly competitive situations, are humble, and try to be as congenial as possible to the people around them. They often are afraid of being rejected by others and, as a result, feel some discomfort when relating to others.

These individuals are probably detached and uninvolved. Cooperative and agreeable people, they may be perceived as easygoing and emotionally stable. However, they may be criticized as being somewhat dull, quiet, indifferent, dependent, or apathetic.

Research suggests that this profile is common among psychiatric inpatients (McCann & Suess, 1988). Tango and Dziuban (1984) found that this profile, at a subclinical level, is correlated with the Strong-Campbell Interest Inventory's vocational interests of music and office practice among college students seeking career counseling. Indecisiveness about career choices was thought to be associated with discomfort with interpersonal contact.

A therapist attempting to work with these clients may have difficulty establishing the therapeutic alliance. The therapist will have to be tolerant of their distant way of relating. A somewhat unexciting course of treatment also can be expected. A supportive relationship will be one in which the therapist takes a protective and parental attitude, reassuring clients that problems can be worked out and that help will be available.

Profile 137: Schizoid-Dependent-Compulsive

This MCMI personality profile emphasizes introversive aspects seen together with dependent and disciplined traits. These individuals are characterized by a lack of interest and awareness of emotional feelings and interpersonal situations. They usually lead relatively unemotional lives: They do not seem particularly happy when things turn out well, nor are they saddened by unfortunate events. They tend to be quiet loners, passive observers who remain uninvolved and seldom take sides or express a strong opinion. Rarely the center of attention, they often fade into the social background.

They have few friends and, when relationships do exist, they tend to be superficial. It is not that such people fear or actively avoid others but that they are somewhat indifferent and apparently have little need to communicate or to obtain support from others.

These clients also think of themselves as unimportant and incapable. Individuals with the same pattern of scores tend to be led by others and to be submissive and dependent. They also tend to shy away from highly competitive situations. They are humble and try to be as congenial as possible to the people around them.

These individuals typically assume that if they do not make mistakes, they can depend on other people to provide for their needs. This perfectionism serves both their dependency needs and fuels their tendency to be distant from others, with its emphasis on controlled and hidden thoughts and feelings. Such individuals often seem rigid, unexpressive, detached, dull, apathetic, and excessively formal. From a more positive perspective, they also appear objective, orderly, dependable, well organized, and responsible.

Profile 138A: Schizoid-Dependent-Negativistic

Individuals with this MCMI profile have an introversive personality style with dependent traits that make them uncomfortable. They tend to be unemotional: When things turn out well for them, they do not seem particularly happy, nor are they saddened by unfortunate events. They tend to be quiet, private people—loners and passive observers who seldom take sides or have a strong position. Rarely the center of attention, these individuals tend to fade into the background. They have few friends, and relationships are usually superficial. It is not that they fear or actively avoid people but that they are somewhat indifferent and apparently have little need to communicate with or to obtain support from others.

Perhaps related to this lack of interpersonal interest and knowhow are the low self-esteem and submissive attitude that typically plague these clients. They avoid competitive situations and try to be congenial and conciliatory. Toward this end, they may cover up aggressive or objectionable feelings.

Some submissive individuals feel comfortable when they are able to establish a dependent relationship with another person who seems to be competent and trustworthy. The lack of emotional interest and awareness exhibited by schizoid-dependent-negativistic clients, however, makes it hard for them to establish a strong relationship of any kind, even a dependent one. These clients often come across as moody or negativistic—their only means of expressing their discomfort with personal relationships.

Profile 170: Schizoid-Compulsive

This MCMI personality profile characterizes individuals who are fairly distant and controlled. Similar people have little interest in, or ability to experience, the subtleties of interpersonal relationships. Because of this, they usually concentrate on matters that do not involve people, such as reading or art. They may be perceived as emotionally insensitive or apathetic to others. As a result, they are likely to have few friends and little real interpersonal involvement.

Additionally, such clients tend to be overly controlled, disciplined, and proper. It is as if the emotions that they feel are so confusing or threatening that they must be hidden. Individuals with similar personality profiles try hard to avoid making mistakes. They are orderly, conscientious, well prepared, and controlled. They try to be efficient, dependable, industrious, and persistent. These individuals usually relate in an overly respectful, ingratiating manner to those in authority. With subordinates, however, they are more likely to be perfectionistic, even disdainful. These individuals often believe in discipline and practice self-restraint. This overcontrol causes them to appear overly formal and proper, and they may be perceived as rigid or indecisive when they have not had a chance to study all possible alternatives. On the positive side, they tend to be well organized and usually do well in situations in which it is important to be accurate and meticulous.

Profile 18A2A: Schizoid-Negativistic-Avoidant

People with these MCMI scores typically are resentful and socially detached. This was the most common profile found among schizophrenics in a Veterans Administration hospital (J. J. Jackson et al., 1991). Antoni, Tischer, Levine, Green, and Millon (1985b) found this personality style to represent a subgroup of the patients obtaining the 24/42 MMPI code.

Similar people have little interest in experiencing the subtle aspects of interpersonal relationships. They may turn their attention instead to areas that do not require social contact, such as reading or art. At worst, these individuals may be seen as emotionally insensitive, distant, and apathetic. Such people probably have few friends and minimal interpersonal involvement.

The MCMI scores also suggested that these individuals generally are unresponsive to stimuli. This may be true regardless of whether the stimulus comes from their own processes or from the outside. Similar individuals are not particularly energetic or enthusiastic, and their thinking is usually vague, unclear, and somewhat impoverished. They typically are not interested in understanding or interpreting past events or in planning for their future. Although they sometimes appear evasive and overly defended, they are more likely to seem apathetic, dull, and uninteresting.

Underlying the detachment from others are conflicts related to feelings of inadequacy and the wish that someone would provide nurturance, shelter, and guidance. These individuals fear, however, that when others get to know them, they will be rejected. At times they may be friendly and cooperative, but they are more typically moody and resentful: Anger and dissatisfaction eventually colors most of their relationships.

Given their personality style, establishing a therapeutic alliance will be difficult. The discomfort that they experience in interpersonal relationships will probably make the sessions unenjoyable. In addition, the therapist will need to be sensitive to them feeling rejected when an uncomplimentary interpretation is made. Finally, their dependency conflict will mean that they are likely to respond resentfully to the therapist's leadership, so that it may be difficult to motivate them to collaborate in their own treatment. The therapist must allow the emotional distance that the clients may need and tolerate their inability to talk about their own life and feelings. If care is taken not to issue directives or advice, the resentments that the clients usually develop when feeling dependent on a relationship may be avoided.

Profile 2A00: Avoidant

This profile describes individuals who are hypersensitive to the possibility of rejection. They assume that people will not value their friendship and fear interpersonal humiliation. Because these "hypersensitive avoidants" (Millon, 1995) feel they have to put their best foot forward and to constantly be on guard, they often are ill at ease in social situations. Even though they often are understanding and compassionate, their perfectionism and anxiety cause them to shy away from social contact and to forfeit the support and acceptance they want from others. As a result, similar individuals tend to be isolated and to function best in situations in which they do not have to interact with many people. Their coping style is characterized by passivity, social withdrawal, a lack of an active interventional approach, and cognitive negativism (Vollrath, Alnæs, & Torgersen, 1994). The use of alcohol and drugs as coping mechanisms also has been reported (Vollrath et al., 1995).

Profile 2A30: Avoidant-Dependent

Individuals with this MCMI profile, referred to as "phobic avoidants" by Millon (1995), usually do not have any close friends, so they tend to remain detached and isolated. They view themselves as weak, inadequate, unresourceful, and unattractive. Strongly wishing to be liked and accepted by others, they nevertheless have a great fear of rejection. They often are guarded and experience social situations negatively. They seem apprehensive, shy, or nervous in social situations. These clients usually avoid relating to others, which forces them to give up the support and affection that the relationship might have brought. Thus, life is experienced as a conflict between taking a risk and accepting the discomfort of forming a relationship, or retreating to the unfulfilling safety of their isolation. Although these individuals usually are sensitive, compassionate, and emotionally responsive, they also are nervous, awkward, mistrustful, and isolated.

This profile has been shown to be common among forensic inpatients (McNiel & Meyer, 1990), patients with an obsessive–compulsive disorder (Joffe, Swinson, & Regan, 1988), and women with a history of sexual abuse (Bryer, Nelson, Miller, & Krol, 1987). Many patients with this personality style have a 28/82 MMPI code type (Antoni et al., 1985a) or a 78/87 MMPI code type (Antoni et al., 1987).

Profile 2A31: Avoidant-Dependent-Schizoid

This MCMI profile characterizes individuals with interpersonal apprehensiveness, feelings of inadequacy, and introversiveness. People with similar scores are preoccupied with being liked and appreciated and consequently constantly anticipate rejection. This creates a bind: By avoiding interactions with others, they feel comfortable and at ease on the one hand and concerned about their lack of social support on the other. Should they actually risk a relationship, the fear of rejection makes them tense, nervous, and uncomfortable and overrides whatever pleasure the relationship brings.

Such people tend to devalue themselves and to think that other people are more capable and more worthy. As a result, they are typically cooperative to the point of submissiveness. Their dependency fits well with the discomfort in interpersonal relationships because it supports the assumption that if others really got to know them, they would see how worthless they really are and would lose interest in their friendship.

Individuals obtaining similar profiles often are unaware of their own emotions and tend to remain aloof and detached. They are distantly complacent, appear somewhat apathetic, and do not experience strong emotional ties with others. They are private individuals, often loners, who may have some acquaintances but typically lack intimate friendships.

Bartsch and Hoffman (1985) found this profile to be prominent in their sample of alcoholics. They believed that drinking may serve to alleviate social anxiety, diminish insecurity, and allow these individuals to establish some social contact. Because of their typical avoidance of social relationships, therapy and involvement in Alcoholics Anonymous would be difficult. Bartsch and Hoffman reported MMPI code type 2478 for this group.

Profile 2A38A: Avoidant-Dependent-Negativistic

Found to be common among women with a history of physical and sexual abuse (Bryer et al., 1987) and alcoholics (Mayer & Scott, 1988), this MCMI profile indicates a fear of rejection, feelings of inadequacy, and a tendency to have mood changes. These individuals want to be liked by others but anticipate that their social approaches likely will be rejected.

People with this personality profile usually underestimate themselves: They feel less capable, less attractive, or worth less as human beings than others. They tend to be unassertive and seldom make demands on others, although they can be controlling in a dependent and submissive manner. They are more comfortable when they can rely on others to make the important decisions in their lives. These individuals assume that people will eventually develop uncomplimentary opinions about them and will reject them.

As a result of this basic personality structure, such people tend to be apprehensive, shy, and nervous in social situations. They are likely to feel caught in a bind: On one hand, they would like to interact with others and to be liked and appreciated. On the other hand, they feel compelled to avoid social situations to avoid the anxiety that the situations evoke.

The psychic conflict manifests itself behaviorally in vacillation and ambivalence. At times open and friendly, they also may be aloof, distant, abrasive, moody, and disinterested in others. Occasionally, similar individuals project the feelings created by this basic conflict, becoming even more distrusting, hostile, and prone to blame others for their failures. This pattern will be short-lived, and these individuals eventually come back to feeling inadequate and blaming themselves for everything that happens to them.

In light of this personality style, these people can be expected to have difficulty establishing a therapeutic alliance. Discomfort in the relationship and mistrustfulness that mitigates against confiding in the therapist will have to be overcome. Even after the relationship has been established, the therapist will need to be careful not to offer interpretations that can be experienced as rejections. The therapist also will need to be able to tolerate moodiness and overt or covert expressions of resentment. These clients may derive much benefit from experiencing the closeness of the therapeutic relationship, once established, because they may not have many other opportunities for emotional closeness.

Profile 2A50: Avoidant-Narcissistic

Individuals obtaining this MCMI personality profile are hypersensitive to the possibility of rejection. They typically assume that people will not value their friendship and often are concerned with the risk of humiliation. This fear causes them to feel ill at ease in social situations. They constantly are on guard, preoccupied with putting their best foot forward. Even though they often are sensitive people who can show understanding and compassion for others, they also tend to be nervous about and uncomfortable with interpersonal contact and will shy away from social situations. They probably would like to have friends and to be well accepted, but their discomfort leads them to forfeit the support that they could have derived from others rather than risk mistreatment. As a result, they tend to be isolated and may function best in situations in which they do not have to interact with many other people.

The fear of rejection has roots in the tendency to overestimate their own value. Individuals obtaining this personality profile typically feel that they are special and superior to others in some way. A tendency to exaggerate their abilities and positive attributes and construct rationalizations to inflate their own worth usually is present. Such people are likely to view themselves as intelligent, outgoing, charming, or sophisticated. They have a need to evoke affection and attention from others. Whenever they feel slighted, rejected, or mistreated by others, they tend to use projection as a defense and depreciate those who refuse to accept or enhance their self-image. Thus, these people may be a bit grandiose, ego centered, and unappreciative of others.

In light of this personality style, these individuals can be expected to have difficulty establishing a therapeutic alliance. A certain amount of discomfort in the relationship and an inability to develop enough trust so that they can truly confide in a therapist will have to be overcome. Even after an alliance has been established, the therapist must be careful not to offer interpretations that can be experienced as rejections and must be able to tolerate expressions of resentment. These clients will feel most enhanced when a therapist treats them with admiration and respect and allows them to be as much in control as possible during the therapy session. A relationship in which they treat the therapist more like a colleague than a superior also will be experienced as ego syntonic and supportive. To the extent that treatment involves giving negative feedback or confronting objectionable behavior or aspects of the personality, the therapeutic situation will be experienced as threatening or stressful. To maintain the therapeutic alliance but contribute to a client's growth, a careful balance must be achieved between uncritical support and the threatening therapeutic work.

Profile 2A6A0: Avoidant-Antisocial

According to the MCMI, these individuals are hypersensitive to the possibility of rejection and look at the environment as a competitive place. Similar people feel that to function in this world, they have to fend for themselves. Somewhat distrusting and suspicious, they also see themselves as assertive, energetic, self-reliant, strong, and realistic. They imagine that they have to be tough to make it in the "rat race." Justifying their assertiveness by pointing to others' hostile and exploitative behaviors, they may be contemptuous of the weak and not care whether they are liked, claiming that "good guys come in last."

Individuals with this type of personality are concerned that others will take advantage of their friendship if they are not careful. This fear causes them to be uncomfortable in social situations because they feel that they constantly have to be on guard. As a result, they tend to be nervous and uncomfortable.

To avoid the discomfort that is commonly attached to interpersonal contact, they shy away from social situations. These people typically like to have friends, but the discomfort associated with the social risk often leads them to forfeit the support that could have been derived from others rather than to take the chance of being mistreated. Such individuals typically are isolated and may function best in situations in which they do not have to interact with many other people.

People obtaining similar MCMI scores usually are impulsive. They typically are perceived as being somewhat aggressive and intimidating, perhaps somewhat cold, callous, or insensitive to the feelings of others. They may be argumentative and contentious, even abusive, cruel, or malicious. When matters go their way, they may act in a gracious, cheerful, and friendly manner. More characteristically, however, their behavior is guarded, reserved, and resentful. Greenblatt and Davis (1992) found this avoidant-antisocial personality to be prevalent among angry Black men in their psychiatric sample.

In light of this personality style, such clients can be expected to have some difficulties in establishing a therapeutic alliance. A certain amount of discomfort in the relationship and an inability to develop enough trust so that they can truly confide in the therapist will have to be overcome. Even after the relationship has been established, the therapist will need to be careful not to offer interpretations that can be experienced as a rejection. To the extent that treatment involves giving clients negative feedback or confronting objectionable aspects of their personalities or behaviors, the therapeutic situation will be experienced as threatening or conflictual. To maintain the therapeutic alliance while contributing to the client's growth, a balance must be struck between uncritical support and the threatening therapeutic work.

Profile 2A8A0: Avoidant-Negativistic

Elevated scores on these MCMI scales indicate a fear of rejection and a tendency to be resentful. Millon (1995) labeled this cluster the "conflicted-avoidant" cluster. People with this personality profile perceive interpersonal situations as risky and likely to lead to humiliation or rejection. Similar individuals would like to be appreciated, but their fear of rejection makes them apprehensive; they would like to meet people and establish strong emotional ties, but they are so uncomfortable in social situations that they tend to avoid interpersonal contacts altogether. These people typically are loners to some degree. They retreat into their own worlds and are interpersonally nervous and uncomfortable. They tend to be sensitive, however, to their own feelings and the emotional reactions that they evoke in others.

Individuals with similar MCMI profiles tend to question their own abilities and see themselves as not being interesting or worthwhile. However, they do not see others as being much better and, in fact, tend to perceive humanity as cold and rejecting. So, in spite of their poor self-image, they do not look up to others and generally are aware of the limitations that other people may have.

When these clients are able to establish significant relationships, the interactions tend to be conflictual. They tend to be moody and resentful. They may be friendly and cooperative at times, but they may become negativistic or hostile, only to feel guilty later and behave contritely. In some cases, these mood fluctuations are less noticeable, with the clients handling the conflict through a more stable form of covert obstructionism.

This profile represents the modal personality makeup for alcoholics (Donat, 1988; Donat, Walters, & Hume, 1991), psychotic Black men in a psychiatric sample (Greenblatt & Davis, 1992), psychiatric patients with mixed diagnoses (T. J. Murphy et al., 1990), psychiatric inpatients who attempted suicide (McCann & Gergelis, 1990), and patients with a dissociative identity personality disorder (Ellason, Ross, & Fuchs, 1995; Fink & Golinkoff, 1990).

In light of this personality style, these individuals can be expected to have some difficulties in establishing a therapeutic alliance. A certain amount of discomfort in the relationship and an inability to develop enough trust so that they can truly confide in the therapist will have to be overcome. Even after the relationship has been established, the therapist will need to be careful not to offer interpretations that can be experienced as a rejection. A tolerance for moodiness and overt or covert expressions of resentment also will be needed. Projected hostility may be minimized by trying not to give advice to such clients and allowing them to control any aspect of the therapy sessions that do not need to be controlled by the therapist. Interpretations dealing with both the fear of rejection and the tendency to blame others also can be helpful. If successful, the clients may derive much benefit from experiencing the closeness of the therapeutic relationship because they may not have many other opportunities for emotional closeness.

Profile 300: Dependent

People obtaining this MCMI profile have a cooperative personality style. These "immature dependent" (Millon, 1995) individuals feel that they are not very able to take care of themselves and must find someone dependable who will protect them and support them, at least emotionally. They tend to feel inadequate or insecure and to see themselves as being less effective or capable than everyone else. They also tend to form strong attachments to people who will be the decision makers. They are followers rather than leaders and are often submissive in social interactions, shying away from competitive situations.

Concerned with the possibility of losing friends, similar individuals may cover up their true emotions when they are aggressive or otherwise objectionable. These are humble people who try to be as congenial as possible to those around them. They probably are well liked but occasionally may be considered wishy-washy because they never take a strong position on controversial issues. They also may be criticized for their submissive dependency, their lack of self-esteem, and their tendency to always look outside of themselves for help. They show a lack of active intervention as their coping style when under stress (Vollrath et al., 1994), as well as a tendency to turn to religion (Vollrath et al., 1995). Similar individuals characterize their family of origin as noncohesive social systems that were controlling, allowed little independence and expressiveness, and were not intellectually or culturally oriented (Baker, Capron, & Azorlosa, 1996; Head, Baker, & Williamson, 1991).

This MCMI profile was found to be the most prevalent profile among psychiatric patients (Donat, Geczy, et al., 1992). Additionally, the profile was commonly found in a group of individuals with head injuries being evaluated for workers' compensation claims (Snibbe, Peterson, & Sosner, 1980), among women who elected mastectomy as opposed to another treatment approach for breast cancer (Wolberg, Tanner, Romsaas, Trump, & Malec, 1987), and among people with bulimia (Tisdale, Pendleton, & Marler, 1990).

In light of this personality style, such individuals can be expected to form a quick alliance with any therapist willing to play a benevolent parental role. An approach in which they are given guidance in an affectionate and understanding manner would be experienced as supportive. It may be difficult if part of the treatment plan is to move clients toward more independence or increase their ability to compete assertively or effectively. If that is the case, these clients may feel vulnerable and threatened and may respond with maladaptive behaviors.

Profile 32A0: Dependent-Avoidant

These "disquieted dependent" individuals (Millon, 1995) tend to have low self-esteem and to see others as being more capable or worthwhile. They likely are followers rather than leaders, often taking passive roles. They would like to seek emotional support and the protection of others but, together with these wishes, they experience discomfort.

The discomfort comes from the assumption that if others get to know them as well as they know themselves, people will develop the same uncomplimentary views that they have of themselves. As a result, these people probably tend to be guarded and apprehensive when relating to others. Similar people try to put their best foot forward and hide their true feelings, especially when the feelings are aggressive or otherwise objectionable. They may seem tense, nervous, and distant. Because they feel ill-at-ease in social situations, they often avoid them, which results in loneliness and isolation.

Research indicates that this personality style prevails among women with eating disorders (Kennedy, McVey, & Katz, 1990; Pendleton, Tisdale, & Marler, 1991) and among nonangry psychotic White men in a psychiatric sample (Greenblatt & Davis, 1992). Similar individuals characterize their family of origin as noncohesive social systems that were controlling, allowed little independence and expressiveness, and were not intellectually or culturally oriented (Baker et al., 1996; Head et al., 1991).

On the positive side, dependent-avoidant individuals try to be cooperative and conciliatory. They can be sensitive and unassuming and maintain any relationship they have been able to establish.

Given the personality style just described, these clients will experience as supportive a relationship in which the therapist has a benevolent and protective attitude toward them. Feeling that the therapist is a powerful expert and will give good advice and guidance will be reassuring for them. Because of their fear of rejection, they may require frequent reaffirmation and the promise of support.

Profile 32A1: Dependent-Avoidant-Schizoid

Common among psychiatric inpatients (Donat, Geczy, et al., 1992) and among individuals in marital therapy (Craig & Olson, 1995), this personality profile characterizes socially detached people with low self-esteem, who tend to perceive others as being more capable and worthy. Similar individuals characterize their family of origin as noncohesive social systems that were controlling, allowed little independence and expressiveness, and were not intellectually or culturally oriented (Baker et al., 1996; Head et al., 1991). This profile has been found to be the modal profile among unipolar depressed patients (Wetzler, Khadivi, & Oppenheim, 1995). Levine, Tischer, Antoni, Green, and Millon (1985) found this personality style to represent a subgroup of the patients with the 27/72 MMPI code.

Similar individuals are likely to be followers rather than leaders, often taking a passive role in social affairs. Although they would like to seek the emotional support and protection of others, they are uncomfortable in social relationships. They also often have trouble understanding the feelings and motivations of others and appear somewhat bland and apathetic.

They tend to assume that if others get to know them as well as they know themselves, people will develop the same uncomplimentary views that they have of themselves. As a result, they are guarded and apprehensive when relating to others. They try to put their best foot forward and to hide their true feelings, especially when the feelings are aggressive or otherwise objectionable. They may seem tense, nervous, and distant. Because they feel ill-at-ease in social situations and lack interest and understanding in the interpersonal area, they often do not have any strong relationships. Thus, they frequently are lonely and isolated from others. However, these clients may be fairly cooperative and gentle, seldom experiencing intense feelings, and feeling fairly pleasant and controlled.

Given the personality style just described, these clients will experience a supportive therapeutic relationship if the therapist has a benevolent and protective attitude toward them. Feeling that the therapist is a powerful expert who will offer helpful advice and guidance will be reassuring for them. Because of their fear of rejection, they may require frequent reaffirmation and the promise of support; the therapist must tolerate clients' discomfort during the sessions.

Profile 32A7: Dependent-Avoidant-Compulsive

This profile characterizes people with a cooperative, avoidant, and disciplined nature. Similar individuals characterize their family of origin as noncohesive social systems that were controlling, allowed little independence and expressiveness, and were not intellectually or culturally oriented (Baker et al., 1996; Head et al., 1991).

Individuals with similar scores tend to have low self-esteem and to see others as being more capable and worthy. They are followers rather than leaders, often assuming passive roles. They would like to seek the emotional support and protection of others but, together with these wishes, they experience a certain amount of discomfort.

The discomfort comes from the assumption that if others get to know them as well as they know themselves, people will develop the same uncomplimentary views that they have of themselves. As a result, such individuals typically are guarded and apprehensive when relating to others. They try to put their best foot forward and have a tendency to hide their true feelings, especially when the feelings are aggressive or otherwise objectionable. They may seem tense, nervous, and distant. Because they feel uncomfortable in social situations, they often avoid them and are frequently lonely and isolated.

Thus, one way in which these individuals defend against the insecurity engendered by their low self-esteem is by counting on the guidance and protection of others. Another defense mechanism that they use is thinking that if they manage to avoid making mistakes, the outcome always will be positive. People with a similar perfectionistic bent are orderly and plan for the future. They are conscientious and do their work on schedule. Other characteristics of these people include efficiency, dependability, industriousness, persistence, extreme respectfulness and ingratiating behavior, perfectionism, and self-discipline. They tend to be indecisive and have significant problems making decisions by themselves. Their perfectionism also may magnify the underlying feelings of inadequacy in that, whenever bad things happen, they will be inclined to look for what mistakes they made that might have led to the undesirable outcome.

In light of this personality style, these clients will experience as supportive a therapeutic relationship in which the therapist has a benevolent and protective attitude. They will be reassured by the feeling that the therapist is a powerful expert who will advise and guide them. Their fear of rejection may require frequent reaffirmation and the promise of support.

Profile 32A8A: Dependent-Avoidant-Negativistic

High scores on these scales characterize people who have cooperative, avoidant, and negativistic personality traits. Individuals with similar scores tend to have low self-esteem. Furthermore, they are likely to assume that if others get to know them, people will develop the same uncomplimentary views that they have of themselves. They would like to seek the emotional support and protection of others but, at the same time, they fear rejection. As a result, they may experience much interpersonal discomfort and tend to be guarded and apprehensive. They may seem tense, nervous, and distant when they are with others. Because they feel ill-at-ease in social situations, they often avoid them and become loners.

Such people are somewhat resentful of others and are inclined to blame negative events on external factors. The anger may be expressed overtly or covertly. In either case, they occasionally may become uncooperative and hard to handle. The projective defense mechanism fits in well with the social avoidance because the hostility tends to alienate others. Projections also give them a rationale for rejecting others before they have a chance to be rejected. At the same time that they resent the control of others, however, they are probably uncomfortable in competitive situations in which they have to act independently and make their own decisions. This discomfort creates a vicious cycle of needing to depend on others but feeling resentful of that need.

Research shows that this personality style prevails among depressed individuals (Piersma, 1986c), especially those with no family history of depression (Joffe & Regan, 1991), and among alcoholics (Craig, Verinis, & Wexler, 1985).

Clients with this dependent, avoidant, and resentful personality style will have difficulty establishing a therapeutic alliance. They may be most at ease in situations in which they feel protected, supported, and safe (i.e., not likely to be rejected or humiliated). This same relationship, however, also is likely to precipitate conflict over dependency, heighten their fear of rejection, and activate their discomfort with intimacy. These clients then may become critical of the therapist, and it may be even more difficult to keep them in treatment. Appropriate interpretations that help them understand how the defensive resentment is generated may increase the clients' understanding, and they may be able to become less dependent, defensive, and conflicted.

Profile 340: Dependent-Histrionic

This MCMI score pattern describes an "accommodating dependent" or "appeasing histrionic" individual (Millon, 1995) with a cooperative personality style and dramatic overtones. The most prominent trait these people display is low self-esteem. They think of themselves as being less gifted and worthy than others. Their poor self-image usually leads to feelings of insecurity and anxiety, especially when they are in competitive situations.

Such people need a lot of attention from others and actively seek affirmation, approval, and affection. They often develop a sensitivity to the moods of others and use this knowledge to evoke the reactions that they desire. They can be charming and outgoing, dramatic, or seductive, usually with the result of having their need for approval met.

These types of people usually are cooperative and congenial, colorful, and in touch with their emotions. However, they may have a difficult time in situations in which they feel alone or have to depend on themselves. The loss of meaningful others often is strongly felt.

With regard to psychotherapy, clients with a dependent-histrionic personality style feel the most comfortable when the therapist re-creates a parental role and offers a good deal of attention, support, nurturance, and protection. In spite of the dependency, similar clients tend to be occasionally contrary and conflictual in the therapeutic relationship as a result of the histrionic overtones. The therapist should be tolerant on these occasions. Therapeutic change may come from processing the perceived lack of support, from encouraging clients to be more independent, and from helping them understand the source of low self-esteem and its relationship to their strong need for attention and support.

Profile 348A: Dependent-Histrionic-Negativistic

People with this MCMI profile have a combination of cooperative, dramatic, and negativistic elements in their personality. Their MCMI scores suggest that they are caught in the bind of having low self-esteem but feeling that they mask it with a confident and self-assured presentation.

Similar individuals think they are less gifted or valuable than others. Their poor self-image leads to feelings of insecurity and results in anxiety when they are in competitive situations. They are followers rather than leaders, usually trying to be cooperative and to get along well with others. They are "people who need people": They tend to relate to others in an easy and meaningful manner but often depend on those relationships to function. Because they trust others to protect and guide them, these people may not be well prepared to take independent responsibility for attaining goals or life accomplishments.

An elevated Histrionic scale score indicates the need for attention from others. Similar people often are conspicuous in their seeking of frequent reaffirmations of approval and affection. Their ability to appreciate the feelings of others may be used to evoke the reactions they desire. They can be charming and outgoing, colorful, dramatic, or seductive. Depending on how functional they are, they may use these traits to cope effectively with the environment or to manipulate or exploit others.

When such people feel inadequate, they are friendly and cooperative. However, they may shift rapidly to a more arrogant and demanding posture to project an image of greater adequacy. They may become bored with stable relationships and displace some of their inner conflicts into interpersonal resentments. Thus, they may seem moody and easily irritated, unpredictable, or negativistic.

Given their personality style, these individuals will benefit from a therapeutic relationship in which the therapist takes a parental role and offers guidance and protection. An emphasis on formalities such as being on time for the session or keeping an interpersonal distance during the session is likely to be perceived as unfriendly and dissatisfying. More ego syntonic to the clients would be a relationship in which they are the center of attention, with demonstrations of affection and support flowing readily from the therapist. The limits to the support that the therapist can offer, however, eventually may become an issue if clients become clingy, demanding, and dissatisfied. Such developments may threaten the therapeutic alliance, but this can be managed by a therapist who makes the clients aware of inappropriate expectations and helps them work through the dependency conflict.

Profile 354: Dependent-Narcissistic-Histrionic

Elevated scores on these MCMI scales characterize people who appear to be cooperative, confident, and dramatic but for whom the most prominent personality trait is low self-esteem. Individuals with similar scores tend to feel less gifted or worthy than others. This poor self-image usually leads to insecurity and anxiety in competitive situations.

Such individuals also tend to publicly overrate their own self-worth. This inclination may come from disparate assumptions that they hold about themselves so that—even though they do not value themselves in some areas—they seem to be highly confident in others. Often, however, this ego inflation is a defensive reaction to the low self-esteem. In either case, there is an obvious conflict between the two images that they try to project. This conflict may play out in vacillations between congeniality and obstructionistic arrogance.

These individuals also need a lot of attention, approval, and affection. People with similar profiles actively pursue the needed attention. They often become sensitive to other people's moods and use this knowledge to evoke the reactions they want. They may seem charming and outgoing, dramatic, or seductive in their relationships with others.

On the positive side, these individuals usually are cooperative and congenial, colorful, and in touch with their emotions, qualities that provide a good foundation for developing effective coping strategies (Leaf et al., 1992; Leaf, Alington, et al., 1991; Leaf, DiGiuseppe, et al., 1990; Leaf, Ellis, et al., 1991; Nakao et al., 1992; Retzlaff & Deatherage, 1993; Strack et al., 1989). Tango and Dziuban (1984) correlated this profile with the Strong-Campbell Interest Inventory's interests in adventure, music, writing, religion, public speaking, and office management and with somewhat exhibitionistic roles (e.g., writer, orator, executive, merchant, adventurer, musician). However, these individuals may have a difficult time in situations in which they feel alone or have to depend on themselves. The loss of meaningful others often is strongly felt.

Profile 356A: Dependent-Narcissistic-Antisocial

According to the MCMI, individuals with this profile have a personality that is driven partly by a sense of personal inadequacy. Similar people often are cooperative and ingratiating. They want to be liked by others and often try to be generous and congenial. In spite of viewing themselves as being less capable than others, however, they feel that they have some quality or innate worth that indeed makes them special and superior to others.

Such people have adapted to these conflictual self-assumptions by developing a posture that allows both of the assumptions to remain in place. Individuals obtaining similar scores emphasize the competitive aspects of the world and see themselves as needing to be tough to come out ahead. They experience the world as a place where everyone is in competition for the same limited assets and focus on the advantages of having personal strength. They often try to hide their own inadequacies because they assume that if others learn about them, the knowledge will become a liability that will work against them. Although they do feel emotionally dependent on others, they try to appear as if they do not need other people and can make it on their own. They try to control others and may be somewhat mistrusting. When confronted by people who question their control, they may have an abrasive or hostile reaction that represents their attempt to bolster their own self-confidence.

On the positive side, this MCMI profile characterizes proud people who portray themselves in a positive light, tend to behave in a congenial and cooperative manner, and may be resourceful in meeting their own emotional needs. These qualities can provide a basis for effective coping strategies (Leaf et al., 1992; Leaf, Alington, et al.,

1991; Leaf, DiGiuseppe, et al., 1990; Leaf, Ellis, et al., 1991; Nakao et al., 1992; Retzlaff & Deatherage, 1993).

Profile 357: Dependent-Narcissistic-Compulsive

This MCMI profile characterizes people who are cooperative, confident, and disciplined but whose most prominent personality trait is low self-esteem. Individuals with similar scores tend to feel less gifted or worthy than others. Their poor self-image usually leads to feelings of insecurity and anxiety when they are in competitive situations. They try to be cooperative and feel most comfortable when they are under the guidance and protection of a powerful mentor.

Even though they do not value themselves in some areas, they seem to be highly confident in others and sometimes may publicly overrate their self-worth. This ego inflation—their propensity to rationalize away their failures and paint themselves in a good light—may be seen as a defensive reaction to the low self-esteem, a way of quieting their insecurities and comforting themselves.

Such individuals also may use compulsive ways of enhancing their self-image. Similar individuals likely are proper and respectful in their relationships with others and adopt a somewhat perfectionistic and moralistic outlook. They usually are hardworking people who see the world in terms of right and wrong (black and white) and who may be somewhat meticulous and picayunish. This proper and disciplined façade frequently is used to emphasize their intrinsic value and combat the fear that they may not be worthwhile.

On the positive side, both the narcissistic and the compulsive elements have been shown to contain effective coping strategies (Leaf et al., 1992; Leaf, Alington, et al., 1991; Leaf, DiGiuseppe, et al., 1990; Leaf, Ellis, et al., 1991; Nakao et al., 1992; Retzlaff & Deatherage, 1993; Strack et al., 1989).

Profile 36A0: Dependent-Antisocial

This MCMI profile defines a cooperative personality style with competitive overtones. The life assumption of individuals with this profile is that they are not capable of taking care of themselves and must find someone dependable who will support and protect them. They tend to feel inadequate or insecure and see themselves as being less effective or able than everyone else. They tend to form strong attachments to people who will be the decision makers and take responsibility for their welfare. Concerned with the possibility of losing friends, they may hide their true emotions when the feelings are aggressive or objectionable. These are humble, congenial people.

Such individuals perceive the environment as a competitive place. As a result, they are somewhat mistrustful and suspicious of others. Typically, their behavior is guarded and reserved, but they hope that, with the help of the people they have risked depending on, they can be strong, realistic, and determined in the rat race of life. Although they do not feel tough or secure by themselves, they look to others to provide protection from a cruel and insensitive world in which people are interested only in personal gain.

In light of the personality style just described, such clients are likely to be guarded and distant at first, but they nonetheless will be able to form an alliance with any therapist willing to play a benevolent parental role. If guidance is given in an affectionate and understanding manner, it will be experienced as supportive. If part of the treatment plan is to move clients toward more independence or increase their ability to compete in an effective or aggressive manner, there may be some difficulties. If that is the case, clients may feel vulnerable and threatened and may respond with maladaptive behaviors.

Profile 370: Dependent-Compulsive

According to the MCMI scores, these individuals tend to have low self-esteem and an orderly and disciplined nature. Similar people believe that other people are more capable, interesting, or valuable than they are. They are humble and personable and often are capable of forming strong interpersonal relationships. They aim to be as congenial as possible to obtain the support they need. As a result, they tend to be fairly submissive, or at least compliant. They shy away from competitive situations in which they feel unsupported and vulnerable. When they feel protected, however, they tend to be at ease and conflict-free.

Thus, one way in which these people defend against their insecurity is by counting on the guidance and protection of others. They also are likely to retreat to a perfectionistic defense that is organized around avoiding mistakes to ensure positive outcomes. Toward that end, they are compulsive and orderly. They prepare in a conscientious manner and complete work on schedule. They try to be efficient, dependable, industrious, and persistent. These individuals often relate in an overly respectful and ingratiating manner, and they can be somewhat demanding. In their quest for perfection, they may be indecisive and have significant problems making decisions by themselves. The compulsive tendency also may serve to strengthen the feelings of inadequacy that are beneath it in that whenever bad events happen, they blame themselves for the outcome.

This personality profile has been found to be prominent among people seeking marital therapy (Craig & Olson, 1995), perhaps because it also is common among men with a history of domestic violence (Hamberger & Hastings, 1986). The profile also is common among people suffering from chronic headaches (Jay, Grove, & Grove, 1987) and among patients with affective disorders in remission who have no family history of depression (Joffe & Regan, 1991). The profile also is prevalent among psychiatric inpatients (Donat, Geczy, et al., 1992) and alcoholics (Mayer & Scott, 1988). Such individuals characterize their family of origin as noncohesive social systems that were controlling, allowed little independence and expressiveness, and were not intellectually or culturally oriented (Baker et al., 1996; Head et al., 1991). They are likely to have a 27/72 MMPI profile (Levine et al., 1985).

Clients with this personality style will benefit from a therapeutic relationship in which the therapist has a benevolent and protective attitude. Feeling that the therapist is a powerful expert who will give appropriate advice and guidance will be reassuring. Such clients can be expected to establish a strong therapeutic alliance without much difficulty and to find such a relationship helpful.

Profile 38A0: Dependent-Negativistic

Individuals with this MCMI personality profile are dependent and negativistic. They tend to feel insecure, to have low self-esteem, and to feel uncomfortable in competitive situations.

Many individuals with low self-esteem look to others for protection and support.

However, individuals with this profile seem to have a conflict in this area. Although they are unsure of their own abilities and need to depend on others, they also tend not to trust others to be reliable or dependable. They resent being in the vulnerable position of needing others and lacking confidence that their needs will be met.

Some people faced with this conflict externalize it by appearing to be cooperative and compliant but actually resist the leader in some way. Others tend to vacillate between friendly cooperation and resentful distrust, only to feel guilty and contrite and begin the cycle again.

Research has shown this style to be common among alcoholics (Retzlaff & Bromley, 1991), drug abusers (Stark & Campbell, 1988), and spouse-abusing men (Hamberger & Hastings, 1986). Patients with this personality profile commonly obtain the MMPI profile codes of 89/98 (Antoni, Levine, Tischer, Green, & Millon, 1986), 27/72 (Levine et al., 1985), or 24/42 (Antoni et al., 1985b).

These clients may need a therapeutic relationship in which the therapist assumes the dominant role and offers parental guidance and protection. The limits to the support that the therapist can offer, however, eventually may become an issue, at which time the clients can become clingy, demanding, and dissatisfied. If not handled properly, such developments may threaten the therapeutic alliance. One way to handle such issues is to make clients aware of their inappropriate expectations and help them work through the dependency conflict.

Profile 38A2A: Dependent-Negativistic-Avoidant

Individuals with this MCMI profile tend to feel that they are not capable or gifted and that if they are left to their own devices, they would not be able to make ends meet. They would like to have someone else take care of them and provide for their needs, but they tend to be distrustful and resent the abilities of others, a fact that eliminates the option of becoming dependent on some benefactor.

These people tend to be moody and to experience sudden, seemingly inexplicable mood shifts. At times they may be friendly and engaging but they typically have periods when they are angry and resentful. Later yet, they may feel guilty and behave contritely. The cycle is completed when they again become friendly and cooperative. In other words, they defend against their insecurities by projecting blame, sometimes onto themselves and sometimes onto others. A variation of the same basic personality makeup involves the use of a negativistic defense. If that is the case, these individuals may try to control resentment through obstructionistic maneuvers that allow the venting of anger in covert ways without blatantly jeopardizing the dependent relationship.

Most individuals with similar MCMI scale scores have considerable feelings of insecurity. They tend to perceive others as being more gifted, more capable, and more worthy. In addition, they fear that others may recognize their lack of value and reject them; they also tend to be nervous and uncomfortable in social situations because they fear that other people do not really like them and that they are imposing. They avoid some of the discomfort by avoiding social relationships altogether. As a result, similar individuals tend to isolate themselves and may establish fairly distant relationships with people they experience as untrustworthy and judgmental.

On the positive side, individuals with this personality style are sensitive people who would like to be appreciated by others and to be able to relate better than they do. They feel conflicted, however, over wanting to depend on others but believing that if they trust others, they will be hurt in the end.

This personality profile was found to be common among depressed patients (Wetzler et al., 1989) and appears to be associated with a poor response to tricyclic anti-depressants (Joffe & Regan, 1989a). Similarly, this profile is common among alcoholics (Retzlaff & Bromley, 1991), especially alcoholic women experiencing major depression (McMahon & Tyson, 1990). The personality profile also can be found with some frequency among spouse-abusing men (Hamberger & Hastings, 1986; Lohr, Hamberger, & Bonge, 1988). In the case of workers' compensation claimants with low back pain, this personality style is thought to have psychosocial stress factors aggravating the pain complaints (Snibbe et al., 1980).

These clients will probably demand much attention and reassurance in the therapeutic situation. In spite of being somewhat distant and mistrustful, similar people react negatively to the unavailability of the therapist or the therapist's attempts to control their behaviors. It may be useful to set clear limits in the therapeutic relationship and to give them as much independence as possible, getting them to make their own decisions rather than offering suggestions or recommendations because any advice given is likely to trigger their dependence–independence conflict.

Profile 400: Histrionic

Referred to as "theatrical histrionics" by Millon (1995), individuals with an elevation in the Histrionic scale show a predominance of dramatic traits in the basic personality structure. They are colorful and emotional and are likely to seek stimulation, excitement, and attention. They tend to react easily to situations around them, often becoming very absorbed, but typically the involvement does not last. This pattern of getting involved and ending up bored is repetitive.

Histrionic individuals are good at making positive first impressions. Their ability to react to unexpected situations, their alertness, and their search for attention make them colorful and charming socialites at parties or other social gatherings. People with this style have been found to have good coping strategies (Leaf et al., 1992; Leaf, Alington, et al., 1991; Leaf, DiGiuseppe, et al., 1990; Leaf, Ellis, et al., 1991; Nakao et al., 1992; Retzlaff & Deatherage, 1993; Retzlaff & Gibertini, 1988; Strack et al., 1989). Such individuals characterize their family of origin as controlling and intellectually or culturally oriented (Baker et al., 1996). The predominant use of repression as a defense was suggested by one study of Italian examinees (Rubino, Saya, & Pezzarossa, 1992).

However, histrionic individuals can be too loud, exhibitionistic, and dramatic. They can be demanding and uncontrollable, especially when they are highly involved. They typically have intense emotional moments in friendships, but these friendships may be short-lived and replaced when boredom sets in. Their dependency has a much different flavor from the dependency of inadequate individuals in that they need the attention of others rather than protection and guidance. As a result, they may be much less submissive than other types of dependent individuals. They cope with stress by seeking emotional support, reinterpreting events in a positive light, and attempting to find humor in their life situations, but they are too inclined to focus on the emotional distress and the discharge emotions (Vollrath et al., 1994).

Given the histrionic personality style, an emphasis on formalities, such as being on time for the session or keeping an interpersonal distance during the session, is likely to feel unfriendly and dissatisfying. The therapist may need to be tolerant of the clients' emotionality and even a certain amount of conflict. The type of relationship that would feel ego syntonic to these clients is one in which they are the center of attention and demonstrations of affection and support flow readily, especially from the therapist to the clients.

Profile 438A: Histrionic-Dependent-Negativistic

This MCMI profile shows a combination of dramatic, dependent, and negativistic traits as components of the basic personality structure. Individuals with this type of personality are colorful and emotional and seek stimulation, excitement, and attention. They react easily to situations around them, often becoming emotionally involved, but typically this involvement does not last. The pattern of getting involved and ending up bored is repetitive.

The scores suggest that these people are caught in the bind of having low self-esteem but having to conceal their self-appraisal and appear confident and self-assured. They tend to feel less gifted or valuable compared with others. Nevertheless, they are aware that dependency on others projects an undesirable image and are uncomfortable with that particular coping strategy. Faced with this conflict, some individuals externalize it by appearing to be cooperative and compliant but actually resisting their leader in some covert way; others may vacillate. At times, they may be friendly and cooperative, but they start to feel resentful and may become angry and aggressive, only to feel guilty and contrite and begin the cycle again. Such a solution allows them to reconcile the wish to be protected and the wish to appear independent and self-sufficient at the expense of being in frequent conflicts with others.

These individuals may be criticized for being somewhat loud, exhibitionistic, or overly dramatic. They need support from others and may be moody or temperamental. However, they often are colorful and expressive people who are able to engage others effectively in a reasonably short period of time. The predominant use of repression as a defense was suggested by one study of Italian examinees (Rubino et al., 1992).

Given this type of personality style, an emphasis on formalities, such as being on time for the session or keeping an interpersonal distance during the session, is likely to feel unfriendly and dissatisfying. The therapist may need to be tolerant of their emotionality and conflict. The type of relationship that would feel ego syntonic to such clients is one in which they are the center of attention and demonstrations of affection and support flow readily, especially from the therapist to the clients. The lack of exciting issues during the sessions, or the limits to the support that the therapist can offer, eventually may become an issue, with clients becoming clingy, demanding, or dissatisfied. If not handled properly, such developments may threaten the therapeutic alliance. One way to handle such issues is to make clients aware of their inappropriate expectations and help them work through the attentional needs and dependency conflict.

Profile 450: Histrionic-Narcissistic

This MCMI profile highlights a need for attention and conspicuousness. These "vivacious histrionic" individuals (Millon, 1995) tend to feel that they are special and may view themselves as being intelligent, outgoing, charming, or sophisticated. They often exaggerate their own abilities, constructing rationalizations to inflate their own worth and belittling others who refuse to enhance the image they try to project. They make good first impressions because they are able to express their feelings, have a flair for the dramatic, and have a natural ability to draw attention to themselves. They also are colorful and may have a good sense of humor.

These people are probably perceived as friendly and helpful; they may actively seek praise and may be entertaining and somewhat seductive. People with histrionic and narcissistic elements have been found to have good coping strategies (Leaf et al., 1992; Leaf, Alington, et al., 1991; Leaf, DiGiuseppe, et al., 1990; Leaf, Ellis, et al., 1991;

Nakao et al., 1992; Retzlaff & Deatherage, 1993; Retzlaff & Gibertini, 1988; Strack et al., 1989). However, they are bored easily and lack self-definition when they are alone. The predominant use of repression as a defense was suggested by one study of Italian examinees (Rubino et al., 1992).

Studies finding this profile in their samples include an investigation of nonpsychiatric individuals with high electroencephalographic alpha waves (Wall, Schuckit, Mungas, & Ehlers, 1990) and drug addicts (Fals-Stewart, 1992). At a subclinical range, this personality was well represented in a group of air force pilot trainees (Retzlaff & Gibertini, 1987a, 1988).

Given this personality style, clients may find it easier to establish a relationship with a therapist who is attentive and inclined to appreciate their charm and successes. Allowing clients to take a leading role in the therapeutic situation and to control as much as possible what goes on in the sessions also would contribute to making the treatment palatable. Once the therapeutic relationship is well established, the therapist will undoubtedly need to offer occasional interpretations that will sound negative if psychological growth is to occur. Care should be taken to choose both the timing and manner of such interpretations to avoid injuring the clients' narcissism beyond a point that they can tolerate.

Profile 456A: Histrionic-Narcissistic-Antisocial

This MCMI defines a dramatic personality style with confident and competitive overtones. Individuals obtaining similar scores have a great need for attention and affection. They constantly seek stimulation and conspicuousness with a dramatic flair. Typically, they are adept at manipulating social situations so that others give them the attention they need. They do this partly by becoming sensitive to others so that they can decide what reactions will evoke the responses they want.

These individuals often easily express their feelings and have fairly intense, short-lived emotions. They may appear outgoing, charming, and sophisticated. People with this profile have been found to have good coping strategies (Leaf et al., 1992; Leaf, Alington, et al., 1991; Leaf, DiGiuseppe, et al., 1990; Leaf, Ellis, et al., 1991; Nakao et al., 1992; Retzlaff & Deatherage, 1993; Strack et al., 1989). However, their other-directedness makes them vulnerable to the lack of acceptance from others. They may be somewhat capricious and intolerant of frustration. At times, their dramatic presentations may appear shallow, phony, or overly seductive rather than expressions of real feelings. They also may have some difficulties in developing a self-identity.

For these individuals, the histrionic style has narcissistic and antisocial components. This finding suggests that, in striving for attention, they may feel that they are special and that they will be successful in most enterprises. They tend to feel that they are better than everyone else, a feeling that is apparent in their interactions with others. They also view the world as being competitive: Everyone is competing for attention, and only those who are better at getting attention will actually have their needs fulfilled. As a result of these attitudes, they may be somewhat abrasive or conflictual at times.

The histrionic-narcissistic-antisocial personality has been found to be common among alcoholics (Bartsch & Hoffman, 1985; Craig & Olson, 1990; Donat, 1988; Donat et al., 1991) and among adult children of alcoholics (Hibbard, 1989). A subclinical version of this profile often was seen in a group of air force pilot trainees (Retzlaff & Gibertini, 1987a).

Given this personality style, these clients may find it easier to establish a relationship with a therapist who is attentive and inclined to appreciate their charm and successes. Allowing the clients to take a leading role in the therapeutic situation and control as much as possible what goes on in the sessions also would help to make the treatment palatable. Accepting the clients' matter-of-fact, tough, and antisocial view of the world should help to establish rapport.

Once the therapeutic relationship is well established, the therapist will undoubtedly need to offer occasional interpretations that will sound negative but have to be made if the clients are to grow psychologically. Care should be taken, however, in choosing the timing and manner of such interpretations to avoid injuring the clients' narcissism beyond the point that they can tolerate.

Profile 458A: Histrionic-Narcissistic-Negativistic

Elevated scores on these MCMI scales indicate a personality composed of dramatic, confident, and oppositionistic traits. These scores characterize people with prominent needs for attention who live fast-paced lives and enjoy stimulation and excitement; they may be thrill-seekers, easily interested in the prospects of some new adventure. Perceived as charming socialites, these people are typically colorful, dramatic, and emotional; they can be flippant, capricious, and demanding but also skilled at attracting others and appearing in a good light. They are easily infatuated, but their enthusiasm is often short-lived. They tend to be immature, unable to delay gratification, are undependable, and often lack discipline. However, they are lively extraverts who present themselves with a certain color and flair.

The MCMI scores also show that these people have a fairly high self-regard. They tend to feel that they are better or more capable than most people. As a result, they are prone to behaving in a confident and self-assured manner and to be comfortable taking a strong position on important issues, even when other people disagree. This trait, however, also may present a problem in that they may treat others in a disdainful and insensitive manner or be threatened when someone questions their superiority.

When these people encounter some sort of opposition, the negativistic elements are likely to emerge. The picture then may be that of angry and provocative individuals who can show their feelings in aggressive or even hostile ways. This highly emotional state is probably short-lived, at which time the other aspects of their personalities will again become more prominent.

Given the personality style just described, these clients may find it easier to establish a relationship with a therapist who is attentive and inclined to appreciate their charms and successes. Allowing such clients to take a leading role in the therapeutic situation and control as much as possible what goes on in the sessions also would help the treatment. Another strategy to remember is that of refraining from giving clients directives or setting up unnecessary rules because they tend to resent controls. Part of the therapist's task is to maintain their clients' perception that the therapist is on their side; otherwise, the relationship becomes competitive and conflictual, and the clients' goals are no longer solving their problems but winning the fight with the therapist.

Once the therapeutic relationship is well-established, the therapist undoubtedly will need to offer occasional interpretations that will sound negative to the clients. The timing and manner of such interpretations should be chosen carefully to avoid injuring the clients' narcissism beyond the point of toleration.

Profile 46A8A: Histrionic-Antisocial-Negativistic

Elevated scores on these MCMI scales characterize the dramatic, competitive, and op-positionistic tendencies of the "disingenuous histrionic" (Millon, 1995) personality style. Individuals with similar scores enjoy being the center of attention. In addition to being somewhat emotional and dramatic and enjoying social situations, they are colorful and lively, but they can be seen as somewhat superficial and not serious enough in their approach to the world. Because they have a tendency to get bored easily, they may not always finish one task before moving on to another.

Another important aspect of the personality pattern characterizing these individuals is a competitive worldview: Such people feel that there is a limited supply of the things for which everyone is striving. As a result, life is a little bit of a rat race and the world is a somewhat cruel and unfriendly place in which no one can really be trusted and in which people have to fend for themselves. Most of these individuals see themselves as tough realists and are always trying to prevent getting into situations in which they may be taken advantage of.

These two tendencies usually cause conflict for similar individuals. The attention-getting tendency is people-loving and tends to make the individuals somewhat dependent on others. The antisocial outlook, on the other hand, makes them somewhat distrusting. Therefore, they typically are caught in this conflict and may resolve it in one of two ways. Some individuals handle the conflict through mood fluctuations. At first they are friendly and cooperative; they then become afraid that they will be taken advantage of and suddenly seem resistant, distant, and mistrustful or even angry and aggressive. In more pronounced cases, they may even become explosive and hard to handle. Other people may handle the conflict with a passive–aggressive maneuver by superficially complying but actually being obstructionistic and thus acting out their aggressive impulses.

Given this personality style, these clients may find it easier to establish a relationship with a therapist who is attentive and inclined to appreciate their charms and successes. Allowing such clients to dominate and control as much as possible what goes on in the sessions also would help the therapy. Another strategy is to avoid giving directives or setting up unnecessary rules because these clients are prone to eventually resent any control. Part of the therapist's task is to maintain their perception that the therapist is on their side; otherwise, the relationship becomes competitive and conflictual and the clients' goals are no longer solving problems but winning the fight with the therapist. On the other hand, it is just as important to stand firm when a rule has been established, making sure that infractions have an appropriate consequence. Clarity, firmness, and certainty about what areas are controlled by whom can eventually lessen some of the conflicts that would otherwise occur.

Once the therapeutic relationship is well established, the therapist undoubtedly will need to offer occasional interpretations that will sound negative to the clients. The therapist should choose carefully the timing and manner of such interpretations to avoid getting involved in a competitive struggle and evoking a defensive and unproductive reaction.

Profile 470: Histrionic-Compulsive

High scores on the Histrionic and Compulsive scales characterize colorful and emotional people who usually seek stimulation, excitement, and attention. They tend to be conspicuous and search actively for affirmation of approval and affection. They often become sensitive to other people's moods and use this knowledge to evoke the reactions they want. They respond readily to situations around them, often becoming emotionally involved, but typically the involvement does not last. These individuals make good first impressions. Their ability to react to unexpected situations, their alertness and interest, and their search for attention make them colorful socialites at parties and similar gatherings.

Similar individuals value an image hinging on propriety and dependability. They also want to appear conscientious, efficient, dependable, industrious, and persistent, and they may place an emphasis, for instance, on "dressing right," having a clean and orderly house, and so on.

In some ways, the histrionic and compulsive tendencies conflict with one another. The histrionic inclination makes people emotional, intense in their relationships, and impulsive. Compulsive people, on the other hand, overcontrol their emotions, are somewhat distant when relating to others, and carefully plan their behaviors. Individuals who have these two tendencies together are often unable to integrate them well and are conflicted as a result. They may then seem moody or emotionally labile. At times, they may be more emotional and intense and then develop some fears about where this behavior would lead and become more rigid and controlled.

Both the histrionic and the compulsive elements, however, have been shown to contain good coping strategies (Leaf et al., 1992; Leaf, Alington, et al., 1991; Leaf, DiGiuseppe, et al., 1990; Leaf, Ellis, et al., 1991; Nakao et al., 1992; Retzlaff & Death-erage, 1993; Strack et al., 1989). The predominant use of repression as a defense was suggested by a study of Italian examinees (Rubino et al., 1992).

Profile 48A0: Histrionic-Negativistic

High scores on these MCMI scales characterize individuals with dramatic and opposi-tionistic traits. Elevations on the Histrionic scale suggest that such people often seek to be the center of attention. They are dramatic, emotional, sensitive, and perceptive about other people's moods, using that knowledge to fulfill their needs for attention and support. They often are colorful socialites who can charm and entertain others and thrive in the superficial relationships of parties and social gatherings. However, they usually need a certain amount of stimulation and become bored easily. When this happens, they are prone to move on to something different without much forethought.

These individuals are probably highly aware of the images that people project. For them, the building of this image is based partly on a negative attitude toward others. These individuals are prone to putting others down or showing disdain. This aspect adds a particular flavor to their basic personality makeup by introducing an aggressive or hostile element.

Some such people handle this aggressiveness by being consistently obstruction-istic, a behavioral pattern that allows them to vent the aggressive element without jeopardizing their ability to gain emotional support and be the center of attention. Otherwise, these people may try to control or repress their angry feelings. In that case, the aggressive element will eventually surface through some kind of hostile explosion. After such an incident, however, the individuals are prone to feel guilty and apologize, an action that they hope will appease the offended party and place them back in their original position. Such a mode of operation may make these people seem moody, overemotional, and unpredictable.

Given this basic personality style, such clients need a therapeutic relationship in which they are the center of attention. Tolerating displays of emotion and accepting a certain amount of conflict will be needed by the therapist. Care must be taken not to unduly foster the clients' enthusiasm and positive responses to the treatment when it occurs and to prepare them for the times ahead when the treatment will become more mundane and they are ready to terminate it. To avoid future resentment, it also may be important to keep some distance and not to intrude in decisions that clients can make on their own.

Profile 500: Narcissistic

High scores on the Narcissism scale of the MCMI characterize "elitist narcissists" (Millon, 1995), whose basic assumption in life is that they are special. These people feel superior to others and have a tendency to exaggerate their abilities and positive attributes, construct rationalizations to inflate their own worth, and depreciate others who refuse to accept or enhance their own self-image.

Such individuals typically view themselves as being intelligent, outgoing, charming, and sophisticated and have a need to be conspicuous and to evoke affection and attention from others. They often make good first impressions because they are likely to have their own opinions and have a natural ability to draw attention to themselves. They are proud people, carry themselves with dignity, and may have a good sense of humor. However, they may have trouble if they do not feel properly recognized or are forced to accept the opinions of others or to compromise.

This personality profile has been found to be predominant among claimants for workers' compensation (Repko & Cooper, 1985) and among women who chose a conservative treatment for breast cancer as opposed to a mastectomy (Wolberg et al., 1987). The profile also is common among alcoholics in the air force (Retzlaff & Gibertini, 1990) and among substance abusers (Craig & Olson, 1990; Craig et al., 1985). Patients with MMPI 42/24 or 89/98 profile codes tend to have this personality profile on the MCMI (Antoni et al., 1985b, 1986). The Narcissistic scale has been shown to represent a healthy aspect of the personality for many individuals (Leaf et al., 1992; Leaf, Alington, et al., 1991; Leaf, DiGiuseppe, et al., 1990; Leaf, Ellis, et al., 1991; Nakao et al., 1992; Retzlaff & Deatherage, 1993; Strack et al., 1989).

Given this personality style, such people can be expected to be most comfortable in situations in which they feel admired or at least respected. If confrontation is used in therapy, much tact has to be exercised so as not to injure clients' narcissism more than they can tolerate. On the other hand, there also is a danger that a therapist would be so supportive of clients' narcissism that no negative feedback is given and growth is not facilitated. Thus, it is important to find ways of helping clients accept their fallibilities and work on their problems without feeling unrecognized or humiliated.

Profile 52A0: Narcissistic-Avoidant

People obtaining this MCMI personality profile assume that they are special and feel superior to most other people. They tend to exaggerate their abilities and positive attributes, construct rationalizations to inflate their own worth, and depreciate others who refuse to accept or enhance their own self-images. Viewing themselves only in positive terms, they tend to think of themselves as intelligent, outgoing, charming, and sophisticated. Any negative attributes that they do accept usually are minimized.

For these people, however, there also is a certain amount of apprehension regarding relationships with others. They tend to feel that other people are not going to appreciate how capable and outstanding they really are. Such individuals are extremely sensitive to any sign of rejection because a rejection is interpreted as a negation of the kind of image that they feel they must have. As a result, when they interact with others, they always feel they have to put their best foot forward. They tend to be tense, nervous, and self-conscious with most of the people with whom they interact. Therefore, their social outlook is conflicted: In some ways they would like to relate to people well so that they would be appreciated, but they are so socially uncomfortable that they find themselves avoiding people altogether much of the time.

Profile 530: Narcissistic-Dependent

This MCMI profile shows predominant confident and cooperative traits in the personality makeup. The juxtaposition of these two styles is a bit unusual and possibly problematic. An elevation on the Narcissistic scale usually indicates that they value themselves highly. Such individuals are prone to assume that they are more capable than others; they think of themselves as being special in some way. As a result, they tend to exaggerate their own positive attributes and to minimize their liabilities. They like to be conspicuous and relate to others with an air of self-assurance. They wish to be leaders, to hold positions of status and power, and are not particularly interested in following somebody else's directions.

The problem with this personality profile is that the second elevation occurs on a scale that is almost the direct opposite of the first. The Dependent scale characterizes individuals who are followers rather than leaders. This score tends to indicate that they are not sure about their own abilities. Given those two divergent assumptions about one's role in life, the test scores suggest that these individuals may experience conflict. At times they may relate in a submissive and overly congenial manner; at other times they may be assertive and try to be dominant.

The task in establishing a therapeutic relationship with clients having this personality style may involve catering to both of the basic emotional needs. The therapist may need to provide the parentallike guidance and support that they seem to need while allowing them to control enough of the situation that they do not feel humiliated. In some ways such individuals will need to be treated like children, but they will still have to be afforded the respect given a peer. The conflict between the two opposing tendencies may lead to some anger and interpersonal discomfort that the therapist will have to handle well for the treatment to be successful.

Profile 540: Narcissistic-Histrionic

The main assumption that these individuals have about themselves is that they are special and probably superior to most other people. Tendencies to exaggerate their abilities and positive attributes, emphasize their past achievements, and depreciate those who refuse to accept their inflated self-images may be present. This narcissism probably is manifested in an air of conviction and self-assurance. When extreme, these individuals are perceived to be conceited and arrogant.

Something that these individuals pay attention to when feeling superior to others is their personal image. They seem to value appearances: A good person is one who looks intelligent, outgoing, competent, sophisticated, and so on. Beneath this surface, however, there is a need for approval and a striving to be conspicuous, to evoke affection, and to attract attention from others. These types of individuals may be impressive at first glance because they may be able to express their thoughts easily, have a flair for the dramatic, and enjoy a natural capacity to draw attention to themselves. However, they may be capricious and intolerant of frustration. They often are emotional, but the emotions may be short-lived. There also is an inclination to be easily bored, at which times they may go do something else. Millon (1995) called this style the "amorous narcissistic" style because of the seductive flavor that they tend to have.

This personality style has been found to be common among drug addicts (Craig & Olson, 1990; Yeager, DiGiuseppe, Resweber, & Leaf, 1992). Generally, however, people with this personality style have been found to have good coping strategies (Leaf et al., 1992; Leaf, Alington, et al., 1991; Leaf, DiGiuseppe, et al., 1990; Leaf, Ellis, et al., 1991; Nakao et al., 1992; Retzlaff & Deatherage, 1993; Strack et al., 1989). In a study of air force pilots in training, at a subclinical level, the individuals were described as sociable, level-headed, and well adjusted (Retzlaff & Gibertini, 1987a).

Clients having this personality style can be expected to be most comfortable in situations in which they feel admired or at least respected, as well as the center of attention. If confrontation is used in therapy, tact has to be exercised so as not to injure their narcissism more than they can tolerate. On the other hand, there also is a danger that a therapist would be so supportive of the clients' narcissism that no negative feedback is given and growth is not facilitated. Thus, it is important to find ways of helping the clients accept their fallibilities and work on their problems without feeling unrecognized or humiliated.

Profile 546A: Narcissistic-Histrionic-Antisocial

High scores on these scales suggest a personality style characterized by confident, dramatic, and competitive elements. The main assumption these individuals hold about themselves is that they are special and superior to most other people. A tendency to exaggerate their abilities and positive attributes, emphasize their past achievements, and depreciate those who refuse to accept their inflated self-image may be present. This narcissism typically is manifested in an air of conviction and self-assurance. When extreme, some individuals are perceived as being conceited and arrogant.

There is evidence that people with this profile pay attention to their personal image when they are feeling superior to other people. They seem to value appearances: A good person is someone who appears intelligent, outgoing, competent, sophisticated, and so on. Beneath this surface, however, there is a need for approval and a striving to be conspicuous, to evoke affection, and to attract attention from others. These individuals may be impressive at first because they easily express their thoughts, have a flair for the dramatic, and enjoy a natural capacity to draw attention to themselves. They may be capricious, however, and intolerant of frustration. They often are emotional, but the emotions may be short-lived; they become bored easily and may move from one enterprise to another.

Another factor in the feelings of superiority may be related to the individuals' tendency to view the environment as a competitive place. They feel that they have to fend for themselves to function. As a result, they are somewhat mistrustful and suspicious. Assertive, energetic, self-reliant, strong, and realistic are adjectives they use to describe themselves. They feel that they have to be tough to survive in a tough world. For them, compassion and warmth are weak emotions that will place them in an inferior position. The competitive outlook fits in well with the feelings of superiority as long as they are in situations in which they have a good chance of "winning."

This profile often has been found among substance abusers (Donat, 1988; Donat et al., 1991; Fals-Stewart, 1992; Retzlaff & Bromley, 1991). It also is indicative of an absence of depression among alcoholics (McMahon & Davidson, 1986b).

Clients with this personality style may require a therapeutic situation in which they feel admired or at least respected. They need to be the center of attention. If confrontation is used in therapy, tact must be used to avoid injuring their narcissism more than they can tolerate. Another problem could arise if clients interpret the confrontation as being part of a competitive relationship and fight it rather than accepting it as useful feedback. On the other hand, there also is a danger that a therapist would be so supportive of the client's narcissism that no negative feedback is given and growth is not facilitated. Therefore, it is important to find ways to help clients accept their fallibilities and work on their problems without feeling unrecognized or humiliated.

Profile 548A: Narcissistic-Histrionic-Negativistic

People who obtain high scores on these MCMI scales assume that they are special and superior to other people. They tend to exaggerate their abilities and positive attributes, construct rationalizations to inflate their own worth, and depreciate others who refuse to accept or enhance their own self-image.

In addition, similar individuals want to appear intelligent, outgoing, charming, and sophisticated and have a need to be conspicuous and evoke affection and attention from others. They typically make good first impressions because they are able to express their feelings, have a flair for the dramatic, and have a natural ability to draw attention to themselves. They are colorful, usually have a good sense of humor, and can be perceived as being friendly and helpful in interpersonal relationships. Actively solicitous of praise, they may be entertaining and somewhat seductive. Their preoccupation with external rewards and approval may leave them feeling empty when they are alone.

These people also tend to be conflicted. On one hand, they see themselves as colorful, more capable, and generally superior to others. On the other hand, however, they depend on a flow of attention and approval from others. With some, this conflict surfaces in a hypersensitive or oppositionistic way of reacting: They may be compliant but resentful. Others handle this conflict by showing mood changes: They may be submissive and compliant at times, become resentful and angry in other instances, and become contrite, apologetic, and overly cooperative in other instances. In terms of research, a variance of this personality style (code 854) was found to be the most common among patients with major depression (Wetzler et al., 1990).

Profile 56A4: Narcissistic-Antisocial-Histrionic

Elevated scores on these scales characterize "unprincipled narcissistic" (Millon, 1995) individuals, who are confident, competitive, and dramatic. A major assumption that they have is that they are special: Such people typically feel superior to most other people. A tendency to exaggerate their abilities and positive attributes, construct arguments to emphasize their own worth, and depreciate those who refuse to accept their self-image may be present. This tendency probably is externalized through an air of conviction, security, and self-assurance. When extreme, these people can be perceived as conceited and arrogant.

Some of the feelings of superiority come from a tendency to view the world in competitive terms. Similar people feel they have to fend for themselves to function. As a result, they are somewhat mistrustful and suspicious. They see themselves as being assertive, energetic, self-reliant, strong, and realistic and feel that they have to be tough to make it in a tough world. These individuals usually justify their aggressiveness by pointing to the hostile and exploitative behavior of others. In their view, compassionate or warm people are weak and will be taken advantage of. This antisocial outlook fits in particularly well with their feelings of superiority if they are in a situation in which they have a chance of winning.

The indications are that these people pay attention to their image when they are feeling superior to others. They seem to value appearances: A good person is someone who appears intelligent, outgoing, charming, sophisticated, and so on. Beneath this surface, there typically is a need for approval and a striving to be conspicuous and to evoke affection and receive attention from others. These individuals usually make good first impressions because they easily express their thoughts and feelings, have a flair for the dramatic, and naturally draw attention to themselves. However, they may be capricious and intolerant of frustration.

This personality style has been found to be common among male inpatients, both in an alcoholic population (Mayer & Scott, 1988) and a more general psychiatric ward (Donat, Geczy, et al., 1992). It also is well represented among drug abusers (Marsh et al., 1988).

Therapy may be more effective for clients with this personality if they feel admired, or at least respected, by the therapist. Similar individuals frequently also need to be the center of attention. If confrontation is necessary, tact must be used so as not to injure their narcissism more than they can tolerate. Moreover, there also is the risk that the clients could interpret the confrontation as part of a competitive relationship and fight it rather than accepting it as useful feedback. On the other hand, it also is possible that a therapist could be so supportive of their clients' narcissism that no negative feedback is given and growth is not facilitated. Therefore, it is important to find ways to help clients accept their fallibilities and work on their problems without feeling unrecognized or humiliated.

Profile 58A0: Narcissistic-Negativistic

This personality profile defines individuals who have a confident and explosive personality. Similar people assume that they are special and superior to most people. They tend to exaggerate their abilities and positive attributes, construct rationalizations to inflate their own worth, and depreciate others who refuse to accept or enhance their own self-image.

Such people typically want to appear intelligent, outgoing, charming, and sophisticated and have a need to be conspicuous, evoking affection and attention from others. They often make good first impressions because they can be friendly and helpful in interpersonal relationships. However, they are unlikely to accept criticism and tend to project whatever feelings of inadequacy they have, attempting to dismiss their failures as resulting from the irresponsibility or incompetence of others.

Individuals with similar MCMI scores tend to be conflicted. On one hand, they want to see themselves as being superior to others. On the other hand, they are insecure and painfully aware of their own limitations. This conflict may surface through mood changes: They may be compliant at times, only to become resentful and angry in other instances and to be contrite, apologetic, and overly cooperative on still other occasions.

Given this personality style, these clients may benefit most from a therapeutic relationship in which they feel admired or at least respected. If therapists confront these clients, they should use tact to avoid injuring their narcissism more than the clients can handle. On the other hand, therapists should not be so supportive of clients' narcissism that no negative feedback is given and the clients do not grow psychologically. Thus, it is important to find ways of helping such individuals accept their fallibilities and work on their problems without feeling unrecognized or humiliated.

In addition, it may be important not to try to control these clients in ways that are not necessary for the therapy to function. Because these individuals are bound to resent any control placed on them, this tactic can prevent the therapeutic relationship from becoming overly conflictual. Such people also may benefit from learning how they normally operate and project negative feelings onto others.

Profile 6A00: Antisocial

These competitive people see their environment as if it was a tournament, and they feel they have to fend for themselves to function. As a result, most individuals with this personality profile are somewhat mistrustful and suspicious of others. They see themselves as being assertive, energetic, self-reliant, strong, and realistic. To make it in the rat race, they have to be tough. These people justify their assertiveness by pointing to the hostile and exploitative behavior of others. They may be contemptuous of the weak and not care whether they are liked because "good guys come in last."

Such individuals are impulsive. They typically are perceived as somewhat aggressive and intimidating. At times, they may appear cold, callous, and insensitive. They may be argumentative and contentious. They may even be abusive, cruel, or malicious. When matters go their way, they may be gracious, cheerful, and friendly. More characteristically, however, their behavior is guarded, reserved, and competitive. When crossed, pushed on personal matters, or faced with embarrassment, they may respond impulsively and become angry, vengeful, and vindictive. This type of personality is found commonly in a therapeutic community for drug addicts and is associated with difficulty obeying rules, staying in treatment, and maintaining abstinence (Fals-Stewart, 1992).

In light of this personality style, the establishment of a therapeutic alliance may be somewhat difficult. Clients are not inclined to see psychotherapy as valuable unless it offers a tangible material benefit, such as a way out of a jam. One approach to establishing an alliance in spite of this difficulty may be to accept, at least temporarily, the same competitive outlook that the clients favor. The therapist then may be in the position to help them explore the behaviors and attitudes that get in the way of their being a "winner."

Profile 6A12A: Antisocial-Schizoid-Avoidant

Competitive, introversive, and avoidant traits characterize this "nomadic antisocial" (Millon, 1995) personality profile of the MCMI. Such individuals see their environment as if it were a tournament, with one person pitted against the other. To be able to function in such a situation, they feel that they have to fend for themselves. Such people are self-sufficient and do not depend on others to fulfill their needs. They may be somewhat mistrustful and suspicious. They see themselves as being assertive, energetic, self-reliant, strong, and realistic. To make it in the rat race, they believe they must adopt a tough stance. Their assertiveness is justified by pointing to the hostile and exploitative behavior of others.

People with this type of personality may be contemptuous of the weak and may appear cold, callous, or insensitive to the feelings of others and may tend to be argumentative and contentious. When matters go their way, they may be gracious, cheerful, and friendly. More characteristically, however, their behavior is guarded, reserved, and aggressive. When crossed, pushed, or embarrassed, they may respond impulsively and become angry, vengeful, and vindictive.

In addition, these individuals keep an emotional distance from others. They are uninterested in interpersonal relations and may not be adept at understanding and enjoying the subtleties of emotions, which could result in apathy about the relationship itself. Moreover, they typically are afraid of being rejected by others who also are looking out for themselves in the competitive world. As a result, social situations are avoided because they are uncomfortable and tension provoking. These individuals restrict the number of relationships they form and tend to have superficial friendships when those exist, alliances that are more like acquaintanceships than strong friendships.

In light of this personality style, the establishment of a therapeutic alliance may be somewhat difficult. Clients are not inclined to see psychotherapy as valuable unless it offers a tangible material benefit, such as a way out of a jam. The fact that they are likely to be threatened or uninterested in emotional closeness also may impede the forming of a relationship. One approach to establishing an alliance in spite of this difficulty may be to accept, at least temporarily, the same competitive outlook that the clients favor. The therapist then may be in the position to help them explore the behaviors and attitudes that get in the way of their being a "winner."

Profile 6A50: Antisocial-Narcissistic

This MCMI personality profile is characterized by competitive and confident traits. Because the environment is perceived to be competitive by nature, people with this profile feel they have to fend for themselves to function. As a result, most individuals with this view are somewhat distant, mistrustful, and suspicious of others. They see themselves as being assertive, energetic, self-reliant, strong, and realistic. For them, one must be tough to make it in this "dog-eat-dog" world. These individuals usually justify their assertiveness by pointing to the hostile and exploitative behavior of others. They may not object if they are not liked; after all, "good guys come in last."

Another aspect of this personality style is an inflated self-image. These people typically see themselves as being more capable, more interesting, and more worthwhile than other people. This tendency often is externalized through an air of conviction, independent security, and self-assurance. When extreme, this tendency may make the bearer appear conceited or arrogant.

Other people may perceive these individuals as being somewhat aggressive and intimidating. Their assertiveness may be sensed as a cold insensitivity to the feelings of others. Such individuals tend to be argumentative and contentious and may even be abusive, cruel, or malicious at times. When things go their way, they may be gracious, cheerful, and friendly. More characteristically, however, they are guarded, reserved, and resentful. When crossed, pushed on personal matters, or faced with embarrassment, they may respond quickly and become angry, vengeful, and vindictive.

This type of personality has been found to be common among the men in a domestic violence abatement program (Hamberger & Hastings, 1986; Lohr et al., 1988). The men were described as self-centered, likely to insist that their values and rules be accepted, and inclined to use others to meet their own needs. They felt entitled to be treated differently from others. This personality style also has been found to be prevalent in correctional inmates (Hart et al., 1991; McNiel & Meyer, 1990) and can be found among alcoholics (Corbisiero & Reznikoff, 1991; Craig et al., 1985). Antoni et al. (1986) found this personality style to represent a subgroup of the patients obtaining the 89/98 MMPI code.

In light of this personality style, establishing a therapeutic alliance may be somewhat difficult. These clients will not see the benefit of psychotherapy unless it offers a tangible material benefit, such as a way out of trouble. They also resent the kind of superior position that the therapist has in the therapeutic situation, perhaps because the therapist is the "expert" whose opinions are solicited during the therapy session.

One approach to establishing an alliance in spite of the difficulties may be to accept, at least temporarily, the same competitive outlook that the clients favor. The therapist then may be in the position to help them explore the behaviors and attitudes that prevent them from being winners. Treating them with as much respect and deference as possible also may contribute to the formation of the therapeutic alliance.

Profile 6A53: Antisocial-Narcissistic-Dependent

This MCMI personality profile indicates the predominance of competitive, confident, and cooperative traits in the personality makeup. The juxtaposition of these three styles is unusual and possibly problematic. An elevation on the Antisocial scale typically is associated with viewing the environment as a contest, a situation in which people are pitted against each other. To be able to function, these individuals feel that they have to fend for themselves. As a result, they are somewhat distant, mistrustful, and suspicious of others. They see themselves as assertive, energetic, self-reliant, strong, and realistic; they feel that they have to be tough to make it in the world.

Another aspect of the personality style portrayed by the MCMI is an inflated self-image. A tendency for the individuals to think that they are more capable, interesting, or worthwhile than other people probably is present. These people like to be conspicuous and admired. Their wish to be leaders and hold positions of status and power, and their lack of interest in following someone else's directions, may become externalized through an air of conviction, independent security, and self-assurance. When extreme, this tendency may make such individuals look somewhat conceited and arrogant.

Similar people may be perceived as aggressive or intimidating; their assertiveness often is sensed as a cold insensitivity to other people's feelings. When events go their way, they may be gracious, cheerful, and friendly. At other times, however, they may be guarded, reserved, and resentful. When crossed, pushed on personal matters, or faced with humiliation, they may become angry and vindictive.

The inflated self-image fits in well with the competitive outlook in that it provides the security that these individuals need to engage in the rivalry they are likely to experience when they are with others. One problem with this personality profile is that the third elevation occurred on a scale that is almost the direct opposite of the first two. The Dependent scale typically characterizes people who are followers rather than leaders. High scores on this scale describe individuals who are unsure of their abilities and would feel more comfortable if they had someone whom they trusted take care of them. One way of integrating all the findings would be to think of these individuals as actually feeling fairly inadequate but compensating against these feelings by putting up an overconfident façade.

In light of this personality style, establishing a therapeutic alliance may be difficult. These people are not likely to see psychotherapy as valuable unless they will benefit from it in a tangible way. They are inclined to resent the kind of superior position the therapist assumes during the sessions. One approach to establishing an alliance may be to accept the same competitive outlook that the clients favor. The therapist then may be able to help them examine the behaviors and attitudes that keep them from being successful. It also will help to treat the clients with special respect and deference.

Profile 6A58A: Antisocial-Narcissistic-Negativistic

Individuals obtaining elevations on these MCMI scales likely will have a competitive personality style with confident and negativistic overtones. In terms of empirical data, this personality profile has been found to be common among alcoholics (Corbisiero & Reznikoff, 1991).

People with this personality style view their environment as primarily competitive and, to be able to function, they feel they must fend for themselves. As a result, they are somewhat distant, mistrustful, and suspicious of others, but they see themselves as being assertive, energetic, self-reliant, strong, and realistic. They feel that they have to be tough to survive in such a competitive environment and justify their assertiveness by pointing to the hostile and exploitative behavior of others. They probably will not care whether other people like them because one does what one must do to get ahead.

An unfortunate effect of adversarial relationships is that the loser suffers as a result of the other person winning. Although this may not be the goal of behaving in a particular way, people with this personality style try not to be bothered by humanistic sentiments or guilt. In fact, they may feel that worrying about such issues implies a weakness or liability instead of something admirable. These people strive to be tough, thick-skinned, streetwise, and capable of taking care of themselves.

Another aspect of the personality style pattern portrayed by these individuals is an inflated self-image. They tend to think they are more able, more interesting, and more worthwhile than others. They have an air of conviction, independent security, and self-assurance. When extreme, these people may appear to be conceited and arrogant.

This personality style also may make the bearer appear aggressive, intimidating, cold, or insensitive. Such individuals tend to be argumentative and contentious and may even be abusive, cruel, or malicious at times. When events go their way, they may be gracious, cheerful, and friendly. More characteristically, however, they are guarded, reserved, and resentful. When crossed, pushed on personal matters, or embarrassed, they may respond quickly and become angry, vengeful, and vindictive.

In fact, high scores on these scales suggest the presence of interpersonal conflicts. At times these people may want to have closer and warmer relationships and may regret having mistreated others in the antisocial struggle. The unresolved conflict is projected in the form of a negativistic resentment or anger. Instead of overtly venting the resentment, some such individuals are more inclined to be obstructionistic.

The predominance of the antisocial personality style probably makes these individuals function particularly well in situations that are inherently competitive, such as some businesses, sales, or competitive sports (e.g., boxing, football). The superficiality in interpersonal relationships and the aggressive attitude, on the other hand, may have a negative effect in situations in which loyalty and team coordination are needed.

In light of the personality style just described, the establishment of a therapeutic alliance may be difficult. These clients may not see value in psychotherapy. Moreover, the therapist's superior position as an expert will be resented.

One way of fostering the relationship may be to accept the competitive outlook that the clients favor. The therapist then may be better able to help them figure out what behaviors and attitudes hinder their becoming a "winner." The therapist also may have to remain unintrusive, careful not to take a stance if it is not necessary. Not taking a strong position will encourage clients to make their own decisions and will decrease the amount of conflict present in the therapeutic relationship.

Giving interpretations at times when clients are using dysfunctional projective mechanisms may be necessary. However, any confrontation has to be carried out with care because these people will be inclined to approach such feedback in a competitive manner and fight the insights that are offered. The therapeutic alliance has to be protected by doing whatever is necessary to keep them feeling that the therapist is on their side.

Profile 6A70: Antisocial-Compulsive

Elevated scores on these MCMI scales indicate predominant competitive and disciplined personality traits. People with this profile view life as a sort of tournament. Everyone, in their view, is competing for the same rewards and these valuables are in limited supply. To be able to function well in this type of situation, they feel they have to fend for themselves. As a result, most such individuals are somewhat mistrustful or even suspicious of others. They see themselves as assertive, energetic, self-reliant, strong, and realistic and feel that they have to be tough to make it in the world. These individuals may be somewhat contemptuous of the weak and not care whether they are liked, claiming that "good guys come in last." Characteristically, their behavior is guarded and reserved.

Additionally, these people assume that the way to become a "winner" is to avoid making a mistake. They usually are orderly and conscientious, plan for the future, prepare well, and do work on schedule. They tend to be efficient, dependable, industrious, and persistent. These individuals often believe in discipline and practice self-restraint, especially when it concerns their own emotions, which are usually kept under control. The overcontrol of the emotions gives them their typical flavor: They are formal and proper and somewhat unlikely to open up and act spontaneously in front of others. They sometimes are perceived as perfectionistic, distant, and inflexible; they tend to be indecisive at times when they have had no chance to study all the possible options. In other words, their strategy to win the rat race is to be careful, deliberate, dependable, and hardworking.

About 15% of the alcoholic population has been found to have this personality style. The group is associated with the MMPI 42 code. Alcohol for these patients is thought to dampen an overly exuberant conscience and to permit escape from responsibility and the expression of anger (Bartsch & Hoffman, 1985). Retzlaff and Gibertini (1987a) found this personality to be common among air force pilot trainees.

Profile 6A8A0: Antisocial-Negativistic

This MCMI personality profile indicates a predominance of competitive traits with negativistic elements. Patients tend to experience life as if it were a tournament. Assuming that everyone is struggling for things that exist in limited supply, they probably are somewhat mistrustful and superficial in the way they relate to others. They need to be strong and self-sufficient. They feel that asking others for help is counterproductive because it lessens their own chances of ending up ahead of those on whom they depend. These individuals are proud of their "realistic" views, which emphasize tangible achievements and material gains.

An unfortunate effect of adversarial relationships is that the loser suffers as a result of the other person winning. Although this may not be the goal of behaving in a particular way, people with this profile probably try not to be bothered by humanistic sentiments or guilt. In fact, they may feel that worrying about those issues implies some weakness or liability instead of something to be admired. They want other people to perceive them as tough, thick-skinned, streetwise, and capable of protecting their own interests.

However, these people may have some conflicts in the way that they relate to others. At times they may want closer and warmer relationships and may regret having mistreated others in their competitive struggle. The unresolved conflict typically is projected in the form of a negativistic resentment or anger. Instead of overtly venting their resentment, some individuals may use an obstructionistic or passive–aggressive strategy.

The predominance of the antisocial personality style probably makes such people function particularly well in situations that are inherently difficult, such as business, sales, or competitive sports. The superficiality in interpersonal relationships and the aggressive attitude, on the other hand, may have a negative effect in situations in which loyalty and teamwork are needed.

In light of the personality style that these clients appear to have, establishing a therapeutic alliance may be difficult. They are not likely to see psychotherapy as valuable unless it offers a tangible material benefit. They also resent the therapist's superior position in the therapeutic situation, perhaps because the therapist is the "expert" whose opinions are solicited during the therapy session. One approach to establishing an alliance is to accept, at least temporarily, the same competitive outlook that the clients favor. The therapist then may be able to help the clients identify the behaviors and attitudes that hinder the chance of their becoming "winners."

The therapist also may have to remain unintrusive and careful not to take a stance. Not taking a stance will encourage the clients to make their own decisions and will decrease the amount of conflict present in the therapeutic relationship. Giving interpretations when the clients are using maladaptive projective mechanisms may be necessary. However, any confrontation has to be done carefully because they will be inclined to react to such feedback in an antisocial manner and to fight the insights that are offered. The therapeutic alliance must be protected, and the therapist has to do whatever is necessary to keep the clients feeling that the therapist is on their side.

Profile 700: Compulsive

Elevated scores on this MCMI indicate the predominance of disciplined traits in the basic personality structure. Individuals with this "conscientious compulsive" (Millon, 1995) type of personality profile place a premium on avoiding mistakes. They usually are orderly and plan for the future. Moreover, they are conscientious, prepare well, and do their work on schedule. They tend to be efficient, dependable, industrious, and persistent. To people in authority, these individuals typically act in a respectful and ingratiating manner. This style of relating often changes when the relationship is with a subordinate. When this is the case, these individuals may become somewhat perfectionistic and demanding.

People with this profile believe in discipline and practice self-restraint, especially when it concerns their own emotions, which are usually kept well under control. The overcontrol of emotions tends to give them a characteristic flavor: They are formal and proper and unlikely to open up and act spontaneously in front of others. Sometimes seen as perfectionistic, distant, or inflexible, these people tend to be indecisive before they have had a chance to study all possible alternatives. However, they are careful, deliberate, righteous, honest, dependable, and hardworking people.

This type of personality style may make it difficult for such individuals to work with some aspects of their environment. For instance, situations that unpredictably change abruptly from one moment to the next or in which following the rules does not lead to the desired outcome can be particularly stressful. However, disciplined individuals are well suited for situations in which it is important to be accurate and meticulous.

People with a compulsive personality style have been found to have good coping strategies, and this has been seen as a possible source of psychological strength (Leaf et al., 1992; Leaf, Alington, et al., 1991; Leaf, DiGiuseppe, et al., 1990; Leaf, Ellis, et al., 1991; Nakao et al., 1992; Retzlaff & Deatherage, 1993). The style has been found to be common among seminarians (Piersma, 1987c) and missionaries (Adams & Clopton, 1990). However, compulsive people also constitute a large portion of the alcoholic population (Craig et al., 1985; Donat, 1988; Donat et al., 1991).

Unfortunately, an elevation on the Compulsive scale also can be obtained by people who are not all that proper or orderly but who are interested in "looking good" in the testing or are defensive psychologically (Craig et al., 1994; Retzlaff, Sheehan, & Fiel, 1991). This is because these people do not endorse personality "flaws" and answer the testing in a perfectionistic manner. If this turns out to be the case, the description has to be changed to emphasize the defensive outlook rather than the meticulousness, orderliness, or the interest in careful planning.

If these clients do have a compulsive personality style, however, they would find it easier to establish a therapeutic alliance with a professional who is formal, proper, punctual, and predictable. Keeping some distance and allowing the clients to control significant parts of the session also would make them feel more at ease. Explanations of the diagnosis, the nature of the "illness," and the expected course of treatment will probably be appreciated. It may, however, be difficult to move such individuals from a superficial therapeutic alliance to a more meaningful dependency on the relationship. Helping them explore the defenses that they use or enhancing their tolerance for allowing others to hold the controls also can be difficult to accomplish.

Profile 72A0: Compulsive-Avoidant

People with high scores on these MCMI scales have disciplined and avoidant tendencies in their personality structure. An important motivational force behind this basic personality structure is the avoidance of mistakes. Such individuals tend to be orderly and plan for the future. To those in authority, they are inclined to be respectful, ingratiating, and dependent. This approach probably changes when they relate to a subordinate. In that case, they may become somewhat arrogant, perfectionistic, or disdainful. They often believe in discipline and practice self-restraint, especially when it concerns their own emotions, which are always kept under control.

There are indications that these people would like to relate to others and enjoy the affection and appreciation of others. People in general, however, present a problem to those with this personality style because they can be emotional and unpredictable. This unpredictability and emphasis on emotional aspects of relationships can make these individuals uncomfortable. Thus, relating to others represents a risk that makes them feel particularly vulnerable. They may be inclined to avoid relationships or to relate in a cold and distant manner to minimize the risks taken.

Individuals with similar MCMI personality scores tend to be proper and formal. They usually are conscientious, well prepared, efficient, dependable, industrious, and persistent. However, they also may be perceived as perfectionistic, rigid, picayunish, and indecisive.

Given this type of personality style, such clients may find it easier to establish a therapeutic alliance with a professional who is formal, proper, punctual, and predictable. Keeping some distance and allowing the clients to control significant parts of the session also will make them feel at ease. Explanations of the diagnosis, the nature of the illness, and the expected course of treatment can be important. However, it may be difficult to move from a superficial therapeutic alliance to a more meaningful dependency on the relationship. Helping such clients explore defenses or to enhance their tolerance for allowing others to be in control also can be difficult to accomplish.

Profile 736A: Compulsive-Dependent-Antisocial

People with this personality profile are disciplined, cooperative, and competitive. This profile has been described in the literature as representing individuals who attempt to avoid expected criticism by presenting themselves in a superficially friendly and compliant manner but who also are fairly guarded and defensive (Donat, Geczy, et al., 1992; Lorr & Strack, 1990). These individuals tend to feel inadequate and have low self-esteem. Superficially, they may appear to be cooperative and congenial and to be searching for support from others. However, they tend to have their own ideas and, although they may sometimes comply with the wishes of others, they are not likely to enthusiastically support someone else's plan.

These people see the world as a competitive place. Because they believe that people are out to satisfy their own needs, they are somewhat mistrustful in their interpersonal relationships; they probably will not share all of their feelings and will harbor suspicions that other people may be trying to use them in some way. Combined with their feelings of inadequacy, the competitive view of the world reinforces the compulsive traits because such individuals feel that they have to avoid making mistakes, which can be used to gain advantage over them.

People with this profile may seem somewhat rigid, unsure, distant, and mistrustful. On the other hand, well-adjusted individuals with this personality cluster may be able to use some of these traits to their benefit. Their disciplined nature may contribute to their being conscientious, hardworking people with an ability to pay attention to detail and follow rules. Their dependent inclinations may translate into a certain congeniality and motivation to be liked and appreciated. Finally, their competitiveness may make them realistic people who are mature enough to appreciate that people do not usually get something for nothing and that one has to look at the risks and alternatives before making a decision.

Profile 738A: Compulsive-Dependent-Negativistic

Disciplined, negativistic, and dependent traits are emphasized by this personality style. This MCMI profile has been described in the literature as representing individuals who attempt to avoid expected criticism by presenting themselves in a superficially friendly and compliant manner but who are fairly guarded and defensive (Donat, Geczy, et al., 1992; Lorr & Strack, 1990). People with high scores on these scales emphasize the need to avoid making mistakes. Such people usually are orderly and plan for the future. They are highly conscientious and well prepared and like to do their work on schedule; they try to be efficient, dependable, industrious, and persistent.

In spite of their perfectionistic inclinations, these people fear that they are not capable enough so that, if left completely to their own devices, they would not be able to make ends meet. They would like to have someone else take care of them and provide for their needs, but they tend to resent any control that others may exert as the price for the emotional support. This resentment eliminates the option of becoming dependent on some benefactor.

The conflict of wanting support but fighting control and dependency also makes these individuals likely to change their overall feelings without an obvious reason. At times, they may be friendly and engaging; they then may become angry and resentful. After that, they may feel guilty and contrite. The cycle is completed when they again become friendly and cooperative. In other words, they defend against their insecurities by projecting blame, sometimes against themselves and sometimes at others. A different style brought about by the same basic conflict involves the use of a passive–aggressive defense. In such cases, they try to control their resentment through obstructionistic maneuvers that allow them to vent their anger in covert ways without blatantly jeopardizing the dependent relationship.

The compulsive element in this personality style may make it difficult for such people to deal with some aspects of their environment. For instance, situations that can change abruptly from one moment to the next, or situations in which following rules does not lead to the desired outcome, can be more stressful for these individuals than for other people. However, such people are well suited for situations in which it is important to be accurate and meticulous.

Given the type of personality style just described, these clients may find it easier to establish a therapeutic alliance with a professional who is formal, proper, punctual, and predictable. Keeping some distance and allowing clients to control significant parts of the session also would make them feel better. Explanations of the diagnosis, the nature of the illness, and the expected course of treatment also can be helpful. Moving these individuals from a superficial therapeutic alliance to a more meaningful dependency on the relationship may be difficult. Helping them explore defenses or enhance their tolerance for not being in control also can be difficult to accomplish. These clients will probably demand some support and reassurance in the therapeutic situation. It may be useful to set clear limits and to give them as much independence as possible, getting them to make their own decisions rather than offering suggestions or recommendations.

Profile 740: Compulsive-Histrionic

Individuals obtaining this MCMI personality profile have predominant disciplined and dramatic traits. In some ways, the dramatic and disciplined tendencies conflict with one another. Dramatic people, for instance, tend to be emotional, intense in their relationships, and impulsive. Disciplined individuals, on the other hand, overcontrol their emotions, are somewhat distant when relating to others, and carefully plan their behaviors. Individuals who have these two tendencies together often are unable to integrate them well and tend to be conflicted. As a result, they may seem moody or emotionally labile. At times they may be more invested and intense, but they then may fear where this behavior would lead and become more rigid and controlled.

The indications would be that these people tend to emphasize appearances, placing a premium on propriety and dependability and living their lives trying to avoid the appearance of making a mistake. A high value may be placed, for instance, on dressing right, having a clean and orderly house, and so on. They probably try to be conscientious, efficient, dependable, industrious, and persistent.

Nevertheless, there is a side to these individuals that is not all that conscientious or dependable and that often breaks through the controls that they try to exert. This is the side that seeks stimulation, excitement, and attention and is colorful and emotional. Thus, at times, these individuals are going to be conspicuous and actively search for affirmation of approval and affection. They often become sensitive to the moods of others and use this knowledge to evoke the reactions they desire. They are highly reactive to their environments and often become deeply involved, but typically this involvement does not last.

Similar people are good at making positive first impressions. The ability to react to unexpected situations, the alertness and interest, and the search for attention help make them colorful at parties and similar gatherings. People with this personality style have been found to have good coping strategies (Leaf et al., 1992; Leaf, Alington, et al., 1991; Leaf, DiGiuseppe, et al., 1990; Leaf, Ellis, et al., 1991; Nakao et al., 1992; Retzlaff & Deatherage, 1993) and to be well represented—with scores at a subclinical range—in well-functioning groups (e.g., Lemkau, Purdy, Rafferty, & Rudisill, 1988). However, similar people typically have difficulty with the balance between the disciplined control of their emotions and their need to get attention, stimulation, and affection.

Given this personality style, forming a therapeutic alliance may be easier if the therapist conducts formal and orderly sessions. Even more important may be making sure that clients are the center of attention and receive a great deal of reassurance, affection, and support.

Profile 750: Compulsive-Narcissistic

The pattern of scores obtained on these scales indicate the prominence of disciplined and confident personality traits, what Millon (1995) called the "bureaucratic compulsive." People with these traits have been found to have good coping strategies (Leaf et al., 1992; Leaf, Alington, et al., 1991; Leaf, DiGiuseppe, et al., 1990; Leaf, Ellis, et al., 1991; Nakao et al., 1992; Retzlaff & Deatherage, 1993; Strack et al., 1989) and, in some cases, to have an enhanced ability to function. However, this type of personality has been found among spouse-abusing men (Lohr et al., 1988).

The disciplined aspects indicate an emphasis on perfectionism and maintaining good control of the environment. People obtaining elevations on these scales are somewhat defensive and unlikely to admit to failures or mistakes. At times they may be seen as too inflexible, formal, or proper and may relate to others somewhat distantly.

Together with the disciplined elements, these individuals have a tendency to feel that they are more special or capable than others. They are field-independent people who rely more on their own feelings or judgments than they do on the opinions of others. A confident air of self-assurance may be present. They may have trouble accepting somebody else's ideas and doing what they are told. Such situations may cause conflict between them and the other people involved.

Given the type of personality style just described, these clients may find it easier to establish a therapeutic alliance with a professional who is formal, proper, punctual, and predictable and able to admire them in some manner. Keeping some distance and allowing them to control significant parts of the session also would make them feel at ease. Other helpful ideas include explaining the diagnosis, the nature of the illness, and the expected course of treatment. It could be difficult to move such individuals from a superficial therapeutic alliance to a more meaningful dependency on the relationship. Helping them explore psychological defenses or enhance their tolerance for not being in control also could be difficult.

Profile 8A00: Negativistic

The Negativistic scale describes resentful individuals. This personality style results from holding two assumptions about the world that are difficult to integrate. Such individuals first assume that they need to rely on others because they are not able to do well without their support; they are "people who need people." The second premise that negativistic individuals hold is that they cannot afford to depend on others. They may feel that others are not interested enough to be dependable, that the dependence on others is not socially acceptable and will make them look bad, and that others would take advantage of them if they are not constantly on guard.

These two assumptions about life typically bring about one of two different behavior patterns. In the passive–aggressive substyle, the conflict is handled by being compliant on the surface but not fully supporting the efforts of others along the way. By contrast, the explosive variant involves a vacillation between feeling lucky and able to get more out of life than expected and feeling cheated or mistreated.

The behavior of negativistic people changes accordingly. At times, these people treat others in an agreeable and friendly manner and, on other occasions, they may be irritable, aggressive, or hostile. At still other times, they may experience guilt and appear eagerly cooperative and remorseful. They frequently may be optimistic and see the future as bright, but this changes, seemingly without reason, into the opposite view. An energetic and productive mood, together with high goals, may characterize them on some occasions but, in other instances, these people are inclined to lower their goals and become less productive.

Similar individuals can be flexible and changeable, sensitive, and responsive to their environments, but they also may seem moody and unpredictable. Projection is an important defense, but the direction of the projection tends to change from self to other or vice versa. Mostly, these people tend to be angry, conflicted, and resentful. They typically are difficult to handle and present some problems wherever they go. A high level of emotional venting as a coping mechanism under stress has been reported (Vollrath et al., 1995). Elevations on the Negativistic scale are accompanied by more elevations of other scales than what can be expected of any of the other 7 basic personality scales (Chick et al., 1994). The style has been reported to be prominent among alcoholics (Craig et al., 1985; Retzlaff & Gibertini, 1990), drug addicts (Craig & Olson, 1990), and chronic pain patients (Jay et al., 1987), and patients with panic disorders who prematurely terminate treatment (J. Reich, 1990).

Given this personality style, it may be useful to try not to control these clients in ways that are not necessary for the therapist and clients to be able to function. Because clients are bound to resent any control that is placed on them, this tactic can prevent the therapeutic relationship from becoming overly conflictual. They also may benefit from learning how they normally operate and tend to project negative feelings onto others.

Profile 8A12A: Negativistic-Schizoid-Avoidant

This MCMI personality profile is indicative of a negativistic personality style with introversive and avoidant elements. This profile was found to be the most common profile in a group of angry, nonpsychotic White men with psychiatric disorders (Greenblatt & Davis, 1992). Elevations of the Negativistic scale are accompanied by more elevations of other scales than what can be expected of any of the other 7 basic personality scales (Chick et al., 1994).

This personality style results from holding two assumptions about the world that are difficult to integrate. Such individuals first assume that they need to rely on others because they are not able to do well without their support; they are "people who need people." The second premise such individuals hold is that they cannot afford to depend on others. They typically feel that others are not interested enough to be dependable.

These two assumptions about life typically cause one of two different behavior patterns. In the passive–aggressive substyle, the conflict is dealt with by being compliant on the surface but not fully supporting the efforts of others along the way. The other variant involves an explosive pattern in which individuals vacillate between feeling that they are lucky and get more out of life than they have a right to expect and feeling cheated or mistreated. Their behavior changes accordingly. At times these people are agreeable and friendly; at other times they may be irritable, aggressive, or hostile; at still other times, they may experience guilt and appear overly cooperative and remorseful. These people frequently may be optimistic and see the future as bright, but this changes, seemingly without reason, into the opposite view. An energetic and productive mood, together with high goals, may characterize some occasions, but in other instances similar individuals are inclined to lower their goals and become less productive.

These people can be flexible and changeable, sensitive, and responsive to their environment, but they also can seem moody and unpredictable. Projection is an important defense that can be aimed at themselves or others. For the most part, though, these individuals tend to be angry, conflicted, and resentful; they often are difficult to handle and may present problems wherever they go.

These individuals also keep an emotional distance from others. To some degree, they are uninterested in interpersonal relations and may not be too adept at understanding and enjoying the subtleties and nuances of emotions. This attribute may lead to their being apathetic about the relationship itself. Moreover, they typically are afraid of rejection. As a result, social situations are uncomfortable and are avoided. Such individuals restrict the number of relationships that they form and tend to have superficial friendships when those do exist, alliances that are more like acquaintanceships than friendships.

In trying to establish a therapeutic relationship, it might be useful for the therapist to avoid trying to control these clients in ways that are not necessary so that the therapist and clients can function. Because the clients probably will resent any control placed on them, the use of minimal controls and directives can prevent the therapeutic relationship from becoming overly conflictual. Clients also may benefit from learning how they normally operate and from exploring their tendency to project negative feelings onto others.

Profile 8A2A0: Negativistic-Avoidant

This MCMI profile defines a personality style characterized by resentment and a fear of rejection. Elevations of the Negativistic scale are accompanied by more elevations of other scales than what can be expected of any of the other 7 basic personality scales (Chick et al., 1994). This profile, with the additional elevation of the Aggressive scale, was part of the most typical profile for individuals diagnosed with a borderline personality disorder (McCann, Flynn, & Gersh, 1992); it was shown to represent 18% of the psychiatric inpatient population, and it is likely that there will be high levels of psychiatric symptoms (Donat, Geczy, et al., 1992). According to Greenblatt and Davis (1992), the negativistic-avoidant style is the most common profile for the angry and psychotic men in their psychiatric sample. This personality style, together with the two variants described next, is so prevalent among men with posttraumatic stress disorder that the presence of this personality style has significant diagnostic value for it (Hyer & Boudewyns, 1987; Hyer et al., 1992; Hyer, Woods, & Boudewyns, 1991; Hyer, Woods, Boudewyns, Bruno, & O'Leary, 1988; Hyer, Woods, Boudewyns, Harrison, & Tamkin, 1990; McDermott, 1987; Munley, Bains, Frazee, & Schwartz, 1994; Sherwood, Funari, & Piekarski, 1990). This style also has been found among alcoholics (Corbisiero & Reznikoff, 1991; Mayer & Scott, 1988; McMahon & Davidson, 1986b; McMahon, Davidson, & Flynn, 1986; Retzlaff & Bromley, 1991), especially those who are depressed (McMahon & Davidson, 1986b), and opiate addicts (Craig et al., 1985), and bulimics (Garner et al., 1990). Unfortunately, this personality style also has been associated with a poor response to treatment (Garner et al., 1990; Hyer, Woods, Bruno, & Boudewyns, 1989; McMahon & Tyson, 1990). Antoni et al. (1985a) found that this personality style represents a subgroup of the patients obtaining the 28/82 MMPI code type.

Individuals with high scores usually have low self-esteem and see themselves as inadequate or unworthy. Projection is an important part of their psychological defenses because the tendency to search for someone to blame is common. In their pessimistic view of the world, other people are typically portrayed as cold and rejecting. Therefore, in spite of their poor self-images, these individuals do not put others up on a pedestal and tend to be aware of the limitations that others may have.

People with this profile have conflicts in their interpersonal relationships. Because they are afraid that they may not be seen in a good light, interpersonal situations are associated with having to take considerable emotional risks. Some individuals are loners who retreat into their own world of fantasy and are nervous and uncomfortable when they are with others. However, they tend to be sensitive people who are aware of their own feelings and the emotional reactions they evoke in others.

Together with the conflict over whether they should relate to others, these individuals tend to be moody and resentful. Thus, they may be friendly and cooperative at times, but then they may become obstructionistic, negativistic, or hostile, only to feel guilty later and behave contritely. In some cases, these mood fluctuations are less noticeable and the conflict is handled through covert obstructionism. This pattern works well because it allows them to cope with the conflict over dependency and their fear of relating to others through the same projective defenses. Thus, the negativistic response allows cooperation without submission and contributes to the formation of relationships that keep others at a distance. The negativism occasionally may have a positive side because there are some individuals who are able to excel while being a rebel.

Patients such as these are likely to be ambivalent about the prospect of therapy and will probably be uncomfortable during the session. The therapist may be able to make establishing the therapeutic alliance easier by finding ways of minimizing the controls and demands that are made on them to make the relationship more conflict-free. Although reassurance of acceptance may be necessary, the therapist should not be too warm and embracing because such an approach may be too threatening to individuals who have to keep some interpersonal distance. In spite of these strategies, the therapist may have to be tolerant of clients who may be irritable, or even hostile, during the sessions.

Once the therapeutic alliance has been established, the therapist might want to use the relationship to help the clients explore their emotional reactions and develop more productive ways of dealing with their feelings. The therapist has to be careful not to be perceived as being on the other side of the fence and joining the mass of individuals who are, in the clients' view, callous and rejecting.

Profile 8A2A3: Negativistic-Avoidant-Dependent

This MCMI profile combines resentment, fear of rejection, and feelings of inadequacy into a personality style. Elevations of the Negativistic scale are accompanied by more elevations of other scales than what can be expected of any of the other 7 basic personality scales (Chick et al., 1994). Moreover, the negativistic-avoidant-dependent profile commonly is associated with a borderline personality disorder (Lewis & Harder, 1991). As a variant of the negativistic-avoidant style, this profile commonly has been found with men suffering from posttraumatic stress disorder (Hyer & Boudewyns, 1987; Hyer et al., 1988, 1991, 1992; Hyer, Woods, Boudewyns, et al., 1990; McDermott, 1987; Munley et al., 1994; Piekarski, Sherwood, & Funari, 1993; Sherwood et al., 1990). The style is common in alcoholics (Bartsch & Hoffman, 1985; McMahon et al., 1986; McMahon et al., 1989b). In alcoholics, the style seems to be associated with higher characterological disturbances and a more continuous alcohol abuse use pattern (McMahon, Davidson, Gersh, & Flynn, 1991). The appearance of this profile also is likely in patients with major depression (Stankovic, Libb, Freeman, & Roseman, 1992) and has been associated with a history of suicide attempts (Joffe & Regan, 1989b). Depressed patients with this personality profile, however, are likely to respond to antidepressants (Joffe & Regan, 1989a), and there is evidence that the MCMI profile will change significantly when the depression improves (Joffe & Regan, 1988; Libb et al., 1990).

Individuals with this personality tend to be moody and to change their overall feelings without any obvious reason. At times, they may be friendly and engaging; they then may become angry and resentful; later yet, they may feel guilty and contrite. The cycle is completed when they again become friendly and cooperative. A different substyle of the same basic personality makeup is found in individuals who vent their resentment through obstructionistic maneuvers that allow them to dissipate their anger without threatening their interpersonal support.

Most of these individuals have considerable feelings of insecurity. They tend to feel that others are more gifted, capable, and worthy than they are. However, they feel that if other people got to know them, the people would recognize their lack of value and reject them. They tend to be nervous and uncomfortable when relating to others because they often feel other people do not actually like them. By avoiding social relationships altogether, they can avoid some of their discomfort. As a result, these people tend to lead lonely lives, fairly distant from the people they see as untrustworthy and judgmental. Similar individuals would like to be appreciated and wish they could relate better than they do.

As clients, these people are likely to be highly ambivalent about the prospect of therapy and will probably be uncomfortable during the sessions. However, their dependency may allow the therapist to have some influence and injects a measure of "likability" (Hyer et al., 1991, p. 179). Establishing a therapeutic alliance may be made easier by finding ways to minimize the controls and demands that are made on such clients to reduce conflict. Reassurance of acceptance may need to be done frequently; care needs to be taken, however, not to make the relationship so warm and embracing that it becomes threatening to the kind of individual who has to be able to keep a certain interpersonal distance. The therapist may have to be tolerant of clients who may be irritable or even somewhat hostile.

Once the therapeutic alliance has been established, the therapist should try to use the relationship to help clients explore their emotional reactions and develop more productive ways of dealing with feelings. This plan has to be executed tactfully, so that the therapist does not come to be perceived as the enemy and joins the mass of individuals who are, in the clients' views, callous and rejecting.

Profile 8A2A6A: Negativistic-Avoidant-Antisocial

This MCMI personality profile characterizes individuals with conflictual, avoidant, and competitive traits. Elevations of the Negativistic scale are accompanied by more elevations of other scales than what can be expected of any of the other 7 basic personality scales (Chick et al., 1994). As a variant of the negativistic-avoidant style, this profile has been found commonly with men suffering from posttraumatic stress disorder (Hyer & Boudewyns, 1987; Hyer et al., 1988, 1991, 1992; Hyer, Woods, Boudewyns, et al., 1990; McDermott, 1987; Munley et al., 1994; Piekarski et al., 1993; Sherwood et al., 1990). This personality (code 86A2A) represents about 10% of the men undergoing treatment for spousal abuse (Hamberger & Hastings, 1986).

Probably the most predominant feature of this personality style is their ambivalence relating to others. Similar people have low self-esteem and feel that they are not particularly able or gifted. They tend to generalize this assessment to also include other people. Thus, even though they do not feel good about themselves, they are inclined to put others down and to judge others as being just as unworthy.

Such people usually feel that they need the help of others to make ends meet. However, they have difficulties accepting the help of others because they see the world as a competitive place where everyone is struggling to obtain the same limited benefits. For them, relying on others risks the possibility that people will take advantage of their trust and use the relationship for their own purposes.

These individuals tend to be extremely sensitive about negative feedback. They fear that others may form poor opinions of them and would not value their friendship. The end result is a constant vigilance for signs of rejection when they are in social situations. They experience interpersonal relationships as anxiety producing and uncomfortable. Because they tend to be nervous when they are relating to others, they often choose to avoid this stress by keeping to themselves. When they do relate, they are distant, superficial, and apprehensive.

These individuals typically experience a great deal of anger. Some such people handle their anger through obstructionistic maneuvers. More typically, however, these are explosive people who demonstrate hostile affectivity, fearlessness, and vindictiveness. Hyer et al. (1991) spoke of this personality style as working on the stance that ''I'm-gonna-get-you-before-you-get-me'' (p. 179). The hostile feelings eventually may subside and leave them in a contrite mood, so that they will try to be friendly and cooperative once more, only to be overcome by resentment later on.

When treating clients with this personality style, the therapist should consider that such clients are likely to be ambivalent about therapy and will be uncomfortable during the sessions. The therapist may be able to facilitate establishing a therapeutic alliance by minimizing the controls and demands made on these clients to reduce conflicts in the relationship. However, the therapist should not be too warm and embracing because this may be threatening to individuals who have to be able to keep some interpersonal distance. In spite of these strategies, the therapist may have to be tolerant of clients who may be irritable or even somewhat hostile.

Once the therapeutic alliance has been established, the relationship could be used to help the clients explore their emotional reactions and develop more productive ways of dealing with feelings. The therapist should be careful not to be perceived as being on the other side of the fence and joining the mass of people who are, in these clients' views, callous and rejecting.

Profile 8A37: Negativistic-Dependent-Compulsive

A combination of resentment, feelings of inadequacy, and a perfectionistic attitude represent the hallmarks of this personality style. People who have this kind of personality do not have a high regard for their abilities or accomplishments and feel that they need the help of others to make ends meet. Their low self-image is partly the result of their high expectations. These people strive to lead a flawless life. They have set ideas about how things should be done and seldom will anyone be able to meet those expectations. Their world is highly idealistic and void of heroes because neither they nor their cohorts can measure up. This kind of situation leaves them in a bind. On one hand, they feel inadequate to meet their own needs and would like to have another person on whom they could depend. However, they have reservations about the abilities of others and often object to the kind of help that they might receive.

As with many individuals bearing this personality style, the psychological adaptation to these forces is evident in the clinical picture. At times these people may seem cooperative and in search of help, attention, and reassurance. However, they also come across as proper, formal, and controlling. Although occasionally they may seem obstructionistic and angry, this anger will be kept well under control and will tend to be vented in covert ways. Elevations on the Negativistic scale are accompanied by more elevations on other scales than what can be expected of any of the other 7 basic personality scales (Chick et al., 1994).

Profile 8A40: Negativistic-Histrionic

This "tempestuous histrionic" (Millon, 1995) personality style describes an individual who is both resentful and dramatic. These people do not have a high opinion of themselves or others. Some individuals who are insecure about their own abilities can obtain peace of mind by finding someone on whom they can depend. The interpersonal attitude that the negativistic-histrionic person tends, however, to eliminate the option of obtaining help as a viable alternative. Similar individuals feel that the dependency on others is not acceptable, that the dependency would make them look bad, and that eventually people would criticize them for needing this type of relationship. As a result, they probably face an unsolvable approach–avoidance conflict: If they do not depend on others, they feel uncomfortable because they fear that they will not be able to provide for their needs. If they do form a dependent relationship, they do not have to worry about making ends meet, but they will become uncomfortable about the type of position in which they will be placed.

The behavior of individuals with the negativistic-histrionic personality style usually fluctuates. At times they may be friendly and congenial. Soon, however, they resent others and may become inappropriately aggressive or even hostile; this also may change and turn into guilt and repentance. The friendly and congenial behavior that may follow completes the behavioral cycle. By contrast, other individuals with similar personality work out their conflicts with a more stable pattern of behavior. This pattern involves appearing to be friendly and congenial on the surface while covertly playing a negativistic and obstructionistic role.

Individuals obtaining similar scores have a great need for attention and affection. They constantly seek stimulation and conspicuousness with a dramatic flair. These individuals often easily express their feelings and have fairly intense, short-lived emotions. When they are at their best, they may appear outgoing, charming, and sophisticated.

Elevations of the Negativistic scale are accompanied by more elevations of other scales than what can be expected of any of the other 7 basic personality scales (Chick et al., 1994). Furthermore, research has shown that about one third of the alcoholics in treatment have a negativistic-histrionic personality style (Donat, 1988; Donat et al., 1991). This personality was the predominant style among patients with a panic disorder (J. Reich, 1990). The style was found with many individuals who had obtained the 78/87 profile code in the MMPI (Antoni et al., 1987).

Given this personality style, it may be best to avoid placing any controls on these clients beyond the minimum. Because these clients are likely to resent any control, this tactic can prevent the therapeutic relationship from becoming overly conflictual. A supportive relationship would be one in which the clients are the center of attention. The therapist should have tolerance for displays of emotion and be able to accept a certain amount of conflict. Care must be taken to prepare the clients for the times ahead when they will be angry at the therapist, the treatment has become mundane, and they are ready to terminate. Such clients also may benefit from learning how they normally operate and about their tendency to project negative feelings onto others.

Profile 8A56A: Negativistic-Narcissistic-Antisocial

This MCMI personality profile defines a conflictual personality style with confident and competitive traits. The combination often leads to resentments and difficulties in handling anger. Many people who have the same pattern of scores appear conflicted and moody and change their feelings and behaviors from one moment to the next. They seem irritable, unstable, or erratic and typically have a low tolerance for frustration. Similar people may vacillate between being enthusiastic and cheerful or resentful and ornery. At times they may feel guilty and try to be friendly and cooperative, but they soon start resenting others and become critical, angry, or spiteful. Instead of being moody or explosive, other people with this pattern of MCMI scores vent their resentment by adopting an oppositional pattern of behavior. Their anger then may be less obvious, but in their negativism, irresponsibility, and passivity, they "get even" by making others angry.

Part of the resentment these individuals experience comes from the perception that they are better than the people around them. They see the world as a competitive place where every person has to fight for the same limited rewards. However, they are unable to integrate those two assumptions about the world because, if they were truly superior, they should have their needs fulfilled without having to compete with "lesser" human beings. It is this conflict and lack of integration that often leads to whatever problems they present in terms of their psychological functioning.

This personality style has been found to be common among drug abusers (Craig & Olson, 1990). Elevations of the Negativistic scale are accompanied by more elevations of other scales than what can be expected of any of the other 7 basic personality scales (Chick et al., 1994).

On the positive side, individuals with this personality style are independent people who do not cling to others. They tend to be proud and avoid situations in which they may be humiliated, an issue that may be important for them.

In light of this personality style, the therapist should pay attention to the clients' narcissistic needs if a strong therapeutic alliance is to be established. There will be a tendency, for instance, for clients to reject any interpretation that sounds critical. Feeling threatened, they may become angry and blame the therapist for real or imagined faults or mistakes. Keeping clients feeling that the therapist is on their side and avoiding competitive or conflictual dealings will require tact and effort. A balance has to be struck between being unconditionally supportive and dealing with their issues in an aggressive manner. Often, such a balance will require the therapist to allow clients much control over the relationship and will call for limiting the areas of exploration in which negative feedback may be given to them.

Profile 8A6A0: Negativistic-Antisocial

The negativistic-antisocial personality style is characterized by resentful and competitive traits, a combination that leads to conflicted and moody individuals who are inclined to change their feelings and behaviors from one moment to the next. Similarly scoring individuals are upset easily and have a low tolerance for frustration. At times they may feel guilty and try to be friendly and cooperative, but they soon start resenting others and become more critical, which may even have an angry or spiteful element.

This kind of vacillation theoretically results from conflictual views about the self and the environment. On one hand, such individuals tend to be aware of their own limitations and may feel that they need to depend on others to provide for some of their needs. On the other hand, they seem to view the world as a competitive place, a rat race in which one has to be strong, dominant, adequate, and willful to survive. These people typically suppress the softer emotions of kindness, generosity, and gentility because of the belief that these emotions will make them weak and vulnerable to the exploitation of others. In their minds, the way to survive is to be assertive, energetic, self-reliant, and on guard. They feel that they must be aware of the possible manipulations of others and try to gain the upper hand whenever possible. Elevations on the Negativistic scale are accompanied by more elevations of other scales than what can be expected of any of the other 7 basic personality scales (Chick et al., 1994).

In light of the negativistic-antisocial personality style, the therapeutic approach that we advocate would be one of remaining unintrusive, being careful not to take a position among the options available unless necessary. This stance will encourage clients to make their own decisions and will decrease conflict in the therapeutic relationship. Interpretations may need to be made when clients use maladaptive projective mechanisms. However, any confrontation has to be done carefully because these clients will be inclined to perceive the feedback in a competitive manner and fight the insights that are offered. The therapist must protect the therapeutic alliance and do whatever is necessary to keep these clients feeling that the therapist is on their side.

Profile 8A6A4: Negativistic-Antisocial-Histrionic

Resentful, competitive, and dramatic elements characterize people with this MCMI personality profile. Such individuals tend to be angry and moody and are inclined to change their feelings and behaviors from one moment to the next. They typically are perceived as obstructionistic, inclined to approach life by turning everything around, and seldom accept views in the manner in which they were presented.

There often is a conflictual aspect to these people's oppositionism, such that they typically are aggressive, if not hostile, in their interactions with others. Similarly scoring individuals tend to emphasize their ability to remain independent and are not inclined to do what others tell them to do. They are competitive by nature and may be seen as behaving in a callous manner in the struggle to get ahead of everyone else. They are likely to be mistrustful, to question the motives of others, and to assume that they have to be vigilant and on guard if they are to protect themselves. These people tend to blame others for anything that goes wrong. They are "touchy" individuals: Excitable and upset easily, they are inclined to treat others in a rough or mean manner and become angry whenever they are confronted or opposed.

The anger and emotional lability that such clients seem to have theoretically results from conflictual views regarding the self and the environment. On one hand, they tend to be aware of their own limitations and may feel that they need to depend on others to provide for some of their needs. On the other hand, they seem to view the world as a competitive place in which one has to be strong, dominant, adequate, and willful to survive. They may be inclined to suppress the softer emotions of kindness, generosity, and gentility, feeling that these emotions will make them weak and vulnerable to the exploitation of others. These individuals typically are vigilant of the possible manipulations of others and try to gain the upper hand whenever possible.

These people's negativism may be fueled partly by their histrionic tendencies. They seem to need to be the center of attention and may become easily bored with any situation that becomes routine. Their contrariness probably serves to fulfill their need for attention—albeit in an abrasive and unproductive manner—because uncooperative behaviors are likely to be noticed. In fact, the oppositionism and the search for attention may create a vicious cycle that may be hard to break because their oppositionism tends to meet several of their psychological needs. Elevations on the Negativistic scale are accompanied by more elevations of other scales than what can be expected of any of the other 7 basic personality scales (Chick et al., 1994).

Profile 8A70: Negativistic-Compulsive

The personality style may be described as resentful and disciplined. A variant of this personality style (code 871 with the Schizoid scale also elevated) was found to be the modal profile for the angry and psychotic Black psychiatric patients (Greenblatt & Davis, 1992). Elevations of the Negativistic scale are accompanied by more elevations of other scales than what can be expected of any of the other 7 basic personality scales (Chick et al., 1994).

The negativistic-compulsive style results from holding two assumptions about the world that are difficult to integrate. These individuals first assume that they need to rely on others because they are not able to do well without their support. The second premise is that they should strive toward perfection on their own. These two assumptions about life typically bring about one of two different behavior patterns.

In the passive–aggressive substyle, the conflict is handled by being compliant on the surface but not fully supporting the efforts of others along the way. By contrast, the moody variant involves a vacillation between feeling lucky and being able to get more out of life than expected and feeling cheated or mistreated. The behavior changes accordingly. At times these people treat others in an agreeable and friendly manner but they also may be irritable or hostile. Still at other times, these people may experience guilt and appear eagerly cooperative and remorseful. An energetic and productive mood, together with high goals, may characterize them on some occasions, but in other instances these people are inclined to lower their goals and become less productive.

Such individuals place a premium on avoiding mistakes. They tend to be orderly and plan for the future. They prepare in a conscientious manner and try to do the work on schedule. They strive to be efficient, dependable, industrious, and persistent. They often relate in an overly respectful and ingratiating manner, but they may be somewhat rigid, perfectionistic, and demanding. They have significant problems making decisions by themselves.

Negativistic-compulsive individuals can be moody and irritable. Projection is an important defense, but the direction of the blame tends to change from the self to others. Mostly, these people tend to be resentful and conflicted. They typically are difficult to handle and present some problems wherever they go.

Given this personality style, it may be useful to try not to control these clients in ways that are not necessary for both the therapist and the clients to be able to function. Because these clients are bound to resent any control that is placed on them, this tactic can prevent the therapeutic relationship from becoming overly conflictual. They also may benefit from learning how they normally operate and tend to project negative feelings onto others.

 **Assessment of Psychopathology**

In this chapter we focus on the use of the MCMI for assessing the different psychopathological patterns. We use mostly the diagnostic entities from the fourth edition of the *Diagnostic and Statistical Manual of Mental Disorders* (*DSM–IV*; American Psychiatric Association, 1994), as well as the *DSM–IV* distinction between clinical syndromes (Axis I) and personality disorders (Axis II).

As useful as the distinction between the two axes may be, it often is difficult to make (Hirschfeld, 1993). Part of the problem is that many of the Axis II prototypes have aspects in common with the Axis I disorders. The borderline personality disorder, for instance, includes affective instability, which also is part of the Axis I affective disorders (Widiger, 1989), and, presumably as a result of this commonality, patients with affective disorders are likely to obtain an elevation on the Borderline scale of the MCMI-I (H. J. Jackson, Rudd, Gazis, & Edwards, 1991). The dependent personality disorder is characterized partly by the kind of helplessness and feelings of inadequacy that also constitute an important aspect of many types of depression (Overholser, 1991). Not surprisingly, as a result, depressed patients generally have elevated the Dependent scale on the MCMI-I (G. E. Alexander, Choca, Bresolin, et al., 1987; G. E. Alexander, Choca, Dewolfe, et al., 1987).

Also blurring the distinction between the two axes is the way that some disorders affect the individual so as to increase his or her chances to meet criteria for other disorders: There is a reasonable amount of literature showing that the emotional state of the individual alters the personality traits that are demonstrated (e.g., Hirschfeld et al., 1983).

Personality traits often are thought to predispose the individual to developing certain clinical syndromes (e.g., schizoid or avoidant personality styles may increase a person's tendency toward schizophrenic symptomatology; Millon, 1981). Whenever there are more specific data about the interaction between the two axes of the *DSM–IV*, we include the information in the discussion.

The MCMI profile of people suffering from a *DSM–IV* syndrome typically have several elevations, more than would be expected if the profile were to reflect only the primary diagnosis. B. K. Campbell and Stark (1991), for instance, gave the MCMI-I to 100 consecutive admissions to a community outpatient drug program. Their substance abusers obtained significantly higher means for 8 of the 20 scales when the scores obtained were compared with those of the normative sample. In some cases, the multiple elevations may be indicative of comorbidities, additional psychiatric problems that merit professional attention. In other cases, however, the multiple elevations may be attributable to a lack of selectivity of MCMI scales or to the natural clustering of particular pathological traits. Thus, an elevation on the Alcohol Abuse scale is almost expected in the case of a cocaine addict because this scale shares items with the Drug Abuse scale and the majority of the cocaine addicts also have abused alcohol. Diagnosticians have to develop the skill of deciding what part of the profile should be seen as part and parcel of a particular diagnosis and what findings are indicative of other problems. In addition to the history and other diagnostic data, clinicians can use the knowledge of what MCMI scales tend to be elevated for particular disorders. This information is offered in Tables 6 and 7. The interpretive logic would be that, if the profile in question looks similar to what is the modal profile for a particular disorder, the findings should not be seen as pointing to additional problems.

In this chapter we discuss personality disorders first because many of them are related to the personality styles discussed in the previous chapter. Along with the *DSM–IV* clinical syndromes, we also review the few articles that have dealt with pathologies that are not recognized *DSM–IV* diagnoses by themselves, such as partner abuse and thought disorders.

Personality Disorders

Table 6 shows our rendition of the data that Millon (1987) presented for the typical patient suffering from the different personality disorders,

Table 6

Expected Primary and Secondary MCMI Elevations With the Different Personality Disorders

Disorder	Highest scale	Other elevations
Schizoid	Schizoid	Avoidant, Schizotypal
Avoidant	Avoidant	Schizoid, Negativistic, Self-Defeating, Dysthymia
Dependent	Dependent	Avoidant, Self-Defeating
Histrionic	Histrionic	Narcissistic
Narcissistic	Narcissistic	Histrionic, Aggressive
Antisocial	Antisocial	Narcissistic, Negativistic, Aggressive, Borderline, Paranoid, Drug Abuse
Compulsive	Compulsive	
Negativistic	Negativistic	Aggressive
Schizotypal	Avoidant	Schizoid, Negativistic, Self-Defeating, Schizotypal, Borderline, Anxiety, Dysthymia, Thought Disorder, Major Depression
Borderline	Borderline	Avoidant, Negativistic, Self-Defeating, Anxiety, Dysthymia
Paranoid	Aggressive	Narcissistic, Antisocial, Compulsive, Paranoid, Anxiety, Dysthymia

adjusted with any relevant literature that we found (e.g., Lewis & Harder, 1991; Retzlaff et al., 1994; Swirsky-Sacchetti et al., 1993). A knowledge of such typical profiles may be helpful in making decisions about patients' diagnoses. The reader should remember that there is much variance within any diagnostic group. When a protocol is obtained that does not fit typical patients within a diagnostic category, the finding often can be used to further understand the patient at hand and does not necessarily mean that the person does not suffer from the particular clinical syndrome.

From our viewpoint, a person can have a personality disorder in one of two ways. Seven of the 10 *DSM–IV* personality disorders constitute syndromes that we would see as exaggerations of basic personality styles. In other words, the clusters of personality traits that we have discussed repeatedly throughout this book are sometimes seen in a pathologically exaggerated or rigid fashion. Such a pattern can then be classified as a personality disorder.

In addition, there are three *DSM–IV* personality disorders that are not represented among the personality styles: the borderline, the schizotypal, and the paranoid. There also are MCMI scales for personality disorders that are considered to be in need of further study and that are not part of the current official nomenclature. The MCMI-II contains two such scales (the Aggressive and the Self-Defeating scales); in addition to those two, the MCMI-III includes a Depressive Personality scale. All 6 of these lifelong dysfunctional characterological tendencies, in our opinion, do not have a "normal" or nonpathological variant; in other words, the pattern is intrinsically pathological even in cases in which the disorder is not severe.

Most research in which the MCMI personality scales were used has dealt with the validity of the scales or the characterological issues related to particular clinical syndromes. (These studies were discussed in chap. 3.) The investigations included here are those that have examined personality styles or personality disorders in their own right.

Overholser, Kabakoff, and Norman (1989) compared individuals with a significant elevation on the Dependency scale with other psychiatric inpatients. They reported that this group was unlikely to be married and more likely to have been hospitalized repeatedly for psychiatric problems. Overholser (1991) also found that patients displaying elevated levels of dependency over a 6-week period of time tend to report a mild but persistently elevated level of depression. The findings were said to agree with previous evidence relating depression to dependency (see the section on affective disorders).

Looking at whether particular professions attract different kinds of characterological pathology, Patrick (1990) evaluated the incidence of pathological narcissism in the clergy. The scores she obtained with the MCMI-I Narcissistic scale generally failed to reveal the presence of narcissistic personalities. On the other hand, judging from the MCMI-I, such narcissism is more likely to occur among adults who are firstborn or only-born children (Curtis & Cowell, 1993).

A cluster analysis of individuals presumed to have a narcissistic personality disorder on the basis of an elevation of the MCMI-II Narcissistic scale was done by DiGiuseppe, Robin, Szeszko, and Primavera (1995). As we have noted, we do not see the mere elevation of an MCMI scale as showing the presence of a personality disorder. To us, the fact that many of the participants had higher scores on personality scales other than the Narcissistic scale made the findings even more uninterpretable.

Hart et al. (1991) examined men with an antisocial personality disorder and found support for Millon's picture of how these individuals would look on the MCMI-II: The convicts they tested obtained their highest elevation on the Antisocial scale, but psychopathy also was associated with elevations on the Narcissistic, Aggressive, and Drug Abuse scales.

Data gathered from a group of borderline patients suggest that difficulties with interpersonal attachments are related to the severe personality scales of the MCMI-I. Specifically, avoidant attachment difficulties may be related to elevated scores on the Borderline scale, whereas difficulties consisting of resistant or hostile attachments are correlated modestly with the Schizotypal and Borderline scales (Sperling, Sharp, & Fishler, 1991).

There have been three studies examining some of the MCMI personality elevations with obsessive–compulsive patients. Joffe et al. (1988) studied 23 patients with obsessive–compulsive disorder matched by age and sex with a group who had major depressive disorder. All were administered the MCMI-I. There were no mean differences between the groups on the personality scales. There was no significant difference in the frequency of personality disorder diagnoses between the two groups. The most common personality constellation of the obsessive–compulsive group was a mixture of avoidant, dependent, and negativistic features. The discussion focused on the high frequency of personality disorders in the obsessive–compulsive group and the lack of compulsive personality disorder diagnosis using the MCMI-I. Similar results were reported by J. S. Silverman and Loychik (1990) after looking at a family with three obsessive–compulsive siblings. The small sample sizes are weaknesses of these studies.

Fals-Stewart and Lucente (1993) did a combined assessment and treatment study with obsessive–compulsive individuals. They cluster analyzed the MCMI-I results of 137 obsessive–compulsive patients and found four cluster types that were reasonably well defined and differentiated. Behavior therapy then was offered to the patients using a mixture of exposure and response prevention exercises. The authors found that patients with little character pathology, or those with dependent and compulsive features, did best in behavioral treatment.

Clinical Syndromes

Table 7 shows our own rendition of the data that Millon presented for typical patients suffering from the different clinical syndromes, adjusted

Table 7

Expected Primary and Secondary MCMI Elevations With Different Clinical Syndromes

Problem area	Highest scale	Other elevations
Anxiety	Anxiety	Avoidant, Negativistic, Self-Defeating
Somatoform	Somatoform	Anxiety, Histrionic, Compulsive
Eating disorder	Borderline	Schizoid, Avoidant, Dependent, Schizotypal
Mania	Hypomania	Histrionic, Narcissistic, Antisocial, Paranoid, Drug Abuse, Psychotic Delusion
Dysthymia	Dysthymia	Avoidant, Negativistic
Alcohol abuse	Alcohol abuse	Negativistic, Antisocial, Dependent, Anxiety, Dysthymia, Drug Abuse
Drug abuse	Drug abuse	Alcohol Abuse, Antisocial, Negativistic, Narcissistic, Histrionic
Schizophrenia	Avoidant	Schizotypal, Schizoid, Dependent, Narcissistic, Negativistic, Self-Defeating
Major depression	Dysthymia	Major Depression, Anxiety, Avoidant, Dependent, Self-Defeating, Negativistic
Delusion	Psychotic Delusion	Psychotic Thinking, Paranoid, Narcissistic, Aggressive

with any other data we found (e.g., Craig, 1993a; Craig et al., 1994; Craig & Weinberg, 1992a, 1992b; Hogg et al., 1990; Hyer, Carson, Nixon, Tamkin, & Saucer, 1987; Kennedy et al., 1990; Retzlaff et al., 1994; Simonsen, Haslund, Larsen, & Borup, 1992; Wetzler et al., 1995; Yeager et al., 1992). The supporting data and Millon's (1987) own conclusions, which are occasionally somewhat different from the ones presented here, can be found in the test manual. As before, knowledge of such typical profiles may be helpful, but considerable variance exists within any diagnostic group.

In the remainder of this chapter, we review the literature on the MCMI and different disorders. Clinicians typically have hypothesized about underlying or predisposing personalities behind most clinical syndromes, and the MCMI has proved to be a good instrument for testing some of the hypotheses. When such data are available, we present them first and then discuss any other information on that disorder.

Schizophrenic Disorders

Hogg et al. (1990) investigated the comorbidity of personality disorders and schizophrenia in a sample of 40 schizophrenics with recent onset. Using the personality scales of the MCMI-I, they found elevations of the Dependent, Narcissistic, and Avoidant scales. Also using the MCMI-I, Greenblatt and Davis (1992) found the Avoidant scale to be effective in predicting psychosis.

Josiassen, Shagass, and Roemer (1988) tried to differentiate between psychotic and nonpsychotic schizophrenics using both the MCMI-I and evoked potentials. The authors reported that the psychotic schizophrenics had a higher mean amplitude of the primary somatosensory potentials.

Anxiety Disorders

Alnæs and Torgersen (1990) compared a group of 84 patients with anxiety disorders with other outpatients using the MCMI-I. They reported that the individuals with "pure" anxiety disorders tended to be more schizotypal than depressed patients. They also were more schizoid and avoidant and less histrionic than patients with other mental disorders except depression. Some caution in accepting these results is in order: Many chi-square analyses were performed between the different groups used in the study. Therefore, some of the findings might have been obtained by chance.

Similarly, Wetzler et al. (1990) compared 20 patients with panic disorders with 23 depressed patients and 24 normal individuals. The findings showed that the patients with panic disorders scored higher than normal individuals on the Schizoid, Avoidant, Negativistic, Schizotypal, Borderline, Anxiety, Somatic Preoccupation, Dysthymic, Psychotic Thinking, and Psychotic Depression scales of the MCMI-I. The patients scored significantly lower than the normal respondents on the Narcissistic and Compulsive scales (Wetzler et al., 1990). Finally, there seems to be a high level of dependency on the MCMI-I among individuals suffering from phobias (J. Reich, Noyes, & Troughton, 1987).

Dissociative Disorders

College students scoring high on the Dissociative Experience Scale (Bernstein & Putnam, 1986) were found to have a significantly higher score on the Borderline scale of the MCMI-I compared with students scoring low on the Dissociative Experience Scale (Ross, Ryan, Voigt, & Eide, 1991). A group of 96 patients with a dissociative identity (multiple personality) disorder was found to have elevations on the Avoidant, Self-Defeating, Borderline, and Negativistic scales of the MCMI-II. Elevated Axis I scales have included Dysthymia and Major Depression (Ellason et al., 1995; Fink & Golinkoff, 1990). The test was able to differentiate between the dissociative identity disorder and schizophrenia but did poorly when the differentiation was between the dissociative identity disorder and borderline personalities (Fink & Golinkoff, 1990).

Affective Disorders

The association between personality traits and affective symptomatology has been well established in the literature. Because most psychological evaluations are done at a time when the patient is symptomatic, there is a need to characterize typical results during the acute episodes as well as during remission.

We compared the personality styles of manic, depressed, and euthymic patients with unipolar or bipolar affective disorders with those of a control group of nonpsychiatric individuals. Depressed patients appeared to be more schizoid, avoidant, dependent, and negativistic and less narcissistic than their euthymic cohorts on the MCMI-I regardless of whether they suffered from a unipolar or bipolar affective disorder (G. E. Alexander, Choca, Bresolin, et al., 1987; G. E. Alexander, Choca, DeWolfe, et al., 1987). These findings generally have been supported by others (Hyer, Harrison, & Jacobsen, 1987; Libb et al., 1990; Stankovic et al., 1992; Wetzler et al., 1990, 1995). Manic bipolar patients have been found to be more histrionic, narcissistic, antisocial, and compulsive than their euthymic cohorts on both the MCMI-I (G. E. Alexander, Choca, DeWolfe, et al., 1987; Alnæs & Torgersen, 1991; Wetzler & Marlowe, 1993) and the MCMI-II (Turley et al., 1992).

In our work, euthymic individuals with a history of unipolar depression were found to be more avoidant and negativistic than other participants on the MCMI-I. Euthymic bipolar patients were more histrionic, narcissistic, and antisocial than the other groups. The normal control group was found to be more compulsive than the psychiatric patients (G. E. Alexander, Choca, DeWolfe, et al., 1987). Our findings conflicted with those of J. Reich and Troughton (1988), who reported no MCMI-I differences between asymptomatic patients with a history of depression and normal respondents. Physiological work using electro-encephalographic alpha activity and the MCMI-I is more consistent with our work, in that the participants with high alpha readings tended to score higher on the Histrionic, Narcissistic, and Hypomania scales regardless of whether they were symptomatic (Wall et al., 1990). These findings were interpreted to indicate an association of extraverted personality traits and high alpha.

The work of Joffe and Regan (1988) also fits in well with our findings. They reported reductions of scores on 6 of the personality scales of the MCMI-I (i.e., the Schizoid, Avoidant, Dependent, Negativistic, Schizotypal, and Borderline) when complete remission was achieved with depressed patients.

Going by these findings, we would caution clinicians that clients who suffer from affective disorders may elevate the measures of personality traits on the MCMI, both during the episode and after remission. Several theories have been proposed to account for such findings. The *common cause theory* proposes a common element, such as a chemical imbalance, that is responsible for both the personality traits and the mood disorder. A family history of depression, for instance, has been found to be associated with higher scores on the Dependent and Compulsive scales of the MCMI-I among depressed patients (Joffe & Regan, 1991). Otherwise, personality traits could be subclinical signs of the mood disorder (the *spectrum model*) or the personality may be predisposing the individual to the affective pathology. It also is possible that personality and mood are independent but capable of affecting each other (the *pathoplasty model*) or that the personality traits are *scars* that are left over from the affective disorder episodes (for reviews of these models, see Farmer & Nelson-Gray, 1990; Klein, Wonderlich, & Shea, 1993). As is now well recognized, this etiological controversy will not be resolved until a longitudinal study is available that assesses participants premorbidly, during the episode, and during remission (Klein, Wonderlich, & Shea, 1993).

Another way of looking at the relationship between affective disorders and personality styles is to conceptualize the personality elements as defining different depressive styles. J. O. Goldberg, Segal, Vella, and Shaw (1989), for instance, found two such styles after administering the MCMI to depressed patients. The first of these types was characterized by elevated scores on the Negativistic scale of the MCMI-I and was seen as being similar to Beck's (1983) "autonomous" depressive. Such individuals are described as typically feeling misunderstood and unappreciated; they tend to anticipate disappointment and to precipitate failures through obstructive behaviors. By contrast, the other type conceptualized by J. O. Goldberg et al. was marked by elevated scores on the Dependent and Avoidant scales of the MCMI and was seen as being similar to Beck's "sociotropic" subtype. These individuals were thought to be self-effacing, noncompetitive people who were constantly seeking relationships in which they could lean on someone for guidance and security.

Similarly, Overholser (1991; Overholser et al., 1989) examined the difference between dependent and nondependent depressed individuals. The data indicated that dependent depressed respondents were more likely to be older and female than nondepressed psychiatric control respondents, were more likely to demonstrate reduced activity and energy levels, and were more likely to have more pathological views of success and happiness than nondependent depressed respondents.

In another study, different types of depression were compared. Individuals who suffered from seasonal depression were compared with other depressed individuals. The findings showed the seasonally depressed individuals had less of an elevation on the Schizotypal and Avoidant scales of the MCMI-I and obtained higher scores on the Narcissistic scale. The findings were interpreted as indicating a lower level of psychopathology for the seasonal group (Schuller, Bagby, Levitt, & Joffe, 1993).

In terms of the psychopathology scales of the MCMI, depression typically has been associated with scales measuring anxious-fearful syndromes as opposed to the extraverted-projective syndromes, which are more typical comorbidities of the manic group. Wetzler and his coworkers (Wetzler et al., 1990; Wetzler & Marlowe, 1993), for instance, repeatedly found depressed patients scoring higher than other respondents on the Schizotypal, Borderline, Anxiety, Dysthymia, and Psychotic Depression scales of the MCMI-I. On the MCMI-II, depressed patients scored significantly higher than other psychiatric patients on Anxiety and Dysthymia and lower on the Aggressive, Paranoid, Bipolar, Drug Abuse, and Delusional Disorder scales (Wetzler & Marlowe, 1993). The manic group tended to score higher than other patients on the Paranoid, Hypomania, Drug Abuse, and Psychotic Delusion scales on both the MCMI-I and MCMI-II (Wetzler & Marlowe, 1993).

Eating Disorders

Norman, Blais, and Herzog (1993) used MCMI-I data to support their claim that 84% of patients with eating disorders suffered from a personality disorder. The fact that practically every person who takes the MCMI will obtain an elevation on one of the personality scales (see the discussion in chap. 6) renders that finding relatively useless.

Tisdale et al. (1990) compared a group of bulimic individuals with psychiatric patients who did not have an eating disorder and with a group of normal control individuals. The data showed that bulimic respondents obtained significantly higher scores on the Dependent, Avoidant, and Schizoid scales; their average score on the Narcissistic scale was significantly lower than the average score of the other two groups. The average base-rate (BR) score obtained by the bulimic patients on the Dependent scale was 75, indicating that most of them had a dependent personality style. The investigators considered their findings to be consistent with previous descriptions of bulimic women as dependent, unassertive, eager to please, and concerned with social approval. This contention has been supported, at least in part, by other studies with the MCMI-I (Kennedy et al., 1990; Norman et al., 1993; Pendleton et al., 1991; Schmidt, Sanders, Burdick, & Lohr, 1991).

In terms of the pathology scales, elevations on the Borderline, Anxiety, and Dysthymia scales have been found among bulimic individuals before treatment (Garner et al., 1990; Kennedy et al., 1990). Elevations on the Schizoid and Schizotypal scales were found with the larger group that included both bulimia and anorexia (Kennedy et al., 1990).

Caution should be exercised not to overdiagnose personality disorders during an acute phase of the disorder because the MCMI-I scores have been found to change considerably after the acute phase has resolved (Garner et al., 1990; Kennedy et al., 1990).

An elevation on the Dysthymia scale of the MCMI-I was found to predict poor treatment outcome among bulimic women (Garner et al., 1990). Sansone and Fine (1992) found that women with eating disorders who obtained elevated Borderline scale scores on the MCMI-I showed greater psychopathology 3 years later and had less life satisfaction than similar patients without the borderline characteristics.

Lundholm, Pellegreno, Wolins, and Graham (1989) compared a group of 173 women receiving treatment for bulimia with 265 university women. They found 27 items from the MCMI-I, mostly dealing with social withdrawal and depression, that successfully differentiated the two groups. Note that these items may not differentiate between individuals with an eating disorder and other psychiatric patients.

Substance Abuse

The idea that substance abuse is fueled by characterological tendencies probably dates back to Freud. The Freudian contention that all alcoholic individuals represented an "oral" personality (the precursor of the modern dependent personality) has not been supported by the literature. Instead, the current thinking is that there are several alcoholic subtypes. In a comprehensive review of the literature, Nerviano and Gross (1983) identified seven such subtypes. Several MCMI-I studies done by different investigators have revealed clusters among alcoholic patients supporting the presence of several of the theoretically derived subtypes (Bartsch & Hoffman, 1985; Craig et al., 1985; Donat et al., 1991; Gibertini & Retzlaff, 1988b; Matano, Locke, & Schwartz, 1994; Mayer & Scott, 1988; Retzlaff & Bromley, 1991).

In most of the MCMI-I studies, there was a group of alcoholic patients with elevated scores on the Negativistic scale. It appeared that they often had additional elevations on the Borderline or Paranoid scales and were thought to be demonstrating moderate-to-severe personality dysfunctions. Specifically, the patients were characterized as having "substantial variations in mood, irritability, suspiciousness" and "an ambivalent and indecisive approach" to life (Bartsch & Hoffman, 1985, p. 711). Drinking is typically done with friends (Donat et al., 1991) and often serves a "self-medicating" function for them (Bartsch & Hoffman, 1985). This group tended to be anxious and demonstrated borderline and paranoid tendencies (Craig et al., 1985), being less likely than other alcoholic groups to "inhibit interpersonal anxieties, frustrations and discouragements" (Donat et al., 1991, p. 343). In terms of its prevalence, this cluster accounted for 38% of Mayer and Scott's (1988) sample. The presence of a massive pathological factor on the MCMI-II of alcoholics, with heavy loadings on the Negativistic and Borderline scales (Litman & Cernovsky, 1993), suggested that this test would lead to the diagnosis of a similar type of alcoholic.

A variant of the negativistic type, characterized by additional elevations on the Avoidant and Schizoid scales of the MCMI-I, was found by several investigators (Corbisiero & Reznikoff, 1991; Retzlaff & Bromley, 1991). With significant elevations on the Anxiety and Dysthymia scales, individuals in this cluster were seen as having widespread symptomatology. They have a "poor and alienated self-image . . . are mistrustful of others, and have difficulty managing and expressing emotions" (Corbisiero & Reznikoff, 1991, p. 295). Scores on the Alcohol Use Inventory showed a serious drinking problem, even though these individuals were typically concerned about their drinking (Corbisiero & Reznikoff, 1991).

Another cluster of patients was defined by elevated scores on the Narcissistic and Histrionic scales of the MCMI-I. For those patients, the drinking was conceptualized as "recreational in nature" and a "manifestation of a lifestyle of self-indulgence and thrill seeking" (Bartsch & Hoffman, 1985, p. 711). According to Donat et al. (1991), these individuals are interpersonally insensitive and value personal willpower and self-reliance. Ironically, they report obtaining few benefits from drinking and are likely not to recognize the deleterious effects that the drinking has in their lives. Matano et al. (1994) saw these individuals as being especially prone to use "ego-protecting defenses" and thought that the first goal of treatment should be to break through the denial. This cluster may account for 22–28% of the alcoholic population (Gibertini & Retzlaff, 1988b; Mayer & Scott, 1988). The emergence of a Histrionic-Narcissistic-Manic factor with the MCMI-II of alcohol abusers (Litman & Cernovsky, 1993) suggested that a similar cluster would be obtained with that version of the inventory.

An antisocial narcissistic alcoholic also has been found with the MCMI-I. Constituting as much as 20% of some alcoholic samples, these individuals have been described as "exploitive, defiant, and often hostile, with an inflated self-image or sense of entitlement, with a lack of sensitivity or indifference to the rights of others" (Corbisiero & Reznikoff, 1991, pp. 295–296). Scores on the Alcohol Use Inventory indicated serious drinking problems and less concern with the drinking than is seen with other alcoholics.

Accounting for about 20% of the samples (Craig et al., 1985; Matano et al., 1994; Mayer & Scott, 1988) were the alcoholic patients with elevated scores on the MCMI-I Compulsive scale. Bartsch and Hoffman (1985) talked about this cluster as representing an "overly exuberant conscience," so that the function of the alcohol is to "permit escape from feelings of responsibility, or permit the expression of anger" (p. 711). They typically are unaware of any positive or negative effects that the drinking may have in their lives (Donat et al., 1991). This type of alcoholic also is represented by one of the factors found with the MCMI-II (Litman & Cernovsky, 1993).

In most of the MCMI-I studies, there was a cluster with schizoid, avoidant, and dependent elements that constituted as much as 28% (Craig et al., 1985) or as little as 5% (Gibertini & Retzlaff, 1988b) of the examinees. Besides the three MCMI-I personality scales that measure those three traits, some of the investigators found elevations on the Borderline and Schizotypal scales (Bartsch & Hoffman, 1985; Donat et al., 1991; Mayer & Scott, 1988). Craig et al. (1985) described these respondents as being "anxious and depressed" (p. 159). Such individuals were thought to demonstrate "widespread and severe maladjustment" and to be typically "caught between feelings of loneliness and social apprehension"; drinking may serve to "mediate social anxiety to a level that produces self-assurance and permits social contact" (Bartsch & Hoffman, 1985, p. 712). They are inclined to become "self-critical, discouraged, and socially withdrawn and, as a result, are more likely than patients in other clusters to engage in solitary drinking" (Donat et al., 1991, p. 343). It is particularly difficult for this group to recognize the cognitive impairment that results from their drinking (Donat et al., 1991). Participation in treatment programs is especially difficult for this type of alcoholic (Fals-Stewart, 1992). Given the level of pathology that these individuals demonstrate, Matano et al. (1994) advised an emphasis on the reduction of the level of distress experienced by the patient as the first goal of treatment.

Retzlaff and Bromley (1991) found a cluster of dependent and anxious individuals who otherwise did not show much other pathology. There appears to be a small group of alcoholics who do not have characterological or emotional problems besides their drinking behavior (Corbisiero & Reznikoff, 1991; Retzlaff & Bromley, 1991). According to scores on the Alcohol Use Inventory, the drinking of these individuals also is likely to be less problematic than the drinking of other alcoholics (Corbisiero & Reznikoff, 1991). Finally, Retzlaff and Bromley (1991) also found a "denial" group that "rejects all personality and clinical symptoms" (p. 306) in a defensive manner.

A similar type of work also has been done with drug abusers. Craig et al. (1985) described two personality clusters. The first group, accounting for 31% of the sample, obtained elevated scores on the Narcissistic and Antisocial scales. This group was seen as characterologically similar to the second group of self-indulgent, thrill-seeking alcoholics described earlier and also was found in a study by Fals-Stewart (1992) in which alcoholics were not differentiated from other substance abusers. Perhaps Bartsch and Hoffman's (1985) argument that individuals belonging to this group use chemicals for "recreational" purposes also can be made for drug abusers.

Craig et al. (1985) reported a second cluster of drug abusers made up of negativistic-avoidant patients who also tended to score highly on the Anxiety and Dysthymia scales. This group was seen as being different from any of the alcoholic clusters and accounted for 28% of the sample.

It is noteworthy that 40% of the Craig et al. (1985) drug abuse sample remained unclustered. Fals-Stewart (1992) was able to assign all patients in his sample using five clusters, but 17% of his sample were alcoholics. Besides the narcissistic-antisocial-histrionics, Fals-Stewart found a cluster of schizoid-avoidants that resembled the fourth cluster of socially withdrawn, severely maladjusted alcoholics described earlier. The individuals falling into this cluster were said to be socially withdrawn and were found to have a poor prognosis (see chap. 10). This cluster also was supported by one of the factors Litman and Cernovsky (1993) uncovered with the MCMI-II.

Another cluster that proved to be difficult to treat in the Fals-Stewart (1992) work was the group exhibiting an elevation on the Antisocial scale of the MCMI-I. This type of substance abuser may correspond to the "antisocial sociopath" of Nerviano and Gross (1983) even though it had not been reported in any of the MCMI-I studies of alcoholics. The cluster appeared to be characterized by a disregard for social rules and conventions: The group contained the largest percentile of patients removed from the program for rule violations (Fals-Stewart, 1992). Fals-Stewart's (1992) work led to two additional clusters, one with no elevation and one with an elevation on the Histrionic scale, that had not been found with either alcoholics or drug abusers in the past.

The issue of whether alcohol and drug-abusing patients are basically similar or different also has been addressed. Craig et al. (1985) argued that if the question is examined from the MCMI-I personality perspective, there are four describable types of alcoholics and two types of drug addicts. Both types of addiction have been found to appeal to narcissistic personality types who also might demonstrate histrionic or antisocial elements. Because this cluster may account for about 25% of the substance abuse population, it could be said that 25% of the two diagnostic groups are basically alike. When the treatment offered is engineered to reflect personality aspects, perhaps these patients could be treated together regardless of the kind of addiction they have. From a characterological viewpoint, however, alcoholics and substance abusers are more different than they are alike. As sophistication increases in measuring characterological tendencies, the old debate becomes obsolete because, even with patients who abuse only one type of substance, the patients are not all alike.

In subsequent work, Craig and Olson (1990) investigated the similarities and differences between cocaine and opiate addicts using the MCMI-I. They reported that these two groups of drug abusers are more similar than different in terms of their personality styles. Nevertheless, they found that cocaine addicts demonstrated more features of an antisocial personality style, whereas the heroin addicts had significantly higher scores on the Alcohol Abuse, Anxiety, and Somatic Preoccupation scales. The finding that cocaine abusers do not show evidence of an affective disorder on the MCMI-I has been used to argue against the hypothesis that the abuse represents attempts at self-medication (Dougherty & Lesswing, 1989).

Using multivariate procedures, Craig and Olson (1990) also were able to distinguish between two different types of cocaine abusers. The first cluster was characterized by high scores on the Narcissistic, Antisocial, Paranoid, and Drug Abuse scales. The patients were described as "arrogant and self-centered" and "driven to act out because of fear or mistrust of others" (Craig & Olson, 1990, p. 235). In addition to elevated scores on the Narcissistic and Antisocial scales, the second cluster showed a very predominant Negativistic scale and elevations on the Paranoid, Avoidant, Drug and Alcohol Abuse, Anxiety, and Dysthymia scales of the MCMI-I. The individuals were seen as driven by their irritability, unpredictable moods, and pessimistic attitudes. They were characterized as suffering from great inner turmoil and feeling "cheated in life, misunderstood, and unappreciated" (Craig & Olson, 1990, p. 235).

Similarly, Craig and Olson (1990) described two kinds of heroin addicts using data from the MCMI-I. The first type was characterized by elevations on the Narcissistic and Antisocial scales. They described these people as showing "arrogant traits of self-worth, an intimidating social manner, tendencies to exploit other people, [and] a lack of personal responsibility" (1990, p. 235). By contrast, the second cluster was characterized by elevated scores on the Negativistic scale, indicating erratic behaviors with a great deal of anger as well as guilt and remorse.

Much of the work that has been done to distinguish different kinds of substance abusers can be thought of as mostly reporting the effects caused by other group differences besides the drug of choice. Cannon, Bell, Fowler, Penk, and Finkelstein (1990) have reported significant differences in age, sex, and race between groups of substance abusers. When such differences are taken into account, the distinguishing features that the different kinds of substance abusers show on the MCMI tend to diminish, if not completely disappear (Donat, Walters, & Hume, 1992).

In addition to characterological problems, researchers have noted a prevalence of depression among alcohol abusers. McMahon and Davidson (1986a) found that 66% of male alcoholics undergoing inpatient treatment obtained elevated scores on the Dysthymia scale of the MCMI. McMahon and colleagues (McMahon & Davidson, 1986b; McMahon & Tyson, 1989, 1990) demonstrated how the MCMI-I can be used to discriminate between the patients who will experience only transient depressive episodes and those for whom the depressive feelings may be more enduring and problematic. In their work, the enduring depression was associated with higher scores on the Negativistic and Avoidant scales and was correlated negatively with Compulsive scale scores. In other words, the more enduring depressive feelings tended to include a pattern of interpersonal ambivalence, low self-image, irritable affectivity or explosive anger, hypersensitivity to rejection, and social isolationism. On the other hand, the more transient episodes tended to be associated with excessive emotional control, fear of social disapproval, and psychological restraint (McMahon & Davidson, 1985b; McMahon & Tyson, 1989, 1990).

McMahon, Schram, and Davidson (1993) further examined the interplay among personality type, alcoholism, depression, and other variables. They attempted to study the relationship of depression, personality subtypes, and social supports. The three personality subtypes included dependent, detached/ambivalent, and independent. There were 125 participants drawn from inpatient and outpatient substance abuse units in the Miami area. The MCMI-I was used, along with a life experience survey, perceived support network inventory, and a depression rating scale. Results indicated that the detached/ambivalent group reported greater levels of depression than the other groups. Both detached/ambivalent and dependent types reported higher levels of depression under high stress than under low stress. Social support was not found to buffer the negative stress effects in any of the groups, contrary to predictions.

Alcoholics also can be differentiated in terms of the level of their social functioning on the basis of the MCMI. McMahon et al. (1986)

found the low-social-functioning group of alcoholics to have a significantly higher mean score on the Schizotypal scale of the MCMI-I and a significantly lower mean on the Compulsive scale.

Additionally, the MCMI-I can be used to describe the pattern of drinking used by alcoholic patients. McMahon and associates (McMahon et al., 1989b; McMahon & Davidson, 1989; McMahon, Davidson, Gersh, & Flynn, 1991) found that continuous drinkers tended to have higher scores on the Psychotic Thinking scale than did episodic drinkers. A group of the alcoholics in the Craig et al. (1985) sample also had such elevations, a finding that was attributed to the possible development of an organic mental disorder that causes "disorganization of thinking, regressive behavior, confusion, and disorientation" (p. 159). McMahon et al. (1989b) found associations of lesser magnitude between continuous drinking and higher scores on the Drug Abuse, Paranoid, and Hypomanic scales. Episodic drinking, on the other hand, was associated with higher scores on the Compulsive scale. On the basis of their data, McMahon et al. characterized continuous drinkers as being more likely to be confused, agitated, and disorganized in their thinking than episodic drinkers; the former also are more likely to feel misunderstood and unappreciated and to be discontented and socially alienated. Although continuous drinkers are likely to be more stable in terms of their social and occupational functioning than episodic drinkers and to have greater prospects for controlled drinking, McMahon and Davidson (1989) cited data indicating that continuous drinkers are more psychologically disturbed and at greater risk for neuropsychological impairment and liver problems.

Children of substance abusers also have been studied with the MCMI. Hibbard (1989) examined whether adult children of alcoholics had greater emotional and characterological problems than did a matched control group of adults with nonalcoholic parents. The MCMI-I and Rorschach were administered; the Rorschach was scored with a specialized method purported to assess object relations. Results indicated that adult children of alcoholics were more pathological in their personality functioning and object relations. Post hoc comparisons of MCMI results demonstrated interactions between group and gender for several scales (i.e., Histrionic, Narcissism, Hypomania, and Dysthymia). Adult children of alcoholics overall scored higher on the Borderline and Negativistic scales and lower on the Compulsive scale than did the control group respondents. These results are only suggestive, however, and must be viewed with caution because of the small sample size ($n =$ 15 in each group).

Given the tendency of many substance abusers to deny or minimize their addiction, the issue of whether they can avoid detection becomes particularly poignant. Craig et al. (1994) found that 52% of their substance abusers were able to fill out the MCMI-II without elevating the substance abuse scales when they were asked to try to hide their addiction. Even with those instructions, however, 48% of the study participants were unable to avoid detection. The patients who were able to fake the test were more likely to have been classified by the clinicians as "mild" abusers than those who could not avoid detection. The test profile obtained by those who avoided detection was the usual "fake good" profile discussed in chapter 5.

Posttraumatic Stress Disorder

Psychologists in the Veterans Administration system have used the MCMI repeatedly to diagnose posttraumatic stress disorder (PTSD) among Vietnam veterans. In an early study, for instance, the profiles of 25 veterans diagnosed as suffering from PTSD were compared with a matched group of psychiatric patients (Robert et al., 1985). Results showed that the PTSD patients had significant elevations in 9 of the 20 MCMI-I scales and that profiles for the two groups were significantly different in shape and scatter. A discriminant analysis correctly classified 88% of the patients (92% of the PTSD respondents and 84% of the comparison respondents).

Investigations dealing with PTSD have consistently reported a modal profile with elevations in the Negativistic and Avoidant scales, the 8A2A codetype profile, on either the MCMI-I (Hyer & Boudewyns, 1987; Hyer et al., 1988, 1991; Hyer, Woods, Boudewyns, et al., 1990; McDermott, 1987; Munley et al., 1994; Sherwood et al., 1990) or the MCMI-II (Hyer et al., 1992). Further personality differentiations also have been made for patients who have schizoid elements as well (the 8A2A1 profile code; Hyer et al., 1991), dependent elements (8A2A13 profile code; Hyer et al., 1991; Piekarski et al., 1993), or antisocial elements (8A2A16A profile code; Hyer et al., 1991; Piekarski et al., 1993).

Several investigators have found that a high Borderline scale score was also a frequently occurring phenomenon on the MCMI-I, as were high scores on the Anxiety, Dysthymia, Alcohol Abuse, and Drug Abuse scales (Busby, Glenn, Steggell, & Adamson, 1993; Hyer et al., 1988, 1991; McDermott, 1987; Robert et al., 1985; Sherwood et al., 1990). The elevation of the Self-Defeating scale on the MCMI-II also appears to be part of the pattern, as is a tendency to have elevated Disclosure and Debasement response style scores (Hyer et al., 1992). These findings suggest a pattern of emotional instability that often is part of the clinical picture of PTSD patients (Hyer, Woods, Boudewyns, et al., 1990).

As helpful as these data may be, the findings do not exclusively identify individuals with PTSD because there may be individuals with other diagnoses who also fit the same pattern of scale elevations. An attempt to develop a PTSD scale from the item pool of the MCMI-I was unsuccessful (Choca et al., 1987). The inclusion of a specially made PTSD scale on the MCMI-III probably has remedied this problem. The MCMI-I also cannot discriminate between PTSD patients who use dissociation as a defense mechanism and those who do not (Hyer, Albrecht, Boudewyns, Woods, & Brandsma, 1993).

Adjustment Disorders

While studying 68 patients requesting cancer evaluations at a breast clinic, Malec, Wolberg, Romsaas, Trump, and Tanner (1988) collected MCMI data before the diagnosis was made and on several occasions thereafter. The data showed that the MCMI-I reflected the emotional changes experienced by some of the patients who turned out to have cancer compared with those whose growths were benign. Although the MCMI scores of the two groups were not statistically different on the initial evaluation, the cancer group had significant elevations on the clinical syndrome scales compared with the noncancer group after the cancer was diagnosed. Specifically, 29% of the cancer patients obtained significant elevations on those scales, whereas only 7% of the noncancer group obtained such elevations. The elevations were obtained mostly on the Anxiety, Dysthymia, and Somatic Preoccupation scales. These elevations were observed even though the patients did not meet the *DSM–III* criteria for a major depressive episode. Malec et al. also reported that, judging from the MCMI-I, the psychological disturbance shown by the cancer group had disappeared 16 months after the diagnosis was made.

In a similar study, Baile, Gibertini, Scott, and Endicott (1993) examined the prevalence and severity of depression and anxiety in individuals undergoing tests for head and neck cancer. The MCMI-I showed a high level of both anxiety and depression in the sample regardless of whether a malignancy was found. There were some personality style differences in the two populations: Patients with benign lesions tended to have peaks on the Histrionic and Negativistic scales, whereas those with cancer tended to have more peaks on the Dependence and Compulsive scales.

The stress experienced by individuals who recently had returned from a "cult" living environment was reflected in elevations on the Anxiety, Dysthymia, and Somatoform scales of the MCMI-I (Martin, Langone, Dole, & Wiltrout, 1992).

Suicide Potential

Clinicians often are faced with evaluating the suicidal risk that a particular patient may present. Joffe and Regan (1989b) provided some evidence that depressed patients showing borderline traits on the MCMI-I are more likely to attempt suicide than those who do not. This finding has some face validity because many of the suicidal items included in the test are keyed into the Borderline scale.

Hull, Range, and Goggin (1992) found the Negativistic, Dysthymia, and Paranoid scales of the MCMI-I to be the best predictors of the results of the Suicidal Behaviors Questionnaire. McCann and Suess (1988) reported that 85% of their psychiatric inpatients with elevations on the Schizoid, Avoidant, Dependent, and Negativistic scales on the MCMI-I demonstrated suicidal ideation and that 65% had made a suicide attempt. Similar results were reported by McCann and Gergelis (1990), suggesting that this personality profile is somewhat of a suicide marker. McCann and Gergelis noted that the findings are consistent with the stress-vulnerability model of suicidal ideation because the model emphasizes the likelihood that individuals who feel alienated, depressed, and unable to cope will experience suicidal thoughts.

Attempts to find a definite MCMI suicide marker, however, have been unsuccessful. Joffe and Regan (1989b) failed to find any difference on the frequency of MCMI-I personality scale elevations of suicide attempters and nonsuicide attempters. The only significant difference found by McCann and Gergelis (1990) between individuals having suicide ideation and those who had attempted to kill themselves was in the Desirability scale of the MCMI-II, on which the attempters obtained a higher score.

Sleep Disorders

One investigation of 6 patients with a sleep terror disorder concluded that the patients also suffered from a personality disorder because they had elevated personality scale scores on the MCMI-II (Llorente, Currier, Norman, & Mellman, 1992). Because the overwhelming majority of individuals who take the MCMI will obtain such elevations, however, the authors' argument is not very convincing.

Neuropsychological Dysfunction

The MCMI often has been used as part of neuropsychological evaluations. Like the Minnesota Multiphasic Personality Inventory (MMPI), the MCMI provides a measure of the overall level of psychopathology and the possibility that the examinee is experiencing a diagnosable emotional problem, such as depression or paranoid delusions. In our opinion, the superiority of the MCMI lies in its focus on personality.

Even individuals who do not have a diagnosable emotional disorder may experience difficulty coping with intellectual losses. A determination of the individuals' basic personality can give clinicians some indication of the way the individuals may be reacting to the stress of the neuropsychological dysfunction. Elevations on the Schizoid or Avoidant scales, for instance, suggest the possibility of social withdrawal and isolation; the Dependent scale warns clinicians of the possibility of clinging dependency; Histrionic scale elevations suggest overemotionality and excessive dramaticism. Individuals with a Narcissistic elevation may be trying to reassert their personal worth by insisting on their superiority; compulsive reactions can be conceived of as an attempt to order life more meticulously at a time when it may appear particularly chaotic. For individuals who respond to their losses with anger or distrust, Narcissistic, Aggressive, or Paranoid scale scores may be elevated.

Clinicians using the MCMI with acutely disturbed individuals should heed our usual caveat about assuming that the score profile obtained reflects premorbid clinical realities. In other words, an elevation of the Dependent scale may often, *but not always*, indicate that the examinee was a dependent type before the onset of the neuropsychological dysfunction. In individuals for whom the MCMI personality profile can be shown to represent their premorbid inclinations, the personality profile can be used to speculate about the underlying dynamics of an emotional disturbance. For intelligent narcissistic individuals, for instance, a loss of intellectual abilities could undermine the basic assumption that they are superior to others; for those with a compulsive nature, the occurrence of unforeseeable and unpreventable brain impairment could shake the lifelong belief that unwanted events can be avoided by not making any mistakes.

Clinicians using the MCMI should remember that scale elevations do not imply causality. The neuropsychological literature has demonstrated that damage to particular areas of the brain can lead directly to mood instability, disinhibition, and so on. Elevations on the MCMI suggest, at best, the clinical picture at the time of the testing and do not reveal the causative factors that may have generated the clinical picture. Whether the elevations represent lifelong pathology, an adjustment reaction to the brain damage, or the direct result of a dysfunctional brain has to be argued on the basis of patients' histories, the neurological findings, or the neuropsychological literature.

Unfortunately, there is limited empirical information on the use of the MCMI as part of a neuropsychological battery. Swirsky-Sacchetti et al. (1993) investigated the cognitive impairment of 10 patients with a borderline personality disorder. They failed to find any difference in the MCMI-I profiles of borderline patients with or without cognitive impairment.

Problem-Solving Deficits

Gilbride and Hebert (1980) examined the MCMI characteristics of good and poor interpersonal problem solvers. The measure of problem-solving ability used was the Means-Ends Problem Solving Procedure, which requires the examinee to finish a story that presents some sort of problem. Black individuals who were poor problem solvers showed significant elevations on the Paranoid and Psychotic Delusions scales compared with good problem solvers of the same race. For White individuals, the poor problem solvers had higher means on the Schizoid and Schizotypal scales.

Chronic Low Back Pain

Papciak and Feuerstein (1991) administered the MCMI-II to 186 chronic back pain sufferers. The Anxiety and Dysthymia scales were found to be modestly but significantly associated with a computerized measure of trunk strength. The authors concluded that the two scales measure psychological factors that negatively affect the recovery of workers' compensation examinees.

Chronic Fatigue Syndrome

The MCMI-II was given to a small sample of patients diagnosed with chronic fatigue syndrome (CFS; also known as chronic Epstein-Barr virus). The score pattern that emerged included elevations on 5 of the personality scales (i.e., Histrionic, Schizoid, Avoidant, Narcissistic, and Aggressive) as well as the Anxiety, Dysthymia, and Somatoform scales. The results were interpreted as indicating the presence of "severe personality pathology and affective distress" (C. Millon et al., 1989, p. 131).

Vorce, Jones, Helder, Pettibon, and Reiter (1995), however, would argue that the MCMI-II elevations are caused partly by the intrinsic nature of CFS and may not be indicative of an additional psychiatric problem. Vorce et al. asked five experts to rate the MCMI-II items in terms of their possible association with CFS. They found that the content of 54 of the MCMI-II items were thought to be part of the CFS symptomatology. Eliminating from this pool of items those items that had a low endorsement rate for CFS patients reduced the number of items to 46. The scales that were most affected were Anxiety, Debasement, Somatoform, Dysthymia, Major Depression, Self-Defeating, Alcohol Dependence, and Negativistic. Vorce et al. noted that most of the affected scales represented constructs (e.g., depression, somatoform disorders) that have been used to explain CFS symptoms. They discussed several possible corrections that could be used to separate more cleanly the diagnosis of CFS from psychiatric disorders.

Sexual Disorders

Several MCMI studies have evaluated men convicted of child molestation or rape. The general MCMI-I profile of sexual offenders portrays such individuals as being more negativistic, dependent, interpersonally isolated, and depressed and less narcissistic than control group examinees (Chantry & Craig, 1993; Langevin et al., 1988). Cluster analyses have led to the characterization of several distinct groups among the sexual offenders. Perhaps one third of these individuals have an avoidant-schizoid-dependent personality on the MCMI-I. A second group, appearing to include many of the rapists, had a narcissistic-antisocial-histrionic personality and elevations on the substance abuse scales. As many as 50% of the sexual offenders, however, obtained no significant MCMI-I elevations (Bard & Knight, 1987; Chantry & Craig, 1994).

Looking at sexual abuse from the victim's viewpoint, P. C. Alexander (1993) showed that MCMI-II findings were not associated with the kind of sexual abuse the person experienced as a child. Rather, her findings pointed to the importance of characteristics in the relationship the person had with the adult abuser. A preoccupied attachment, as measured on the Relationship Questionnaire, was associated with dependent, self-defeating, and borderline personality attributes. Fearful attachment, on the other hand, was linked to higher scores on the Avoidant and Self-Defeating scales of the MCMI-II.

Legal Offenders

Working with a population of emotionally disturbed incarcerated men, Blackburn (1986) characterized four personality types that he labeled *primary psychopath, secondary psychopath, controlled,* and *inhibited.* Distinguished by elevations on the Narcissistic, Antisocial, and Histrionic scales of the MCMI-I (Blackburn, 1996), the primary psychopath profile has also been found prominent among Canadian prisoners (Weekes & Morrison, 1993). The secondary psychopath is defined by elevations on the Negativistic, Avoidant, Schizoid, and Antisocial scales (Blackburn, 1996) and bears some resemblance to one of the clusters reported by Weekes and Morrison (1993). Primary and secondary psychopaths have more convictions for assaultive crimes than the other two types and have spent a significantly longer period of time incarcerated (Blackburn, 1975, 1996). Studies have also found a group of patients with a compulsive personality (Blackburn, 1996; Weekes & Morrison, 1993); and a fourth group where the prominent feature was their social detachment (indicated by elevations on the Schizoid and Avoidant scales; Blackburn, 1996).

Partner Abuse

Hastings and Hamberger (1988) did a substantial amount of work using the MCMI-I to characterize male patients who abuse their relational partners. In support of the contention that wife batterers often suffer from a personality disorder, Hastings and Hamberger found marked differences in the MCMI-I personality elevations between the batterers and a control group of nonbatterers. These findings have been replicated with the MCMI-II (Beasley & Stoltenberg, 1992; Hart et al., 1993; C. M. Murphy, Meyer, & O'Leary, 1993).[1] Batterers with a poor premorbid history (defined by a lack of a high school education, unemployment, a history of alcohol abuse, or a history of having witnessed or experienced abuse) showed more elevations on the MCMI-I than did batterers with a good premorbid history (Hastings & Hamberger, 1994).

Hamberger and Hastings (1988a, 1991) distinguished wife abusers from a nonabuser control group. The differences in MCMI-I scale elevations suggested that wife abusers may have difficulty regulating affective states and feel uncomfortable in intimate relationships. These individuals were seen as being more alienated, in more need of approval, and more sensitive to rejection than the nonbatterers. According to the MCMI-I scores, the batterers were more prone to experience anxiety and depression, have somatic complaints, and abuse drugs or alcohol than the members of the control group. Whenever alcohol abuse was present, as revealed by elevations of the MCMI-I scale, this problem was associated with an even greater tendency toward overall pathology and a propensity toward interpersonal ambivalence and alienation (Hamberger & Hastings, 1987, 1991; Hastings & Hamberger, 1988).

Using the MCMI-II, Dutton (1994) discussed the prevalence of the negativistic-avoidant personality profile when the test results of men in treatment for wife assault were compared with a control sample of blue-collar workers. He interpreted the findings as indicating that wife assaulters are caught in a bind between perceived abandonment and being smothered.

As informative as this characterization may be, it is of limited clinical utility when one must evaluate or treat a particular individual. Per-

---

[1]Hart, Dutton, and Newlove (1993) diagnosed numerous abusers with a personality disorder entirely on the basis of the MCMI-II. They assumed that mere elevations on the personality scales of the MCMI-II could be used to diagnose personality disorders, an assumption that we see as untenable (Choca, Shanley, et al., 1992). In our opinion, the fact that no control group was used further compromised the power of their conclusions. The problem was corrected, however, by the work of Beasley and Stoltenberg (1992), who did use a control group.

haps of even greater clinical value is the factor analysis that Hamberger and Hastings (1986, 1988a) carried out using the 8 personality scales of the MCMI-I. This procedure led to the emergence of three factors associated with wife batterers. The findings allow the classification of such individuals in a way that elucidates the psychodynamics behind the spouse abuse. Using the proposed system, three "pure" types are recognized: borderline-schizoid, narcissistic, and dependent.

The borderline-schizoid typically shows a prominence on those two MCMI-I scales. Other scales that may be elevated with this group are the Negativistic and Avoidant scales (Lohr et al., 1988). These men were described as withdrawn, moody, and hypersensitive to interpersonal slights. Hamberger and Hastings (1986, 1988a) characterized such individuals as "Dr. Jekyll and Mr. Hyde" types who can be very calm and sociable one moment but then turn uncontrollably hostile the next because of the unpredictable lability. These individuals theoretically require a symbiotically supportive relationship that offers external validation of their value and existence. If the partner fails to recognize their worth, these individuals are devastated and physically express their anger. Once the incident is over, however, they tend to express considerable guilt and remorse. The relationship between a borderline personality structure and wife abuse has been supported by Dutton's (1994) work using the MCMI-II and the Borderline Personality Organization Inventory (Oldham et al., 1985). People having this cluster type are considered to hold more irrational beliefs than those in other clusters of relational partner abusers (Lohr et al., 1988).

By contrast, individuals obtaining elevated scores on the Narcissistic scale of the MCMI-I have self-centered approaches to life. These men typically feel that they are important people and demand respect and admiration. A refusal to look at them with awe invites threat and aggression. Hamberger and Hastings (1986, 1988a) felt that, for this type of person, the abuse is like a punishment that is handled in a matter-of-fact manner because of the sense of superiority and entitlement that leads them to believe it is appropriate for them to show others the error of their ways. The presence of a narcissistic group also has been supported by other studies (Lohr et al., 1988).

Finally, dependent individuals lack self-esteem and feel in dire need of support from others. It is the failure of other people to meet their dependency needs that is eventually translated into rebellious and hostile feelings.

In addition to individuals who are "pure" types, Hamberger and

Hastings (1986, 1988a) found many who represent a combination of the pure types, as well as some individuals whose scores on the MCMI-I personality scales would not be indicative of any personality tendencies.

Another system for classifying wife abusers was used by Dutton (1994). Dutton used the results of the Psychological Maltreatment of Women Inventory (Tolman, 1989) to classify wife abusers into a dominance/isolation group, for whom the issues are the rigid observance of traditional sex roles, demands for subservience, and isolation from resources, and an emotional/verbal-abuse group, who tend to withdraw emotional resources, take part in verbal attacks, and engage in behaviors that degrade women. The dominance/isolation group was mostly associated with the Negativistic and Self-Defeating scales of the MCMI-II, whereas the emotional/verbal-abuse group was characterized by elevations on the Aggressive-Sadistic and Narcissistic scales.

The usefulness of this kind of information can be applied readily when evaluating a wife batterer who meets one of the described types. If that is the case, clinicians can use the MCMI to theoretically predict the kind of situation that evokes the aggressive feelings within the context of the family system. The information also can be used in working with patients to make them aware of the personal issues that they are reacting to when they act in a hostile manner toward their wives. The critical issues of treatment completion and recidivism also have received some attention in the literature (see chap. 10).

Marital Discord

Craig and Olson (1995) examined 75 women and 70 men seeking marital therapy. A cluster analysis of MCMI-II results led to the characterization of four different types of individuals who seemed inclined to have difficulties in their marriages. The first type is a narcissistic-aggressive-histrionic individual; Craig and Olson thought that such individuals would form either a conflictual or an overadequate controlling relationship with their spouse depending on the type of person they married. The second type is characterized by generalized maladjustment and elevations on the Negativistic, Aggressive, Self-Defeating, Narcissistic, and Borderline scales. Such individuals also would be expected to form a conflictual or dictatorial relationship with their spouse. Finally, there were two types of dependent individuals: an anxious dependent-avoidant-schizoid type and a dependent-compulsive type. It was assumed that these individuals likely would play the underadequate role in an overadequate–underadequate relationship. The psychotherapeutic goals offered for the different types of relationships are reviewed in chapter 10.

Victims of Abuse

The MCMI-I was given to 30 clients of a university counseling center who had reported receiving physical, sexual, or emotional abuse as children. This group scored higher on the Borderline scale than did a control group of 54 nonabused clients even though the group score was not clinically elevated (a BR score average of 73). The 19 clients who reported only emotional abuse did not differ from the clients reporting sexual or multiple forms of abuse (Braver, Bumberry, Green, & Rawson, 1992). Recall that the Borderline scale of the MCMI-I was originally called Cyclothymia and mostly measured mood instability.

Abortions in Adolescents

N. B. Campbell, Franco, and Jurs (1988) studied young women who had abortions as adolescents or adults on the MCMI-I and Beck Depression Inventory. The authors reported that 25% of their overall sample had significant elevations on the Anxiety, Dysthymia, and Somatoform scales. It is unclear how this would compare with other comparable clinical populations. Campbell et al. also included some data demonstrating that those who had abortions as adolescents had greater elevations on four scales of the MCMI-I. However, their mean scores were well below BR scores of 75 (range = 58.9–63.4). Thus, their conclusions about the meanings of these differences seem suspect.

The MCMI and Other Psychological Instruments

In this chapter we review investigations in which two versions of the MCMI, or the MCMI and another instrument, were given to the same individuals. Our review is intended to serve three purposes. First, some of the studies address the concurrent validity of the MCMI, such as when the test led to similar results to those obtained with other tools. Second, in comparing different instruments, these studies can make clinicians aware of situations in which the use of the MCMI may be more or less advantageous than the use of the other instrument. Finally, some of the studies offer information that clinicians can use to integrate the findings of the two sources. Although the other source of information typically has been another psychological test, the procedures for integrating MCMI results with clinician ratings using canonical variates are available in the literature (Robbins & Patton, 1986).

In his review of the literature involving the MCMI and the Minnesota Multiphasic Personality Inventory (MMPI), Gallucci (1990) criticized the available studies for not meeting the five criteria he proposed as optimal. In particular, Gallucci noted that few of the studies estimated the incremental validity that is gained from using more than one test. That criticism would apply not only to the MMPI studies discussed later, but to almost all of the studies in this chapter. In theory, having the results from more than one psychological instrument would increase the amount of certainty that clinicians would have about the diagnosis of a particular patient. In practice, however, that potential has been hard to actualize. A study by Marlowe and Wetzler (1994), for instance, showed little improvement in diagnostic efficiency over single scale elevations when the MCMI-I, the MCMI-II, the MMPI, the SCL-90-R, and the psychiatrist's diagnosis were used.

In any event, we first discuss the instruments that are most similar, in structure or scope, to the MCMI-III. Other instruments designed to measure personality traits are discussed next, followed by the instruments that emphasize the clinical syndromes.

The MCMI-I and the MCMI-II

Millon (1987) reported high correlations between the corresponding scales of these two versions. Hyer et al. (1992) gave both versions to 100 veterans diagnosed with posttraumatic stress disorder (PTSD). Although their correlations were not as high as Millon's, the corresponding scales were found to be similar enough that the two versions can be "used interchangeably," at least with a PTSD group (Hyer et al., 1992, p. 878). When the patients were grouped together, both of the MCMI versions resulted in the typical PTSD profile, with elevations in the Avoidant and Negativistic scales. Even the high-point codes showed some stability, as one or both of the highest two elevations of the MCMI-I turned out to be elevated on the MCMI-II 85% of the time. However, the data also showed significant differences between the two instruments. The base-rate (BR) scores on the MCMI-II were significantly higher for most of the scales and the 2-point code involved the same two scales in only 17.5% of the cases (Hyer et al., 1992).

The MCMI and the Millon Behavioral Health Inventory

Like the MCMI, the Millon Behavioral Health Inventory (MBHI) is rooted in Millon's theory and contains the eight basic personality prototypes that Millon (1969) proposed. In addition to the personality scales, the MBHI contains scales designed to measure attributes thought to be relevant in the treatment of medically ill patients. Wise (1994b) administered both these inventories to a group of psychiatric patients with medical symptoms. In looking at the personality scales, his data showed that the two tests were not significantly different in the number of scales that were elevated. A significant and positive correlation was found between the complementary scales of the two instruments. However, the actual code-type correspondence was a disappointing 30% for single scales and 21% for 2-point codetypes.

The MCMI and the Personality Adjective Check List

Strack (1987, 1990) developed the Personality Adjective Check List (PACL) to measure the 8 basic Millon personality scales in normal individuals. When both instruments were given to a sample of 140 university students, six of the eight PACL scales obtained their highest correlation with their MCMI-II counterpart (Strack, 1991a). One of the exceptions was the Introversive scale of the PACL, which was not only related to the Schizoid scale of the MCMI-II, but it also was negatively related to the Avoidant and the Histrionic scales. The PACL's Forceful scale was more associated with the Dependent (negatively) and the Narcissistic scales than with its MCMI-II counterpart (Antisocial).

Strack's (1991a) factor analysis of the two scales together led to four factors that accounted for 77% of the variance. Three of these factors (labeled Social Dominance Versus Submissiveness, Emotionality Versus Restraint, and Social Introversion Versus Extraversion) showed the theoretically expected loadings on both the MCMI-II and the PACL. The last factor, thought to measure general maladaptiveness, loaded only on 5 of the 8 scales of the MCMI-II.

The correlations obtained by Strack (1991a) between the matching scales of the two instruments ranged from .41 to .72. These values seemed to indicate that the scores produced by the two instruments have definite similarities but are far from equivalent. The difference between the two could be explained partly by the difference in format (the PACL is an adjective checklist as opposed to a true–false questionnaire), the presence or absence of items designed to measure pathological traits, and the adjustments made to the Millon typologies of the MCMI-II in order to align the descriptions with the revised third edition of the *Diagnostic and Statistical Manual of Mental Disorders* (*DSM–III–R*; American Psychiatric Association, 1987).

The MCMI and the Wisconsin Personality Disorders Inventory

The Wisconsin Personality Disorders Inventory (WPDI) is a self-report questionnaire designed to measure the 11 personality disorders of the

DSM–III–R from the interpersonal perspective of Benjamin's (1974, 1984) Structural Analysis of Social Behavior (SASB). The SASB is based on Leary's circumplex model (see the historical section in chap. 1 for more information). The instrument consists of 360 items that are rated on a 10-point scale (Klein et al., 1993). All but 2 (Narcissistic and Antisocial) of the scales of the WPDI were significantly correlated with the corresponding personality scale of the MCMI-I. The reported correlations range from −.26 to .68.[1] When corrected for attenuation, the average correlation between the two instruments was .46 (Klein et al., 1993). Except for two scales, these questionnaires measure constructs that have much in common, even though they clearly are different tools.

The MCMI and the Inventory of Interpersonal Problems

The Inventory of Interpersonal Problems is a self-report inventory designed to assess maladaptive interpersonal dispositions (L. M. Horowitz, Rosenberg, Baer, Ureño, & Villaseñor, 1988). Alden, Wiggins, and Pincus (1990) developed scales for this instrument that allow placement of the individual on the nurturant-cold and domineering-unassertive axes of the circumplex. Using the MCMI-I and the Alden scales, Matano and Locke (1995) found that schizoid, avoidant, and negativistic alcoholics were excessively guarded interpersonally, narcissistic patients were too domineering, compulsive individuals were unassertive, antisocials were guarded and domineering, and dependent individuals were both open and unassertive.

The MCMI and the NEO Personality Inventory

The NEO Personality Inventory (Costa & McCrae, 1985) was designed to measure personality in accordance with the five-factor model (Neuroticism, Extraversion, Openness to Experience, Psychoticism, and Agreeableness). In terms of that model, Costa and McCrae reported that the Schizoid scale of the MCMI-I was related negatively to the Ex-

---

[1]The report that the two compulsive scales had a significant negative correlation seemed odd to us, but the issue is not addressed in the paper. Klein (personal communication, January 11, 1994) thought that the finding is attributable to discrepancies between the MCMI compulsive prototype and that of the revised third edition of the *Diagnostic and Statistical Manual of Mental Disorders*. We are not convinced that this factor could explain a negative correlation but have no better explanation.

traversion scale, specifically showing low warmth, gregariousness, positive emotions, assertiveness, and openness to feelings. In addition to being related negatively to Extraversion scores, avoidants in Millon's (1969) typology scored highly on the Neuroticism scale, showing problems with self-consciousness, depression, and vulnerability. Dependent scale scores were related to low Openness to Experience scores and to high Agreeableness scores in terms of the five-factor model. Histrionic individuals obtained positive correlations with the Extraversion scale and negative correlations with the Conscientiousness scale. The high Extraversion scores were thought to be attributable to histrionic individuals' gregariousness, positive emotions, assertiveness, and excitement seeking. Individuals who had high scores on the Narcissistic scale were found to have high scores on the Extraversion scale and low scores on the Agreeableness scale. These people were high in assertiveness and saw themselves as being low in self-consciousness and vulnerability. The Antisocial scale also was correlated negatively with Agreeableness scores. Compulsive individuals were found to have extremely high scores on the Conscientiousness scale. Finally, scores on the Negativistic scale have been correlated with Neuroticism scores (Costa & McCrae, 1990; McCrae, 1991).

The MCMI and the Gordon Personality Profile Inventory

The Gordon Personality Profile Inventory (GPPI) is another measure of the five-factor model of personality. Dyer (1994) administered this inventory and the MCMI-II to a group of 50 participants. His data showed the MCMI-II Schizoid and Avoidant scales characterize individuals lacking assertiveness, goal-directed behavior, and drive. Dependent participants turned out to be cautious and behaviorally inhibited. Unexpectedly, histrionic people showed a capacity for original thinking on the GPPI. The Antisocial Scale of the MCMI-II correlated negatively with both the Cautiousness and Vigor scales of the GPPI. Correlating negatively with GPPI's Responsibility, Personal Relations, and Vigor was the MCMI-II's Aggressive Scale, but the Self-Defeating Scale had a negative correlation with every GPPI scale. Compulsive participants tended to be routine oriented, behaviorally inhibited, emotionally contained, and responsible. The Negativistic and Borderline scales had significant negative correlations with all but one of the GPPI scales. Finally, schizotypal individuals were found to be introverted, socially isolated, irresponsible, and lacking in drive.

The MCMI and the 50-Bipolar Self-Rating Scales

A third measure of the "Big Five" personality factors, the 50-Bipolar Self-Rating Scales (50-BSRS) is a 50-item self-report questionnaire (L. R. Goldberg, 1992). When both the MCMI-II and the 50-BSRS were given to psychiatric patients, the Schizoid, Schizotypal, and Avoidant scales were found to be related negatively to Extraversion, Emotional Stability, and Openness to Experience; the Avoidant scale also was related to low Agreeableness. Dependent individuals are thought of as introverted and closed to experience, whereas histrionics are agreeable, undependable, and open to experience. Narcissists and antisocials are both extraverted, but the narcissists also are open to experience. The Compulsive scale was characterized as measuring introversion and conscientiousness. MCMI-II Negativists were disagreeable, neurotic, and undependable on the 50-BSRS. The MCMI borderline prototype was shown to be related to disagreeableness and lack of conscientiousness, and paranoids were unstable. Finally, those with high scores on the Self-Defeating scale were introverted, disagreeable, undependable, and neurotic, whereas those with high scores on the Aggressive scale were disagreeable, neurotic, and open to experience (Soldz et al., 1993b).

The MCMI and the Eysenck Personality Questionnaire

Similar constructs as those used by the five-factor model are represented by the Psychoticism, Extraversion, and Neuroticism scales of the Eysenck Personality Questionnaire (Eysenck & Eysenck, 1975). Using a psychiatric sample, Gabrys et al. (1988) found an association between low Psychoticism scores and a compulsive personality style, whereas high Psychoticism scores led to elevations of the Schizoid, Avoidant, and Negativistic scales of the MCMI-I. Introversion was related to the Schizoid, Avoidant, Dependent, Negativistic, Schizotypal, Borderline, Anxiety, Somatoform, Dysthymia, Psychotic Thinking, and Major Depression scales. Finally, examinees scoring low on Neuroticism tended to score high on the MCMI-I's Histrionic, Narcissistic, and Compulsive scales.

The MCMI and the Sixteen Personality Factor Questionnaire

The Sixteen Personality Factor Questionnaire (16PF) has validity scales that appear similar to the Desirability and Debasement scales of second and third editions of the MCMI. Because of this apparent similarity, the 16PF has been used to study the performance of the MCMI Modifying Indices. The Fake-Bad scale of the 16PF has a significant positive correlation with the Disclosure and Debasement scales of the MCMI-II. On the other hand, the Motivation Distortion (Fake-Good) scale of the 16PF is correlated positively with the Desirability scale and correlated negatively with both the Disclosure and Debasement scales (Grossman & Craig, 1994).

On the personality scales, DeLamatre and Schuerger (1992) found support for the convergent validity of 10 of the 11 MCMI-I scales and the 16PF dimensions. General convergence also was reported using five broad factors (i.e., Extraversion, Anxiety, Practicality, Independence, and Self-Control) from a new version of the 16PF and the MCMI-I (Terpylak & Schuerger, 1994).

Hyer, Woods, Boudewyns, et al. (1990) gave both the MCMI-I and the 16PF to a group of veterans diagnosed with PTSD. Their findings were always consistent with Millon's (1977) conceptualizations of the different MCMI scales. For example, the Schizoid and the Avoidant scales were related inversely to the Assertiveness scale and related positively to the Self-Sufficiency scale of the 16PF. The Avoidant scale also was related to the Anxiety scale. The Dependent scale was related positively to the Sensitivity scale but related inversely to the Self-Sufficiency scale. Patients with high scores on the Histrionic scale also tended to have high scores on the Intelligence, Assertive, Happy-Go-Lucky, Boldness, Extraversion, Tough Poise, and Independence scales of 16PF. Both the Narcissistic and the Antisocial scales appeared to be associated with assertiveness and independence; the Narcissistic scale also was correlated with the Happy-Go-Lucky, Boldness, and Extraversion scales, whereas the Antisocial scale was found to be associated with the Tough Poise scale and related negatively to the Sensitivity scale. Correlating positively with the Conformity and Self-Discipline scales, the Compulsive scale of the MCMI was related negatively to the Tension, Anxiety, and Tough Poise scales. Finally, judging from these two inventories, respondents with negativistic personality styles tend to be tense, anxious, and not inclined to be warm, emotionally stable, happy-go-lucky, conforming, bold, and self-disciplined. Correlations for the Schizotypal, Borderline, and Paranoid scales of the MCMI-I also are included, along with the correlations obtained by the symptom formation scales on the traits of the 16PF (Hyer, Woods, Boudewyns, et al., 1990).

Craig and Olson (1992) administered the MCMI-II and the 16PF to 75 women and 70 men involved in outpatient marital therapy. They found 75 significant correlations between the Millon personality scales and the 16PF and 40 significant correlations between the latter test and Millon clinical syndrome scales. All the obtained correlations were thought to reflect a "meaningful and logical" relationship between the two tests (Craig & Olson, 1992, p. 703).

The MCMI and Other Measures of Narcissism

The MCMI has received some attention for its ability to measure narcissism. Prifitera and Ryan (1984) administered both the MCMI-I and the Narcissistic Personality Inventory (NPI), which was developed by Raskin and Hall (1979) using a counterbalanced design and psychiatric patients. Prifitera and Ryan reported a correlation of .66 between the Narcissistic scale of the MCMI-I and the NPI. They also found significant correlations between the NPI and the Histrionic and Negativistic scales of the MCMI. They explained the latter correlations on the basis of the similarities between the narcissistic personality prototype and the prototypes for the histrionic and negativistic individuals. Finally, Prifitera and Ryan used the two scales to classify their sample into low and high narcissism and found that the instruments agreed on the classification 74% of the time.

In a similar study done with undergraduates, Auerbach (1984) showed a statistically significant correlation of .55 between the Narcissistic scale of the MCMI-I and the NPI. Auerbach found it troublesome, however, that the coefficient of homogeneity for the MCMI Narcissistic scale was low, thus suggesting that the scale may be measuring more than one concept in the case of college students. Moreover, neither the Narcissistic scale nor the NPI correlated significantly with the Marlowe-Crowne Social Desirability Scale (Crowne & Marlowe, 1964), possibly pointing out that the concept of narcissism may not be related to a wish to be perceived as being socially desirable.

Using the NPI and clinical ratings to choose narcissistic patients, Chatham and her coworkers compared the narcissistic group with a control group of nonnarcissistic psychiatric patients. The study showed that the narcissistic respondents tended to score higher on the Histrionic, Narcissistic, and Antisocial personality scales and on the Paranoid, Hypomanic, and Drug Abuse scales of the MCMI-I. The findings characterized the narcissistic group as being more extraverted, aggressive, dramatizing, suspicious, and energetic than nonnarcissistic psychiatric patients (Chatham et al., 1993).

In their work with wife abusers, Beasley and Stoltenberg (1992) found the NPI to be less responsive than the MCMI-II to the narcissistic characteristics of their sample. They blamed their finding on the NPI having been developed to tap less extreme levels of narcissism than the MCMI-II.

The MCMI and Other Measures of the Borderline Personality

Lewis and Harder (1991) correlated the score of the Borderline scale of the MCMI-I with results obtained from Kernberg's (1977) Structural Interview, from the Diagnostic Interview for Borderline Personality Disorders (Gunderson & Singer, 1975), and from the Borderline Syndrome Index (Conte, Plutchik, Karasu, & Jerrett, 1980). The data showed the MCMI-I scale to have the most robust correlation with the other instruments.

The MCMI and the Defense Mechanism Inventory

According to the data obtained by Whyne-Berman and McCann (1995), elevations on the Antisocial scale of the MCMI-II are associated with acting-out defenses. Compulsive traits are found in individuals who use reaction formation as a defense, and paranoid tendencies are tied to projection. A negativistic style uses displacement. Finally, the Self-Defeating scale is related to the mechanism of devaluation. Although many significant correlations were found between these two instruments, the correlations tended to be modest (no higher than .38), indicating that the instruments measure different constructs.

The MCMI and the COPE

The COPE is a 60-item self-report inventory designed to measure the frequency of habitual coping strategies (Carver, Scheier, & Weintraub,

1989). Data from this inventory led to the clustering of the MCMI-II personality scales into three groups according to the predominant coping strategy used. The first group, including the Aggressive, Narcissistic, Antisocial, Paranoid, and Histrionic scales, characterized individuals who typically cope with stress by venting emotions. The second group, containing the Negativistic, Borderline, and Self-Defeating scales, showed deficits of active coping and a tendency to disengage from goals, both mentally and behaviorally. Finally, the third group emphasized passivity, social withdrawal, and cognitive negativism as coping strategies. This group included the Schizotypal, Schizoid, and Compulsive scales (Vollrath et al., 1994). COPE scores were used subsequently to predict change in the MCMI-II personality scale scores (Vollrath et al., 1995).

The MCMI and Measures of Rationality and Self-Regard

The main focus of rational–emotive therapy is to help clients fight irrational thoughts that, according to Ellis (1977), have self-defeating consequences that interfere with their survival and happiness. Two studies examined the relationship of the MCMI-I and various experimental measures of rationality of thinking and positive self-regard. Results of both studies indicated that the Histrionic, Narcissistic, Antisocial, and Compulsive scales are correlated with rationality and positive self-regard, whereas most of the other MCMI scales tend to be correlated with irrationality. In both articles, the correlation found between the other personality scales (i.e., Schizoid, Avoidant, Dependent, Negativistic, Schizotypal, and Borderline) and irrational ways of thinking was noted (Hyer, Harrison, & Jacobsen, 1987; Leaf, Ellis, et al., 1991).

The MCMI and Measures of Perfectionism

We were able to find one study that examined the MCMI-I and two obscure measures of perfectionism. This was a simple correlational study, somewhat limited by the modest sample size ($N = 91$; Broday, 1988). There were two interesting findings: The Negativistic scale was the most highly correlated with perfectionism, and the Compulsive scale was correlated inversely with perfectionism.

The MCMI and the Reciprocal Attachment Questionnaire

Elevations of the Dysthymia scale of the MCMI-I were used to distinguish a group of 42 depressed patients from a similar group of nondepressed patients. Five of the 11 scales of the Reciprocal Attachment Questionnaire were found to be significantly elevated for the depressed group (Pettem, West, Mahoney, & Keller, 1993).

The MCMI and the MMPI

The biggest competitor of the MCMI has been, of course, the MMPI. These two tests are used in the same settings and are designed to measure patterns of emotional disturbance. There is evidence that they are indeed highly similar from a global or structural viewpoint. Sexton et al. (1987), for example, demonstrated that the MCMI-I and a short version of the MMPI (the MMPI-168) had conceptually identical factor structures and were equally useful in predicting discharge diagnoses in an inpatient psychiatric unit. Ownby, Wallbrown, Carmin, and Barnett (1990, 1991) examined the two inventories together using a population of male criminal offenders. Ownby et al. reported that 29% of the MMPI variance was accounted for by the MCMI-I, whereas 36% of the MCMI-I variance was redundant with the MMPI scores of the same individual.

A combined factor analysis of the MCMI-I and the MMPI in a male criminal offender population of 2,245 participants was conducted by Ownby, Wallbrown, Carmin, and Barnett (1990). Results indicated that there were important areas of overlap for the two instruments in terms of measuring the same aspects of the participants' functioning. Results also indicated that each of those instruments contains unique sources of variance. Ownby et al. recommended the use of both instruments as complementary components within an objective assessment battery. They also argued cogently that the consistently found factor structures for the MCMI-I and the MMPI reflect clinical realities, not just test artifacts attributable to overlapping items and scales.

Similar results were obtained by Ward (1994) using the second version of both of these instruments. Principal-components analysis led to seven components with the MMPI-2 and five components with the MCMI-II. The first two principal components, labeled *emotional maladjustment* and *antisocial traits*, were well correlated (.68 and .63, respectively) and accounted for large portions of the explained variance (58% of 76% for the MMPI-2 and 57% of 82% for the MCMI-II).

Smith et al. (1988) administered the MMPI and the MCMI-I to 106 consecutive new admissions to a private outpatient mental health clinic. Twelve of the 20 MCMI-I scales were correlated highly with the MMPI, whereas 8 scales failed to show positive correlations with any MMPI scale. A similar lack of convergence was found between the clinical syndrome scales of the MCMI-II and the MMPI-II, leading to the conclusion that the two tests differ substantially in how they measure psychopathology (Blais, Benedict, & Norman, 1994).

In terms of the equivalence of specific scales, McNiel and Meyer (1990) reported great similarity between the weight factor (now called the Disclosure Index) of the MCMI-I and the F and K scale scores of the MMPI. Their investigation with correctional inmates and forensic inpatients revealed that the MCMI index is correlated negatively with the F scale score and correlated positively with the K score.

Morey and Le Vine (1988) examined the convergence between the MCMI-I personality scales and the personality scales that Morey and colleagues (Morey, Blashfield, Webb, & Jewell, 1988; Morey et al., 1985) had earlier derived for the MMPI-I. Their results indicated significant convergence across the two instruments. Other studies have shown 5 of the 11 Morey et al. (1985) scales (i.e., Schizoid, Avoidant, Dependent, Histrionic, and Narcissistic) to be highly correlated with their corresponding MCMI-I scales (McCann, 1989; Schuler, Snibbe, & Buckwalter, 1994). Three other scales (i.e., Negativistic, Schizotypal, and Borderline) were found to correlate in one study (McCann, 1989) but not in another (Schuler et al., 1994). Morey and Le Vine (1988) argued that the poorest convergence involved scales measuring *DSM–III* disorders that were least consistent with the Millon prototypes (i.e., the Compulsive, Antisocial, and Negativistic personality scales), an argument that is supported by Wise's data (1994a). Similar findings have been reported for the convergence of the personality scales of the MCMI-II and the MMPI-2 (Wise, 1996). In the final assessment, it seems that the corresponding personality scales of these two instruments have some commonalities (an average correlation of .54, according to Wise [1996]) but that they are clearly different measures.

The Narcissistic scale of the MCMI-I has been shown to be correlated with three of the four experimental scales designed to measure narcissism with the MMPI (Chatham et al., 1993).

The depression scales of these two inventories appeared to be interchangeable. According to Millon (1987), the correlation between these two scales is .70. The Depression scale of the MMPI also was modestly correlated with the Borderline and Dysthymia scales of the MCMI-I. In a study comparing depressed patients with patients suffering from other psychiatric disorders, Wetzler et al. (1989) found that both of these inventories were efficient in predicting the diagnosis of major depression. On the basis of their data, Wetzler et al. argued that the instrument to be used should be chosen with a specific goal in mind: If one wishes to rule out a major depression, the MMPI Depression scale would be the most useful; the strength of the MCMI-I, on the other hand, is in its higher overall accuracy (Wetzler et al., 1989).

Millon (1987) also reported that the MCMI-I Borderline scale was modestly correlated with the Psychasthenia scale, whereas the Schizotypal and Thought Disorder scales were modestly correlated with the Schizophrenic scale of the MMPI.

The convergences of ancillary scales of the MMPI have also been studied. Zarrella, Schuerger, and Ritz (1990) predicted 19 of the 20 MCMI-I scales using Wiggins's MMPI scales (1969), Harris and Lingoes's MMPI scales (1968), and Serkownek's MMPI scales (1975). Hyer, Woods, Summers, Boudewyns, and Harrison (1990) compared Kleiger and Kinsman's MMPI Alexithymia scale (1980) with the scales of the MCMI-I. Consistent with the concept of alexithymia as an impaired ability to experience, label, or express emotions, Zarrella et al. found the Alexithymia scale to be related to the Schizoid and Narcissistic scales of the MCMI, even though only a small amount of the variance could be accounted for.

On the other hand, the concordance shown between MMPI and MCMI scales has been far from perfect. Millon's (1987) own figures showed little or no relation between the scales of these two inventories, a finding that has been supported by others (Marsh et al., 1988). At least with a population of criminal offenders, the paranoid scales of the two inventories appeared to be measuring different aspects of paranoia and produced appreciably different results. The same conclusion was reached with regard to the Hysteria scale of the MMPI and the Somatic Preoccupation scale of the MCMI-I (Ownby et al., 1991).

McCann (1991) examined the convergent and discriminant validities of the MCMI-II and the MMPI personality disorder scales using multitrait–multimethod procedures and factor analyses. Using both overlapping and nonoverlapping scales, he determined the effects of item overlap. He concluded that item overlap did not have a general impact on validity but that some MCMI-II scales demonstrated better validity in nonoverlapping form (the Negativistic and Borderline scales in particular) and that some scales (the Paranoid in particular) performed best in the overlapping form. He concluded that the convergent and discriminant validities of these scales were established generally by the results of his study of 80 psychiatric inpatients. His findings also indicated that the Antisocial and Negativistic scales of the MCMI-II performed better and represented significant improvements over the original MCMI-I scales. In the factor-analytic studies performed, he found that the MMPI factors reflected the *DSM–III–R* personality disorder clusters, whereas the MCMI-II scales yielded a factor structure that reflected Millon's (1969) dimensions of personality.

One MCMI personality scale that consistently has shown a low correlation with its MMPI counterpart has been the Compulsive scale. McCann (1992) examined the issues involved by examining the factor structure of both the MMPI and the MCMI-II scales on the same sample. Judging from his data, the low correlation can be explained partly by noting that the MMPI Compulsive scale does not measure the issue of restraint or the tendencies not to be gregarious and sensation-seeking.

A different approach to that of examining the similarities between the MMPI and the MCMI is to determine how these two inventories complement each other. A series of articles by Antoni and other Millon associates suggested that the MCMI can add to the information derived from the MMPI. Their investigations were based on data collected by approximately 175 clinicians on more than 3,000 patients. Their reports revealed a number of personality patterns that commonly occur with people obtaining particular MMPI profiles.

Patients who obtain an MMPI 28/82 code type (i.e., elevations on the Depression and Schizophrenia scales), for instance, can be characterized as depressed people who have difficulties being assertive. They often are stubborn, irritable, resentful, and moody and are typically thought to be in a state of inner turmoil. They are conflictual people who tend to feel guilty whenever their conflicts are externalized. Prone to depression, such individuals also may be anxious or agitated or demonstrate psychomotor retardation (Dahlstrom, Welsh, & Dahlstrom, 1972; Graham, 1977; Greene, 1980; Lachar, 1974).

A somewhat similar MMPI profile is the 24/42 code type (i.e., elevations on the Depression and Psychopathic Deviance scales). Like people with a 28/82 code type, these individuals are prone to have periods of guilt and depression. By contrast, however, these patients' depression commonly results from their being "caught" in some way (e.g., were fired from a job because of dishonesty) so that they are seen as "psychopaths in trouble." By nature, these individuals tend to be impulsive, unable to delay gratification, and have little respect for the norms of society. Substance abuse is common (Dahlstrom et al., 1972; Graham, 1977; Greene, 1980; Lachar, 1974).

For both of these two "depressed" MMPI profiles, three main MCMI-I styles have been reported (Antoni et al., 1985a, 1985b). The *interpersonally acting-out group* has elevated MCMI scores on the Antisocial and Narcissistic scales (Scales 5 and 6A). People in this group are arrogant, aggressive, and self-centered and may drift toward paranoidlike behaviors if they are repeatedly unable to secure support and reinforcement. The *interpersonally acting-in group* has elevated scores on the Schizoid scale of the MCMI. In addition to the MMPI characterization, these individuals also can be described as people who think of themselves as weak and ineffectual and tend to become alienated from both themselves and others. Decompensation for this group is expected to take the form of a schizotypal personality pattern with behavioral eccentricities and cognitive slippage. Finally, the *emotionally acting-out group* has elevations on the Negativistic, Dependent, and Histrionic scales of the MCMI (Scales 8A, 3, and 4). They can be described as having a labile affect and being inclined to vacillate between depressive moods and euphoric or hostile episodes.

Another common MMPI profile that is associated with a depressed affect is the 27/72 (i.e., elevations on the Depression and the Psychasthenia scales). Individuals who obtain such a profile are usually described as anxious worriers and indecisive, insecure people who have a dependent personality style. They have high expectations of themselves and feel guilty when they fail to accomplish their personal goals. Their depression typically involves a pessimistic view of their problems, a tendency to brood and ruminate, and complaints of tiredness and exhaustion (Dahlstrom et al., 1972; Graham, 1977; Greene, 1980; Lachar, 1974).

In terms of the MCMI-I, three different styles of the MMPI 27/72 profile have been noted (Levine et al., 1985). The *fearful dependent group* has elevated scores on the Avoidant, Schizoid, and Dependent scales of the MCMI (Scales 2A, 1, and 3). These individuals typically have strong dependency needs and would like to be accepted by others, but their fear of rejection makes them apprehensive. As a result, they usually are loners who withdraw from others to defend against possible rejection.

The *conforming-dependent group* is characterized by elevations on the Compulsive and Dependent scales of the MCMI (Scales 7 and 3). These people react to the risk of rejection by submitting to the wishes of others and conforming to societal norms rather than avoiding interpersonal relationships. Finally, Levine et al. noted a third group characterized by elevations on the Negativistic and the Dependent scales of the MCMI-I (Scales 8A and 3). These *ambivalent dependent individuals* deal with interpersonal risks by becoming conflictual, vacillating in their moods, and acting out their frustrations.

Individuals characterized by MMPI code 78/87 are introspective worriers. Harboring feelings of inferiority, such people are likely to interact in a passive dependent manner and to be nervous when they are with others. They typically have rich fantasy lives and spend a great deal of time daydreaming. The diagnosis of a schizoid personality or a schizophrenic reaction is common (Dahlstrom et al., 1972; Graham, 1977; Greene, 1980; Lachar, 1974).

With the 78/87 MMPI group, Antoni et al. (1987) found three patient groups that were distinguishable in terms of their MCMI scores. The *interpersonally acting-in group* has elevated scores on the Schizoid and Avoidant scales of the MCMI-I. In addition to the inferiority feelings and passive dependence described by the MMPI scores, these individuals can be characterized by withdrawal and lack of interpersonal relationships; their insecurities surface as a lack of assertiveness and an inability to act in a decisive and self-initiating manner. By contrast, Antoni et al. uncovered two other groups that tend to dissipate their issues in emotional ways. The *emotionally acting-out group* has elevations on the Negativistic, Histrionic, and Avoidant scales of the MCMI-I. Caught in a conflict between their dependency and strivings toward autonomy, these individuals tend to have labile affect and to vacillate between angry defiance and feelings of guilt accompanied by inner turmoil. Finally, there was a group with primary elevations on the Avoidant and Dependent scales of the MCMI that was labeled the *emotionally acting-in group*. Antoni et al. conceptualized such individuals as struggling with a conflict between taking the risk of relating interpersonally or leading a life of loneliness and isolation. In the authors' minds, these are people who not only feel inadequate about their own abilities but also have a great fear of rejection so that they find it difficult to establish interdependent relationships with others.

Finally, the MMPI code type 89/98 (i.e., elevations on the Schizophrenia and Hypomania scales) also has been examined (Antoni et al., 1986). This profile usually is characterized by a lability of mood, confusion, disorientation, restlessness, indecisiveness, and hyperactivity. Typical individuals are fearful of relating to others and engage in excessive daydreaming instead of developing strong social ties. Their reality testing may be marginal, and autistic thinking and hallucinations or delusions may be present. They are self-centered and infantile, often demanding a great deal of attention and becoming resentful and hostile when their demands are not met. Although they have a need to achieve, feelings of inferiority and inadequacy often contribute to a mediocre performance. Projection, regression, and inappropriate affect are common. Diagnostically, they are mostly categorized as either schizophrenic or manic (Graham, 1977; Greene, 1980; Lachar, 1974).

Data collected by Antoni et al. (1986) showed a set of six MCMI-I profiles that appeared most frequently with people obtaining the 89/98 MMPI profile. These groups were further refined such that the individuals were characterized primarily as narcissistic (i.e., an elevation on Scale 5 of the MCMI), antisocial (i.e., an elevation on Scale 6A), or dependent/negativistic (i.e., elevations on Scales 3, 8A, or both).

The information from the MCMI-I then was used to further explain these individuals' style. In the case of narcissists, the manic- and schizophreniclike clinical picture was thought to be fueled by feelings of grandiosity and a disregard for social constraints. When their charm is not impressive to others and their arrogant presentation does not obtain the needed support, these individuals respond with the defensive picture drawn by the MMPI or by acting-out behaviors such as substance abuse.

Respondents with a primarily antisocial personality style make up the largest group. The psychopathology was said to be driven by a mistrust of others and an angry rejection of social norms. In their view of the world as cruel and competitive, these individuals feel that they have to compensate for their inner sense of weakness by avoiding close relationships and projecting blame.

Finally, the dependent/negativistic personality substrate was thought to explain the clinical syndrome described by the MMPI as a response to conflicts over dependency. Anticipating disillusionment in their desperate need for closeness and support, such individuals become suspicious of others and fearful of their domination. The inner turmoil caused by their unresolvable conflict eventually is translated into the social, thought process, and mood disturbances described by the MMPI.

The MCMI and the Diagnostic Inventory of Personality

The Diagnostic Inventory of Personality (DIPS) is a psychiatric questionnaire containing 171 items and designed to measure clinical syndrome (Axis I) groups (e.g., alcohol abuse, drug abuse, schizophrenia, paranoia, affective disorders, anxiety disorders). It has three scales tapping personality (Axis II) pathology (i.e., the Withdrawn Character, Immature Character, and Neurotic Character scales). The DIPS has been administered to psychiatric patients who also took the MCMI-I. The pattern of correlations showed the DIPS to measure the same clinical syndromes as those measured by the MCMI-I scales (Leroux, Vincent, McPherson, & Williams, 1990).

The MCMI and the SCL-90

There also has been some interest in examining the SCL-90 (Derogatis, 1983) and the MCMI. According to Millon (1982), only four of the SCL-90 scales are modestly related (correlations in the .60s) to scales of the MCMI-I. Of these, the Depression scale is again noteworthy, having commonalities with the Psychotic Depression, Dysthymia, Negativistic, and Borderline scales of the MCMI-I. Wetzler et al. (1989) found the Dysthymia scale of the MCMI-I and the Depression scale of the SCL-90 to be equally efficient in diagnosing major depressions.

Additionally, Millon (1982) reported modest correlations between the SCL-90's Interpersonal Sensitivity scale and the Avoidant, Negativistic, Schizotypal, Borderline, Psychotic Thinking, and Psychotic Depression scales of the MCMI-I. Anxiety, as measured by the SCL-90, seemed similar to the Anxiety, Psychotic Depression, and Borderline scales of the MCMI-I. Finally, the Psychotic Thinking and Psychoticism scales were modestly related (Millon, 1982). A factor analysis of both scales together has led to two interbattery factors thought to represent anxious depression and emotionality, and paranoid thinking (Strauman & Wetzler, 1992).

The MCMI and the California Psychological Inventory

Because the MCMI provides measures of personality styles, it should be related to other personality trait inventories such as the California Psychological Inventory (CPI). Holliman and Guthrie (1989) administered both the MCMI-I and the CPI to 237 college students. As expected, they reported a significant overlap in the variance between the two tests such that about 40% of the variance of either test could be accounted for by the other.

The measures of social withdrawal and detachment of the MCMI-I were predictably related to low scores on the interpersonal interaction scales of the CPI. Specifically, the Schizoid, Avoidant, and Dependent scales of the MCMI-I correlated negatively with the Class I scales of the CPI (i.e., the Dominance, Capacity for Status, Sociability, Social Presence, Social Acceptance, and Sense of Well-Being scales). The Histrionic, Narcissistic, and Antisocial scales, on the other hand, were positively correlated with these Class I scales of the CPI. Another significant finding was that the MCMI-I Compulsive scale was associated with higher scores on the Class II scales of the CPI (i.e., Responsibility, Socialization, Self-Control, Tolerance, Good Impression, and Communality). Holliman and Guthrie (1989) felt that the Compulsive scale may be a measure of good adjustment to some degree, at least with a college population. Finally, the Negativistic scale of the MCMI-I showed its highest correlations with scales related to delinquency and criminal behavior (negatively correlated with Responsibility, Socialization, Achievement via Conformance, and Intellectual Efficiency).

The MCMI and the Psychopathy Checklist, Revised

When both of these instruments have been given to convicts, the Psychopathy Checklist, Revised (PCL-R) total scores correlated most highly with the Antisocial scale of the MCMI-II. Significant associations also were found between the PCL-R total scores and the Narcissistic, Aggressive, Negativistic, Borderline, Paranoid, Drug Dependence, Thought Disorder, and Delusional Disorder scales (Hart et al., 1991).

The MCMI and the Profile of Mood States

Correlations between the MCMI-I and the Profile of Mood States (POMS) also are available. For example, associations have been found between the Avoidant and Negativistic scales of the MCMI and the Depression and Confusion scales of the POMS (McMahon & Davidson, 1985a). The Anxiety, Dysthymia, and Psychotic Depression scales were found to be related to the Tension, Depression, Fatigue, and Confusion scales of the POMS (McMahon & Davidson, 1986a). All of the reported relationships, however, were modest: The best correlation was .56.

The MCMI and the Beck Depression Inventory

A reasonable amount of agreement has been found between the Dysthymia scale of the MCMI-I and the Beck Depression Inventory (J. O. Goldberg et al., 1987; O'Callaghan et al., 1990).

The MCMI and the Alcohol Use Inventory

Donat (1994) cluster-analyzed Alcohol Use Inventory (AUI) scores on alcoholic inpatients for whom he also had MCMI-II results. Using this method, he characterized five different groups on the basis of AUI and MCMI-II scores.

The first group typically obtained one single elevation on the Gregarious scale of the AUI and tended to be histrionic-narcissists on the MCMI-II. These features, and the absence of high scores on other scales, suggest that drinking serves a social function for this group. Despite the fact that these patients may be healthier emotionally than other groups, their reliance on alcohol to fulfill interpersonal needs may pose a problem in their recovery. There is the potential, however, for the productive use of social methods of recovery maintenance, such as Alcoholics Anonymous.

The second group was characterized by elevations on the marital scales of the AUI and no notable features on the MCMI-II. The findings suggested a vicious cycle in which the drinking aggravated existing marital problems, and the marital problems, in the patients' view, provoked them to drink. Because the quality of the marital relationship appeared to be tied to the drinking, consideration of the use of marital or couples therapy was recommended.

By contrast, the third cluster was represented by individuals who had low scores on the same marital scales of the AUI, but MCMI-II scores showed antisocial, aggressive, and drug-abusing tendencies. These patients were considered to be more self-directed and likely to place a high value on willpower and self-control. They typically are less concerned with the impact that their substance abuse may have on others and may experience caregivers as intrusive. For such patients, the treatment should emphasize the fact that the substance abuse interferes with their ability to reach their personal goals. They must learn that in order to be in command of their lives, they must control their substance-abusing tendencies.

In contrast to the first group, the fourth group is characterized by low scores on the Gregarious scale and high scores on many of the other scales of the AUI (i.e., scales measuring compulsiveness, sustained drinking, loss of control, role maladaptation, and the experience of delirium and hangovers). MCMI-II scores showed elevations on the Avoidant, Antisocial, Negativistic, Self-Defeating, and Borderline scales. These profiles indicated high levels of emotional distress and few coping skills. The patients reported that they often drank alone and appeared to match the advanced stage of the traditional disease process of alcoholism. Therapy designed to manage the patients' social anxiety and depression was recommended.

Finally, the fifth group tended to be older and to have more women than the other groups. People in this group were characterized by low scores on the Gregarious scale and elevations on a scale indicating that the patients drink to manage their moods. The MCMI-II composite had an elevation on the Compulsive scale and relatively low scores on the Narcissistic, Antisocial, Aggressive, and Negativistic scales. Patients with such profiles tended to deny the presence of alcohol-related problems. The emphasis appeared to be one of maintaining strict control over emotions. The findings suggested that these individuals will drink alone in their struggle with emotional distress. Therapeutic interventions to help them deal with their distress also may be helpful with this group.

The MCMI and the Eating Disorder Inventory

Lundholm (1989) gave the MCMI-I and the Eating Disorder Inventory to a group of 135 undergraduate women. Findings showed that elevations of the Alcohol Abuse scale were associated with significantly higher scores on the Interoceptive Awareness, Ineffectiveness, Maturity Fears, Interpersonal Distrust, and Bulimia scales of the Eating Disorder Inventory.

The MCMI and Projective Techniques

We often have used the MCMI in conjunction with projective tests. Information about a particular person obtained from different sources can be used to either support some finding or add additional information about the patient. When scores on the Dysthymia scale of the MCMI are elevated, for instance, we search for other evidence of depression. Perhaps the presenting complaints involved affective symptoms, the Rorschach Inkblot Test was constricted and showed a repeated use of the blackness of the inkblot as a determinant, and the Thematic Apperception Test (TAT) stories betrayed a preoccupation with problematic or depressing situations. Having such confirmation from several sources of information increases our level of confidence on the relevance of our test findings and allows us to decide eventually, for instance, whether the patient meets *DSM–IV* criteria for a particular disorder.

The fact that projective tests can be used to gather evidence about the clinical syndromes is well-known and needs no further discussion here. At one time we strongly believed that clients' personality styles were reflected in the way they performed on projective instruments. For example, in the first edition of this book, we proposed that schizoid or avoidant personality styles would lead to signs of social detachment on the projective tests, such as a low number of human responses on the Rorschach or the portrayal of distant relationships on the TAT. A submissive and noncompetitive way of relating to others possibly could be shown in the TAT stories of dependent individuals. Histrionic individuals were expected to be superficial and have a great deal of color on the Rorschach, as well as to generate dramatic and interesting TAT stories. The grandiosity of narcissists and their arrogant style of relating theoretically should be apparent in the projective measures. The Rorschach of compulsive individuals undoubtedly would be too constricted and reveal a preoccupation with detail.

Intent on supporting some of our hypotheses, we collected MCMI and Rorschach results on a group of 670 patients referred for emotional evaluations (Choca, Van Denburg, Mouton, & Shanley, 1992). We assembled eight groups representing individuals with schizoid, avoidant, dependent, histrionic, narcissistic, competitive/antisocial, compulsive, and negativistic personalities. The assignment to a particular group was made by an experienced clinician on the basis of both MCMI and historical data. Patients' personalities were further characterized with regard to their functional level as constituting only personality traits, a personality style, or a personality disorder. Each respondent then was matched with a control patient who had the same primary Axis I psychopathology but a different personality makeup.

Having compiled the 8 personality groups and the 8 control groups with mixed personalities, we examined the effect that the personality had on Rorschach variables. We had at our disposal the 87 different variables and markers that are generated by the Hermann Rorschach computer program (Choca & Garside, 1992) and that include all the Exner scores and ratios. Because the personality groups were not large enough to support the use of all 87 variables, we selected the Rorschach variables to be used on theoretical grounds. The number of supportable variables and the variables selected varied from one personality group to another. For our schizoid group with 34 individuals, for instance, we selected the total number of responses (R), the number of unusual or minus form quality responses (FQu and FQ−), the number of whole human responses (H and (H)), and the number of responses that used the white section of the inkblot (S) as the variables to be compared. The histrionic group was larger ($n = 66$) and supported the selection of seven variables (R, FQu, FQ−, FC, CF, C, and W). The method was repeated for the other six personality styles as well.

Our findings showed almost no significant differences between the personality and control groups. This is not to say that some of the protocols were not casebook examples of what a particular personality should look like on the Rorschach. Some of our histrionic respondents, for example, did show the elevated number of whole and color responses that theoretically would be expected. The problem was that many other histrionic respondents did not show those signs and that the entire group was not different from its control. Although Rorschach experts routinely refer to this test as measuring personality variables, it is noteworthy that none of the personologists support the use of this test as a measure of personality style (e.g., see the section on problems in projective methods in McCrae & Costa, 1990).

In spite of our own findings, we still routinely use the Rorschach and think that the scores of this test give valuable clinical information. Our experience has taught us to remain a bit closer to the actual data than we would have in the past. An elevated number of whole responses, for instance, undoubtedly says something about the examinee and may even indicate that the person tends to have a global and superficial view of the world; the jump from that kind of interpretation to saying that the person is histrionic, however, is probably not warranted. On the basis of our findings, we strongly advise against interpreting negative Rorschach findings: The assertion that a person is not schizoid, compulsive, or negativistic because the Rorschach protocol is not what theoretically would be expected for that personality style is risky.

That projective tests can be a good complement to the information obtained from psychiatric questionnaires such as the MCMI clearly can be seen by the fact that such combination represents the most popular clinical battery used with psychiatric patients. In such a battery, the Rorschach allows clinicians to evaluate the quality of patients' thought processes and their approaches to life. The psychiatric inventory typically provides a sophisticated way of looking at what patients think of themselves. TAT stories are often an indication of the life problems that the individuals are facing and the way those issues play out in their interpersonal relationships.

Determining what the usual personality style of a particular individual is can help us decide which of the feasible interpretations of a particular marker in the projective techniques is the most valid. Constriction on the Rorschach, for example, can be the result of personality traits or the reflection of an acute emotional state such as a depression. If patients who had a constricted Rorschach protocol are, according to the MCMI, highly compulsive, we still would have to wonder about the degree to which the lack of determinants and the underproductivity were the result of their compulsive bent as opposed to a reflection of the lack of energy and enthusiasm that often accompanies a despondent mood. If the patients were to have almost any other personality style, however, the constriction of the protocol could be confidently seen as indicating depression.

Similar considerations can be applied to evaluating patients' contact with reality. Blatantly psychotic responses are, of course, pathological regardless of patients' personality styles. Milder forms of thought disturbances, however, are probably much more likely to be present with histrionic or negativistic individuals than with compulsive individuals. Thus, in our experience, the protocols of histrionic patients are bound to contain personal references, boundary problems in terms of mixing one response with another, and color or movement responses that are not carefully linked to the form of the inkblot. Thus, we are much more prone to disregard mild lapses in thought processes when patients have a histrionic personality style than another style.

9

Case Reports

In this chapter we offer some of our own testing reports as examples of how the MCMI can be integrated with historical information or data obtained from projective measures into descriptive and useful narratives. We have changed the identifying information to protect the client's confidentiality.

The case study presentations begin with the report of psychological testing. Each case report contains a thorough review of the history and a discussion of the findings. A review of the logical steps taken in interpreting the MCMI data follows. Finally, we present the raw data for each case so that clinicians may conduct their own analyses. For the raw data presented, the Rorschach Inkblot Test results were done with the help of the Hermann computer program sold by Multi-Health Systems (Choca & Garside, 1992). The Thematic Apperception Test (TAT) results were taped at the time of administration and were transcribed thereafter.

In writing reports it often is useful to have a scheme around which to organize them. This idea has been described in detail elsewhere (Choca & Van Denburg, 1996) and involves the use of one of four different organizational strategies that we label *personality, developmental, motivational,* and *diagnostic.*

The typical report using a *personality scheme* begins with a description of the individual's basic personality style. Once the personality has been described, the rest of the data can be presented as they relate to the personality style. If there was a clear precipitant to the onset of the symptomatology, the importance of that event often can be discussed in terms of the values and assumptions of the individual's personality style. Using this model, the psychopathology can be explained as exaggerations of the basic personality style, as maladjustments caused by the interaction between that personality style and the environment, or as some reflection of the personality traits.

The common thread in the different parts of the report in the *developmental scheme* is the tracing of the client's history to explain how the client developed the way he or she did. This scheme may involve speculations about the etiological underpinnings of the personality style, a description of the personality style per se, and a review of the effect that the personality style might have had during the different stages of development to bring about the experiences that the individual had at that stage. The psychopathology then is understood in terms of a failure to complete successfully developmental tasks along the way.

The *motivational scheme* is particularly useful when the client's life has revolved around striving toward a particular conscious or unconscious goal. In such cases, the report can be organized around the client's striving. The personality then may be seen as resulting from such a striving (e.g., the person who resolved early in life that he or she would avoid making mistakes and developed a compulsive personality style) or as influencing the different attempts that the client has made to reach his or her goal. The psychopathology then can be explained as reactions the person had to difficulties in striving for the goal.

Finally, with patients presenting a difficult differential diagnosis question, it may be useful to follow what we call a *diagnostic organizational scheme*. Such a report would revolve around the issues involved in the differential diagnosis, perhaps discussing the different criteria for the diagnoses under consideration and offering the evidence that the testing has provided in support of or against each of the criteria. This system may be used for the Axis I syndromes first and then repeated for the Axis II personality structure.

These schemes should be thought of as a way of conceptualizing and organizing the report and should not inhibit readers from developing some of their own. In addition, the manner of presentation can be varied for any one of the schemes; in other words, a report following the personality scheme does not always need to begin with a description of the personality, as suggested earlier, because one could do it just as well in the reverse order. The schemes also could be intermixed (e.g., the report of a schizophrenic using the diagnostic organizational scheme could switch, at some point, into the developmental scheme and discuss how the psychotic episodes have prevented the individual from accomplishing various developmental tasks in his or her life).

We chose the cases that follow because they represent the different kinds of pathology rather than because they exemplify the different diagnostic schemes, but clinicians may be able to see more than one organization being used in the reports.

Thought Disturbance in a Schizoid Personality Disorder

Referral Information

Donald Green was a 26-year-old black man who was admitted into the psychiatric unit while he was in a psychotic state. Mr. Green had come to believe that he could control the weather with his thoughts. He placed tapes across his chest in response to the request of the voices he heard. Four days before admission, Mr. Green shaved his head because he believed there were "things" living in his head and that he could get rid of them by doing that. He admitted feeling that he was "more than one person" and could hear "two voices," one male and one female, when he spoke. He also tended to be somatically preoccupied: He reportedly had been suffering from headaches and abdominal pain for some time and was complaining of a cracking noise in his left shoulder.

A psychological evaluation was requested to help with the differential diagnosis. In particular, the issue was whether Mr. Green was suffering from a schizophrenic disorder. At the time of the testing, Mr. Green was being treated with Stelazine.

Psychiatric History

This was the first time that the patient had received psychiatric treatment. Mr. Green denied abusing alcohol or drugs and knew of no family member who had a history of psychiatric problems.

Medical History

Mr. Green was hospitalized at a medical hospital in July 1985 with complaints of headaches and abdominal pain. That was the only other time he had been in the hospital. During the current admission, a computed tomography scan of the brain and an electroencephalogram were taken and found to be within normal limits.

Family History

Mr. Green had considerable difficulty detailing his history. He often claimed not to know what different members of the family did for a living or other important pieces of information. At other times, his answers were confusing, and it took great effort to clarify what he was trying to say.

Mr. Green was born in New York City and was raised in the Brooklyn area. He was the oldest of six children, who were raised together, but he had three younger stepsisters who were not raised with him. Mr. Green was born out of wedlock. His biological father was a 53-year-old machinist whom the patient saw annually. His father left the relationship with Mr. Green's mother early on, married someone else, and had three daughters from that marriage.

Mr. Green's mother was a 51-year-old woman employed by a hospital in Brooklyn. He described her as being very religious and seemed to have positive feelings toward her. She married when Mr. Green was young but is now divorced.

The ex-husband, Mr. Green's stepfather, was in his 50s. Mr. Green referred to this man as his "father" because he was the male figure in the home throughout most of Mr. Green's childhood. The stepfather worked as a mail carrier but quit his job some time ago and moved out of state. Mr. Green therefore did not see him frequently.

The patient was the oldest of his siblings and was followed by William. A 25-year-old single man, William did not have a place to stay and had been living in the streets. Gwen was Mr. Green's 24-year-old sister who was single and lived with him. He characterized her as a "pain" because she had a "big mouth." Gwen worked at the same Brooklyn hospital as their mother. David was a 22-year-old Marine stationed elsewhere. A 21-year-old brother, Rodney, obtained a college degree on a football scholarship and lived in California. Brenda, aged 9, was the last of the siblings raised together. She was still living with her mother.

Mr. Green was married in 1983. The marriage lasted 2 years. His ex-wife was still single, and they saw each other fairly often. She was characterized as being straightforward. They had a 2-year-old daughter who was not a problem.

Mr. Green readily admitted that he had no friends. For social enjoyment, he went out dancing but picked different partners and did not have a steady companion.

Educational History

While he was in high school in Brooklyn, Mr. Green worked just hard enough to get by. He was never placed in a special education program, but he always was a below-average student. The patient attended a technical school for 2 years, but he ended up feeling "wiped out" and dropped out to go to work.

Occupational History

Mr. Green worked at a freight company for 9 years until that company was purchased by a trucking company. For the 6 months that preceded his hospitalization, he had been employed as a dispatcher by the latter company and apparently had had no problems with his job.

Mental Status Examination

At the time of this evaluation, Mr. Green was alert, oriented, verbal, and coherent. His speech and language functions were intact. The other intellectual functions examined (e.g., memory, figure reproductions, mental control, abstractions) also were within normal limits. His ability to perform calculations could not be tested because he refused to cooperate: He stated that he never calculated anything and would not make the necessary effort. His thought processes were jumbled at times, and his thought content was marked by delusions and auditory hallucinations. He was evasive and superficial. Affective responses often were inappropriate in that he sometimes joked constantly and refused to take the testing seriously. At other times, he seemed angry with the examiner. His mood was generally within normal limits and had a good range of emotions. Anger, however, was prevalent in his comments and sarcastic remarks. There was no suicidal or homicidal ideation. He was mildly restless and needed to stand up or walk around several times during the testing. Although he tried to appear relaxed, he seemed tense and apprehensive about the testing. He had no insight and claimed that there was nothing wrong with him, even when he spoke of fairly severe psychiatric symptoms. Mr. Green was only minimally cooperative; he often tried to avoid having to give information and completed the entire procedure rapidly.

Discussion

Unfortunately, all the data obtained was consistent with the presence of a schizophrenic process. About the only requirement that did not appear to be met for a schizophrenic disorder was that of duration: Mr. Green had not been in a psychotic state for 6 months at the time of the evaluation.

Specifically, Mr. Green showed a defective contact with reality, which was clinically obvious in his auditory hallucinations, deluded thinking, and possible somatic delusions. His Rorschach results, on the other hand, uncovered vague and confused thinking as well as occasional illogical reasoning. As seen on this test, his communications often were so egocentric that they seemed not to be intended to share information: His thinking frequently could be understood only after repeated questioning to clarify all of the steps in the chain of associations that he had not communicated.

Mr. Green seemed bizarre, both inside and outside of the testing. This effect often was created by the content of his responses, as was the case when he made several inappropriate sexual responses on the Rorschach. At other times, the bizarre quality was produced by the lability of the affect and by the defenses that he was using. The lability left the examiner off-balance, not knowing what to expect next. On the Rorschach, a constriction and an inability to share his feelings and use his psychic resources was intermixed with an uncontrolled expression of emotions. On the surface, the mood lability materialized in the following manner: It seemed as if Mr. Green first attempted to deny troublesome thoughts through humor. He repeatedly made humorous discounting remarks about the testing to the examiner, not taking the diagnostic procedure seriously. This defense did not last long, and he eventually projected his discomfort through sarcasm or a mildly insulting comment about the procedure or the examiner.

Almost all his MCMI pathology scale scores were elevated, showing that, even by his own assessments, Mr. Green was having many emotional problems and functioning poorly. In fact, the scores were so elevated that they probably constituted a "cry for help," an attempt on Mr. Green's part to communicate that things were not going well with him.

As far as his personality structure was concerned, Mr. Green's scores have to be taken with caution. The elevations he obtained showed negativistic, schizoid, avoidant, and dependent components in his personality. It is possible that some of these traits had been acutely exacerbated by the patient's psychotic state because he might have become more isolated, distrusting, and resentful as a result of his psychosis. As a result, the validity of the personality findings will remain questionable until the acute episode goes into remission.

If the personality style remains as shown by the MCMI after remission, the patient would be seen as having a resentful, introversive, and insecure personality. Individuals with similar styles tend to be moody and to change their overall feelings without any obvious reason. At times, they may be friendly and engaging; they then become angry and resentful; later yet, they may feel guilty and contrite. The cycle is completed when they again become friendly and cooperative. A different substyle of the same basic personality makeup can be observed in individuals who vent their resentment through obstructionistic maneuvers that allow them to dissipate their anger without threatening their interpersonal support.

Most of these individuals have considerable feelings of insecurity. They tend to feel that others are more gifted, more capable, or more worthy. They feel, however, that if others get to know them, their own lack of value would be recognized and they would be rejected. Such individuals also tend to be nervous and uncomfortable when relating to others; they often feel that the other person does not really like them and that they are imposing. They frequently avoid some of the discomfort of relating by avoiding social relationships altogether. As a result, these people tend to lead lonely lives, being fairly distant from others, whom they view as untrustworthy and judgmental.

Individuals with similar MCMI scores are sensitive people. They would like to be appreciated by others and wish they could relate better than they do. They are caught, however, between wanting to depend on others but feeling that if they trust others, they will be hurt in the end. The emotional changes and other possible maladaptive developments are simply the surface behaviors that their basic conflict brings about.

All of Mr. Green's personality findings were consistent with what was known about his premorbid functioning. For example, Mr. Green admitted having no friends and his mother apparently described him as a "sensitive" individual who was "a loner, given to daydreaming." Thus, he seemed to have a schizoid personality disorder that preceded the psychotic episode.

The psychological strengths uncovered by the evaluation included the absence of a cognitive or memory impairment and at least average intellectual abilities. The patient also had a good work history and seemed to function, even if at a marginal level, before the onset of the psychosis. Therefore, it is possible that when the patient recovers from his psychotic episode, he may be able to return to his previous level of functioning.

Mr. Green's stories on the TAT were varied and did not suggest that he was preoccupied with any interpersonal issue. As a result, it was difficult to identify any troublesome situations in his life. Because he had several inappropriate sexual responses on the Rorschach and because the story evoked by the heterosexual intercourse card of the TAT involved the murder of the woman, the findings probably indicated difficulty with that kind of sexual intimacy.

Diagnostic Assignments and Recommendations

  I Schizophreniform disorder (295.40)
 II Schizoid personality disorder (301.20)
III No known contributing medical problems

Recommendations

Continued evaluation for the use of psychotropic medications seems indicated. In addition, the formation of a therapeutic alliance would be beneficial. The problem with the latter recommendation is that any kind of close relationship will be threatening to Mr. Green and therefore difficult to establish.

MCMI Interpretive Logic

Because the Validity Index score was 0, one could assume that the examinee read and understood the test items. The elevations on the Disclosure and Debasement scales suggest a tendency to exaggerate the symptomatology, which is further supported by the numerous elevations on the severe symptom scales. The finding is interpreted as a "cry for help" in the discussion. An 8A12A personality profile was obtained. Because the personality elevations might have been aggravated by the acute psychotic symptomatology, a note of caution is included in the report. Because there were signs of characterological dysfunction before the onset of the clinical syndrome, the personality structure is seen as constituting a personality disorder. The numerous elevations in the clinical syndrome scales, especially in the more severe syndromes, is consistent with the presence of a psychotic state.

Test Results

The Millon Clinical Multiaxial Inventory–Third Edition

Scale	Abbreviation	Base-Rate Score
Modifying Indices		
Disclosure	X	85**
Desirability	Y	65
Debasement	Z	95**
Validity (raw score)	V	0
Personality Style Scales		
Schizoid	1	99**
Avoidant	2A	92**
Dependent	3	88**
Histrionic	4	69
Narcissistic	5	64
Antisocial	6A	65
Compulsive	7	30
Negativistic	8A	105**
Severe Personality Scales		
Depressive	2B	83*
Aggressive	6B	45
Self-Defeating	8B	61
Schizotypal	S	85**
Borderline	C	81*
Paraphrenic	P	108**
Clinical Syndrome Scales		
Anxiety	A	109**
Somatoform	H	81*
Bipolar: Manic	N	119**
Dysthymia	D	94**
Alcohol Dependence	B	94**
Drug Dependence	T	97**
Posttraumatic Stress Disorder	R	76*
Severe Clinical Syndrome Scales		
Thought Disorder	SS	101**
Major Depression	CC	88**
Delusional Disorder	PP	114**

Note. Scores below the cutoff of 75 are shown without asterisks.
*Score elevation was between 75 and 84.
**Score elevation was 85 or above.

Rorschach Protocol

1. Card I   Reaction time: 16 s
SCORE: W oF   o   A   P   1.0
bee
INQUIRY: prongs, wings

2. Card I   Reaction time: 19 s
SCORE: W vF   o   Art   1.0
blotches on a blot folded in half
INQUIRY: just the way they looked

3. Card I   Reaction time: 39 s
SCORE: W oF   o   A   (P)PSV   1.0
INQUIRY: same thing, wing

4. Card I   Reaction time: 9 s
SCORE: W vF   u   Art
somebody sat in some ink or something
INQUIRY: it just looks like the mark that would be left if you sat on some
paint

5. Card II   Reaction time: 333 s
SCORE: D oF   o   Ad
butterfly
INQUIRY: tail end, long tail sticking out, something doesn't make sense
LOCATION: Bottom central detail

6. Card II   Reaction time: 201 s
SCORE: Dd oF   o   Ls   PER
Positions, church steeple
INQUIRY: I've seen church steeples shaped like that
LOCATION: midcenter

7. Card II   Reaction time: 57 s
SCORE: D oM   ao   (2)(H)   P   3.0
two ladies beating the drums; the titties are together, though.
Two ladies or two men, I don't know
INQUIRY: Heads, breasts, kettle; mixing ups some kind of potion.
Two witches.

8. Card II   Reaction time: 12 s
SCORE: D oF   o   Cg
Bow tie
INQUIRY: looks like one

9. Card II   Reaction time: 5 s
SCORE: D oF   u   (2)An   INC1.DV1   3.0
Two hearts joined together
INQUIRY: shape
I don't understand why you are showing me such pictures

Rorschach Protocol (contd.)

10. Card IV   Reaction time: 4 s
SCORE: W om   pu   Hh   2.0
A bell
INQUIRY: The Liberty Bell. Shape, little hanger in the middle. It's hung by here

11. Card IV   Reaction time: 61 s
SCORE: W oM.FD   p−   H.Sx   P   2.0
A guy laying on his back with his feet up and his dick between his legs
INQUIRY: laughs
Laying on his back? you are looking at his feet first

12. Card V   Reaction time: 5 s
SCORE: W oF   o   A   P
A bat
INQUIRY: wings

13. Card VI   Reaction time: 19 s
SCORE: D oFC'   −   Hh.Bl   (P)CONTAM   2.5
A blood stain on a fur rug, a bear skin rug
INQUIRY: the whole thing could be a blood stain rug? the way it looks
Bl? this spot here (darker cn)
LOCATION: bottom D

14. Card VI   Reaction time: 24 s
SCORE: Rejected
Blood stain
INQUIRY: part of Number 13, does not want by itself.

15. Card VII   Reaction time: 4 s
SCORE: W vF   u   Art   2.5
Black ink spot
INQUIRY: just the way it looks

16. Card VIII   Reaction time: 15 s
SCORE: D oF   o   (2)A   P
Pair of lions, like the Lowenbrau bottle with the two lions on it
INQUIRY: two cats on side

17. Card IX   Reaction time: 29 s
SCORE: W vm   −   Fi
A solar flare
INQUIRY: Shooting out. It can reach way over here too (expanding the gray D on top to W)

Rorschach Protocol (contd.)

18. Card X   Reaction time: 4 s
SCORE: W vCF   –   An.Sx   DV
Picture of the ovaries and stuff like that
INQUIRY: Two blue spots reminds me of a picture I drew in grammar school. I saw three levels, too.
? (can't explain)
LOC? wants W

19. Card X   Reaction time: 5 s
SCORE: D oF   o   Ls
Could be the Eiffel Tower too.
INQUIRY: the shape

Rorschach Score Sequence

Card	No.	Time (seconds)	Scoring					
I	1	46	W	oF	o	A	P	1.0
I	2	19	W	vF	o	Art		1.0
I	3	39	W	oF	o	A	(P)PSV	1.0
I	4	9	W	vF	u	Art		
II	5	333	D	oF	o	Ad		
II	6	201	Dd	oF	o	Ls	PER	
II	7	57	D	oM	ao	(2)(H)	P	3.0
II	8	12	D	oF	o	Cg		
II	9	5	D	vF	u	(2)An	INC1.DV1	3.0
IV	10	4	W	vm	pu	Hh		2.0
IV	11	61	W	oM.FD	p–	H.Sx	P	2.0
V	12	5	W	oF	o	A	P	
VI	13	19	D	oFC'	–	Hh.B1	(P)CON	2.5
VI	14	24	Rejected					
VII	15	4	W	vF	u	Art		2.5
VIII	16	15	D	oF	o	(2)A	P	
IX	17	29	W	vm	–	Fi		
X	18	4	W	vCF	–	An.Sx	DV1	
X	19	5	D	oF	o	Ls		

Rorschach Structural Summary

Global

	n	%
R	18	
Rejects	1	
P	5	28
(P)	2	11
(2)	3	17
Fr	0	0
rF	0	0
3r+(2)		17
RT Ach	23 s	
RT Ch	74 s	
AFR		29
Zf	10	
ZSum	18	

Location

	n	%
W	8	44
D	7	39
Dd	1	6
DW	2	11
S	0	0
POSITION		
▲	18	100
◄	0	0
►	0	0
▼	0	0
DEV QUAL		
+	0	0
v/+	0	0
o	11	61
v	7	39
RATIOS		
W	8	
M	2	
W	8	
D	7	

Determinants

	n	%
M	2	11
FM	0	0
m	2	11
FT	0	0
TF	0	0
T	0	0
FY	0	0
YF	0	0
Y	0	0
FV	0	0
VF	0	0
V	0	0
FC'	1	5
C'F	0	0
C'	0	0
FC	0	0
CF	1	5
C	0	0
Cn	0	0
FD	1	5
F	12	63
Blends	1	
RATIOS		
a	1	6
p	2	11
M	2	
wtd C	1.0	
M+wtd C	3	
FM+m	2	
Y+T+V+C'	1	
ΣFMmYTVC'	3	
FC	0	
CF+C	1	

Contents

	n	%
CONT	10	
H	1	5
(H)	1	5
Hd	0	0
(Hd)	0	0
A	4	18
(A)	0	0
Ad	1	5
(Ad)	0	0
Ab	0	0
Al	0	0
An	2	9
Art	3	14
Ay	0	0
Bl	1	5
Bt	0	0
Cg	1	5
Cl	0	0
Ex	0	0
Fi	1	5
Fd	0	0
Ge	0	0
Hh	2	9
Ls	2	9
Na	0	0
Sc	0	0
Sx	3	14
Vo	0	0
Xy	0	0
RATIOS		
H+HD	2	
A+AD	5	
H+A	6	
HD+AD	1	
A%		23

Quality

	n	%
OF ALL		
+	0	0
o	10	55
u	4	22
−	4	22
OF F		
+	0	0
o	9	75
u	3	25
−	0	0
DV1	2	
DV2	0	
INC1	1	
INC2	0	
DR1	0	
DR2	0	
FAB1	0	
FAB2	0	
ALOG	0	
CON	1	
AB	0	
CP	0	
AG	0	
MOR	0	
CFB	0	
PER	1	
COP	0	
PSV	1	

Thematic Apperception Test Stories

1. A little boy sitting in a dark room wishing he had a violin and according to the picture he has got his violin and now he has to learn to read the music. I don't see no future there.

Thematic Apperception Test Stories (contd.)

2. I see a girl going to school and she is watching her parents fixing the yard or planting seeds for next summer. (Oh, there are two ladies.) One is going to school and one is watching the man work. The horse and the man be serious. I hope he will get good crops.

3BM. It looks like someone is praying, or either hurting, in pain, or they are looking for their keys and they are right by their foot and they don't see them. The lady is sitting in an awkward position hoping that she can find her keys and they are right next to her feet and she hasn't found them yet, but according to this picture she should see them.

4. I see a man and a woman standing outside of a doorway or a window. He is fixing to go get in some trouble he ain't got no business getting into and she is saying, "Baby, will you please wait and think about it?" He just froze there so he didn't go.

6BM. I don't see nothing in this one, just a lady and a man. The woman is looking out of the window, the guy is grabbing his hat or something, I don't know. It looks like half of this part was cut out. Maybe somebody died and they are both sad about it.

7BM. Father and son, the son is trying to do what he wants to do and the father is saying, "Look, would you listen? I got the gray hair here." Hopefully the guy will get wise.

8BM. It looks like somebody got shot and the doctor is trying to remove the bullet and the woman is walking away with the gun. I wouldn't come near, I don't know he might die.

10. A mother and daughter—I couldn't tell you what is happening in this picture. It looks like they are knee-deep in trouble for sure. It looks like she is whispering in her ear. I don't know what will happen.

12M. I can't tell if her eyes are open or closed. Are her eyes open or closed? Someone is laying on the bed and somebody came and knelt beside them in the bed; maybe he is trying to hypnotize her and showing his right hand. I don't know. The outcome of that is she should wake up.

13MF. Well, it looks like she did not wake up. He just killed her. Now he is upset at what he has done. The outcome of that is straight to jail. Do not pass go. You now collect $200.

16. Spades. Those who went bowling before would have wished they hadn't. This reminds me of space because the paper is blank, or a full moon because the paper is blank, that is about it.

Thematic Apperception Test Stories (contd.)

17BM. It looks like somebody is climbing a rope. They are pulling on a serious bill or coming down a rope and looking somewhere else as they do it. It is a fireman coming down a rope and he is trying to get to the squad before it becomes more than just a one alarm fire, so he is in a hurry. He forgot his clothes though. He was in a real hurry.

18BM. This I couldn't tell you nothing about. It looks like a fat man with a nice jacket. He has got hands all in his back. Somebody is grabbing him from behind. It looks like he is trying to get shook up real good there. No maybe he is going to jail. He is handcuffed and the cops got their hands on him taking him away.

Affective Disorder With a Dependent Personality Style

Referral Information

Paul D'Angelo was a 32-year-old White man who was admitted into the psychiatric ward after becoming paranoid at his job. The patient explained that when a wallet belonging to another employee was stolen, a supervisor threatened to fire all the employees unless the wallet was found. Even though he had nothing to do with the incident, he felt the need to openly deny that he had done anything wrong and thought that others were talking about him behind his back. He became tense and somewhat agitated and was not able to sleep well. He became insecure and indecisive and believed that he was unable to cope with the demands of his daily life.

On admission into the unit, Mr. D'Angelo was described as guarded and agitated and was said to be preoccupied with his genitals. Flight of ideas and ideas of reference also were noted. He was diagnosed as having an agitated depression. At the time of the testing, he was on Navane and Norpramine.

Psychiatric History

Mr. D'Angelo was seen by a physician on consultation during a medical hospitalization in August 1986. At the time he complained of labile emotions and mood swings that had been bothering him for several months. The physician felt that the patient was depressed and prescribed antidepressants. Mr. D'Angelo received follow-up treatment from another physician and was kept on antidepressants. According to the patient, his emotional difficulties began after his wife and his mother quarreled; he had taken his wife's side and had not been on speaking terms with his mother before this admission.

Mr. D'Angelo admitted having a problem with excessive drinking in the past, but he has had only an occasional beer since he was put on medication last August.

The family history is remarkable in that Mr. D'Angelo's father reportedly has a bipolar affective disorder. His mother and three of his brothers were alleged to be alcoholics.

Medical History

The patient's medical history is unremarkable except for a bout of pneumonia that required hospitalization when he was 15 years old. A medical evaluation by a physician at a hospital the previous August led to negative findings. A computed tomography scan of the brain taken during this latest admission also was within normal limits.

Family History

Mr. D'Angelo was born and raised in the Los Angeles area, the youngest of five siblings in a Catholic Italian family. His 65-year-old father was in and out of hospitals all of his life. The father was a building inspector and worked for the city until 4 years ago. His father was characterized as a mild-mannered individual, a "weak" person needing to take direction from the patient's mother. One of the issues that led to the falling out with his mother was Mr. D'Angelo's disapproval of her decision to put his father in a nursing home. In spite of the patient's feeling that the nursing home is the best place for his father, he resented that the decision was made only on the basis that the mother was "tired of him." The father had been in the nursing home since the previous July.

Mr. D'Angelo's mother (aged 57 years) used to be a clerk at a community center but was not currently employed. The patient talked about her as a "good mother" in spite of her drinking six beers every day. He characterized all family members as inclined to ignore their problems. It was apparently this characteristic that led to the fight between his wife and his mother a year ago: His wife reportedly confronted her mother-in-law about the fact that many of the siblings were drinking excessively, an issue that the mother allegedly did not want to face.

The oldest of the siblings is Tom (aged 39). Tom is an alcoholic and an inpatient in the psychiatric ward at the same hospital where the patient is now; Tom was in detox at the time of the testing. A plumber, Tom had difficulty finding work during the past 5 years, perhaps because of his alcohol abuse. Tom is married and has two children. As an adult, the patient has been closer to Tom than to any of the other brothers. The frequency of their contacts, however, varied considerably depending on whether their wives were getting along well.

The second brother is 38-year-old Danny. Danny lives in Texas with his new wife. He is an epileptic on anticonvulsant medication and also is thought to be an alcoholic. Danny is a driver for a major beer company.

Frank (aged 37) is disabled with a left-sided partial hemiparesis. He was hurt when he dove into the shallow end of a swimming pool. Frank never married and is cared for by his mother.

The brother immediately preceding the patient is Tony, a 35-year-old handyman who lives in Montana. Tony is married and has two children. One of the children has a defect in the spinal cord that caused paralysis of the lower extremities.

Mr. D'Angelo married his current wife 9 years ago. The wife is a 33-year-old housewife. She was characterized as a beautiful woman who is outgoing, straightforward, and energetic and was thought to be very good to him. The D'Angelos have two children. Tiffany is 7 years old and Chip is 5. Both were doing well and had presented no problems.

Educational History

Mr. D'Angelo went to a Catholic elementary school and graduated from a public high school in Los Angeles. He was an "average" student and never had any significant difficulties in school.

Occupational History

After his high school graduation, Mr. D'Angelo went to work for a car dealership. He was first employed unloading new cars but was able to learn the repair work and became an assistant mechanic. He worked for that employer for 12 years, was very satisfied with his current position, and felt that his supervisor was happy with his work.

Mental Status Examination

At the time of the evaluation, the patient was alert, oriented, verbal, and coherent. His speech and language functions were intact. The other intellectual functions examined—including memory, calculations, figure reproductions, mental control, and abstractions—also were within normal limits. His thought process was orderly and effective. The thought content was unremarkable. The presence of paranoid delusions, ideas of reference, and preoccupation with his genitals was noted on admission. His affective responses always were appropriate. Mood was within normal limits and demonstrated a good range of emotions, but this apparently constituted a change from his previous dysphoria. There was no suicidal or homicidal ideation. Psychomotor activity was within normal limits at the time of the testing, although the patient reportedly was originally in an agitated state. Mr. D'Angelo was anxious, asked how he was doing on several occasions, and showed a fine hand tremor when he was required to draw figures. He associated this tremor with his being tense and claimed that he did not have it the rest of the time. He was friendly and cooperative and posed no problems during the test administration.

Discussion

The scores that Mr. D'Angelo obtained on the MCMI indicated that he has a dependent personality. Individuals with similar personalities assume that they are not very capable of taking care of themselves and must find someone who is benevolent and dependable and would support them, at least emotionally. They tend to form strong attachments to people who would then take a dominant role in decision making. They are followers rather than leaders and often are submissive in interpersonal affairs, shying away from highly competitive situations. Concerned with losing friends, they hide their feelings, especially when such feelings are aggressive or objectionable. These are unconceited people who try to be as congenial as possible to the people around them. Mr. D'Angelo is probably well liked but may be occasionally considered wishy-washy because he never takes a strong position on controversial issues. Similar individuals could be criticized for their inclination to be submissive, their lack of self-esteem, and their constant looking outside themselves for help.

Mr. D'Angelo has been able to establish himself well, both socially and occupationally, and leads a fairly independent life. As a result, his personality style cannot be considered dysfunctional or to constitute a personality disorder. Nevertheless, the dependent personality style can explain the kind of stress that Mr. D'Angelo has been under. It seemed that his mother was the all-powerful figure in his childhood home, the "stronghold" of the family on whom the patient had learned to depend. Although his loyalties have shifted to his wife and his acquired family, it seems that he still needs the support of his mother to feel comfortable. Thus, when the quarrel ensued between his mother and wife, Mr. D'Angelo's insecurities increased and he started having emotional problems. It is interesting that the issues at work revolved around the possible loss of support from another authority figure, a supervisor, and that the patient strongly wished to reassure everyone of his innocence so that there would be no chance that this support also would be compromised.

At the time of testing, Mr. D'Angelo was not actively psychotic. Nevertheless, several of his Rorschach responses showed faulty reality contact. Although the number of such responses was not extreme, it was significantly higher than the normal range. In addition, the patient often saw "eyes" as an important part of his responses and was reminded of a "mask" on many of the cards, both of which are thought to be associated with paranoid defenses.

The presence of anxiety and depression was repeatedly observed throughout the testing. For example, most of the TAT stories revolved around negative or depressive events such as a car accident, a man who is about to leave his wife, a son who leaves his mother, a dying father, a man who is emotionally distressed after having sex with a prostitute, and so on. Consistent with the preoccupation with his genitals that he demonstrated at the beginning of the hospitalization, his MCMI scores also indicated the presence of somatic concerns. Finally, there were indications that Mr. D'Angelo abuses alcohol as a way of defending against his anxieties.

On the positive side, there were no signs of cognitive deficits in the mental status examination. The impression was that Mr. D'Angelo had average intellectual capacities. That he also has achieved all of the major developmental milestones of the past is impressive. Thus, Mr. D'Angelo has established himself independently, has a good family and a good job, and has no great conflicts in his life. Once he has been able to reconstitute the sources of support that he needs, he may be able to return to his premorbid level of functioning.

Diagnostic Assignments and Recommendations

   I Major depression with psychotic features (296.34)
  II Dependent personality style with no personality disorder
 III No known medical problem contributing

Recommendations

Continued evaluation for the use of psychotropic medications to control the symptomatology seems indicated. In addition, Mr. D'Angelo may benefit from psychotherapy. Given his personality style, he will obtain support from a therapeutic relationship that is protective and guiding in a parental-like manner.

MCMI Interpretive Logic

Because the Validity Scale score was 0, the test gave no indications of the patient having difficulties understanding or responding appropriately to the items. The modifying indexes all were unremarkable. The personality profile (300) indicated a dependent personality, and the history showed that the patient had been highly functional and did not point to the presence of a personality disorder. Other elevations showed the patient to be depressed, anxious, and somatically preoccupied. The mild elevation of the Borderline scale was seen as resulting from mood instability rather than from any of the other aspects associated with the borderline personality disorder.

Test Results

The Millon Clinical Multiaxial Inventory–Third Edition

Scale	Abbreviation	Base-Rate Score
Modifying Indices		
Disclosure	X	60
Desirability	Y	65
Debasement	Z	26
Validity (raw score)	V	0
Personality Style Scales		
Schizoid	1	51
Avoidant	2	60
Dependent	3	80*
Histrionic	4	65
Narcissistic	5	28
Antisocial	6A	18
Compulsive	7	64
Negativistic	8A	24

The Millon Clinical Multiaxial Inventory–Third Edition (contd.)

Scale	Abbreviation	Base-Rate Score
Severe Personality Scales		
Depressive	2B	78*
Aggressive	6B	0
Self-Defeating	8B	61
Schizotypal	S	72
Borderline	C	78*
Paraphrenic	P	22
Clinical Syndrome Scales		
Anxiety	A	84*
Somatoform	H	92**
Bipolar: Manic	N	4
Dysthymia	D	84*
Alcohol Dependence	B	70
Drug Dependence	T	49
Posttraumatic Stress Disorder	R	57
Severe Clinical Syndrome Scales		
Thought Disorder	SS	58
Major Depression	CC	47
Delusional Disorder	PP	9

Note. Scores below the cutoff of 75 are shown without asterisks.
*Score elevation was between 75 and 84.
**Score elevation was 85 or above.

Rorschach Protocol

1. Card I   Reaction time: 0 s
SCORE: W oF   0   A   P   1.0
Wasp or bee
INQUIRY: Tail, wide wing span

2. Card I   Reaction time: 22 s
SCORE: W SoFT   0   (Ad)   1.0
Mask
INQUIRY: Of a wolf, outline, two sets of eyes, whiskers (?) shaggy outline; face of a wolf

3. Card I   Reaction time: 7 s
SCORE: W o   ma   0 Hh
Glider plane
INQUIRY: Flying over. They build them in such weird shapes these days

Rorschach Protocol (contd.)

4. Card II   Reaction time: 4 s
SCORE: D   oFC   0   (2)H   P   3.0
Two women, old
INQUIRY: In black dress and red faces. They could be two chickens, too, with the beaks

5. Card II   Reaction time: 3 s
Score: D   SvFC'   0   Hh   4.5
A night light in the blackness.
INQUIRY: Imprint of a lampshade in the middle of the dark
LOCATION: black and white center

6. Card II   Reaction time: 10 s
SCORE: D   oFMa   0   (2)(A)   (P)   3.0
Two chickens touching hands
INQUIRY: Looking at each other, from a cartoon

7. Card III   Reaction time: 10 s
SCORE: D   oF   –   Ad   3.0
Two people looking at each other
INQUIRY: The looks. Some kind of animal face or something at a distance; nostrils, eyes
LOCATION: the usual P including orange cn D. Patient is seeing only two faces

8. Card III   Reaction time: 3 s
SCORE: D   oMa   0   H   P
Two women
INQUIRY: the way they look

9. Card III   Reaction time: 4 s
SCORE: D   oF   u   (Ad)
Two eyes in a mask
INQUIRY: Mask of a wasp or something, face. It's a very ugly creature. Head of a wasp

10. Card IV   Reaction time: 15 s
SCORE: W   oF   0   (A)   P
A giant monster with a long tail hanging down the middle. Two big feet, two small claws
INQUIRY: Head, pinhead

11. Card V   Reaction time: 5 s
SCORE: W   oFC'   0   A   INC1   1.0
Butterfly with a woman's face, maybe
INQUIRY: In the fine blackness you can see two eyes and a nose

Rorschach Protocol (contd.)

12. Card V   Reaction time: 1 s
     SCORE: D   oMp   0   (2)Hd   2.5
     Two heads looking down
     INQUIRY: Forehead, nose and mouth

13. Card VI   Reaction time: 9 s
     SCORE: W   vmp   0   (A)   2.5
     A cat flattened out on the pavement after it got run down by a steam-roller

14. Card VI   Reaction time: 5 s
     SCORE: D   oMp   0   (2)Hd.Cg   6.0
     Two opposing faces looking out
     INQUIRY: King with a crown, long beard, nose

15. Card VI   Reaction time: 41 s
     SCORE: W   vF   u   An   2.5
     The inside anatomy of something
     INQUIRY: The amoebas or something, like that in somebody's body

16. Card VII   Reaction time: 4 s
     SCORE: D   oMp   0   (2)Hd   P   3.0
     Two women looking at each other
     INQUIRY: Faces, hats

17. Card VII   Reaction time: 4 s
     SCORE: D   oFM   p0   (2)(Ad)   3.0
     Two pigs looking away from each other
     INQUIRY: Round nose, something you might see in a cartoon, eye

18. Card VII   Reaction time: 2 s
     SCORE: D   oFM   p0   A   1.0
     Upside-down butterfly
     INQUIRY: Body, wings spread out
     LOCATION: bm D

19. Card VIII   Reaction time: 6 s
     SCORE: DdS-F   –   (Ad)   4.0
     Mask of a wasp or something
     INQUIRY: I see a face in here somewhere
     LOCATION: circular area taking the cn part of both of the top Ds (green and blue)

20. Card VIII   Reaction time: 7 s
     SCORE: D –F   –   Hd.Cg   3.0
     Face of a man with a hat
     LOCATION: top and cn D (green and blue)

Rorschach Protocol (contd.)

21. Card VIII   Reaction time: 2 s
SCORE: Dd omp   0   (2)Hd
Maybe a couple of legs fused together
INQUIRY: Couldn't find at first
LOCATION: tiny projections at cn bm of blue D

22. Card IX   Reaction time: 12 s
SCORE: W −F   −   Ad   ▼   5.5
Some kind of insect's face, upside-down
INQUIRY: Eyes, stinger, nose

23. Card IX   Reaction time: 20 s
SCORE: Dd vF   u   Na
Map of river with tributaries
INQUIRY: Lake, river, and tributaries
LOCATION: inside darker edge of orange D

24. Card IX   Reaction Time: 5 s
SCORE: Dd oMp   0   (2)Hd   4.5
Two faces looking away on the green part
INQUIRY: Nose, eyes
LOCATION: outside edge

25. Card X   Reaction time: 7 s
SCORE: D S+F   +   Hd
Two faces, one on bottom, one on top
INQUIRY: Eyes (yellow), nose (green cn), mustache (green)
LOCATION: white space with defined by pink in bm

26. Card X   Reaction time: 3 s
SCORE: D oFMa   0   (2)A   P   4.5
Two crabs meeting at top
INQUIRY: claws (green)
LOCATION: blue D

27. Card X   Reaction time: 13 s
SCORE: DdS oF   −   (Hd)   6.0
Face
INQUIRY: eyes (tiny circular s defined by blue D in cn and pink D
LOCATION: circular area bound by the pink D, the wishbone on top and the green D on bm

Rorschach Protocol (contd.)

28. Card X   Reaction time: 3 s
   SCORE: Dd oF   O   Hd
   Three sets of eyes
   LOCATION: tiny details in three different places of the blot
29. Card X   Reaction time: 11 s
   SCORE: D oFMa   O   (2)A   4.0
   Butting heads here (top gray)
   INQUIRY: like two animals butting heads

Rorschach Score Sequence

Card	No.	Time (seconds)	Scoring					
I	1	0	W	oF	o	A	P	1.0
I	2	22	W	SoFT	o	(Ad)		1.0
I	3	7	W	om	ao	Hh		
II	4	4	D	oFC	o	(2)H	P	3.0
II	5	3	D	SvFC'	o	Hh		4.5
II	6	10	D	oFM	ao	(2)(A)	(P)	3.0
III	7	10	D	−F	−o	Ad		3.0
III	8	3	D	oM	ao	H	P	
III	9	4	D	vF	u	(Ad)		
IV	10	15	W	oF	o	(A)	P	
V	11	5	W	oFC'	o	A	INC1	1.0
V	12	1	D	oM	po	(2)Hd		2.5
VI	13	9	W	vm	o	(A)		2.5
VI	14	5	D	oM	o	(2)Hd.Cg		6.0
VI	15	41	W	vF	u	An		2.5
VII	16	4	D	oM	po	(2)Hd	P	3.0
VII	17	4	D	oFM	po	(2)(Ad)		3.0
VII	18	2	D	oFM	po	A		1.0
VIII	19	6	DdS	vF	−	(Ad)		4.0
VIII	20	7	D	vF	−	Hd.Cg		3.0
VIII	21	2	Dd	om	po	(2)Hd		
IX	22	12	W	−F	−	Ad		▼5.5
IX	23	20	Dd	vF	u	Na		
IX	24	5	Dd	oM	po	(2)Hd		4.5
X	25	7	D	S+F	+	Hd		
X	26	3	D	oFM	ao	(2)A	P	4.5
X	27	13	DdS	−F	−	(Hd)		6.0

Rorschach Score Sequence (contd.)

Card	No.	Time (seconds)	Scoring				
X	28	3	Dd	oF	o	Hd	
X	29	11	D	oFMa	o	(2)A	4.0

Rorschach Structural Summary

Global	n	%	Location	n	%	Determinants	n	%	Contents	n	%	Quality	n	%
R	29		W	8	28	M	5	17	CONT	6		OF ALL		
Rejects	0		D	15	52	FM	5	17				+	1	0
			Dd	6	21	m	3	10	H	2	6	o	20	69
P	6	21	DW	0	0	FT	1	3	(H)	0	0	u	3	10
(P)	1	3	S	5	17	TF	0	0	Hd	8	26	–	5	17
						T	0	0	(Hd)	0	0			
(2)	10	34				FY	0	0	A	6	19	OF F		
Fr	0	0	POSITION			YF	0	0	(A)	3	10	+	1	0
rF	0	0	▲	28	97	Y	0	0	Ad	2	6	o	3	25
3r+(2)		34	◄	0	0	FV	0	0	(Ad)	4	13	u	3	25
			►	0	0	VF	0	0	Ab	0	0	–	5	42
RT Ach	10	s	▼	1	3	V	0	0	Al	0	0			
RT Ch	7	s				FC'	2	7	An	1	3			
						C'F	0	0	Art	0	0	DV1	0	
AFR		61	DEV QUAL			C'	0	0	Ay	0	0	DV2	0	
			+	1	3	FC	1	3	Bl	0	0	INC1	1	
			v/+	0	0	CF	0	0	Bt	0	0	INC2	0	
			o	18	62	C	0	0	Cg	2	6	DR1	0	
Zf	22		v	10	34	Cn	0	0	Cl	0	0	DR2	0	
ZSum	72					FD	0	0	Ex	0	0	FAB1	0	
						F	12	41	Fi	0	0	FAB2	0	
									Fd	0	0	ALOG	0	
						Blends	0		Ge	0	0	CON	0	
									Hh	2	6	AB	0	
			RATIOS			RATIOS			Ls	0	0	CP	0	
			W	8		a	5	17	Na	1	3	AG	0	
			M	5		p	6	21	Sc	0	0	MOR	0	
									Sx	0	0	CFB	0	
			W	8		M	5		Vo	0	0	PER	1	
			D	15		wtd C	.5		Xy	0	0	COP	0	
												PSV	1	
						M+wtd C	6							
						FM+m	8							
						Y+T+V+C'	3		RATIOS					
									H+HD	10				
						Σ FMmYTVC'	11		A+AD	15				
						FC	1		H+A	11				
						CF+C	0		HD+AD	14				
									A%		48			

Thematic Apperception Test Stories

1. This is a little boy looking at a violin. He looks kind of sad. The violin could be broken or something. It looks like before he wanted to play the violin and now that he has got the violin he doesn't know if he can play it. In the future he will be a great violinist.

2. This looks like a guy plowing the field getting ready to plow some corn with the fork. It could have been the winter snows. There is a lady looking on with a book. It looks like it is going to be a good harvest in the future, although he is doing it by hand. It is like winter and now it is spring where the guy is plowing the field and in the fall it will be a good harvest.

3BM. This is a picture of a man or woman sobbing over something. It looks like I see a set of keys lying on the floor. Maybe she was in a car accident or something and she is crying about what happened, but in the future she will learn not to drink and drive. Maybe she was drunk when she was driving, caused an accident. She will quit drinking from the picture.

4. It kind of reminds me of a [sic] old navy World War II movie star and actress. They are all talking on the porch, maybe before they were in dancing or something. It looks like maybe she said something to make him mad and he is getting ready to leave. He will be leaving her. She is trying to hold him back. It looks like she said something to make him mad and he is leaving, either that or he is going off to war or something.

Substance Abuse in a Borderline Personality Disorder

Referral Information

Janet Olsen was a 35-year-old woman who was admitted to a chemical abuse program for detoxification and treatment. The patient stated that, in addition to her drinking, she had been feeling lonely and isolated and had been having crying spells. She felt abused by the other family members and feared that she "couldn't trust anybody." Finally, she felt that she was "falling apart" and was "losing control" of her life.

Among the recent stressors that might have been associated with the presenting complaints is that the family had moved into their present area recently and the patient felt that she did not have any good friends. Mrs. Olsen has heard rumors that her husband was having an affair and explained that her husband was an amphetamine abuser. She has had trouble controlling her 15-year-old daughter and was concerned about facial scars that her 13-year-old daughter received in an accident. The family had financial difficulties and was still involved in a legal suit to recover their losses from the accident in which the daughter was injured.

The course of treatment during the current admission was marked by obvious symptoms of alcohol withdrawal during the first few days, including hand tremors. The current evaluation was requested to learn more about the patient, particularly whether she was suffering from an affective disorder.

Psychiatric History

This was the second psychiatric admission for Mrs. Olsen. The first admission took place when she was 20 years old and her first husband sent her away. At the time, she spent 2 weeks at a hospital in Nashville, Tennessee. The patient recalled that in 1978, she attempted to kill herself and her children by turning on the gas but then changed her mind and received no treatment for her depression. Mrs. Olsen had been drinking continuously for the previous 8 months, during which time she has had amnesic episodes and two blackouts. There also was weekly abuse of marihuana and cocaine. Before admission, she had been on Elavil and Xanax, which were given to her last April by a general practitioner.

Her family history is remarkable in that her mother suffered from a psychiatric disorder and was in an institution for 6 years. Her father was an abusive alcoholic, a problem that one of her brothers and one of her sisters still have. In addition, the same sister was said to have emotional problems and to be under psychiatric care.

Medical History

Mrs. Olsen has never had any major medical problems or serious accidents. She had a dilation-and-curettage procedure about 8 years ago.

Social History

Mrs. Olsen was born and raised in Nashville. Both parents reportedly abused the children physically, and she was sexually abused by her father and two of her brothers. She remembers her childhood as being difficult and traumatic. Her father, who was referred to as a ''jerk'' and was an alcoholic, died of liver failure when the patient was an adult. Her mother had to be psychiatrically hospitalized for 6 years when Mrs. Olsen's father went into the military and was said to have lived a "rough" life. The mother lived with the youngest sister in Nashville and was apparently dying of complications associated with her diabetes.

Mrs. Olsen was the fourth of five children. Her older sister died of diabetes before the age of 40. The rest of the siblings still live in Nashville. Her older brother, Joe, is in his 40s and works as a plumber. He is married to a nonsighted and physically challenged woman. According to the patient, David (aged 37) is an alcoholic who abuses his wife. Mrs. Olsen came next and was followed by Nancy (aged 27), an alcoholic with other emotional problems. Nancy's boyfriend killed her children when "they would not stop wetting the bed."

Mrs. Olsen moved to Kentucky 14 years previously while she was still married to her first husband. She married him when she was 18 years old to "get out" of her parents' home. She claimed that the first husband physically abused her. Her first hospitalization took place, however, when they were not getting along and he had sent her back to Tennessee. The couple were apart for perhaps a year, during which time Mrs. Olsen had a boyfriend and lived in Virginia. She eventually went back to her first husband, but the marriage ended in divorce 9 years ago.

After separating from her first husband, Mrs. Olsen went to live with her current husband and his girlfriend. It was at that time that she tried to kill herself and the children. Three years ago, however, after the girlfriend left, Mrs. Olsen married her present husband.

Her current husband, Kevin, was a 35-year-old appliance salesperson. He is an outgoing man who seems to love being the center of attention when he is in public, but he is quiet at home. The husband was reportedly bothered by Mrs. Olsen's inability to "carry on an intelligent conversation," something that suggested to her that she was not the "right" woman for him, and this made her feel guilty. She thought about going back to school as a way to remedy the situation. The husband is addicted to amphetamines and recently changed jobs.

Mrs. Olsen has a 15-year-old daughter from her first husband. Eleanor was described as "confused" and occasionally suicidal. She recently went into a hospital emergency room stating that she had been raped. There have been conflicts between the patient and Eleanor because Mrs. Olsen disapproved of Eleanor's friends. Other problems included her poor school performance and her being injured when she was struck by a car.

The second of Mrs. Olsen's daughters, Cathy, was born from the relationship the patient had with a boyfriend during her first marriage. Cathy is 13 years old and had been a poor student. She was hurt 4 months earlier when a store's plate glass window shattered as she was standing next to it waiting for a bus. Cathy was left with facial scars. The family hoped to obtain plastic surgery for Cathy with money from their lawsuit against the store owner.

Angela (aged 11) was fathered by the patient's first husband during the period when they were reconciled. Angela is a quiet child. She is involved in church activities and is doing better in school than her siblings. However, Angela had experienced emotional problems, perhaps as a result of her feeling responsible for her parents' divorce. She had seen a psychiatrist at a mental health center.

Finally, Mrs. Olsen had a fourth child by her current husband. Donald was born before the couple was married and had another last name. He has a difficult time in school and is currently in special education. In addition, he has allergies and has to take a medication that tends to make him lethargic.

Educational and Occupational History

Mrs. Olsen finished eighth grade before dropping out of school. She explained that she ''failed a few years'' and was told that she read at a fourth-grade level. The patient had been a housewife most recently but had been employed as a file clerk intermittently throughout her adult life.

Mental Status Examination

At the time of the evaluation, this right-handed individual was alert, oriented, verbal, and coherent. Her speech and language functions were intact. Most of the other intellectual functions examined showed mild deficits. Her memory was somewhat impaired (e.g., she could only remember one out of three words after a 5-min delay). She had trouble doing simple subtractions, even when she was allowed to use paper and pencil; she was never able to accurately do simple multiplications. She had trouble thinking of different meanings for the same word, and proverb interpretations were concrete. The figure reproductions were within normal limits. Her thought processes were disordered, confused, and circumstantial. Mrs. Olsen often experienced blocking, such that she would not offer information unless asked directly. At times, she talked as if she took for granted that the examiner knew something that she had not yet disclosed. There also were several instances in which she stated that she did not want to talk about something or seemed uncomfortable and asked questions about who would have access to that information. No delusions or hallucinations seemed to be present. Her affective responses always were appropriate. Her mood was within normal limits, and she demonstrated a good range of emotions. There was no suicidal or homicidal ideation. Her psychomotor activity and anxiety levels were within normal limits. The patient was friendly and cooperative.

Discussion

Mrs. Olsen appeared to suffer from a borderline personality disorder. Her history, for instance, showed affective instability, the tendency to act out sexually, an inclination to attempt suicide as a way to solve her problems, and difficulties with self-image. Those symptoms are the hallmarks of this disorder according to the fourth edition of the *Diagnostic and Statistical Manual of Mental Disorders* (*DSM–IV*).

Consistent with the borderline diagnosis, the MCMI described Mrs. Olsen as showing a pervasive instability in terms of moods, interpersonal relationships, and self-image. Her scores indicated that she typically responds in an impulsive and overemotional way and that her affective response tends to be labile, at times showing apathy and numbness while demonstrating excessive intensity or involvement. Sadness, hopelessness, and aimlessness often were underlying the more obvious emotional responses.

Underneath the borderline surface is a personality makeup consisting of introversiveness, a fear of rejection, and inadequate, self-defeating tendencies. Her MCMI scores suggested that she wants to be liked by others but expects that her social approaches will be rejected. As a result, Mrs. Olsen is likely to be apprehensive. Probably perceived as a nervous individual, she tends to feel uncomfortable in social situations. This type of person often is caught in a bind: She would like to interact with others and to be liked and appreciated, but she tends to avoid social situations to avoid the anxiety that these situations evoke.

At times, Mrs. Olsen may appear to be dependent and submissive. People with similar personality profiles usually underestimate themselves: When they compare themselves with others, they feel that they are less capable or less worthy. In fact, the indications were that the patient has such a poor self-image that she feels uncomfortable when she is treated nicely and may seek out situations in which she will be hurt or rejected. It is as if she has come to expect mistreatment and routinely has, almost by design, the type of interpersonal interactions that could be expected to bring about the abuse. When abuse has taken place, it might have been provoked, at least partly, by the resentments that Mrs. Olsen commonly harbors. Even though she is inclined to put herself down, the indications were that she is just as likely to devalue others. Similar people show their resentment in a somewhat insulting or even hostile way of interacting and appear to derive some pleasure from humiliating others. This, in return, creates ill-will from others, which activates the person's own resentment in an angry and frustrating vicious cycle.

The testing was most informative because it offered a rare glimpse of the dynamics that possibly were connected with the borderline personality disorder. It seemed as if she did not feel appreciated by either of her parents and might have had a poor relationship with all of her siblings. Her own self-esteem was not enhanced by her school experiences either, because her intellectual abilities were low enough that she was seen as "retarded." The one area in which she probably felt wanted was sexually. Unfortunately, she was abused sexually by her father and brothers, which caused her to be conflicted and confused. Ultimately, she became "ashamed" of her lack of education and human potential and obtained gratification in life primarily through her ability to please men sexually. In what seemed like a replay of her childhood home situation, the picture she has of herself is negative and unrewarding.

Consistent with all of these dynamics, two themes were prevalent in the TAT stories. These themes were the theme of shame, which often was associated with a lack of education, and the theme of difficulties in her romantic relationships.

The shame theme started on the first TAT card with the boy afraid to "take the chance of trying to learn how to play the violin." It continued on with the following comments obtained on Card 2: "It is quite possible that she is ashamed of her mother. Maybe her mother is not well educated and she is getting a more proper education. Look at the difference of clothing. Look at how nice she looks and look at mama." Although her response to Card 2 betrays a concern that her children would be ashamed of her, the most prevalent preoccupation involved her husband and the way he feels ashamed of the wife. It was noteworthy that the issue was often deeper than abandonment. It is not just that the men leave her after they have sex, but that they abuse her again: Her men have a need to bolster their own self-esteem by denigrating hers.

The theme of being taken advantage of in her romantic relationships was recurrent: The "husband" on Card 3GF was said to be an "alcoholic" and was "cheating" on his wife. In response to Card 4, she stated that the husband "can't even look at her face," that he is a "jerk" who will "end up leaving her." Finally, on a card that portrays two people in a gentle embrace, it was striking how far Mrs. Olsen had to distance herself from the two people: She first placed them in a group different from her own and she minimized the emotional ties by making them into distant friends.

The patient's low self-esteem, her shame, probably dates back to a childhood sense of deprivation, as suggested in the following excerpt: "It reminds me of me. But I never had any dolls. I never had nice clothes either. . . . Because I was quiet and shy and I wasn't doing any good in school, they told my mother that I was retarded, deformed in the mind. . . . The little girl is in pain. She has buried herself."

In addition to the characterological problems discussed so far, the testing generated concerns about the presence of other kinds of psychopathology. Mrs. Olsen, for example, had significant problems with her thinking processes, which was evident in the faulty reality contact on her Rorschach responses and the disturbed thought processes observed during the interview. Given that she apparently has never been delusional, these problems could be blamed on the combination of the borderline personality disorder and low intellectual abilities. However, the indications would be that she has some propensity toward thought disturbances as part of the borderline syndrome.

The presence of alcohol abuse also was indicated. Substance abuse frequently has been found with individuals having Mrs. Olsen's combination of borderline, schizoid, avoidant, and dependent personality elements. Similar people have been described as being anxious and depressed and demonstrating widespread and severe maladjustment. They are thought to be typically caught between feelings of loneliness and social apprehension. Their drinking may serve to alleviate social anxiety to a level that produces self-assurance and permits social contact. Participation in treatment programs is especially difficult for this type of alcoholic.

Finally, there were signs that she experiences periods of despondency and depression and a high level of anxiety. At least at the time of the testing, neither of these problems seemed pronounced enough to constitute a separate disorder. Rather, these problems were seen as part of the borderline character pathology that has been described already.

Diagnostic Assignments and Recommendations

   I Alcohol intoxication
      Alcohol abuse disorder
  II Borderline personality disorder
 III No known medical problems contributing

Recommendations

Mrs. Olsen needs to take her drinking problem seriously and to commit herself to actively participating in Alcoholics Anonymous. That her husband also is a substance abuser presents additional difficulties; an effort probably should be made to have the two of them treated during the same period of time if permanent gains are to be made. The use of family therapy to evaluate and improve the relationships at home also is recommended.

    Mrs. Olsen would benefit from individual psychotherapy. It would be helpful if she could gradually learn to develop closeness and positive feelings for another person. An exploration of her low sense of self and her feeling of being abused by others could lead to growth-producing insights.

MCMI Interpretive Logic

The Validity scale and modifying indexes were all unremarkable and can be disregarded. The elevations on severe personality scales indicate that the patient has a personality disorder. The elements of this disorder are organized in the narrative under the umbrella of the borderline personality. In keeping with the seriousness of the personality disorder, the discussion uses more pejorative terms (e.g., self-defeating) in addition to the milder terms that can be used to describe particular personality traits (e.g., submissive). Given this personality disorder and the patient's history, the elevations on mood disorder scales (i.e., Depressive Personality and Dysthymia) are interpreted to be part of the borderline syndrome.

Test Results

The Millon Clinical Multiaxial Inventory–Third Edition

Scale	Abbreviation	Base-Rate Score
Modifying Indices		
Disclosure	X	50
Desirability	Y	65
Debasement	Z	55
Validity	V	0
Personality Style Scales		
Schizoid	1	115**
Avoidant	2	109**
Dependent	3	96**
Histrionic	4	0
Narcissistic	5	26
Antisocial	6A	54
Compulsive	7	62
Negativistic	8A	87**
Severe Personality Scales		
Depressive	2B	103**
Aggressive	6B	42
Self-Defeating	8B	76*
Schizotypal	S	63
Borderline	C	92**
Paraphrenic	P	60
Clinical Syndrome Scales		
Anxiety	A	107**
Somatoform	H	87*
Bipolar: Manic	N	70
Dysthymia	D	112**
Alcohol Dependence	B	78*
Drug Dependence	T	59
Posttraumatic Stress Disorder	R	65
Severe Clinical Syndrome Scales		
Thought Disorder	SS	81*
Major Depression	CC	73
Delusional Disorder	PP	72

Note. Scores below the cutoff of 75 are shown without asterisks.
*Score elevation was between 75 and 84.
**Score elevation was 85 or above.

Rorschach Protocol

1. Card I   Reaction time: 0 s
SCORE: D −F   −   (2)A
Butterfly
INQUIRY: flares out, four butterflies
LOCATION: top outside D and the outside D

2. Card I   Reaction time: 5 s
SCORE: D −F   −   (2)A
(Second set of butterflies from Response 1)

3. Card I   Reaction time: 5 s
SCORE: W −F   −   A   1.0
Like the nest of bats, queen, and family, getting closed in for protection or food. This one is saying I'm the king, I'm under control. Vampire, because I saw a vampire movie last night.
INQUIRY: we would kill them when we were kids

4. Card II   Reaction time: 6 s
SCORE: D o   Ma   0   (2)H   P   3.0
This is kind of silly. Reminds me of a cartoon, clapping hands, dancing. Could be regular dancers too.

5. Card III   Reaction time: 3 s
SCORE: D o   Ma   0   (2)H   P   3.0
Reminds me of waiters for some reason. It's like they are wearing tuxedos. They are holding their hats. It looks like they are gentlemen (laughs). It could also be dancers because of the heels and the different positions.

6. Card IV   Reaction time: 28 s
SCORE: W o   F   0(A)   P   2.0
Monster, something evil. I don't like this one at all. Makes me feel fear. I do not like it.
INQUIRY: tail

7. Card V   Reaction time: 6 s
SCORE: W o   F   0A   P   1.0
Butterfly
INQUIRY: wings and body

8. Card V   Reaction time: 5 s
SCORE: W o   Mp   0   H.Cg   1.0
A dancer in Vegas wearing a costume.
INQUIRY: the dancer is here in the middle and this is the costume. Is got the arms spread out like this

Rorschach Protocol (contd.)

9. Card V   Reaction time: 18 s
SCORE: Dd   F   Hd   PER
Reminds me of something ugly. It looks like my mother because she was. . . . I don't want to look at it.
INQUIRY: the face. The face she used to look at me. (Talks about the last time she saw her mother.)
LOCATION: face in Dd cn top below the "ears"

10. Card VI   Reaction time: 13 s
SCORE: W   vma   u   Na   2.5
Earthquake, ground is cracking, earth is opening up.

11. Card VI   Reaction time: 4 s
SCORE: W   vma   u   Na.Ex   2.5
Could be a volcano
INQUIRY: this part over here and here is the lava coming out

12. Card VI   Reaction time: 6 s
SCORE: W   vma   u   Fi   2.5
Fourth of July with flairs going up

13. Card VI   Reaction time: 2 s
SCORE: Dd   vF   u   Hd
Evil face
LOCATION: top cn inner detail

14. Card VII   Reaction time: 7 s
SCORE: W   vMa   (2)H.Hh   (P)   2.5
Oh, goodness. See saw in the park with pony tails. That's cute.
INQUIRY: two girls here

15. Card VII   Reaction time: 23 s
SCORE: D   vFMp   u   A.Hh   PER   1.0
We have dogs. They really surprise you. Dogs: Sandy and Bandit on top of the picnic table.
INQUIRY: Picnic table with our dogs
LOCATION: picnic table = bm D; dogs = mid D; top D not included

16. Card VII   Reaction time: 21 s
SCORE: D   Ma   (2)Hd   Ag   3.0
Two people staring at each other, like a contest of outstaring.
Or full of anger.
LOCATION: top D, head only

17. Card VIII   Reaction time: 33 s
SCORE: W   vCF   u   Na   PER   4.5
Oh, at least this one has some color, more cheerful. Like Christmas colors. Tree with birds on the side of the tree. I love going into the forest preserve. I only see nice things on this.

Rorschach Protocol (contd.)

18. Card IX   Reaction time: 11 s
       SCORE: W   vma   u   Hh   5.5
       Fountain, middle part shooting up. Water going in separate directions

19. Card IX   Reaction time: 4 s
       SCORE: D   Ma   (2)(H)   4.5
       Sword fighting up here
       INQUIRY: two creatures fighting with swords
       LOCATION: orange D

20. Card X   Reaction time: 13 s
       SCORE: D   F   (2)A
       Clams or crabs, different kinds of fish
       INQUIRY: it looks like a clam with something sticking out
       LOCATION: side brown D

21. Card X   Reaction time: 2 s
       SCORE: D   F   (2)A   PER
       Goldfish
       INQUIRY: we used to have a couple of aquariums.
       LOCATION: yellow D with red circle in midfield

22. Card X   Reaction time: 5 s
       SCORE: D   −F   −   A
       Lobster
       INQUIRY: it looks like one
       LOCATION: blue D

23. Card X   Reaction time: 17 s
       SCORE: D   F   (2)A
       Worms. Pretty colors, a pleasure to look at, no fear
       LOCATION: green bm

Rorschach Score Sequence

Card	No.	Time (seconds)		Scoring				
I	1	0	D	−F	−	(2)A		
I	2	5	D	−F	−	(2)A		
I	3	5	W	−F	−	A		1.0
II	4	6	D	M	a	(2)H	P	3.0
III	5	3	D	M	a	(2)H	P	3.0
IV	6	28	W	F		(A)	P	2.0
V	7	6	W	F		A	P	1.0
V	8	5	W	M	p	H.Cg		1.0
V	9	18	Dd	F		Hd	PER	
VI	10	13	W	vm	au	Na		2.5

Rorschach Score Sequence (contd.)

Card	No.	Time (seconds)		Scoring				
VI	11	4	W	vma	u	Na.Ex		2.5
VI	12	6	W	vma	u	Fi		2.5
VI	13	2	Dd	vF	u	Hd		
VII	14	7	W	vMa		(2)H.Hh	(P)	2.5
VII	15	23	D	vFMp	u	A.Hh	PER	1.0
VII	16	21	D	Ma		(2)Hd	Ag	3.0
VIII	17	33	W	vCF	u	Na	PER	4.5
IX	18	11	W	vma	u	Hh		5.5
IX	19	4	D	Ma		(2)(H)		4.5
X	20	13	D	F		(2)A		
X	21	2	D	F		(2)A	PER	
X	22	5	D	−F	−	A		
X	23	17	D	F		(2)A		

Rorschach Structural Summary

Global	n	%	Location	n	%	Determinants	n	%	Contents	n	%	Quality	n	%
R	23		W	10	43	M	6	26	CONT	7		OF ALL		
Rejects	0		D	11	48	FM	1	4				+	0	0
			Dd	2	9	m	4	17	H	4	15	o	12	52
P	4	17	DW	0	0	FT	0	0	(H)	1	4	v	7	30
(P)	1	4	S	0	0	TF	0	0	Hd	3	11	−	4	17
						T	0	0	(Hd)	0	0			
(2)	10	43				FY	0	0	A	9	33	OF F		
Fr	0	0	POSITION			YF	0	0	(A)	1	4	+	0	0
rF	0	0	▲	23	100	Y	0	0	Ad	0	0	o	6	54
3r+(2)	43		◄	0	0	FV	0	0	(Ad)	0	0	v	1	09
			►	0	0	VF	0	0	Ab	0	0	−	4	36
RT Ach	10 s		▼	0	0	V	0	0	Al	0	0			
RT Ch	10 s					FC'	0	0	An	0	0			
						C'F	0	0	Art	0	0	DV1	0	
AFR	44		DEV QUAL			C'	0	0	Ay	0	0	DV2	0	
			+	0	0	FC	0	0	Bl	0	0	INC1	0	
			o	11	48	CF	1	4	Bt	1	4	INC2	0	
			v	8	35	C	0	0	Cg	1	4	DR1	0	
Zf	17		−	4	17	Cn	0	0	Cl	0	0	DR2	0	
ZSum	46					FD	0	0	Ex	1	4	FAB1	0	
						F	11	48	Fi	1	4	FAB2	0	
									Fd	0	0	ALOG	0	
						Blends	0		Ge	0	0	CON	0	
									Hh	3	11	AB	0	
									Ls	0	0	CP	0	

Rorschach Structural Summary (contd.)

Global		Location			Determinants			Contents			Quality		
n	%		n	%		n	%		n	%		n	%
		RATIOS			RATIOS								
		W	10		a	9	39	Na	3	11	AG	1	
		M	6		p	1	4	Sc	0	0	MOR	0	
								Sx	0	0	CFB	0	
		W	10		M	6		Vo	0	0	PER	4	1
		D	11		wtd C	1.0		Xy	0	0	COP	0	
											PSV	0	
					M+wtd C	7							
					FM+m	5							
					Y+T+V+C'	0		RATIOS					
								H+HD	8				
					ΣFMmYTVC'	5		A+AD	10				
					FC	0		H+A	15				
					CF+C	1		HD+AD	3				
								A%		37			

Thematic Apperception Test Stories

1. This reminds me of a young boy looking at a violin. He is trying to figure out can I play it or should I take that chance of trying to learn how to play it. The way his eyes look, it doesn't look like he really wants to learn how to play according to his eyes, because they look awfully uninterested in it. They look sad and down and his mouth looks sad. It doesn't look like he wants to play it.

2. This reminds me of farmers living out in the country. It looks like a man is plowing, fixing the field for corn and this looks like the mother leaning against the tree. This looks like the daughter looking back at her mother. It looks like she is going to school or to church the way she is dressed. It looks like that to me. That could be a Bible or it could be a schoolbook of some kind. It looks like the woman is pregnant with child unless she is overweight. It just looks like a family, a farmer. It looks like there is water out in the back. That's what it looks like to me. If you look at it from my point of view, I'd like to be where they are. I envy them, I honestly do because it doesn't look like they are really pleased by their mouths. This woman looks like she is contented. He looks like he is strong. He is healthy but she doesn't look too happy the way her mouth is, down. It is quite possible that she is ashamed of her mother. Maybe her mother is not well educated and she is getting more proper education. Look at the difference of clothing. Look at how nice she looks and look at mama. Mother doesn't have her hair fixed up nicely and you can see that mama is plain, but it looks like the daughter has some makeup on. It looks like to me she is just going to take off and leave her mother.

Thematic Apperception Test Stories (contd.)

3GF. It looks like she is crying. It looks like she is upset. She is trying to decide if she should walk out of that door or shouldn't I? Should I go get help or shouldn't I? She looks very unhappy, very unhappy and as for myself the way she is trying to force herself out I think she will make it. She could be unhappy about anything. She could find that her husband is an alcoholic. She could find out that her husband is cheating on her. It looks like to me she wants to go and get help.

4. It looks like she is really in love with him and he is turning away from her. He is turning his head away. He can't even look her in the face, look her in the eye. That is terrible. What a jerk. Look at the love in her face. He is going to end up leaving her and she is going to have a broken heart and she is going to cry.

6GF. It looks like they are having some kind of discussion or something. He said something and she looked back. He is looking at her and saying, "Do you understand what I am saying?" and her eyes are going, I understand what he is saying but I don't really want to tell him how I feel because if I tell him how I feel it is just going to cause problems and why should I do that? She just keeps it to herself.

7GF. That doesn't remind me of a mother; it looks like a house maid. It is a child and the child looks lonely. He is holding a little doll. The woman looks sad. She wants to communicate with the child because she can tell the child is, you know. You know what that reminds me of? But I never had any dolls. It reminds me of me. But I never had any dolls. I never had nice clothes either. You know what they used to say about me, my sisters and brothers, because I was quiet and shy and I wasn't doing good in school? They told my mother that I was retarded, deformed in the mind. It wasn't that. It was just that it did no good to speak out. It did no good. That is what it reminds me of. The little girl is in pain. She has like buried herself. I hope that woman can reach her. She has a book in her hand. Maybe she is trying to read something to the child. Maybe communication wasn't doing too good so she got a book to read to the child to see if she could communicate with the child like that or maybe the child is supposed to be listening—you know you could look at this at a different angle, honestly, if you think about it. Maybe my mind was just in a depressing way, right. Because it is possible that the woman, she is no mother, I can see that according to her clothing and maybe she is trying to help the child with remembering things. She could be reading to the child. Like myself, if someone reads to me or if I read out loud, I remember better.

Thematic Apperception Test Stories (contd.)

9GF. It looks like they are at the beach, the ocean, trees, water, waves. It looks like this young woman is going down the beach and this one is like spying on her, watching her. This one isn't quite as pretty as this one. This one looks more intelligent. This one looks more prettier. Maybe she envies her because she is prettier. The problem does not get solved. The women do not really communicate to understand why they have these feelings towards each other. They will stay away from each other.

10. It looks like someone is hugging somebody. It looks like a father hugging his son. It sure don't look like no woman, no young girl. You know how I've seen on TV, I've also seen it here, you know how a priest leans over and kisses the forehead of a woman, Catholic people, that's what it reminds me of too. It looks like they are showing caringness, you know, feelings. You know how even though you don't love that person, you just want to hug them as a friend.

13MF. You know what this reminds me of. He just had sex with her and after he is done he is ashamed of her and he is hiding, "Aw, I'm ashamed of you." It's done and over. I got what I wanted. I'm not trying to be nasty but I got to tell you what is on my mind. That's the reason it aggravates me about men, honestly, because you know, that irritates me, it really aggravates me. Everything is fine and dandy until after they have sex and then they are done with the woman. They say I'm ashamed of you. They get what they wanted. So rather than deal with saying goodbye they say I'm ashamed of you.

16. I can tell you right away because this is what I want. I want it bad. I want to go visit Florida and see the white sand, the beautiful waves, the sail boats, people surfing, and way out there, see Pensacola is a navy town, and when you look way, way out, well way back, well it has been years. I don't know if they have the ships out in the Gulf again. That's what I see. I see Pensacola Beach on the Gulf side. I go back not so much to visit my friends but I want to visit the town because the town then I disliked because it has too many memories. I want to go back and see it as something beautiful, something I can say yes, it has changed. I see happiness. I don't have to look at Pensacola as something ugly and disgusting.

Thematic Apperception Test Stories (contd.)

17GF. This is like a bridge of some kind. That could be the sun or the moon. This is the water and the boats. This is like a shed of some kind. This woman is looking down at the water. It looks like fishermen. Not really, not fishermen. It looks like they are carrying some heavy packages of some kind. Have you ever seen those old-fashioned potato sacks? Well, that is what it reminds me of, some kind of grain of some kind. I don't really see a story, to tell you the truth. It is a young girl just looking down in the water watching the people. Well, she was all alone and now she is happy they are back so she won't have to be alone anymore.

Anxiety Disorder in an Avoidant Personality

Referral Information

Ms. Wolcott is a 62-year-old single White woman who had been admitted into the psychiatric ward with complaints of intense anxiety, panic attacks, and depression. The patient had been sleeping and eating poorly, was experiencing a low energy level and a lack of motivation, and was anhedonic. She was unable to stay home alone or function independently. Ms. Wolcott also had several somatic complaints such as a strange feeling on the back of her neck, shortness of breath, a tingling sensation on the head, and stomachaches. Among the stressors noted was the death of her mother a month earlier, her being withdrawn from the chronic use of a minor tranquilizer, and a lack of social contacts.

The course of treatment during the hospitalization was marked by many requests from the patient to be placed back on Ativan. Sinequan was given for a day or so, but it was discontinued when the patient complained about the amount of sedation she experienced. At the time of the testing, Ms. Wolcott was kept on Tolectin and Buspar.

Psychiatric History

Ms. Wolcott explained she has been "nervous" all of her life. She was admitted into the medical ward of a hospital 20 years ago, and it was at that time that she was placed on benzodiazepam. She only recently stopped taking this drug as prescribed by her family physician. Last November, already suffering from the problems that led to the current admission, Ms. Wolcott spent a week in a medical ward at the same hospital she had been in 20 years before. A history of psychiatric problems in the family was denied.

Medical History

Ms. Wolcott had a tonsillectomy at the age of 9 and had gall bladder surgery 6 years ago. Laboratory tests during the current admission were said to indicate subclinical hypothyroidism.

Family History

Ms. Wolcott was born and raised in Madison, Wisconsin. Her father died 15 years ago at the age of 72. He worked for a heating and air conditioning company and was characterized as a wonderful man who was liked by everyone. Ms. Wolcott always had a good relationship with him.

As close as Ms. Wolcott was to her father, she had an even closer relationship with her mother. The patient explained that she had lived with her mother all of her life and that, when her mother had to be placed in a nursing home before her death, her absence left the patient feeling lonely. The mother worked for 20 years as a bookkeeper in an office supply store. She is remembered as "the best," but the patient recalled how her mother unfortunately tried to shelter her too much from the world.

Ms. Wolcott never married. She was the youngest of two siblings. Her 66-year-old brother is an aerospace engineer. He recently accepted a job at the University of Louisville and moved to Kentucky. Her brother is married and has a daughter. He is expected to live with the patient temporarily until he could find a place for himself and his family.

Ms. Wolcott explained that she has always been shy and "never went out to make friends." In fact, the patient admitted that she seldom went out with anyone outside the family. As long as she was employed, she had a group of acquaintances at work. However, she lost those contacts when she retired and had been very isolated, especially after her mother went into the nursing home.

Educational History

Ms. Wolcott recalled that after graduating from grammar school, she was sent to a boarding school for 2 years. She went to the boarding school on the advice of her grammar school principal, who felt that she needed to be "away from the home." She apparently never adjusted to the boarding school and felt lonely and homesick. Thus, at the end of 2 years, she was allowed to return home and continued her studies in a local business school. Ms. Wolcott was an average student and never presented any academic difficulties.

Occupational History

The patient retired 4 years ago from the company where she did book-keeping work for 37 years. She explained that, at the end of her tenure there, she was expected to do tasks (e.g., moving files from one room to another) that she was not physically able to do anymore. Up until that time, however, she had apparently performed her functions well. Because her mother became sick right after the patient's retirement and has since died, Ms. Wolcott has not enjoyed her retirement. She currently feels she needs to create some activities and some way to structure her life.

Mental Status Examination

At the time of the evaluation, the patient was alert, oriented, verbal, and coherent. Her speech and language functions were intact; the other intellectual functions examined also were within normal limits. These functions included memory, calculations, figure reproductions, mental control, and abstractions. Her thought process was orderly and effective. Her thought content was remarkable only in that she was originally preoccupied with the fear that she would not be given her medication on time. She talked about the death of her mother several times but did not seem unduly preoccupied with that loss. There were no indications of delusions or hallucinations. The affective responses always were appropriate. Although her mood was within normal limits, it tended to be serious. There was no verbalized suicidal or homicidal ideation. The psychomotor activity and anxiety levels were within normal limits. Ms. Wolcott was very anxious at the beginning, repeatedly asking questions while taking the paper-and-pencil questionnaire and wondering whether she could do an adequate job in the testing. As time went on, however, she seemed to become more comfortable and relaxed. She was friendly and cooperative throughout.

Discussion

The test results were consistent with the presence of a generalized anxiety disorder. In addition, the indications were that Ms. Wolcott was mildly depressed. Her Rorschach responses, for instance, were somewhat unproductive and constricted, and her TAT stories often alluded to the death of someone in the family, as in the following story obtained on Card 3GF: "It looks like somebody is in the depths of despair. Looks like she is crying, very sad about something. She could have been happy before this happened. I would say someone close to her died and her future would be that she will get over her grief." Among the other stories with similar depressive themes, the one that is noteworthy is her response to Card 14, on which the protagonist commits suicide by jumping out a window.

Judging from her MCMI scores, at the basis of Ms. Wolcott's problems is a personality style with schizoid, avoidant, dependent, and compulsive components. The indications from the history were that the patient met criteria for an avoidant personality disorder. Note that this type of personality is prevalent among individuals with an anxiety disorder, the "anxious" cluster of the *DSM–IV* personality prototypes. Although it was possible that the acute anxiety episode had aggravated the patient's personality traits, the history pointed to the lifelong prevalence of these tendencies.

Individuals with similar MCMI scores tend to have low self-esteem; they see others as being more capable or valuable than they are. They are followers rather than leaders, often taking a passive role in interpersonal affairs. They would like to seek the emotional support and protection of others but, together with that wish, they experience discomfort in social situations.

The discomfort comes from the assumption that if others get to know them as well as they know themselves, these people would develop the same uncomplimentary views that they hold of themselves. Similar people try to put their best foot forward and have a tendency to cover up their true feelings, especially when these feelings are aggressive or otherwise objectionable. They may seem tense, nervous, and distant. Because they feel ill at ease in social situations, they often avoid such affairs and frequently are lonely and isolated.

One way in which Ms. Wolcott defends against the insecurity that her low self-esteem may bring is by counting on the guidance and protection of others. The second defense mechanism she uses is thinking that, if she manages to avoid making a mistake, she always can expect the outcome to be a positive one. Individuals with a similar compulsive bent are orderly and plan for the future. They prepare in a conscientious manner and do the work on schedule. They try to be efficient, dependable, industrious, and persistent. These individuals often relate in an overly respectful and ingratiating manner. They may be somewhat perfectionistic and self-disciplined. They tend to be indecisive, especially when they have to make a decision by themselves. The compulsive inclination also may serve to strengthen the feelings of inadequacy that are beneath it in that, whenever bad events take place, Ms. Wolcott will be inclined to look for what mistakes she made that might have led to the undesirable outcome.

The extent to which this dependent, anxiously shy, and compulsive personality style was caused by an overprotective mother is debatable. What seems undeniable, however, is that it fits in well with the relationship that the patient had with her mother. The mother was the protective figure and was the only real safe relationship that she had.

Perhaps as a result of this good fit, the indications were that the patient's personality style was exaggerated enough to be dysfunctional. Her MCMI scores suggested that she is isolated and has few real relationships. Individuals obtaining similar scores are somewhat eccentric. They may have a rich fantasy life and may mix their own personal idiosyncrasies with other material in their conversations; they appear anxious and apprehensive and may have flat affect.

Finally, her responses to the projective measures depict a fairly immature and infantile individual who is not well developed psychologically. The impression was that the personality structure was impaired enough to constitute a personality disorder.

Encumbered with this personality disorder, Ms. Wolcott has been able to make only a marginal adjustment in her adult life. She was never able to establish significant relationships outside of the family and seemed to cope psychologically only with the help of her family; even with that support, she became dependent on tranquilizers as the only way to control the anxieties she experienced. The loss of her job a few years before the testing has further jeopardized the kind of adjustment that she was able to make.

Regarding psychological strengths, Ms. Wolcott is very personable and shows no evidence of intellectual or memory deficits. She also has some insight into her problems and seemed well motivated.

Diagnostic Assignments and Recommendations

I Generalized anxiety disorder
  Benzodiazepine dependence
  Uncomplicated bereavement

II Avoidant personality disorder with schizoid, dependent, and compulsive elements

III No known medical problems contributing

Recommendations

Continued evaluation for the use of psychotropic medications to reduce the patient's anxiety is indicated. In addition, Ms. Wolcott may benefit from a period of psychotherapy. Given her personality style, she can be expected to experience as supportive a relationship in which the therapist has a benevolent and protective attitude toward her. Feeling that the therapist is a powerful expert who will advise and guide her appropriately will be reassuring for Ms. Wolcott. The patient's fear of rejection may require frequent reaffirmation and promise of support.

MCMI Interpretive Logic

The Validity and modifying indexes all are at an acceptable level and can be disregarded. The elevation of the schizotypal personality raises the question of her having a personality disorder. After a review of the items endorsed, it is evident that most of the items dealt with the patient's social isolation; the elevations on the Schizoid and Avoidant scales give further support to this personality structure, and the history meets criteria for the avoidant personality disorder. The discussion also works to blend in the compulsive aspects. Finally, the elevations of clinical syndrome scales, with the support of information from other sources, served to arrive at the diagnosis of a generalized anxiety disorder.

Test Results

The Millon Clinical Multiaxial Inventory–Third Edition

Scale	Abbreviation	Base-Rate Score
Modifying Indices		
Disclosure	X	55
Desirability	Y	57
Debasement	Z	37
Validity (raw score)	V	0

The Millon Clinical Multiaxial Inventory–Third Edition (contd.)

Scale	Abbreviation	Base-Rate Score
Personality Style Scales		
Schizoid	1	85**
Avoidant	2	85**
Dependent	3	94**
Histrionic	4	3
Narcissistic	5	24
Antisocial	6A	35
Compulsive	7	95**
Negativistic	8A	7
Severe Personality Scales		
Depressive	2B	73
Aggressive	6B	32
Self-Defeating	8B	52
Schizotypal	S	80*
Borderline	C	53
Paraphrenic	P	74
Clinical Syndrome Scales		
Anxiety	A	76*
Somatoform	H	84**
Bipolar: Manic	N	0
Dysthymia	D	75*
Alcohol Dependence	B	35
Drug Dependence	T	0
Posttraumatic Stress Disorder	R	66
Severe Clinical Syndrome Scales		
Thought Disorder	SS	68
Major Depression	CC	44
Delusional Disorder	PP	70

Note. Scores below the cutoff of 75 are shown without asterisks.
*Score elevation was between 75 and 84.
**Score elevation was 85 or above.

Rorschach Protocol

1. Card I   Reaction time: 2 s
SCORE: W o FMa.FC'   0   A   P   1.0
butterfly
Flying bat, more than a butterfly
INQUIRY: It's black. Wing spread, the body and the feet

2. Card II   Reaction time: 4 s
SCORE: W o vFMa.FC   u   A   4.5
Oh my God, two colors! Could be a flying insect but it's so big. Here is the body and these are the wings
INQUIRY: wings, two different colors, this glow is like the end lights up.

3. Card III   Reaction time: 9 s
SCORE: D o   Ma   0   (2)H   P   3.0
Two people stirring up a pot
INQUIRY: repeats

4. Card III   Reaction time: 3 s
SCORE: D o   FC   0   A   CONT
a butterfly between them
INQUIRY: the wings, the color, the shape

5. Card IV   Reaction time: 8 s
SCORE: W o   F   0   (A)   P   2.0
Oh my! Some kind of a monster from a creepy show
INQUIRY: Big feet, floppy arms. Like King Kong.

6. Card V   Reaction time: 7 s
SCORE: W o   F   0   A   P   1.0
They are all very similar, they would have to be.
Some kind of butterfly, the legs sticking out
INQUIRY: the wings, the legs, the thing coming out on top.

7. Card VI   Reaction time: 8 s
SCORE: W vF   u   (2)(A)   2.5
These are all very similar. Wings sticking out. Some kind of a creepy character. Some kind of a monster. Head there, there are a couple of eyes there.
INQUIRY: I don't know what kind of a monster would have two sets of wings.

8. Card VII   Reaction time: 5 s
SCORE: D o   F   0   (2)Ad   1.0
That don't look like nothing. Too much space in between. There is a face on each one of these.
INQUIRY: two faces on each side. The eye, the nose, the mouth. The ear and the snout.
LOCATION: 2nd D from top, below the usual girl's face

Rorschach Protocol (contd.)

9. Card VII   Reaction time: 9 s
SCORE: D o   F   0   A   1.0
butterfly
INQUIRY: the wings with the body in the middle
LOCATION: bottom D

10. Card VII   Reaction time: 10 s
SCORE: D v F   u   A   ▼1.0
a long tail
INQUIRY: a tail, a body and the head. It's kind of an animal.
LOCATION: top D with card upside down

11. Card VIII   Reaction time: 18 s
SCORE: D o   F   0 (2)A   P   3.0
This is different. I see two rats on each side.
INQUIRY: long tail, head

12. Card VIII   Reaction time: 3 s
SCORE: D o   FC   0   A
butterfly
INQUIRY: the wings, the color, the body.
LOCATION: bottom D

13. Card VIII   Reaction time: 2 s
SCORE: D v   FMa   u (2)A   3.0
two insects
INQUIRY: they are getting together.
LOCATION: uppermost green D

14. Card IX   Reaction time: 7 s
SCORE: D o   F   0   A   2.5
They get worse. That looks like a big butterfly.
INQUIRY: the wings and the body
LOCATION: midsection

15. Card IX   Reaction time: 10 s
SCORE: Rejected
The line going down the middle makes you think that it is the body of
an insect. Maybe more than one kind because of the different colors.
INQUIRY: (cannot find and rejects)

16. Card X   Reaction time: 7 s
SCORE: D o   F   0   A   P   4.0
An animal with a lot of feet
INQUIRY: the feet. It's a crab or something
LOCATION: upper blue D

Rorschach Protocol (contd.)

17. Card X   Reaction time: 6 s
SCORE: D   o   FC   0 (2)A
two rats
INQUIRY: black rats. There are two of them
LOCATION: top gray D

18. Card X   Reaction time: 6 s
SCORE: Dd v   F   v   Xy   4.0
An X-ray of the inside of a body.
INQUIRY: this part coming down here
LOCATION: center bottom up to the blue D

Rorschach Score Sequence

Card	No.	Time (seconds)	Scoring					
I	1	2	W	FM.FC′	a	A	P	1.0
II	2	4	W	vFM.FC	au	A		4.5
III	3	9	D	M	a	(2)H	P	3.0
III	4	3	D	FC		A		
IV	5	8	W	F		(A)	P	2.0
V	6	7	W	F		A	P	1.0
VI	7	8	W	vF	u	(2)(A)		2.5
VII	8	5	D	F		(2)Ad		1.0
VII	9	9	D	F		A		1.0
VII	10	10	D	vF	u	A		▼1.0
VIII	11	18	D	F		(2)A	P	3.0
VIII	12	3	D	FC		A		
VIII	13	2	D	vFM	au	(2)A		3.0
IX	14	7	D	F		A		2.5
X	16	7	D	F		A	P	4.0
X	17	6	D	FC		(2)A		
X	18	6	Dd	vF	u	Xy		4.0

Rorschach Structural Summary

Global	n	%	Location	n	%	Determinants	n	%	Contents	n	%	Quality	n	%
R	17		W	5	29	M	1	5	CONT	3		OF ALL		
Rejects	0		D	11	65	FM	3	16				+	0	0
			Dd	1	6	m	0	0	H	1	6	o	12	71
P	6	35	DW	0	0	FT	0	0	(H)	0	0	u	5	29
(P)	0	0	S	0	0	TF	0	0	Hd	0	0	–	0	0
						T	0	0	(Hd)	0	0			
(2)	6	35				FY	0	0	A	12	71	OF F		
Fr	0	0	POSITION			YF	0	0	(A)	2	12	+	0	0
rF	0	0	▲	16	94	Y	0	0	Ad	1	6	o	7	70
3r+(2)		35	◄	0	0	FV	0	0	(Ad)	0	0	u	3	30
			►	0	0	VF	0	0	Ab	0	0	–	0	0
RT Ach	7 s		▼	1	6	V	0	0	Al	0	0			
RT Ch	6 s					FC'	1	5	An	0	0			
						C'F	0	0	Art	0	0	DV1	0	
AFR		70	DEV QUAL			C'	0	0	Ay	0	0	DV2	0	
			+	0	0	FC	4	21	Bl	0	0	INC1	0	
			o	12	71	CF	0	0	Bt	0	0	INC2	0	
			v	5	29	C	0	0	Cg	0	0	DR1	0	
Zf	14		–	0	0	Cn	0	0	Cl	0	0	DR2	0	
ZSum	34					FD	0	0	Ex	0	0	FAB1	0	
						F	10	53	Fi	0	0	FAB2	0	
									Fd	0	0	ALOG	0	
						Blends	2		Ge	0	0	CON	0	
									Hh	0	0	AB	0	
			RATIOS			RATIOS			Ls	0	0	CP	0	
			W	5		a	4	24	Na	0	0	AG	0	
			M	1		p	0	0	Sc	0	0	MOR	0	
									Sx	0	0	CFB	0	
			W	5		M	1		Vo	0	0	PER	0	
			D	11		wtd C	2.0		Xy	1	6	COP	0	
												PSV	0	
						M+wtd C	3							
						FM+m	3							
						Y+T+V+C'	1		RATIOS					
									H+HD	1				
						ΣFMmYTVC'	4		A+AD	15				
						FC	4		H+A	15				
						CF+C	0		HD+AD	1				
									A%	88				

Thematic Apperception Test Stories

1. That looks like a boy studying his lesson. He looks like 5 or 6 years old and that would be before his school days, I would say. Well, he will go on to have a career in his life, whatever he wants to do in his life.

2. This looks like a farm. A man is working with a horse. This might be his wife and daughter. He's probably been a farmer all his life. His daughter is going to school and his wife is standing here and he's working with a plow horse. The girl looks like she is going to school with books in her hand. She will go on to do better things too. If she continues with her studies she will make something out of her life.

3GF. It looks like somebody is in the depths of despair, looks like she's crying, very sad about something. She could have been happy before this happened. I'd say somebody close to her died and in her future she will get over her grief. Just like me when my mother died.

4. Looks like two movie stars in two movies that I saw not too long ago. These people remind me of a musical I saw. They fell in love with each other. He left her and never came back to her. Looks like he's pulling away from her. He's a riverboat gambler, but he left her and finally came back after he found out she had a child and it was his.

6GF. This woman is talking to a man standing behind her and turning around. The look on her face, he must have startled her. Well, she might have been married and is falling in love with him, both nice looking people and that's what will happen in the future.

7GF. That's a mother talking to her daughter who is holding a doll, both sitting on a couch talking about something. She looks like she's got a book in her hand. She must be reading to her but she doesn't look like she is paying any attention to her. If she was paying any attention to her mother she would get something out of it. They are all cooking out there.

9GF. This girl is running away for some reason. This one is standing behind a tree with something in her hand. I can't make it out. She is watching her run away wondering where she is going but she looks frightened. This is water, maybe she sees someone in the water that needs help and she is running to help that person. See, she's got a towel in her arms and she will save the person that needs help.

10. This is two middle-aged people that have been married for a long time and they still love each other. He is kissing her on the forehead. It looks like they are married for almost 50 years and will be married for the rest of their life.

Thematic Apperception Test Stories (contd.)

13MF. The man is in despair over the death of his wife. She is not already gone. She will die and that will be it.

14. It looks like he's ready to jump out the window. A small picture, looks like somebody is jumping out the window in a dark room. Either he's thinking about doing himself in or trying to escape from something. Whoever is bothering or whatever is bothering him, maybe despondent over something.

15. Looks like a man in a graveyard, he's praying for something he's buried there. It's an old gravestone. He came to visit somebody's grave and he's praying for them. Nothing can happen if the person is dead there, then nothing can happen.

17GF. This looks like a house, but there's some people outside the house, or one person at least. It looks like there's other people too. There is somebody on the roof, another building here and the sun is shining. There's a boat here. They are getting out of the boat, in the water. Somebody's looking down on them. There's a high wall around the house, high windows. They can get out of the boat right there. The sun shining down and somebody's looking down. It almost looks like they are up to no good to me. They are bringing something to this house on the rafters by boat. This looks like a woman here and these are men. They look like smugglers and might hide it in this house here and if they get caught they will get thrown in jail.

18GF. This looks like a very sad woman. She is holding her daughter in her arms and she must be very ill. That's why she looks so sad, because her daughter is so ill. There is a staircase here. I don't know if somebody fell down the stairs and got hurt. She was laying there and she picked her up in her arms and she could have died or be seriously injured in the fall. Hopefully, she will recover if she is still living. You always hope for something better.

10 Psychotherapy and the MCMI

We hope that psychological assessment techniques are used not only to help diagnose and classify people reliably and validly but also as an aid in choosing the most helpful methods of treatment. Ideally, the determination of certain diagnoses and personality profile types through personality testing should lead to logical prescriptions for a distinct type of psychotherapeutic treatment that is specific to that particular personality profile. This hope was guiding our therapeutic suggestions for the MCMI personality styles contained in chapters 4–7. However, as we discuss, we have relied primarily on a speculative application of personality theory and our own clinical experience in developing our ideas regarding the type of therapeutic relationship and techniques that would be most useful with the specific personality styles.

However, our speculations may not need to be as far afield these days. Since the first edition of this book, interest in psychological testing and therapy treatment planning has grown. There has been at least one large book dealing with the application of test findings to therapy (Maruish, 1994), and a book dedicated exclusively to the integration of the MCMI and psychotherapy (Retzlaff, 1995b). Millon (1995), in his recent revision of his *Disorders of Personality* and in a book chapter (Millon & Davis, 1995), has extended his writing on the treatment of the varying personality types. Millon presumed that knowing a patient's personality type (which could be gained through viewing a MCMI profile) should assist in the more efficacious application of therapy techniques to alter certain personality features and symptomatic presentations.

Retzlaff's (1995b) book is especially interesting because it outlines how to use the MCMI-III with different theories and models of treatment. Thus, approaches such as behavior therapy, self psychology, cognitive therapy, and object relations theory are applied to Millon's domain model. The different personality types are discussed within the different theoretical models, and case examples are provided, along with MCMI-III findings, that integrate test results and treatment approaches.

Psychological Testing and Treatment Recommendations

If we take a skeptical approach, a priori objections to the notion that psychological testing can lead to useful therapy "prescriptions" include the argument that the information most germane to understanding and helping someone in psychotherapy can be gathered only through the face-to-face interpersonal contact of the therapy interview. It also can be argued that testing interferes with the developing therapeutic process. Dewald (1967), in a psychoanalytic perspective, noted that the use of psychological tests

> may have an impact on the developing therapeutic situation and relationship, since they tend to bypass the patient's conscious participation and suggest that the therapist may have semimagical means or methods of understanding the patient. (p. 297)

Dewald (1967) also suggested that introducing psychological testing later in treatment can be complicated and problematic because

> the patient will have significant doubts about the therapist's confidence in himself and in the choice of treatment being undertaken, or they [sic] will indicate to the patient that the therapist has significant doubts about the patient's capacities and progress. (p. 297)

Others have argued that knowing a patient's psychological assessment makes no difference in subsequent therapy process or outcome. A variant of this second objection was discussed by Beutler (1989), who felt that "psychotherapies do not exert diagnosis-specific benefits" (p. 273) and that "psychiatric diagnoses have proved to be of little value either to the development of individual psychotherapy plans or to the differential prediction of psychotherapy outcome" (p. 271). Beutler instead sought to develop and understand nondiagnostic dimensions and factors that may lead to the best type of psychotherapeutic strategy. He called for improving therapist–patient matching, increasing the specificity of interventions, and clarifying treatment-setting decisions. It is interesting, however, that despite his reservations about the value of diagnosis for psychotherapy, Beutler did not fully disregard diagnosis as a potentially important variable to be taken into account, nor did he posit that a thorough assessment is not useful. He did not address explicitly the role of psychological testing in providing some of the information (other than a simple diagnostic label) that he felt is helpful in making treatment decisions. In more recent writings, however, Beutler seems to have changed his views somewhat and has discussed the use of psychological testing to measure pretreatment client variables (Beutler & Consoli, 1993).

A third argument against the use of psychological testing in psychotherapy is that its results actually bias or negatively skew the therapist's attitude toward the patient. In other words, it may be that the test results turn the relationship into an evaluative, pathologizing, or judgmental one. This is most often the objection of those from the humanistic, or client-centered, school, who tend to undervalue and even demean the usefulness of psychological testing.

For example, Rogers (1951) was explicit in deemphasizing the use of the diagnostic process in psychotherapy. He thought that diagnosis, either through interviewing or psychological testing, "places the clinician in a godlike role which seems basically untenable from a philosophical point of view" (Rogers, 1951, p. 221). He felt that the use of diagnosis to determine treatment modalities or approaches "tends to be palliative and superficial, rather than basic" (Rogers, 1951, p. 221) and that "a diagnosis of the psychological dynamics is not only unnecessary but in some ways is detrimental or unwise" (Rogers, 1951, p. 223). The basic thrust of Rogers's objections is that diagnosis leads to the client losing a sense of responsibility for self-knowledge and that such assessment possibly leads to some form of social control "of the many by the few" (Rogers, 1951, p. 224).

This particular a priori criticism of the role of psychological assessment and diagnosis also might be an objection from someone who is a follower of Langs's (1973) psychoanalytic viewpoint, wherein the use of psychological testing is construed as a "therapeutic frame" violation. For example, Langs presented a case in his book *The Technique of Psychoanalytic Psychotherapy* that argues against the use of psychological testing. In that case, an adolescent boy who had been in treatment for 2 years (with one of Langs's supervisees?) was given psychological testing before going to college. This testing was done at the request of the boy's parents for unknown reasons. The boy responded poorly to the testing in that his subsequent behavior and fantasies in subsequent sessions were marked by paranoid concerns and withdrawal. Langs (1973) interpreted this scenario as follows:

> The implications of this vignette are clear: The therapist's use of testing evoked an iatrogenic regression and paranoid disturbance in the patient which was—on the patient's part—in keeping with his latent psychopathology. It is clear that the two-person ground rule should be followed without exception in almost all psychotherapies and that the infractions come primarily from the therapist's deficient understanding of proper principles of technique and from his countertransference difficulties. (p. 196)

Several points should be made regarding this example. First, few would disagree that giving psychological testing later in treatment has much different effects and meanings than does an early assessment. It is an empirical question whether the meanings of a later testing can be sufficiently discussed and worked through in a satisfactory way or whether there are so many problems that testing should be reserved only for early in treatment. Langs (1973) felt in his example that at termination "the therapeutic alliance remained compromised to the end" (p. 196). Second, it is unclear whether the adolescent in the example was upset about taking the psychological tests or whether he was more bothered by his parents' intrusion into his treatment. Finally, Langs generalized from this negative experience with one case of a disturbed adolescent to a prescription for all intensive therapies with all patients.

The issue of whether test results would make a difference in the therapy process or outcome is an empirical question. To answer the question, researchers would have to study two matched, roughly equivalent groups of therapists in which one group of therapists is given psychological testing data and the other group is not; the investigation then would have to include acceptable psychotherapy process–outcome measures. To simplify this type of study, one might have to circumscribe the problems studied or shorten the length of treatment, as M. J. Horowitz et al. (1984) have done. In this case, all patients were experiencing grief reactions from the death of a parent. To our knowledge, there has been no study of this.

Despite the a priori objections to using psychological testing to determine treatment method and strategy, numerous clinicians have attempted to do so, although the assessment methods and strategies have differed considerably. The question of the usefulness of test results in treatment planning was discussed by Meehl in 1960 and later reprinted in his 1973 book *Psychodiagnosis: Selected Papers*. He wrote of a study with Bernard C. Glueck in which they surveyed different therapists about the ultimate usefulness of "pretreatment personality assessment" (Meehl, 1973, p. 118). Most groups, except followers of George Kelly, responded negatively. Meehl wrote that "the over-all percentage who believe that such prior knowledge of the client's personality greatly speeds therapy is only 17 percent" (1973, p. 118).

However, Meehl (1973) found that by using the Q-sort technique, therapists quickly form a stable image of the patient. In fact, it appeared that "somewhere between the second and fourth therapeutic hour it has stabilized approximately to the degree permitted by the terminal sort-resort reliabilities" (p. 122). Of course, a stable view of the patient is not equivalent to the validity of the perception, but this finding does bear on the pragmatic or cost–benefit usefulness of testing and assessment. Summarizing these findings, Meehl (1973) wrote that

> since the commonest justification for expenditure of psychometric time is the utility to the therapist of "advance knowledge," . . . the skepticism expressed by our sample of psychotherapists, taken in combination with the convergence curves for the therapist's perception of his patient, put this widely held belief badly in need of experimental support. (p. 132)

Unfortunately, Meehl and his colleagues never went on to test this belief (Meehl, personal communication, 1990).

Although Meehl's group of therapists in 1960 were highly skeptical about the value of psychological testing in psychotherapy, recent surveys of clinical psychologists have demonstrated that a substantial number continue to conduct psychological testing (Berndt, 1983; Norcross & Prochaska, 1982; Wade & Baker, 1977) and to apply their findings to their treatment recommendations. Moreover, articles and books continue to argue for the usefulness of psychological testing in making treatment recommendations (Honigfeld, 1971; Hyer, 1994; Maruish, 1994; Retzlaff, 1995b; van Reken, 1981; Weiner, 1972).

Most authors who discuss the actual application of psychological testing to treatment use projective tests and primarily are psychodynamically oriented. In many cases, the articles are anecdotal case reports. For example, Cerney (1978) wrote about the use of an entire test battery to predict the outcome of psychotherapy, to function as an objective measure to assist in examining the process of treatment, and to point out possible pitfalls in psychotherapeutic treatment. Aronow and Reznikoff (1971) provided a case study of the application of projective tests in treatment. Walker (1974) noted the usefulness of the word-association sentence method in predicting psychotherapy outcome. Lovitt (1988) provided support for his contention that "intensive study of each person's personality structure or coping style is necessary for a proper match between the patient and a treatment approach" (p. 518).

Mortimer and Smith (1983), from a psychodynamic perspective, wrote of the usefulness of psychological testing in three long-term treatment cases. Although their article also was anecdotal, its encouragement of explicit focus in treatment and clear case description are laudable. The test report of a battery of tests was used to provide explicit direction on a different focal point in each case. In one situation, the test report focused on the patient's ego deficits; in another, it focused on the centrality of a certain impulse-defense configuration; and in the third, it focused on a possible transference paradigm and core neurotic conflict. Mortimer and Smith noted that

> as psychotherapists, we have become convinced that an unfocused or inaccurately focused treatment may be a considerable disservice to the patient. . . . The test report is a useful tool to help establish a central focus initially and to regain it when the report is reviewed. . . . When we determine the relative centrality of the different facets which the patient presents to us in testing, we are able to help psychotherapists determine where to focus their efforts and attention. (1983, p. 138)

Workers at the Menninger Foundation, long a bastion of the sophisticated use of psychological tests, continue to publish work on using projective testing in psychotherapeutic treatment. Colson, Pickar, and Coyne (1989) used the Rorschach to help predict possible patient factors leading to treatment difficulties in a long-term inpatient setting. There were some significant findings, although they cautioned that "the findings are few and of low magnitude. . . . Hence examiners should be cautious about using Rorschach findings to draw inferences about the course of hospital treatment" (1989, p. 56). Schectman detailed how sensitive use of projective instruments can help therapists to better understand and deal with varying transference–countertransference dilemmas of borderline patients. In-depth use of such testing explicating countertransference possibilities can help clinicians to continue with such difficult patients: "What sustains us is our slow, but persistent, increased understanding of such patients, and of those dark parts of ourselves" (Schectman, 1989, p. 317).

Different from the traditional psychological testing instruments,

Kiesler (1986a) used an interpersonalist assessment technique (either the Impact Message Inventory or Check List of Psychotherapy Transactions) before psychotherapy. He then formulated specific interventions and techniques to modify the interpersonal patterns if the patterns interfered with a person's life in or out of therapy. Kiesler's model is useful in that it highlights the inherently interactional basis of psychopathology and the therapeutic relationship. That is, Kiesler paid close attention to how the patient and the therapist reciprocally affect one another to produce any given dynamic moment in treatment. By conceptualizing treatment as interactional, the therapist then can begin to acknowledge his or her contribution to treatment and better understand how the patient's (or the therapist's) characteristic interpersonal style can be either an impediment or asset to therapeutic change.

Since our first edition, another interpersonalist has published a useful text integrating assessment and treatment of the varying personality subtypes. Benjamin (1993) used her Structural Analysis of Social Behavior (SASB) and INTREX questionnaires to draw helpful diagnostic distinctions, which then can be used to formulate treatment goals and plans. This model sketches out primary interpersonal styles that deal with the dimensions of love–hate, enmeshment–differentiation, and focus on self or other. She also provided some useful core wishes that the varying personality types will bring into any new interpersonal transaction, such as psychotherapy. For example, she wrote that the dependent personality believes "you must take care of everything for me. You do it so well, and I do it so badly" (Benjamin, 1993, p. 105). She later provided chapters on each personality type that include case examples, SASB patterns, expected transference reactions, and treatment implications.

Followers of George Kelly continue to value and publish articles and books on how their particular assessment methodology (the Role Construct Repertory Test) can be used to develop treatment strategies. Kelly (1969a) defined constructs as "the axes of reference man contrives to put his psychological space in order and to plot his varying courses of action" (p. 36). Kelly's followers are convinced that use of their assessment methodology helps to alert clinicians to repetitive or limited constructs that patients bring to treatment. This could lead to explicit therapeutic strategies, including selecting other constructs, making constructs more explicit, testing constructs for their validity and consistency, and altering the range or meaning of a construct (Kelly, 1969b; Neimeyer, 1987).

There is a book by Butcher (1990) and at least one published article by Trimboli and Kilgore (1983) concerning the Minnesota Multiphasic Personality Inventory (MMPI) and treatment considerations. More directly germane to treatment issues, Trimboli (1979) offered unpublished material on ways in which the MMPI might be used to guide therapy. All these authors discussed the ways in which the MMPI can be used psychodynamically to provide treatment implications. They also discussed each scale of the MMPI separately, making specific predictions about factors such as transference constellations, reasonable treatment goals, and issues of therapeutic timing and strategy.

Butcher (1990) wrote a comprehensive text on how the MMPI-2 can be used in objective assessment, treatment selection, and therapy planning. He provided methods for using each individual scale to predict treatment responsiveness, organized the material related to special scales of the MMPI and treatment evaluation, and addressed how to give feedback to patients who have taken the MMPI. One weakness of the book is that although Butcher (1990) claimed his treatment suggestions from high-point codes were culled "from the empirical literature on the MMPI in treatment contexts" (p. viii), he failed to cite any of those studies, which might lead readers to be skeptical of some of Butcher's suggestions.

There are few studies that have examined empirically the integration of psychological testing and psychotherapy outcome. W. H. Anderson and Bauer (1985), working with the MMPI, discussed how patients with a certain MMPI code type (2/4) present in psychotherapy and how successful treatment can be undertaken or altered to deal with the 2/4 personality characteristics. They contrasted successful and unsuccessful therapeutic work with these particular patients and provided rough guidelines for therapists working with "2/4" patients.

In another empirical study, Merbaum and Butcher (1982) examined the relation between therapists' ratings of patients' "likability," predictions of therapy benefit, and psychopathology as assessed by the MMPI. They found moderately strong associations between the patients rated by therapists as "difficult" and the patients' levels of self-reported pathology as reflected on the MMPI results. There also were strong associations between how "easy" patients were viewed as being by therapists and the estimated benefit from treatment. However, there were no differences between either easy or difficult patients and the actual number of therapy sessions completed. Merbaum and Butcher speculated that there is a relation between patients' pathology and their subsequent likability. Another interpretation may be that, because therapists tend to rate likable patients as having a superior prognosis, a self-fulfilling prophecy takes place. This has implications for the use of testing data early in treatment: It could be argued that therapists might become discouraged by a patient's pathological presentation on the testing and prematurely develop negative feelings about the eventual treatment outcome.

In a theoretical article related to concepts underlying the MCMI, Millon (1988) offered a new model of conceptualizing psychotherapy. He wrote of a model for interweaving diagnostic information and psychological treatment for those disorders. His "personologic psychotherapy" attempts to address environmental stressors, personality factors, and constitutional variables. He differentiated between "functional" and "structural" personality processes and highlighted particular combinations that lead to different character pathology. Millon strongly supported the idea that assessment makes a difference in treatment technique but that simply making a diagnosis is not enough. Millon (1988) stated that "which attributes should be selected for therapeutic intervention is not, therefore, merely a matter of making 'a diagnosis,' but requires a comprehensive assessment, one that appraises not only the overall configuration of attributes, but differentiates their degrees of salience" (p. 215).

Millon was not specific in what treatment methods clinicians should apply, but he believed in basing interventions on empirically verified procedures that should be tailored to the patients' problem. He objected to application of the same therapy model to all emotional difficulties and hoped instead that clinicians would combine techniques to achieve a whole that is greater than the sum of its parts. The foci of such therapy would vary, but, for example, it might involve simultaneous interventions at the level of interpersonal behavior à la Sullivan or modifications of dysfunctional beliefs or a faulty self-image through cognitive–behavioral modalities à la Aaron Beck (Beck & Freeman, 1990). Others have argued that because the distinction between functional and dysfunctional personality traits is thought to lie in the extremeness and the rigidity of the traits, personality-oriented psychotherapists should attempt to help the patient become less extreme and less rigid with regard to the personality traits in question (Sim & Romney, 1990). Still others (Turkat, 1988, 1990; Turkat & Maisto, 1985) have offered specific guidelines and various techniques to use with personality disorders. However, such work is at a formative stage, and even the author of one "cookbook" admits that "scientific evidence to support or refute the validity of the approach is lacking" (Turkat, 1990, p. 16).

From an empirical viewpoint, the MCMI has been used in several studies to assess possible changes in personality that might occur as a result of using various treatment modalities. Clinical populations studied have included alcoholics and drug abusers (McMahon, Flynn, & Davidson, 1985a), private psychiatric inpatients (Piersma, 1986b, 1989a), Vietnam veterans with posttraumatic stress disorder (PTSD; Hyer et al., 1989), and spouse abusers (Hamberger & Hastings, 1988b). A consistent finding across these four studies is that, regardless of whether there was clinical improvement, personality style scales remained fairly stable from pre- to posttest assessments and were more stable than symptom scales (e.g., level of anxiety, depression).

Three other studies using the MCMI have touched briefly on the use of the MCMI in treatment contexts. Cantrell and Dana (1987) used the MCMI-I as a screening instrument with patients at a community mental health center. They demonstrated that the MCMI-I was poor at predicting premature termination of treatment, although there was evidence that dropouts scored significantly higher on the Dependent scale than patients who stayed in treatment long enough to be assigned a therapist. Moreover, there was a slight but significant correlation between the total number of therapy sessions attended and scores on the Compulsive scale. These conclusions should be regarded as tentative because the sample size was relatively small ($N = 72$) and did not support the number of statistical tests performed on the data.

McMahon and Davidson (1986b) used the MCMI to examine depressed and nondepressed alcoholics treated in a Veterans Administration inpatient unit. Patients were originally divided into the two groups on the basis of their scores on the Dysthymia scale. They demonstrated that these two groups could be differentiated on the basis of having a detached (schizoid or avoidant) personality style or because they were suffering from disorganized or distracted mentation (Schizotypal and Psychotic Thinking scale scores). Because the depressed alcoholics also had a longer history of alcohol abuse and more physical and psychological symptoms, McMahon and Davidson recommended that this subgroup "would benefit most from an intensive, comprehensive, and long-term therapeutic program" (1986b, p. 183).

From a biological perspective, Joffe and Regan (1989a) examined patients who did and did not respond to tricyclic antidepressant treatment to determine whether there would be personality differences between the two groups. The MCMI, Beck Depression Inventory, Hamilton Rating Scale for Depression, and Schedule for Affective Disorders and Schizophrenia were administered. In the remission phase, there were no significant differences between responders and nonresponders on the MCMI. In the depressed phase, responders scored higher on the Antisocial and Paranoia scales. The MCMI tended to overdiagnose personality disorders in the depressed phase. There was no difference in frequency of personality disorders between responders and nonresponders. The findings of this study are limited because of the relatively small sample ($N = 42$).

One issue of concern involves the validity of the models presently used to generate treatment recommendations from test results. At least with the MMPI, there is no shortage of automated programs (Graham, 1987). Many of these programs offer psychotherapeutic suggestions specific to a given code type. Unfortunately, these computerized services do not publish the method used in developing interpretations or therapy recommendations (Matarazzo, 1986). Moreover, they do not provide data on how accurate or helpful the suggestions were with given personality types. This is not to say, of course, that such a process of validating recommendations would be easy (Fowler & Butcher, 1986) but simply to highlight the current knowledge in this area.

For example, one of the more publicized and favorably received computerized MMPI programs, the Caldwell Report, provides "treatment considerations" for the different MMPI code point types (Graham, 1977). These considerations include rough estimates of suicidal potential, possible indications for medications, predicted course of treatment, and suggestions of differing techniques that "have been beneficial in similar cases" (Caldwell, 1975, 1984). Caldwell has not, to our knowledge, published an explanation of how he obtained these results or data on their reliability and validity.

There have been many other attempts by computerized services to suggest treatment possibilities on the basis of MMPI results. To use another example, in the MMPI program by Strassberg, Cooper, and Marks (1987) available for use with personal computers, multiple treatment recommendations and suggestions are given. These include the degree of psychological mindedness, potential transference constellations, and medication possibilities. Strassberg et al. mentioned in the report that their suggestions for treatment and diagnostic interpretation were based on their clinical experience and on the work of others. They cautioned that their information and suggestions are "suggestive and tentative" and "should be treated as hypotheses which are essentially untested outside of clinical work" (1987, p. 1).

Graham (1987) believed that such caveats are not sufficient and cautioned that

> all of the studies that have tried to establish the validity of (computerized or automated) interpretive systems have had serious shortcomings. . . . No study to date has evaluated an entire interpretive system. The external criterion measures used in most studies have been limited in scope and of questionable reliability. (p. 242)

He further stated that it is essential that only qualified professionals use the reports and that other assessment data are integrated with the test findings. He concluded by saying that "the level of accuracy of the interpretive statements is at best modest, but in many cases it is no less than the accuracy of clinician-generated descriptions of clients based on MMPI data" (Graham, 1987, p. 242).

Thus, it is obvious that much work needs to be done to establish the validity and reliability of treatment suggestions given certain test results. However, in lieu of such hard data and given that many clinicians already do make inferences for therapy on the basis of the testing they do with their patients or on even less reliable information, it might be useful to explore further what approaches could be used to generate treatment suggestions from MCMI results.

Using the MCMI in Psychotherapy: Supportive Versus Insight Orientations

What we can offer at this point are our own thoughts on how the results of the MCMI can be used to develop a treatment plan with psychotherapy patients. We begin by examining the issue of whether to recommend supportive or insight-oriented treatment. Dewald (1967, 1971) held that the vast majority of patients who seek psychotherapy actually are served best by supportive measures. He felt that insight-oriented, or exploratory, approaches are too anxiety provoking and potentially overwhelming for most patients. Dewald appeared to feel that most patients have ego weaknesses or flawed self-identities that need "bolstering" or rebuilding rather than "deconstruction" or "reconstruction." He provided some clinical examples about how to generate supportive interventions for certain character types, such as giving a compulsive patient a less time-consuming substitute symptom. Unfortunately, Dewald failed to provide a comprehensive theoretical model of matching supportive techniques and treatment tactics with the patient's personality type.

Werman (1984), like Dewald, believed that many patients are better served by supportive rather than insight-oriented, or exploratory, methods. He also believed that many patients are too fragile to be able to handle interpretations of the unconscious, underlying dynamics or even most aspects of the transference. Werman provided a rough cataloging of intervention strategies for supportive therapy, but he did not say much about the diagnoses of patients better suited for supportive treatment or about the results of psychological testing of such patients.

Kernberg (1984) differed from Werman (1984) and Dewald (1967, 1971) in his view of supportive psychotherapy. Kernberg felt that many patients can benefit more from an exploratory, expressive type of treatment. He tended to reserve supportive measures primarily for borderline patients with antisocial tendencies or for focused, narrow goals when, because of financial or other constraints, a more leisurely expressive and exploratory approach is not possible.

A useful review of the supportive treatment literature was provided by Winston, Pinsker, and McCullough (1986). They summarized the major definitions, issues, and techniques of supportive psychotherapy. Of particular interest is the catalog and explanations they offered of the divergent techniques of supportive work. They concluded by urging better delineation of supportive treatment and encouraged those in training positions to supervise and teach supportive treatment with as much interest as they would in teaching the uncovering, or expressive, modalities. Winston et al. called for systematic research on the efficacy of such methods and readily acknowledged the dearth of empirical work in this area.

There is a tradition in psychoanalysis and in many forms of psychoanalytic therapy that discourages attempts to match therapy techniques to character patterns or constellations. Some might even object to a systematic method of choosing a given treatment modality or focus, particularly within expressive insight-oriented treatment. However, there are some notable exceptions. F. Alexander and French (1946), for instance, advocated briefer treatment methods in which the therapist would attempt to provide whatever the patient had not been given by his or her original caretaker. For example, if the patient had been treated harshly and coldly as a child, the therapist would try to be as warm and nurturing as possible to ostensibly compensate for the deficits. This approach has met with a great deal of criticism and scorn, although some recent psychoanalytic writers (e.g., Levy, 1987; T. Sha-piro, 1988, 1989) have seen the value in maintaining an explicit focus of the treatment strategy or aims in psychotherapy or psychoanalysis.

Levy (1987) argued that the analytical ideal of full neutrality, and the wait for the unfolding of the unconscious, is an artificial ideal. When being supervised on analytical treatment cases, Levy found that his supervisors would instruct him to focus on certain problems, ignore others, and, in general, adjust his technique to the patient's character type. He mentioned that such focusing and direction is a common part of the "unofficial" clinical lore of analytical therapists but that it is rarely discussed explicitly in the literature or in public forums.

Levy (1987) pointed out that one of the rare exceptions of strategic applications of technique on the basis of diagnosis or character pathology within the history of psychoanalytic literature was offered by Glover (1955). In a chapter on the analyst's case list in his book *Psychoanalytic Therapy*, Glover (1955) discussed the numerous cases an analyst or analytically oriented therapist might encounter and generally divided the cases according to their "accessibility" or, as he put it, "the transference potential of the patient" (p. 185).

Within varying categories (e.g., anxiety hysteria, reactive depressions, obsessional neurosis, manic–depressive states), Glover (1955) speculated on the ultimate transference constellation, the most helpful and salient foci of the treatment, the types of crises in treatment, and particular qualities of the termination process. He provided rough guidelines for the best "lines of approach" for each given case.

In Glover's (1955) approach, he wrote of the paranoid patient:

> Of the three main character reactions manifested by the paranoiac ego, viz. suspicion, sensitiveness to contact and a defensive aggressiveness, the factor of suspicion calls for priority of attention. It should be ventilated from the first session of analysis; also from the first session the transference aspects should be raised in the slightly indirect form of ventilating the patient's reactions to treatment. . . . During these two early phases of analysis the delusional or near-delusional products of the patient should not be subject to interpretation but should be treated with non-committal receptivity. (p. 252)

Thus, it can be seen that Glover (1955) recommended specific technical maneuvers that take into account transference disposition, personality style, symptomatology, and timing within the treatment rather than the traditional analytical advice to remain more uniformly detached and silent, allowing the transference to unfold before making interpretations or providing direction.

More recently, other psychoanalytic clinicians have discussed explicitly the importance of needing to adapt the therapy technique to the differing psychopathology or character structure of the patient. Giovacchini (1984, 1987), Kernberg (1975), Kohut (1971, 1977), and D. Shapiro (1989), among others, have discussed in great detail the understanding and treatment of patients with borderline, narcissistic, or other character disorders. Those authors, to varying degrees, have developed particular techniques or guidelines for the specific treatment of the given character pathology. For example, Giovacchini (1987) wrote that

> formulating a continuum of psychopathology based on the quality of object relations is useful for understanding patients and, to some extent, for anticipating transference development in treatment. . . . Furthermore, the reason for making a diagnostic judgment—and some psychoanalysts doubt that there is any—is to help the clinician find dominant patterns of adaptations and defenses that permit conclusions about character structure and give some order and predictability to the treatment process. (p. 322)

Thus, Giovacchini (1987) viewed diagnosis of character structure to be particularly useful in providing some broad outlines of possible transference manifestations so that there can be some planning of the therapeutic task ahead. He probably would emphasize assessment of the patient's history of object relations, as well as what led the patient to seek therapy. Although he did not mention it, psychological testing also could presumably be used to gain understanding into likely character traits and potential transference manifestations so that tentative treatment planning could occur.

Another recent contributor within psychoanalytic circles, T. Shapiro (1988, 1989) encouraged an intelligent integration of diagnostic classification and the methods and models of psychoanalysis. Shapiro wrote of the history of psychoanalytic or psychoanalytically informed diagnostic categorizations of the borderline patient. He, like Levy (1987), claimed that treatment of patients requires strategy, a strategy that is made more intelligible with firm diagnostic information. In the example of the borderline patient, he noted the following:

> Of crucial importance for the conceptual soundness of borderline personality disorder or organization is the differentiation of therapeutic effect, with specific groups differentiated by the psychoanalytically guided techniques available. (T. Shapiro, 1989, p. 192)

Although he did not mention psychological tests directly, presumably T. Shapiro (1989) would approve of the analytically informed usage of any psychological means to refine the "clinical truth" (p. 193) of clinical classifications so that wise treatment decisions can be made.

Along with the work done by those from a more classical analytical model, there has been a burgeoning of work from theorists within the interpersonalist camp that has examined treatment planning, predictions of process, and elucidation of strategies with differing personality styles. Kiesler (1977, 1979, 1982, 1986a, 1986b); McCullough (1984), and T. Van Denburg (1987), among others, have developed systematic methods to assess and direct treatment of patients with varying personality styles (e.g., borderline, passive-dependent, chronically dysthymic) from an interpersonal approach. The central assumptions of the interpersonalists' model were derived from Sullivan's (1953) seminal ideas that personality is "the relatively enduring pattern of recurrent interpersonal situations which characterize a human life" (pp. 110–111).

Kiesler's (1983) operationalization of Sullivan's (1953) ideas, following Leary's (1957) lead, is founded on the assumption that human interactions are a function of two basic motivations: the need for control (e.g., domination) and the need for affiliation (e.g., love, friendship). Kiesler (1983) constructed what he called the "interpersonal circle" to explain and classify the varying interactions that people engage in with one another. Kiesler posited that psychopathology is partially a function of rigid and extreme interpersonal behavior that is carried out across situations. Although the normal or healthy person is flexible and adaptable in his or her actions with significant others, the maladjusted individual reenacts the same inflexible and limited roles with whomever he or she comes into contact. Kiesler extended these ideas to psychotherapy and theorized that patients will bring the same patterns to treatment, thus exerting the same interpersonal pulls in therapy that they exhibit in their outside lives. The therapist should be savvy enough to spot such interpersonal transactions and intervene accordingly in the treatment. Kiesler and his associates (Kiesler, 1982, 1986b; Kiesler, Van Denburg, Sikes, Larus, & Goldston, 1990) have demonstrated that the third edition of the *Diagnostic and Statistical Manual of Mental Disorders* personality disorders can be reliably and validly described using interpersonal taxonomies and that there are beginnings of the application of such methodology to the treatment of specific disorders and styles (Andrews, 1984; Cashdan, 1982; Coyne, 1976; Kiesler, 1977, 1985, 1986a;

Klerman, Weissman, Rounsaville, & Chevron, 1984; Young & Beier, 1982).

Writers from other schools of therapy have begun to take the interpersonalist's lead and see the importance of changing treatment plans or relationship stances based on the characteristics of the client. In a recent issue of *Psychotherapy*, there was a special section with six articles from varying viewpoints that discussed matching client needs with therapist relationship stances. Although "the published literature on the subject is meager, and most clinicians are unable to verbalize or operationalize the grounds on which they tailor their interpersonal stance to different clients" (Norcross, 1993, p. 402), the papers in the special section were a beginning attempt to articulate how psychotherapists shift their styles to better match with clients' characteristics and needs.

We often tell our supervisees that in doing supportive psychotherapy, they need to individualize the treatment. However, we think that one problem with the concept of "supportive" therapy is that the treatment is often unclear and poorly defined. What often is meant by the term *supportive therapy* is simply that the therapist will be making an effort to be understanding, conciliatory, sympathetic, compassionate, and nonconfrontative and that no demands will be made of the patient that the latter could find threatening or difficult. If those attributes are present in the relationship, it generally would be thought that the relationship would feel comfortable to the client and would contribute to the reduction of tension. In spite of the merits of that general approach to therapy, the prescription of the same mode of interaction for every patient can be criticized as being unduly simplistic and one that does not recognize the individual's uniqueness or the therapist's level of sophistication. This mode of therapy possibly could be prescribed for an individual who does not have the resources needed for a meaningful change, at least at the beginning of therapy.

The results of the MCMI can provide one way of refining the system by allowing easy and effective consideration of the client's personality style. Knowing the individual's basic life assumptions and the cluster of traits that make up the client's personality structure allows the practitioner to set up an interpersonal environment during the session that is designed to be experienced by the client as egosyntonic and congenial to his or her own way of operating.

Table 8, taken from a training manual we recently wrote (Choca & Van Denburg, 1996), offers some of the interpersonal characteristics

Table 8

Supportive Interventions for the Different Personality Styles

Style	Supportive attribute
1. Schizoid	Accept interpersonal distance
	Problem solve in practical matters
	Do not emphasize insight
	Do not emphasize relationships
2. Avoidant	Reassure
	Be careful with negative interpretations
	Be relaxed
3. Dependent	Be dominant
	Be protective
4. Histrionic	Allow patient to be center of attention
	Be emotionally demonstrative
5. Narcissistic	Allow patient to be dominant
	Be careful with negative interpretations
6. Competitive	Accept competitive assumption
	Show how the client is not competing well in terms of his or her psychological functioning
	Be firm when limits are tested
7. Compulsive	Be on time
	Be organized
	Accept a hierarchical view of the world
8. Negativistic	As much as possible, do not tell patient what to do (any controls will be used as an issue by the patient)
	Tolerate and interpret moods

that theoretically would lead to a supportive therapeutic experience with the different personality styles. Note the flexibility that this additional level of sophistication allows. Looking at any particular type of intervention (e.g., confrontation), the consideration of the personality style allows the practitioner to avoid such interventions with some individuals (i.e., avoidant or dependent clients) while using it with others (i.e., competitive clients). With most of our clients, the issues become more complex than the table would lead one to believe because most people have a combination of more than one personality style. Thus, the therapist would have to mix and integrate the recommendations that are given in the table to do justice to most patients.

Especially in the case of individuals whose personality traits are too extreme or too rigid and who may be considered to have a personality disorder, care should be taken not to emphasize the ego-syntonic recommendations to the point of fostering further pathology. For the supportive relationship to remain beneficial, the therapist has to operate at clients' levels so that the relationship is comfortable without being antitherapeutic. With dependent individuals, for instance, if the therapist is to take responsibility for things that clients can handle by themselves, the interventions would be seen as encouraging the individuals to become more dependent than they already are, a regressive tactic.

From our viewpoint, the issue of supportive versus insight-oriented therapy cannot involve the choice of one to the exclusion of the other. Most therapists adjust their treatment to fit patients' needs while attempting, at least to some degree, to increase their understanding of the way they function. The more capable, psychologically developed, functional, and motivated therapy candidates are, the more feasible it may be to emphasize the goal of raising their level of functioning or understanding. Whyne-Berman and McCann (1995) made the same point in terms of the sophistication of individuals' defense mechanisms, with the more primitive defenses calling for a more directive or supportive approach.

Personality theory and the MCMI also can be useful with an insight-oriented treatment plan. In the majority of the patients we see, especially after the acute symptomatology diminishes, clients are left to struggle with cumbersome or pathological personality traits. Knowing what those traits are and having some understanding of the theoretical etiologies of those traits can provide invaluable help in designing the treatment strategies.

Using the MCMI in Psychotherapy: Brief Versus Long Term

The literature on brief therapy focuses more on ways in which psychotherapy can be altered or planned to appropriately deal with divergent personality types or diagnoses. This is no doubt about the need to be as judicious as possible, given either internally or externally imposed treatment-length constraints.

Most, but not all, brief therapy theorists begin their therapeutic assessment procedure by limiting the patient populations who can be treated with their methods. Davanloo (1979), Sifneos (1972), Mann (1973), and Malan (1976) attempted to screen patients for more serious psychopathology before attempting brief treatment. Thus, they likely would exclude personality types and disorders such as borderline, narcissistic, schizoid, schizotypal, and paranoid clients from being treated with their methods.

In contrast to the majority of brief therapists, Strupp and Binder (1984) reported that they "have seen that the range of patients thought to be treatable has been progressively extended" and that "the best available evidence (of when brief therapy is appropriate) remains clinical experience" (p. 56). They later reiterated this position and advocated that brief therapists use a "time limited attitude" (Binder, Henry, & Strupp, 1987). Consistent with Strupp and his colleagues' perspective, Donovan (1987) wrote a useful and insightful article on the ways in which brief therapy methods can be broadened to treat a wider variety of patient types and personality disorders. He postulated that all personality disorders can be traced to a nuclear conflict: the holding of a core pathogenic belief about the self. The belief can take a variety of forms, but it usually pertains to issues involving the modulation of self-esteem. These problems with self-esteem, Donovan continued, are a direct derivative of interactions with early caretakers.

To help patients in brief therapy using Donovan's (1987) ideas, the therapist must first do a focal inquiry of pathogenic convictions about the self. This requires "the taking of an empathic object relations history" (Donovan, 1987, p. 176). Along with this inquiry comes facing and dealing with potentially disorganizing and intense affect. However, the therapist should not make matters worse by prematurely confronting or interpreting in a manner that causes patients to be retraumatized. Donovan seemed to be saying that if patients can trust the relationship enough and be understood, powerful affect will emerge. Finally, an attempt is made to reframe the pathogenic belief about the self, and the therapist "must offer himself as an alternative self object" when "the patient is most vulnerable and most in need of this function" (Donovan, 1987, p. 176). By examining patients' object-relations histories and sensitively determining what they can bear to hear about themselves, Donovan would implicitly be taking into account patients' personality style, even though he did not use that exact language.

M. J. Horowitz et al. (1984), writing from within the brief treatment field, stated that

> the question of which kind of therapy is best for a particular person is unanswered by available research data. This is especially the case with reference to character style or the nature of Axis 2 [sic] diagnosis (presence of personality disorders) in the American Psychiatric Association's *Diagnostic and Statistical Manual.* (p. 31)

Nonetheless, M. J. Horowitz et al. did attempt to provide explicit "road-maps" and clinical landmarks for the psychotherapy of divergent personality types, including hysterical, compulsive, narcissistic, and border-line patients.

M. J. Horowitz et al. (1984) intentionally restricted their book and study to helping patients who were in the midst of a grief reaction caused by the death of a parent. They proposed that different personality styles have different defensive structures, varying cognitive patterns, and divergent interpersonal behavior. Because of these multiple variations, the reaction to the loss and grief differ. This necessitates that the therapist be flexible in his or her approach so that psychotherapeutic interventions can be best geared to the unique personality qualities of each patient.

M. J. Horowitz et al. (1984) described their use of a "configurational analysis" to examine all cases presented to their research group and used this analysis to order data more systematically than often is the case in ordinary case conferences and case studies. Factors such as *DSM–III* diagnosis, "states of mind," role relationships, and modes of information processing were considered, both within and outside of treatment. According to Horowitz et al., "case formulation may help a therapist to understand relationship problems based on individual personality styles" (1984, p. 57). Treatment had to be uniquely tailored to the individual case because, in spite of the fact that each patient had a parent die shortly before beginning therapy, there were "individualized variations in response, resting in part on personality style" (M. J. Horowitz et al., 1984, p. 57). In the chapters covering the varying personality styles, the authors sought to "emphasize the difficulties in establishing a therapeutic alliance with persons who have different personality styles" and "describe the process in therapy by which this came about" (M. J. Horowitz et al., 1984, p. 67).

MCMI Personality Styles and the Therapeutic Relationship

As already mentioned, Lovitt (1988) argued that "intensive study of each person's personality structure or coping style is necessary for a proper match between the patient and a treatment approach" (p. 518). Although that suggestion may be ideal, in most settings clinicians generally have to accept patients as they are referred or assigned. In either case, in theory, the MCMI results could help with the matching or at least could indicate the kind of relationship that would result between two specific individuals on the basis of their particular personality styles.

Such a pragmatic, real-world model was suggested by Sweeney, Clarkin, and Fitzgibbon (1987). They supported the use of the MCMI as a test that could be used profitably in initial screenings to make treatment recommendations within an acute inpatient setting. Sweeney et al. called for a more focused problem-oriented assessment method that is economically practical and backed by empirical support.

Several researchers have explored the relation between single personality traits and treatment parameters. For instance, Fry (1975) found that a directive and controlling therapist produced more satisfaction for patients who look outside of themselves for their locus of control. Canter's (1966, 1971) work indicated that the characteristic of authoritarianism was related to patients' preferences for different therapeutic approaches. The intraception trait on the Edwards Personal Preference Schedule (Edwards, 1959) has been correlated with an orientation toward insight in therapy (Birch, 1976; Gibeau, 1975). In addition, numerous researchers have examined the relation between "therapeutic behaviors" such as openness, empathy, and genuineness and the therapist's personality traits (S. Anderson, 1968; Bent, Putnam, Kiesler, & Nowicki, 1976; Beutler, Johnson, Neville, Workman, & Elkins, 1973; Brewer, 1974; C. Palmer, 1975; Wright, 1975).

It seems logical that an individual's personality style will significantly influence the quality of the interpersonal relationship that he or she establishes. In a pilot study conducted at our medical center (Choca, Silverman, & Gerber, 1980; J. T. Silverman, 1979), we examined the quality of the kind of relationship that patients established with their therapists in terms of strength, dominance, and conflictualness. As expected, the findings showed that schizoid individuals tended to establish relationships that were seen by the therapist as having low strength; an unpredicted significant correlation was found between Compulsive scale scores of the MCMI-I and the staff's strength rating. Our data suggested that histrionic and antisocial patients were inclined to play a more dominant role. Finally, the Antisocial and the Compulsive scale scores were significantly related to the amount of conflict that the patient perceived in the relationship.

In a well-designed recent study, Muran, Segal, Samstag, and Crawford (1994) looked at the relationship between pretreatment interpersonal variables and the therapeutic working alliance. The MCMI and Inventory of Interpersonal Problems were given to 32 patients before beginning brief (20-session) cognitive therapy. The patients then completed the Working Alliance Inventory after the third session of treatment. Positive correlations were found between measures of the working alliance and the interpersonal qualities of a friendly-submissive nature. Hostile-dominant problems were related negatively to the development of the working alliance.

Personality Enlightened Therapy for PTSD

The holistic assessment and treatment of PTSD proposed by Hyer and colleagues (Hyer et al., 1991; Hyer, Davis, Woods, Albrecht, & Boudewyns, 1994) starts with a lifestyle analysis that relies on patients' early recollections and family configuration; the private logic or beliefs that patients endorse also are taken into consideration. The system then investigates patients' personalities, typically with the help of the MCMI. The importance of taking into consideration characterological factors in the treatment of PTSD also has been emphasized by others (e.g., Sherwood et al., 1990). Finally, the PTSD symptoms are evaluated. The goal is to understand the symptoms that are informed by patients' lifestyles and their personalities.

In their writings, Hyer et al. (1991, 1994) offered many insights and advice in handling patients with different MCMI profiles. They characterized the general "traumatic personality" as a negativistic-avoidant style. These individuals are "oversensitive, fearful, self-preoccupied, disgruntled, uneasy, irritable . . . unsettled . . . anxious, complaining, and powerless" (Hyer et al., 1991, p. 176). Given this personality, the overall treatment approach must be one that emphasizes the increase of control as a therapeutic goal. This control would include attempts at "reduction of vacillating and self-defeating patterns" (Hyer, 1994, p. 237).

More specific advice also is available for the three personality subtypes that have been found. Individuals who have schizoid elements along with the negativistic-avoidant personality (the 8A2A1 code type) "appear cognitive and affectively confused" and experience themselves as "strange, lost and despairing" (Hyer et al., 1991, p. 178). A reasonable therapeutic approach is to respect the detachment and to build trust over time. By contrast, patients with benign but annoying dependent traits (the 8A2A13 code type) have a poor self-image and are submissive, a fact that tends to increase compliance. By far the most difficult patients are said to be those with an antisocial bent (the 8A2A16A code type). Their interpersonal distrust often makes the building of a working alliance difficult. In his later work, Hyer (1994) discussed how the self-defeating code type added to the 8A2A1 profile "floods the avoidant and ambivalent character traits with a repetitive series of misfortunes" (p. 239). This group also "tends to increase problems and undermine progress in treatment" (Hyer, 1994, p. 239). Hyer et al. (1994) also noted that elevations in any of the severe personality scales (e.g., Borderline), which occurs in as many as 60% of these patients, further complicates the treatment and aggravates the prognosis. Although Hyer (1994) took pains to say that this material is best viewed as a "clinical taxonomy and represents anything but perfect classification" (p. 240), recent empirical work using the cluster analysis technique tended to support his assumptions (Hyer et al., 1994).

Marital Therapy

As detailed in chapter 7, Craig and Olson (1995) used the MCMI-II to characterize four types of individuals who are likely to seek marital therapy. The authors then considered the possible combinations of the four different types and the therapeutic interventions that may be useful.

For example, the couple consisting of a narcissistic-aggressive-histrionic individual and a negativistic-aggressive-borderline individual is likely to have a conflictual marital relationship. It is suggested that the therapist focus on the conflicts and attempt to decrease the frequency and intensity of the quarreling.

When the narcissistic-aggressive-histrionic individual is matched with either of the two dependent types, the theoretical result will be an overadequate–underadequate relationship, in which the dependent spouse may complain of the partner being too bossy and controlling. A similar overadequate–underadequate relationship can be expected to result from the marriage of a negativistic-aggressive-borderline individual with either of the two dependent types. In those cases, Craig and Olson (1995) contended that the dependent spouse needs to see how his or her own behaviors allow the other to be controlling, whereas the overadequate spouse needs to explore the effect that a more egalitarian relationship would have on his or her own self-esteem.

A different problem is foreseen with the marriage of two individuals with dependent personality styles. The difficulties of the resulting underadequate–underadequate relationship may be that each of the partners would want the other to take the lead. In those cases, Craig and Olson (1995) recommended individual therapy along with the conjoint sessions designed to reduce the sensitivity to rejection and fear of making decisions.

Treatment Outcome Studies

The MCMI has been used to document the effects of treatment. A test–retest design using the MCMI-I, for instance, was used to show a change toward a more extraverted mode of functioning in the case of morbidly obese patients who received gastric stapling surgery and lost weight (Chandarana, Conlon, Holliday, Deslippe, & Field, 1990). Piersma and Smith (1991) used the Dysthymia scale of the MCMI-II to show symptom improvement in a group of hospitalized depressed individuals.

McMahon et al. (1985b) reported a reduction of the MCMI-I scores for a heterogeneous psychiatric population and two groups of substance abusers after 1–3 months of treatment. Similar results were reported by Piersma (1986d) for psychiatric inpatients; this was further confirmed with the MCMI-II (Piersma, 1989b). The increase of the Histrionic and Narcissistic scale scores and the decrease of the Disclosure and Debasement indexes also can be taken as signs of improvement during treatment. The Anxiety, Dysthymia, and Major Depression scales of the MCMI-I were used to show the benefits of short-term cognitive therapy done with individuals chosen through a suitability interview (Safran, Segal, Vallis, Shaw, & Wallner Samstag, 1993).

Peniston and Kulkosky (1990) compared the effect of alpha–theta brain-wave relaxation training with the use of group therapy and lectures in the treatment of alcoholics. The findings indicated that the group treated with the relaxation technique decreased their MCMI-I scores on 13 of the 20 scales. By contrast, the respondents receiving only group therapy and lectures obtained significant decreases on 2 scales and showed an increase on Compulsive scale scores.

Martin et al. (1992) examined the MCMI-I findings of former cult members, most of whom attended a residential treatment program for "deprogramming." Those who attended the program were assessed before and 6 months after treatment. Pretreatment–posttreatment measures with the MCMI-I showed a strong treatment effect. There were surprising changes in some personality constellations and lower test–retest correlations than reported in previous studies.

The trend of MCMI score reduction after treatment, however, was not always found. Judging from MCMI-I results, an intense 5-week inpatient treatment of veterans with PTSD did not lead to a reduction in the symptomatology (Hyer et al., 1989). Hyer et al. reported higher scores on 17 of the 20 scales after treatment, even though none of the changes were significant. They tentatively concluded that chronic PTSD is resistant to short-term treatment. Results of a later study by another group showed better results with patients who completed a 140-day treatment program. In that case, 12 of the 20 scale scores decreased. The fact that more than half of the sample dropped out of treatment before completing the program and were not included in the analysis undoubtedly pushed the data in the positive direction (Funari, Piekarski, & Sherwood, 1991).

In terms of predictor variables, higher scores on the Histrionic and Narcissistic scales of the MCMI-I and MCMI-II have been found to be associated with better outcomes (Chambless et al., 1992; Leaf, Ellis, Mass, DiGiuseppe, & Alington, 1990; Vaglum et al., 1990). Higher levels of schizoid, avoidant, and schizotypal traits have been associated with poorer outcomes (Chambless et al., 1992; Leaf, Ellis, Mass, et al., 1990; Vaglum et al., 1990).

Predictor-variable investigations dealing with specifically defined areas of pathology also are available. Fals-Stewart and Lucente (1993) used a mixture of exposure and response prevention behavior therapy exercises to treat obsessive–compulsive personality disorder. The authors found that patients with little character pathology, or those with dependent and compulsive features, did best in behavioral treatment.

In spite of the failure of Craig's (1984) early attempt to predict treatment dropout of substance abusers with the MCMI-I, others have reported significant findings. Fals-Stewart (1992) found two substance abuse subtypes that respond poorly to treatment in a drug-free therapeutic community. The first of these subtypes was characterized by a single elevation on the Antisocial scale of the MCMI-I. Members of this group were thought to have little regard for social rules and proved more likely than others to be expelled from treatment as a result of program rule violations. The second substance abuse subtype with a poor prognosis was characterized by elevations on the Schizoid and Avoidant scales. Such individuals were thought to experience great discomfort in a milieu emphasizing interpersonal interactions and become "self-critical, discouraged, and socially withdrawn" (Fals-Stewart, 1992, p. 524). Both of the poor prognostic groups stayed a fewer number of days in the program and remained alcohol- or drug-free for a shorter period of time. Similar work was reported by Simonsen et al. (1992), who found the Negativistic scale of the MCMI-I to be predictive of early dropout from an outpatient clinic for alcoholics. Finally, McMahon, Kelley, and Kouzekanani (1993) documented the same trend with cocaine abusing men on the MCMI-II. Their data showed that "a fiercely independent orientation with manipulative, exploitive, and confrontive interpersonal features" (McMahon et al., 1993, p. 153) leads to a lack of toleration for the kind of pressure for change that is typically a part of community-oriented treatment.

With a narrower sample of drug abusers, Stark and Campbell (1988) reported that patients staying in treatment had a higher baserate (BR) score on 6 of the MCMI-I scales than did immediate dropouts. Because 4 of these scales (i.e., the Paranoid, Psychotic Thinking, Psychotic Depression, and Psychotic Delusion) measure the most severe areas of pathology, the authors concluded that chronically mentally ill patients become dependent on the clinic for their basic psychological needs and tend to remain longer. However, the means reported all were at subclinical levels (58–61), hovered around the average for psychiatric patients (BR score of 60), and were not indicative of psychopathology. An alternate explanation would be that the immediate dropout group included patients in at least partial denial who endorsed fewer symptoms than the average psychiatric patient. If this turns out to be the case, it would then be signs of denial on the MCMI that would be predictive of early dropout from treatment.

McMahon et al. (1986) found that high-social-functioning alcoholics made significantly greater gains on the MCMI-I as a result of a behaviorally oriented therapeutic community treatment than did the low-social-functioning alcoholics. Although their findings may be plagued by the problem of distinguishing between the severity of the alcoholism and the level of social functioning, McMahon et al. saw their data as indicating that lower functioning alcoholics may need social skills training in addition to the conventional treatment for alcoholism.

Elevations on the Dysthymia scale of the MCMI-I were associated with poor outcome in the treatment of women with bulimia nervosa. Several of the MCMI scales showed significant improvement after treatment, including the Avoidant, Negativistic, Anxiety, and Dysthymia scales. Consistent with other outcome studies, a tendency to elevate the

Compulsive scale during treatment also was reported with this group (Garner et al., 1990).

Low therapist ratings of therapeutic response to inpatient treatment for PTSD were found to be associated with elevations on the Hypomania scale of the MCMI-I. The inventory, however, failed to predict treatment dropout (Munley et al., 1994).

Looking at the completion of treatment for the prevention of partner abuse, Faulkner, Cogan, Nolder, and Shooter (1991) were unable to find significant MCMI-I predictors. The characteristics of recidivists after spouse abuse abatement counseling also have been investigated. The data show that elevations on the substance abuse scales of the MCMI-I are associated with continued abuse even after completion of a treatment program. This finding is explainable in terms of the obvious link between substance abuse, the loss of control, and the lowering of inhibitions in many individuals. It is recommended that such individuals be involved in treatment for their substance abuse, in addition to the treatment for partner abuse. Recidivists also scored significantly higher on the Histrionic and the Narcissistic scales. Perhaps individuals with such elevations have more difficulty, because of their narcissistic needs, appreciating the partner's perspective and have more trouble seeing themselves as being in need of change (Hamberger & Hastings, 1990).

Summary and Conclusions

There does not appear to be sufficient empirical evidence to support the rational "prescription" of specific therapeutic modalities or psychotherapeutic techniques given certain psychological test findings. Even attempts to do something as crude as predict, through testing or other means, who will and who will not remain in treatment has been problematic (Affleck & Garfield, 1961; Garfield & Bergin, 1978; Rouff, Van Denburg, Newman, & Choca, 1995). Although there are some suggestions in the literature that individuals with certain personality constellations are more likely to terminate treatment earlier (e.g., Auld & Eron, 1953; Baekland & Lundwall, 1975; Lorr, Katz, & Rubinstein, 1958), rigorously controlled recent studies have failed to demonstrate that psychological tests (in this case the MMPI) or other methods can predict premature termination of psychotherapy (Dubrin & Zastowny, 1988). Thus, clinicians are forced to use theory, speculation, and clinical hunches to suggest treatment methods that might lead to successful process or outcome of treatment given certain testing findings.

This is essentially the approach we took in our suggested treatment recommendations with the Millon Clinical Multiaxial Inventory. Furthermore, we focused our attention and treatment advice solely on individual psychotherapy with a given patient. It is possible, of course, that the MCMI, and other test instruments, might be given when the patient is involved in family, marital, or group treatment in an outpatient or inpatient setting. It would be up to individual clinicians how they choose to apply our suggestions to varying therapeutic settings and situations. Moreover, as suggested by Graham (1987) and Hyer (1994), we advocate the understanding and integration of other assessment materials and clinical case histories before any firm and definitive treatment methods are initiated. Finally, we hold firmly that only qualified professionals with full training in psychological testing, diagnosis, and psychotherapy use the MCMI as an instrument to guide treatment directions.

References

Abraham, K. (1927). The influence of oral eroticism on character formation. In D. Bryan & A. Strachey (Trans.), *Selected papers on psychoanalysis* (pp. 393–406). London: Hogarth. (Original work published 1924)

Adams, W., & Clopton, J. (1990). Personality and dissonance among Mormon missionaries. *Journal of Personality Assessment, 54,* 684–693.

Adler, A. (1956). The style of life. In H. L. Ansbacher & R. R. Ansbacher (Eds.), *The individual psychology of Alfred Adler* (pp. 172–203). New York: Basic Books.

Affleck, D., & Garfield, S. (1961). Predictive judgments of therapists and duration of stay in psychotherapy. *Journal of Clinical Psychology, 17,* 134–137.

Ahrens, J., Evans, R., & Barnett, R. (1990). Factors related to dropping out of school in an incarcerated population. *Educational and Psychological Measurement, 50,* 611–617.

Alden, L. E., Wiggins, J. S., & Pincus, A. L. (1990). Construction of the circumplex scales for the Inventory of Interpersonal Problems. *Journal of Personality Assessment, 55,* 521–536.

Alexander, F., & French, T. (1946). *Psychoanalytic therapy.* New York: Ronald Press.

Alexander, G. E., Choca, J. P., Bresolin, L. B., DeWolfe, A. S., Johnson, J. E., & Ostrow, D. G. (1987, May). *Personality styles in affective disorders: Trait components of a state disorder.* Paper presented at the convention of the Midwestern Psychological Association, Chicago.

Alexander, G. E., Choca, J. P., DeWolfe, A. S., Bresolin, L. B., Johnson, J. E., & Ostrow, D. G. (1987, August). *Interaction between personality and mood in unipolar and bipolar patients.* Paper presented at the 95th Annual Convention of the American Psychological Association, New York.

Alexander, P. C. (1993). The differential effects of abuse characteristics and attachment in the prediction of long term effects of sexual abuse. *Journal of Interpersonal Violence, 8,* 346–362.

Allen, J. G. (1993). Books in brief. *Bulletin of the Menninger Clinic, 57,* 135.

Alnæs, R., & Torgersen, S. (1990). MCMI personality disorders among patients with major depression with and without anxiety disorders. *Journal of Personality Disorders, 4,* 141–149.

Alnæs, R., & Torgersen, S. (1991). Personality and personality disorders among patients with various affective disorders. *Journal of Personality Disorders, 5,* 107–121.

American Psychiatric Association. (1980). *Diagnostic and statistical manual of mental disorders* (3rd ed.). Washington, DC: Author.

American Psychiatric Association. (1985). *DSM-IIIR in development: Draft.* Washington, DC: Author.

American Psychiatric Association. (1987). *Diagnostic and statistical manual of mental disorders* (3rd ed., rev.). Washington, DC: Author.

American Psychiatric Association. (1993). *DSM-IV draft criteria.* Washington, DC: Author.

American Psychiatric Association. (1994). *Diagnostic and statistical manual of mental disorders* (4th ed.). Washington, DC: Author.

Anderson, S. (1968). Effects of confrontation by high and low-functioning therapists. *Journal of Counseling Psychology, 15,* 411–416.

Anderson, W., & Bauer, B. (1985). Clients with MMPI high D-PD: Therapy implications. *Journal of Clinical Psychology, 41,* 181–188.

Andrews, J. (1984). Psychotherapy with the hysterical personality. *Psychiatry, 47,* 211–232.

Anrig, G. R. (1987). "Golden Rule": Second thoughts. *APA Monitor, 18,* p. 3.

Antoni, M., Levine, J., Tischer, P., Green, C., & Millon, T. (1986). Refining personality assessments by combining MCMI high-point profiles and MMPI codes, Part IV: MMPI 89/98. *Journal of Personality Assessment, 50,* 65–72.

Antoni, M., Levine, J., Tischer, P., Green, C., & Millon, T. (1987). Refining personality assessments by combining MCMI high-point profiles and MMPI codes, Part V: MMPI 78/87. *Journal of Personality Assessment, 51,* 375–387.

Antoni, M., Tischer, P., Levine, J., Green, C., & Millon, T. (1985a). Refining personality assessments by combining MCMI high-point profiles and MMPI codes, Part I: MMPI 28/82. *Journal of Personality Assessment, 49,* 392–398.

Antoni, M., Tischer, P., Levine, J., Green, C., & Millon, T. (1985b). Refining personality assessments by combining MCMI high-point profiles and MMPI codes, Part III: MMPI 24/42. *Journal of Personality Assessment, 49,* 508–515.

Aronow, E., & Reznikoff, M. (1971). Application of projective tests to psychotherapy: A case study. *Journal of Personality Assessment, 35,* 379–393.

Auerbach, J. S. (1984). Validation of two scales for narcissistic personality disorder. *Journal of Personality Assessment, 48,* 649–653.

Auld, F., & Eron, L. (1953). The use of Rorschach scores to predict whether patients will continue psychotherapy. *Journal of Consulting Psychology, 17,* 104–109.

Baekland, F., & Lundwall, M. (1975). Dropping out of treatment: A critical review. *Psychological Bulletin, 82,* 738–783.

Bagby, R. M., Gillis, J. R., & Dickens, S. (1990). Detection of dissimulation with the new generation of objective personality measures. *Behavioral Sciences and the Law, 8,* 93–102.

Bagby, R. M., Gillis, J. R., & Rogers, R. (1991). Effectiveness of the Millon Clinical Multiaxial Inventory validity index in the detection of random responding. *Psychological Assessment, 2,* 285–287.

Bagby, R. M., Gillis, J. R., Toner, B. B., & Goldberg, J. (1991). Detecting fake-good and fake-bad responding on the Millon Clinical Multiaxial Inventory-II. *Psychological Assessment, 3,* 496–498.

Bagby, R. M., Joffe, R. T., Parker, J. D. A., & Schuller, D. R. (1993). Reexamination of the evidence for the DSM-III personality disorder clusters. *Journal of Personality Disorders, 7,* 320–328.

Baile, W., Gibertini, M., Scott, L., & Endicott, J. (1993). Prebiopsy assessment of patients with suspected head and neck cancer. *Journal of Psychosocial Oncology, 10,* 79–91.

Baker, J. D., Capron, E. W., & Azorlosa, J. (1996). Family environment characteristics of persons with histrionic and dependent personality disorders. *Journal of Personality Disorders, 10,* 82–87.

Baldessarini, R. J., Finklestein, S., & Arana, G. W. (1983). The predictive power of diagnostic tests and the effect of prevalence of illness. *Archives of General Psychiatry, 40,* 569–573.

Bard, L., & Knight, R. (1987). Sex offender subtyping with the MCMI. In C. Green (Ed.), *Conference on the Millon inventories* (pp. 133–137). Minneapolis, MN: National Computer Systems.

Bartsch, T. W., & Hoffman, J. J. (1985). A cluster analysis of Millon Clinical Multiaxial Inventory (MCMI) profiles: More about a taxonomy of alcoholic subtypes. *Journal of Clinical Psychology, 41,* 707–713.

Beasley, R., & Stoltenberg, C. D. (1992). Personality characteristics of male spouse abusers. *Professional Psychology: Research and Practice, 23,* 310–317.

Beck, A. T. (1983). Cognitive therapy of depression: New perspectives. In P. Clayton & J. E. Barrett (Eds.), *Treatment of depression: Old controversies and new approaches* (pp. 265–290). New York: Raven Press.

Beck, A., & Freeman, A. (1990). *Cognitive therapy of personality disorders.* New York: Guilford Press.

Benjamin, L. S. (1974). Structural analysis of social behavior. *Psychological Review, 81,* 392–495.

Benjamin, L. S. (1984). Principles of prediction using Structural Analysis of Social Behavior (SASB). In R. A. Zucker, J. Aronoff, & A. J. Rabin (Eds.), *Personality and the prediction of behaviors* (pp. 121–173). New York: Guilford Press.

Benjamin, L. S. (1993). *Interpersonal diagnosis and treatment of personality disorders.* New York: Guilford Press.

Benjamin, L. S. (1995). *Interpersonal diagnosis and treatment of personality disorders* (2nd ed.). New York: Guilford Press.

Ben-Porath, Y., & Waller, N. (1992a). Five big issues in clinical assessment: A rejoinder to Costa and McCrae. *Psychological Assessment, 4,* 23–25.

Ben-Porath, Y., & Waller, N. (1992b). "Normal" personality inventories in clinical assessment: General requirements and the potential for using the NEO Personality Inventory. *Psychological Assessment, 4,* 14–19.

Bent, R., Putnam, D., Kiesler, D., & Nowicki, S. (1976). Correlates of successful and unsuccessful psychotherapy. *Journal of Consulting and Clinical Psychology, 44,* 149.

Berndt, D. (1983). Ethical and professional considerations in psychological assessment. *Professional Psychology: Research and Practice, 14,* 580–587.

Bernstein, E., & Putnam, F. (1986). Development, reliability, and validity of a dissociation scale. *Journal of Nervous and Mental Disease. 174,* 727–735.

Bersoff, D. N. (1988). Should subjective employment devices be scrutinized? It's elementary, my dear Ms. Watson. *American Psychologist, 12,* 1016–1018.

Beutler, L. (1989). Differential treatment selection: The role of diagnosis in psychotherapy. *Psychotherapy, 26,* 271–281.

Beutler, L., & Consoli, A. (1993). Matching the therapist's interpersonal stance to clients' characteristics: Contributions from systematic eclectic psychotherapy. *Psychotherapy, 30,* 417–422.

Beutler, L., Johnson, D., Neville, C., Workman, S., & Elkins, D. (1973). The A-B-therapy-type distinction, accurate empathy, nonpossessive warmth and therapist genuineness in psychotherapy. *Journal of Abnormal Psychology, 82,* 273–277.

Binder, J., Henry, W., & Strupp, H. (1987). An appraisal of selection criteria for dynamic psychotherapies and implications for setting time limits. *Psychiatry, 50,* 154–166.

Birch, W. (1976). The relationship between personality traits and treatment outcome in a therapeutic environment. *Dissertation Abstracts International, 37*, A3508.

Birtchnell, J. (1991). The measurement of dependence by questionnaire. *Journal of Personality Disorders, 5*, 281–295.

Bishop, D. R. (1993). Validity issues in using the Millon-II with substance abusers. *Psychological Reports, 73*, 27–33.

Blackburn, R. (1975). An empirical classification of psychopathic personality. *British Journal of Psychiatry, 127*, 456–460.

Blackburn, R. (1986). Patterns of personality deviation among violent offenders: Replication and extension of an empirical taxonomy. *British Journal of Criminology, 26*, 254–269.

Blackburn, R. (1996). Replicated personality disorder clusters among mentally disordered offenders and their relation to dimensions of personality. *Journal of Personality Disorders, 10*, 68–81.

Blais, M. A., Benedict, K. B., & Norman, D. K. (1994). Associations among the MCMI-II clinical syndrome scales and the MMPI-2 clinical scales. *Assessment, 1*, 407–413.

Blatt, S. J., & Auerbach, J. S. (1988). Differential cognitive disturbances in three types of borderline patients. *Journal of Personality Disorders, 2*, 198–211.

Bonato, D. P., Cyr, J. J., Kalpin, R. A., Prendergast, P., & Sanhueza, P. (1988). The utility of the MCMI as a DSM-III Axis I diagnostic tool. *Journal of Clinical Psychology, 44*, 867–875.

Bornstein, R. F. (1995). Sex differences in objective and projective tests: A meta-analytic review. *Assessment, 2*, 319–331.

Braver, M., Bumberry, J., Green, K., & Rawson, R. (1992). Childhood abuse and current psychological functioning in a university counseling center population. *Journal of Counseling Psychology, 39*, 252–257.

Brewer, B. (1974). Relationships among personality, empathic ability and counselor effectiveness. *Dissertation Abstracts International, 35*, A6449.

Broday, S. (1988). Perfectionism and Millon basic personality patterns. *Psychological Reports, 63*, 791–794.

Bronisch, T., & Klerman, G. (1991). Personality functioning: Change and stability in relationship to symptoms and psychopathology. *Journal of Personality Disorders, 5*, 307–317.

Brown, H. P. (1992). Substance abuse and the disorders of the self: Examining the relationship. *Alcoholism Treatment Quarterly, 9*, 1–27.

Bryer, J. B. (1990). Inpatient psychiatric outcome: A research program and initial findings for adults. *Psychiatric Hospital, 21*, 79–88.

Bryer, J. B., Martines, K. A., & Dignan, M. (1990). Millon Clinical Multiaxial Inventory Alcohol Abuse and Drug Abuse scales and the identification of substance abuse patients. *Personality Assessment, 2*, 438–441.

Bryer, J. B., Nelson, B. A., Miller, J. B., & Krol, P. A. (1987). Childhood sexual and physical abuse as factors in adult psychiatric illness. *American Journal of Psychiatry, 144*, 1426–1430.

Busby, D. M., Glenn, E., Steggell, G. L., & Adamson, D. W. (1993). Treatment issues for survivors of physical and sexual abuse. *Journal of Marital and Family Therapy, 19*, 377–391.

Buss, A. (1989). Personality as traits. *American Psychologist, 44*, 1378–1388.

Butcher, J. N. (1990). *MMPI-2 in psychological treatment.* New York: Oxford University Press.

Butcher, J. N., Braswell, L., & Raney, D. (1983). A cross-cultural comparison of American Indian, Black and White inpatients on the MMPI and presenting symptoms. *Journal of Consulting and Clinical Psychology, 51,* 587–594.

Butcher, J., & Owen, P. (1978). Objective personality inventories: Recent research and some contemporary issues. In B. Wolman (Ed.), *Clinical diagnoses of mental disorders: A handbook* (pp. 475–546). New York: Plenum.

Butcher, J. N., & Rouse, S. V. (1996). Personality: Individual differences and clinical assessment. *Annual Review of Psychology, 47,* 87–111.

Butler, S. F., Gaulier, B., & Haller, D. (1991). Assessment of Axis II personality disorders among female substance abusers. *Psychological Reports, 68,* 1344–1346.

Butters, M., Retzlaff, P., & Gibertini, M. (1986). Non-adaptability to basic training and the Millon clinical multiaxial inventory. *Military Medicine, 151,* 574–576.

Caldwell, A. (1975). *A handbook of MMPI personality types.* Unpublished manuscript.

Caldwell, A. (1984). *The Caldwell report: A sample.* Santa Monica, CA: Clinical Psychological Services.

Calsyn, D. A., & Saxon, A. J. (1990). Personality disorder subtypes among cocaine and opioid addicts using the Millon Clinical Multiaxial Inventory. *International Journal of the Addictions, 25,* 1037–1049.

Calsyn, D. A., Saxon, A. J., & Daisy, F. (1990). Validity of the MCMI drug abuse scale with drug abusing and psychiatric samples. *Journal of Clinical Psychology, 46,* 244–246.

Calsyn, D. A., Saxon, A. J., & Daisy, F. (1991). Validity of the MCMI Drug Abuse Scale varies as a function of drug choice, race, and Axis II subtypes. *American Journal of Drug and Alcohol Abuse, 17,* 153–159.

Campbell, B. K., & Stark, M. J. (1991). Psychopathology and personality characteristics in different forms of substance abuse. *International Journal of the Addictions, 25,* 1467–1474.

Campbell, N. B., Franco, K., & Jurs, S. (1988). Abortion in adolescence. *Adolescence, 23,* 813–823.

Cannon, D., Bell, W., Fowler, D., Penk, W., & Finkelstein, A. (1990). MMPI differences between alcoholics and drug abusers: Effect of age and race. *Psychological Assessment, 2,* 51–55.

Canter, F. (1966). Personality factors related to participation in treatment of hospitalized male alcoholics. *Journal of Clinical Psychology, 22,* 114–116.

Canter, F. (1971). Authoritarian attitudes, degree of pathology and preference for structured versus unstructured psychotherapy in hospitalized mental patients. *Psychological Reports, 28,* 231–234.

Cantrell, J. D., & Dana, R. H. (1987). Use of the Millon Clinical Multiaxial Inventory (MCMI) as a screening instrument in a community mental health center. *Journal of Clinical Psychology, 43,* 366–375.

Carver, C. S., Scheier, M. F., & Weintraub, J. K. (1989). Assessing coping strategies: A theoretically based approach. *Journal of Personality and Social Psychology, 56,* 267–283.

Cash, T. F., Mikulka, P. J., & Brown, T. A. (1989). Validity of Millon's computerized interpretation system for the MCMI: Comment on Moreland and Onstad. *Journal of Consulting and Clinical Psychology, 57,* 311–312.

Cashdan, S. (1982). Interactional psychotherapy: Using the relationship. In J. Anchin & D. Kiesler (Eds.), *Handbook of interpersonal psychotherapy* (pp. 215–226). Elmsford, NY: Pergamon Press.

Cattell, R. B. (1946). *The description and measurement of personality.* New York: World Book.

Cattell, R. B. (1965). *The scientific analysis of personality.* Chicago: Aldine.

Cattell, R. B. (1986). *Manual for the Sixteen Personality Factor Questionnaire*. Savoy, IL: Institute for Personality and Ability Testing.

Cerney, M. (1978). Use of the psychological test report in the course of psychotherapy. *Journal of Personality Assessment, 42*, 457–463.

Chambless, D. L., Renneberg, B., Goldstein, A., & Gracely, E. J. (1992). MCMI diagnosed personality disorders among agoraphobic outpatients: Prevalence and relationship to severity and treatment outcome. *Journal of Anxiety Disorders, 6*, 193–211.

Chandarana, P. C., Conlon, P., Holliday, R. L., Deslippe, T., & Field, V. A. (1990). A prospective study of psychosocial aspects of gastric stapling surgery. *Psychiatric Journal of the University of Ottawa, 15*, 32–35.

Chantry, K., & Craig, R. J. (1993). Psychological screening of violent offenders with the MCMI. *Journal of Clinical Psychology, 50*, 430–435.

Chantry, K., & Craig, R. J. (1994). MCMI typologies of criminal sexual offenders. *Sexual Addiction and Compulsivity, 1*, 215–226.

Chatham, P., Tibbals, C., & Harrington, M. (1993). The MMPI and the MCMI in the evaluation of narcissism in a clinical sample. *Journal of Personality Assessment, 60*, 239–251.

Chick, D., Martin, S. K., Nevels, R., & Cotton, C. R. (1994). Relationship between personality disorders and clinical symptoms in psychiatric inpatients as measured by the Millon Clinical Multiaxial Inventory. *Psychological Reports, 74*, 331–336.

Chick, D., Sheaffer, C. I., Goggin, W., & Sison, G. F. (1993). The relationship between MCMI personality scales and clinician-generated DSM-III-R personality disorder diagnosis. *Journal of Personality Assessment, 61*, 264–276.

Choca, J., Bresolin, L., Okonek, A., & Ostrow, D. (1988). Validity of the Millon Clinical Multiaxial Inventory in the assessment of affective disorders. *Journal of Personality Assessment, 53*, 96–105.

Choca, J., & Garside, D. (1992). *Hermann: A Rorschach administrator and scoring assistant* (2nd ed.) [Computer program]. Toronto, Ontario, Canada: Multi-Health Systems.

Choca, J., Greenblatt, R., Tobin, D., Shanley, L., & Van Denburg, E. (1989, August). *Factor analytic structure of MCMI items*. Paper presented at the 97th Annual Convention of the American Psychological Association, New Orleans, LA.

Choca, J., Okonek, A., Ferm, R., & Ostrow, D. (1982, May). *The relationship of personality style and lithium efflux in affective disorders*. Paper presented at the convention of the American Psychiatric Association, Toronto, Ontario, Canada.

Choca, J. P., Peterson, C. A., & Shanley, L. A. (1986a). Factor analysis of the Millon Clinical Multiaxial Inventory. *Journal of Consulting and Clinical Psychology, 54*, 253–255.

Choca, J., Peterson, C., & Shanley, L. (1986b, August). *Racial bias and the MCMI*. Paper presented at the 94th Annual Convention of the American Psychological Association, Washington, DC.

Choca, J. P., Retzlaff, P., Strack, S., Mouton, A., & Van Denburg, E. (in press). Factorial elements of the MCMI-II personality scales. *Journal of Personality Disorders*.

Choca, J., Shanley, L., Peterson, C., & Hong, J. (1987, August). *A PTSD scale for the MCMI*. Paper presented at the 95th Annual Convention of the American Psychological Association, New York.

Choca, J., Shanley, L. A., Peterson, C. A., & Van Denburg, E. (1990). Racial bias and the MCMI. *Journal of Personality Assessment, 54*, 479–490.

Choca, J., Shanley, L. A., Van Denburg, E., Agresti, A., Mouton, A., & Uskokovic, L.

(1992). Personality disorder or personality style: That is the question. *Journal of Counseling and Development, 70,* 429–431.

Choca, J., Silverman, J., & Gerber, J. (1980). *The effect of the patient's personality style on the therapeutic relationship and therapy outcome ratings.* Unpublished manuscript.

Choca, J., & Van Denburg, E. (1996). *Manual for clinical psychology trainees* (3rd ed.). New York: Brunner/Mazel.

Choca, J. P., Van Denburg, E., Bratu, M. E., & Meagher, S. (1995, March). *Personality changes of psychiatric patients with aging.* Paper presented at the midwinter meeting of the Society for Personality Assessment, Denver, CO.

Choca, J. P., Van Denburg, E., Mouton, A., & Shanley, L. (1992). *The Rorschach: A test with no personality.* Unpublished manuscript.

Clarkin, J. F., Widiger, T. A., Frances, A., Hurt, S. W., & Gilmore, M. (1983). Prototypic typology and the borderline personality disorder. *Journal of Abnormal Psychology, 92,* 263–275.

Colligan, R., Morey, L., & Offord, K. (1994). The MMPI/MMPI-2 personality disorder scales: Contemporary norms for adults and adolescents. *Journal of Clinical Psychology, 43,* 366–375.

Colson, D., Pickar, D., & Coyne, L. (1989). Rorschach correlates of treatment difficulty in a long-term psychiatric hospital. *Bulletin of the Menninger Clinic, 53,* 52–57.

Comrey, A. L. (1978). Common methodological problems in factor analytic studies. *Journal of Consulting and Clinical Psychology, 46,* 648–659.

Conte, H. R., Plutchik, R., Karasu, T. B., & Jerrett, I. (1980). A self-report borderline scale: Discriminate validity and preliminary norms. *Journal of Nervous and Mental Disease, 168,* 428–435.

Corbisiero, J. R., & Reznikoff, M. (1991). The relationship between personality type and style of alcohol use. *Journal of Clinical Psychology, 47,* 291–298.

Costa, P. T., & McCrae, R. R. (1985). *The NEO Personality Inventory manual.* Odessa, FL: Psychological Assessment Resources.

Costa, P. T., & McCrae, R. R. (1990). Personality disorders and the five-factor model of personality. *Journal of Personality Disorders, 4,* 362–371.

Costa, P., & McCrae, R. (1992a). Normal personality assessment in clinical practice: The NEO Personality Inventory. *Psychological Assessment, 4,* 5–13.

Costa, P., & McCrae, R. (1992b). Reply to Ben-Porath and Waller. *Psychological Assessment, 4,* 20–22.

Costello, R. M., Fine, H. J., & Blau, B. I. (1973). Racial comparisons on the Minnesota Multiphasic Personality Inventory. *Journal of Clinical Psychology, 29,* 63–65.

Costello, R. M., Tiffany, D. W., & Gier, R. H. (1972). Methodology issues and racial (black–white) comparisons on the MMPI. *Journal of Consulting and Clinical Psychology, 38,* 161–168.

Coyne, J. (1976). Toward an interactional description of depression. *Psychiatry, 39,* 28–40.

Craig, R. J. (1984). Can personality tests predict treatment dropouts? *The International Journal of Addictions, 19,* 665–674.

Craig, R. J. (1988). A psychometric study of the prevalence of DSM-III personality disorders among treated opiate addicts. *The International Journal of Addictions, 23,* 115–124.

Craig, R. J. (1993a). Contemporary trends in substance abuse. *Professional Psychology: Research and Practice, 24,* 182–189.

Craig, R. J. (1993b). *Psychological assessment with the Millon Clinical Multiaxial Inventory (II): An interpretative guide.* Odessa, FL: Psychological Assessment Resources.

Craig, R. J., Kuncel, R., & Olson, R. E. (1994). Ability of drug abusers to avoid detection of substance abuse on the MCMI-II. *Journal of Social Behavior and Personality, 9,* 95–106.

Craig, R. J., & Olson, R. E. (1990). MCMI comparisons of cocaine abusers and heroin addicts. *Journal of Clinical Psychology, 46,* 230–237.

Craig, R. J., & Olson, R. E. (1992). Relationship between MCMI-II scales and normal personality traits. *Psychological Reports, 71,* 699–705.

Craig, R. J., & Olson, R. E. (1995). MCMI-II profiles and typologies for patients seen in marital therapy. *Psychological Reports, 76,* 163–170.

Craig, R. J., Verinis, J. S., & Wexler, S. (1985). Personality characteristics of drug addicts and alcoholics on the Millon Clinical Multiaxial Inventory. *Journal of Personality Assessment, 49,* 156–160.

Craig, R. J., & Weinberg, D. (1992a). Assessing alcoholics with the Millon Clinical Multiaxial Inventory: A review. *Psychology of Addictive Behaviors 6,* 200–208.

Craig, R. J., & Weinberg, D. (1992b). Assessing drug abusers with the Millon Clinical Multiaxial Inventory: A review. *Journal of Substance Abuse Treatment, 9,* 249–255.

Cronbach, L. J. (1975). Five decades of public controversy over mental testing. *American Psychologist, 30,* 1–14.

Crowne, D., & Marlowe, D. (1964). *The approval motive.* New York: Wiley.

Curtis, J., & Cowell, D. (1993). Relation of birth order and scores on measures of pathological narcissism. *Psychological Reports, 72,* 311–315.

Dahlstrom, W. G., Lachar, D., & Dahlstrom, L. E. (1986). *MMPI patterns of American minorities.* Minneapolis: University of Minnesota Press.

Dahlstrom, W. G., Welsh, G. S., & Dahlstrom, L. E. (1972). *An MMPI handbook: Clinical interpretations* (Vol. 1). Minneapolis: University of Minnesota Press.

Davanloo, H. (1979). Technique of short-term psychotherapy. *Psychiatric Clinics of North America, 2,* 11–22.

Davis, W. E., Beck, S. J., & Ryan, T. A. (1973). Race-related and educationally-related MMPI profile differences among hospitalized schizophrenics. *Journal of Clinical Psychology, 29,* 478–479.

Davis, W. E., & Greenblatt, R. (1990). Age differences among psychiatric inpatients on the MCMI. *Journal of Clinical Psychology, 46,* 770–774.

Davis, W. E., Greenblatt, R., & Choca, J. (1990). *Racial bias and the MCMI-II.* Unpublished manuscript.

Davis, W. E., Greenblatt, R. L., & Pochyly, J. M. (1990). Test of MCMI Black norms for five scales. *Journal of Clinical Psychology, 46,* 175–178.

DeJong, C. A. J., van den Brink, W., Jansen, J. A. M., & Schippers, G. M. (1989). Interpersonal aspects of the DSM-III Axis II: Theoretical hypotheses and empirical findings. *Journal of Personality Disorders, 3,* 135–146.

DeLamatre, J. E., & Schuerger, J. M. (1992). Personality disorder concept scales and 16 PF dimensions. *Psychological Reports, 70,* 839–849.

del Rosario, P. M., McCann, J. T., & Navarra, J. W. (1994). The MCMI-II diagnosis of schizophrenia: Operating characteristics and profile analysis. *Journal of Personality Assessment, 63,* 438–452.

Denton, L. (1988, August). Board votes to oppose Golden Rule technique. *APA Monitor, 19,* p. 7.

Derogatis, L. (1983). *The Symptom Checklist-90 Manual II.* Towson, MD: Clinical Psychometric Research.

Dewald, P. (1967). Therapeutic evaluation and potential: The psychodynamic point of view. *Comprehensive Psychiatry, 8,* 284–298.

Dewald, P. (1971). *Psychotherapy: A dynamic approach.* New York: Basic Books.

DeWolfe, A. S., Larson, J. K., & Ryan, J. J. (1985). Diagnostic accuracy of the Millon test computer reports for bipolar affective disorder. *Journal of Psychopathology and Behavioral Assessment, 7,* 185–189.

DiGiuseppe, R., Robin, M., Szeszko, P. R., & Primavera, L. H. (1995). Cluster analysis of narcissistic personality disorders on the MCMI-II. *Journal of Personality Disorders, 9,* 304–317.

Divac-Jovanovic, M., Svrakic, D., & Lecic-Tosevski, D. (1993). Personality disorders: Model for conceptual approach and classification: I. General model. *American Journal of Psychotherapy, 47,* 558–571.

Dohrendwend, B. S., & Dohrendwend, B. P. (1981). Life stress and illness: Formulation of the issues. In B. S. Dohrendwend & B. P. Dohrendwend (Eds.), *Stressful life events and their contexts* (pp. 1–27). New York: Prodist.

Donat, D. C. (1988). Millon Clinical Multiaxial Inventory (MCMI) clusters for alcohol abusers: Further evidence for validity and implications for medical psychotherapy. *Medical Psychotherapy, 1,* 41–50.

Donat, D. (1991, August). *Personality (MCMI) subtypes among public psychiatric inpatient admissions.* Paper presented at the 99th Annual Convention of the American Psychological Association, San Francisco, CA.

Donat, D. C. (1994). Empirical groupings of perceptions of alcohol use among alcohol dependent persons: A cluster analysis of the Alcohol Use Inventory (AUI) scales. *Assessment, 1,* 103–110.

Donat, D., Geczy, B., Helmrich, J., & LeMay, M. (1992). Empirically derived personality subtypes of public psychiatric patients: Effect on self-reported symptoms, coping inclinations, and evaluation of expressed emotion in caregivers. *Journal of Personality Assessment, 58,* 36–50.

Donat, D., Walters, J., & Hume, A. (1991). Personality characteristics of alcohol dependent inpatients: Relationship of MCMI subtypes to self-reported drinking behavior. *Journal of Personality Assessment, 57,* 335–344.

Donat, D., Walters, J., & Hume, A. (1992). MCMI differences between alcoholics and cocaine abusers: Effect of age, sex, and race. *Journal of Personality Assessment, 58,* 96–104.

Donovan, J. (1987). Brief dynamic psychotherapy: Toward a more comprehensive model. *Psychiatry, 50,* 167–183.

Dorr, D., Barley, W., Gard, B., & Webb, C. (1983). Understanding and treating borderline personality organization. *Psychotherapy: Theory, Research and Practice, 20,* 397–404.

Dougherty, R. J., & Lesswing, N. L. (1989). Inpatient cocaine abusers: An analysis of psychological and demographic variables. *Journal of Substance Abuse Treatment, 6,* 45–47.

Dubrin, J., & Zastowny, T. (1988). Predicting early attrition from psychotherapy: An analysis of a large private practice cohort. *Psychotherapy, 25,* 393–408.

Dubro, A. F., Wetzler, S., & Kahn, M. W. (1988). A comparison of three self-report questionnaires for the diagnosis of the DSM-III personality disorders. *Journal of Personality Disorders, 2,* 256–266.

Duthie, B., & Vincent, K. R. (1986). Diagnostic hit rates of high point codes for the Diagnostic Inventory of Personality and Symptoms using random assignment, base rates, and probability scales. *Journal of Clinical Psychology, 42,* 612–614.

Dutton, D. C. (1994). The origin and structure of the abusive personality. *Journal of Personality Disorders, 8,* 181–191.

Dyer, F. J. (1994). Factorial trait variance and response bias in MCMI-II personality disorder scale scores. *Journal of Personality Disorders, 8,* 121–130.

Edwards, A. L. (1959). *Edwards Personal Preference Schedule*. San Antonio, TX: Psychological Corporation.

Ellason, J. W., Ross, C. A., & Fuchs, D. L. (1995). Assessment of dissociative identity disorder with the Millon Clinical Multiaxial Inventory-II. *Psychological Reports, 76,* 895–905.

Ellis, A. (1977). The basic clinical theory of Rational–Emotive Therapy. In A. Ellis & R. Grieger (Eds.), *Handbook of rational–emotive therapy* (pp. 3–34). New York: Springer.

Endler, N. S., & Edwards, J. M. (1988). Personality disorders from an interactional perspective. *Journal of Personality Disorders, 2,* 326–333.

Endler, N. S., & Magnusson, D. (1976). Toward an interactional psychology of personality. *Psychological Bulletin, 83,* 956–974.

Eysenck, H. J. (1976). *The measurement of personality*. Baltimore: University Park Press.

Eysenck, H. J., & Eysenck, S. B. G. (1975). *The Eysenck Personality Questionnaire*. San Diego, CA: Educational and Industrial Testing Service.

Fals-Stewart, W. (1992). Personality characteristics of substance abusers: An MCMI cluster typology of recreational drug users treated in a therapeutic community and its relationship to length of stay and outcome. *Journal of Personality Assessment, 59,* 515–527.

Fals-Stewart, W. (1995). The effect of defensive responding by substance-abusing patients on the Millon Clinical Multiaxial Inventory. *Journal of Personality Assessment, 64,* 540–551.

Fals-Stewart, W., & Lucente, S. (1993). An MCMI cluster typology of obsessive-compulsives: A measure of personality characteristics and its relationship to treatment. *Journal of Psychiatric Research, 27,* 139–154.

Farmer, R., & Nelson-Gray, R. (1990). Personality disorders and depression: Hypothetical relations, empirical findings, and methodological considerations. *Clinical Psychology Review, 10,* 453–476.

Faulkner, K. K., Cogan, R., Nolder, M., & Shooter, G. (1991). Characteristics of men and women completing cognitive/behavioral spouse abuse treatment. *Journal of Family Violence, 6,* 243–254.

Fink, D., & Golinkoff, D. (1990). MPD, borderline personality disorder and schizophrenia: A comparative study of clinical features. *Dissociation, 8,* 127–134.

Finn, S. E. (1982). Base rates, utilities, and the DSM-III: Shortcomings of fixed rule systems of psychodiagnosis. *Journal of Abnormal Psychology, 91,* 294–302.

Flynn, P. M., & McMahon, R. C. (1983a). Indicators of depression and suicidal ideation among drug abusers. *Psychological Reports, 52,* 784–786.

Flynn, P. M., & McMahon, R. C. (1983b). Stability of the drug misuse scale of the Millon Clinical Multiaxial Inventory. *Psychological Reports, 52,* 536–538.

Flynn, P. M., & McMahon, R. C. (1984a). An examination of the factor structure of the Millon Clinical Multiaxial Inventory. *Journal of Personality Assessment, 48,* 308–311.

Flynn, P. M., & McMahon, R. C. (1984b). Stability of the Drug Abuse scale of the Millon Clinical Multiaxial Inventory. *International Journal of the Addictions, 19,* 459–468.

Fowler, R. D., & Butcher, J. N. (1986). Critique of Matarazzo's views on computerized testing: All sigma and no meaning. *American Psychologist, 41,* 94–96.

Fry, D. (1975). Interaction between locus of control, level of inquiry and subject control in the helping process: A lab analogue study. *Journal of Counseling Psychology, 22,* 280–287.

Funari, D. J., Piekarski, A. M., & Sherwood, R. J. (1991). Treatment outcomes of Vietnam veterans with posttraumatic stress disorder. *Psychological Reports, 68,* 571–578.

Gabrys, J. B., Utendale, K. A., Schumph, D., Phillips, N., Peters, K., Robertson, G., Sherwood, G., O'Haire, T., Allard, I., Clark, M., & Laye, R. C. (1988). Two inventories for the measurement of psychopathology: Dimensions and common factorial space on Millon's clinical and Eysenck's general personality scales. *Psychological Reports, 62,* 591–601.

Gallucci, N. T. (1990). On the synthesis of information from psychological tests. *Psychological Reports, 67,* 1243–1260.

Garfield, S., & Bergin, A. (1978). *Handbook of psychotherapy and behavior change: An empirical analysis.* New York: Wiley.

Garner, D. M., Olmsted, M. P., Davis, R., Rockert, W., Goldbloom, D., & Eagle, M. (1990). The association between bulimic symptoms and reported psychopathology. *International Journal of Eating Disorders, 9,* 1–15.

Genther, R. W., & Graham, J. R. (1976). Effect of short-term public hospitalization for both Black and White patients. *Journal of Consulting and Clinical Psychology, 44,* 118–124.

Gibeau, E. (1975). An exploratory study of selected relationships among counseling orientations, theoretical orientations, personality and counselor effectiveness. *Dissertation Abstracts International, 36,* A1303–A1304.

Gibertini, M., Brandenburg, N. A., & Retzlaff, P. D. (1986). The operating characteristics of the Millon Clinical Multiaxial Inventory. *Journal of Personality Assessment, 50,* 554–567.

Gibertini, M., & Retzlaff, P. D. (1988a). Factor invariance of the Millon Clinical Multiaxial Inventory. *Journal of Psychopathology and Behavioral Assessment, 10,* 65–74.

Gibertini, M., & Retzlaff, P. D. (1988b, August). *Personality and alcohol use patterns among inpatient alcoholics.* Paper presented at the 96th Annual Convention of the American Psychological Association, Atlanta, GA.

Gilbride, T. V., & Hebert, J. (1980). Pathological characteristics of good and poor interpersonal problem-solvers among psychiatric outpatients. *Journal of Clinical Psychology, 36,* 121–127.

Giovacchini, P. (1984). *Character disorders and adaptive mechanisms.* Northvale, NJ: Jason Aronson.

Giovacchini, P. (1987). *A narrative textbook of psychoanalysis.* Northvale, NJ: Jason Aronson.

Glass, M., Bieber, S., & Tkachuk, M. (1996). Personality styles and dynamics of Alaska Native and nonnative incarcerated men. *Journal of Personality Assessment, 66,* 583–603.

Glover, E. (1955). *The technique of psychoanalysis.* London: Bailliere, Tindall & Cox.

Goldberg, J. O., Segal, Z. V., Vella, D. D., & Shaw, B. F. (1989). Depressive personality: Millon Clinical Multiaxial Inventory profiles of sociotropic and autonomous subtypes. *Journal of Personality Disorders, 3,* 193–198.

Goldberg, J. O., Shaw, B. F., & Segal, Z. V. (1987). Concurrent validity of the Millon Clinical Multiaxial Inventory depression scales. *Journal of Consulting and Clinical Psychology, 55,* 785–787.

Goldberg, L. R. (1992). The development of markers of the Big-Five factor structure. *Psychological Assessment, 4,* 26–42.

Graham, J. R. (1977). *The MMPI: A practical guide.* New York: Oxford University Press.

Graham, J. R. (1987). *The MMPI: A practical guide* (2nd ed.). New York: Oxford University Press.

Green, C. J. (1982). The diagnostic accuracy and utility of MMPI and MCMI computer interpretive reports. *Journal of Personality Assessment, 46,* 359–365.

Green, S. B., & Kelley, C. K. (1988). Racial bias in prediction with the MMPI for a juvenile delinquent population. *Journal of Personality Assessment, 52,* 263–275.

Greenblatt, R. L., & Davis, W. E. (1992). Accuracy of MCMI classification of angry and psychotic Black and White patients. *Journal of Clinical Psychology, 48,* 59–63.

Greenblatt, R. L., & Davis, W. E. (1993). The MCMI in the diagnosis and assessment of schizophrenia. In R. J. Craig (Ed.), *The Millon Clinical Multiaxial Inventory: A clinical research information synthesis* (pp. 93–109). Hillside, NJ: Erlbaum.

Greenblatt, R. L., Mozdzierz, G. J., Murphy, T. J., & Trimakas, K. (1986, March). *Nonmetric multidimensional scaling of the MCMI.* Paper presented at the conference on the Millon Clinical Inventories, Miami, FL.

Greenblatt, R. L., Mozdzierz, G. J., Murphy, T. J., & Trimakas, K. (1992). A comparison of non-adjusted and bootstrapped methods: Bootstrapped diagnosis might be worth the trouble. *Educational and Psychological Measurement, 52,* 181–187.

Greene, R. L. (1980). *The MMPI: An interpretative manual.* New York: Grune & Stratton.

Grossman, L. S., & Craig, R. J. (1994). Comparison of the MCMI-II and 16PF validity scales. *Journal of Personality Assessment, 64,* 384–389.

Guilford, J. P. (1936). *Psychometric methods.* New York: McGraw-Hill.

Guilford, J. P. (1952). When not to factor analyze. *Psychological Bulletin, 49,* 26–37.

Gunderson, J. G., & Singer, M. T. (1975). Defining borderline patients: An overview. *American Journal of Psychiatry, 132,* 1–9.

Gutmann, D. L. (1980). The post-parental years: Clinical problems and developmental possibilities. In W. H. Norman & T. H. Scaramella (Eds.), *Midlife developmental and clinical issues* (pp. 38–52). New York: Brunner/Mazel.

Gutmann, D. L. (1987). *Reclaimed powers: Towards a new psychology of men and women in later life.* New York: Basic Books.

Gynther, M. D. (1972). White norms and Black MMPIs: A presentation for discrimination? *Psychological Bulletin, 78,* 386–402.

Gynther, M. D. (1981). Is the MMPI an appropriate assessment device for Blacks? *Journal of Black Psychology, 7,* 67–75.

Gynther, M. D. (1989). MMPI comparisons of Blacks and Whites: A review and commentary. *Journal of Clinical Psychology, 45,* 878–883.

Gynther, M. D., & Green, S. B. (1980). Accuracy may make a difference, but does a difference make for accuracy? A response to Pritchard and Rosenblatt. *Journal of Consulting and Clinical Psychology, 48,* 268–272.

Hamberger, L. K., & Hastings, J. E. (1986). Personality correlates of men who abuse their partners: A cross-validation study. *Journal of Family Violence, 1,* 323–341.

Hamberger, L. K., & Hastings, J. E. (1987, April). *The male batterer and alcohol abuse: Differential personality characteristics.* Paper presented at the meeting of the Western Psychological Association, Long Beach, CA.

Hamberger, L. K., & Hastings, J. E. (1988a). Characteristics of male spouse abusers consistent with personality disorders. *Hospital and Community Psychiatry, 39,* 763–770.

Hamberger, L. K., & Hastings, J. E. (1988b). Skills training for treatment of spouse abusers: An outcome study. *Journal of Family Violence, 3,* 121–130.

Hamberger, L. K., & Hastings, J. E. (1990). Recidivism following spouse abuse abatement counseling: Treatment program implications. *Violence and Victims, 5,* 157–170.

Hamberger, L. K., & Hastings, J. E. (1991). Personality correlates of men who batter and nonviolent men: Some continuities and discontinuities. *Journal of Family Violence, 6,* 131–147.

Hamberger, L. K., & Hastings, J. (1992). Racial differences on the MCMI in an outpatient clinical sample. *Journal of Personality Assessment, 58,* 90–95.

Harris, R., & Lingoes, J. (1968). *Subscales for the Minnesota Multiphasic Personality Inventory.* The Langley Porter Clinic. Mimeographed.

Hart, S. D., Dutton, D. G., & Newlove, T. (1993). The prevalence of personality disorder among wife assaulters. *Journal of Personality Disorders, 7,* 329–341.

Hart, S., Forth, A., & Hare, R. (1991). The MCMI-II and psychopathy. *Journal of Personality Disorders, 5,* 318–327.

Hastings, J. E., & Hamberger, L. K. (1988). Personality characteristics of spouse abusers: A controlled comparison. *Violence and Victims, 3,* 31.

Hastings, J. E., & Hamberger, L. K. (1994). Psychosocial modifiers of psychopathology for domestically violent and nonviolent men. *Psychological Reports, 74,* 112–114.

Hathaway, S. R., & McKinley, J. C. (1967). *Minnesota Multiphasic Personality Inventory manual.* New York: Psychological Corporation.

Head, S., Baker, J., & Williamson, D. (1991). Family environment characteristics and dependent personality disorder. *Journal of Personality Disorders, 5,* 256–263.

Head, S. B., & Williamson, D. A. (1990). Association of family environment and personality disturbances in bulimia nervosa. *International Journal of Eating Disorders, 9,* 667–674.

Helmes, E. (1989). Stability of the internal structure of the Millon Clinical Multiaxial Inventory. *Journal of Psychopathology and Behavioral Assessment, 11,* 327–338.

Helmes, E., & Barilko, O. (1988). Comparison of three multiscale inventories in identifying the presence of psychopathological symptoms. *Journal of Personality Assessment, 52,* 74–80.

Hess, A. K. (1985). Review of Millon Clinical Multiaxial Inventory. In J. V. Mitchell, Jr. (Ed.), *Ninth mental measurement yearbook* (pp. 984–986). Lincoln, NE: Buros Institute.

Hibbard, S. (1989). Personality and object relational pathology in young adult children of alcoholics. *Psychotherapy, 26,* 504–509.

Hibbs, B. J., Kobos, J. C., & Gonzalez, J. C. (1979). Effects of ethnicity, sex and age on MMPI profiles. *Psychological Reports, 45,* 591–597.

Hills, H. A. (1995). Diagnosing personality disorders: An examination of the MMPI-2 and the MCMI-II. *Journal of Personality Assessment, 65,* 21–34.

Hippocrates. (1950). The sacred disease. In J. Chadwich & W. N. Mann (Trans.), *The medical works of Hippocrates* (pp. 179–193). Springfield, IL: Charles C Thomas. (Original work ca. 460–357 B.C.)

Hirschfeld, R. M. A. (1993). Personality disorders: Definition and Diagnosis. *Journal of Personality Disorders, 7,* 9–17.

Hirschfeld, R. M. A., Klerman, G. L., Clayton, P. J., Keller, M. P., McDonald-Scott, P., & Larkin, B. H. (1983). Assessing personality: Effects of the depressive state on trait measurement. *American Journal of Psychiatry, 140,* 695–699.

Hoffman, B., Choca, J., Gutmann, D., Shanley, L., & Van Denburg, E. (1989, August). *Personality changes with aging in male psychiatric patients.* Paper presented at the 97th Annual Convention of the American Psychological Association, New Orleans, LA.

Hogg, B., Jackson, H., Rudd, R., & Edwards, J. (1990). Diagnosing personality disorders in recent-onset schizophrenia. *Journal of Nervous and Mental Disease, 178,* 194–199.

Holcomb, W. R., & Adams, N. (1982). Racial influences on intelligence and personality measures of people who commit murder. *Journal of Clinical Psychology, 38,* 793–796.

Holliman, N. B., & Guthrie, P. C. (1989). A comparison of the Millon Clinical Multiaxial Inventory and the California Psychological Inventory in assessment of a nonclinical population. *Journal of Clinical Psychology, 45,* 373–382.

Honigfeld, G. (1971). In defense of diagnosis. *Professional Psychology, 2,* 289–291.

Horowitz, L. M., Rosenberg, S. E., Baer, B. A., Ureño, G., & Villaseñor, V. S. (1988). Inventory of Interpersonal Problems: Psychometric properties and clinical applications. *Journal of Consulting and Clinical Psychology, 56,* 885–892.

Horowitz, M. J., Marmar, C., Krupnick, J., Wilner, N., Kaltreider, N., & Wallerstein, R. (1984). *Personality styles and brief psychotherapy.* New York: Basic Books.

Hull, J. S., Range, L. M., & Goggin, W. C. (1992). Suicide ideas: Relationship to personality disorders on the MCMI. *Death Studies, 16,* 371–375.

Hunt, C., & Andrews, G. (1992). Measuring personality disorder: The use of self-report questionnaires. *Journal of Personality Disorders, 6,* 125–133.

Hyer, L. (Ed.). (1994). *Trauma victim: Theoretical issues and practical suggestions.* Muncie, IN: Accelerated Development Incorporated.

Hyer, L. A., Albrecht, J. W., Boudewyns, P. A., Woods, M. G., & Brandsma, J. (1993). Dissociative experiences of Vietnam veterans with chronic posttraumatic stress disorder. *Psychological Reports, 73,* 519–530.

Hyer, L., & Boudewyns, P. A. (1987). The 8-2 MCMI code in a PTSD typology. *Center for Stress Recovery Newsletters, 4,* 7–8.

Hyer, L., Carson, M., Nixon, D., Tamkin, A., & Saucer, R. T. (1987). Depression among alcoholics. *International Journal of Addiction, 22,* 1235–1241.

Hyer, L., Davis, H., Woods, G., Albrecht, J. W., & Boudewyns, P. (1992). Relationship between the Millon Clinical Multiaxial Inventory and the Millon II: Value of scales for aggressive and self-defeating personalities in posttraumatic stress disorder. *Psychological Reports, 71,* 867–879.

Hyer, L., Davis, H., Woods, G., Albrecht, W., & Boudewyns, P. (1994). Cluster analysis of MCMI and MCMI-II on chronic PTSD victims. *Journal of Clinical Psychology, 50,* 502–515.

Hyer, L., Harrison, W. R., & Jacobsen, R. H. (1987). Later-life depression: Influences of irrational thinking and cognitive impairment. *Journal of Rational–Emotive Therapy, 5,* 43–48.

Hyer, L., Woods, M., & Boudewyns, P. A. (1991). A three tier evaluation of PTSD among Vietnam combat veterans. *Journal of Traumatic Stress, 4,* 165–195.

Hyer, L., Woods, M. G., Boudewyns, P. A., Bruno, R., & O'Leary, W. (1988). Concurrent validation of the Millon Clinical Multiaxial Inventory among Vietnam veterans with posttraumatic stress disorder. *Psychological Reports, 63,* 271–278.

Hyer, L., Woods, M., Boudewyns, P., Harrison, W., & Tamkin, A. (1990). MCMI and 16PF with Vietnam veterans: Profiles and concurrent validation of the MCMI. *Journal of Personality Disorders, 4,* 391–401.

Hyer, L., Woods, M., Bruno, R., & Boudewyns, P. (1989). Treatment outcomes of Vietnam veterans with PTSD and the consistency of the MCMI. *Journal of Clinical Psychology, 45,* 547–552.

Hyer, L., Woods, M. G., Summers, M. N., Boudewyns, P., & Harrison, W. R. (1990). Alexithymia among Vietnam veterans with posttraumatic stress disorder. *Journal of Clinical Psychiatry, 51,* 243–247.

Ibsen, H. (1879). A doll's house. In *Eleven plays of Henrik Ibsen* (pp. 3–92). New York: Random House.

Inch, R., & Crossley, M. (1993). Diagnostic utility of the MCMI-I and MCMI-II with psychiatric outpatients. *Journal of Clinical Psychology, 49,* 358–366.

Jackson, H. J., Gazis, J., Rudd, R. P., & Edwards, J. (1991). Concordance between two personality disorder instruments with psychiatric inpatients. *Comprehensive Psychiatry, 32,* 252–260.

Jackson, H. J., Rudd, R., Gazis, J., & Edwards, J. (1991). Using the MCMI-I to diagnose personality disorders in inpatients: Axis I/Axis II associations and sex differences. *Australian Psychologist, 26,* 37–41.

Jackson, J. J., Greenblatt, R. L., Davis, W. E., Murphy, T. J., & Trimakas, K. (1991). Assessment of schizophrenic inpatients with the MCMI. *Journal of Clinical Psychology, 47,* 505–510.

Jaffe, L. T., & Archer, R. P. (1987). The prediction of drug use among college students from MMPI, MCMI, and Sensation Seeking scales. *Journal of Personality Assessment, 51,* 243–253.

Jay, G. W., Grove, R. N., & Grove, K. S. (1987). Differentiation of chronic headache from non-headache pain patients using the Millon Clinical Multiaxial Inventory (MCMI). *Headache, 27,* 124–129.

Jensen, A. R. (1980). *Bias in mental testing.* New York: Free Press.

Joffe, R. T., & Regan, J. J. (1988). Personality and depression. *Journal of Psychiatric Research, 22,* 279–286.

Joffe, R., & Regan, J. (1989a). Personality and response to tricyclic antidepressants in depressed patients. *Journal of Nervous and Mental Disease, 177,* 745–749.

Joffe, R., & Regan, J. (1989b). Personality and suicidal behavior in depressed patients. *Comprehensive Psychiatry, 30,* 157–160.

Joffe, R. T., & Regan, J. J. (1991). Personality and family history of depression in patients with affective illness. *Journal of Psychiatric Research, 25,* 67–71.

Joffe, R. T., Swinson, R. P., & Regan, J. J. (1988). Personality features of obsessive–compulsive disorder. *American Journal of Psychiatry, 145,* 1127–1129.

Josiassen, R. C., Shagass, C., & Roemer, R. (1988). Somatosensory evoked potential correlates of schizophrenic subtypes identified by the Millon Clinical Multiaxial Inventory. *Psychiatric Research, 23,* 209–219.

Jung, C. G. (1933). *Modern man in search of a soul.* New York: Harcourt, Brace.

Kaser-Boyd, N. (1993). [Review of the book *Interpretive guide to the Millon Clinical Multiaxial Inventory*]. *Journal of Personality Assessment, 61,* 206–209.

Kelly, G. (1969a). Ontological acceleration. In B. Maher (Ed.), *Clinical psychology and personality: The selected papers of George Kelly* (pp. 7–45). New York: Wiley.

Kelly, G. (1969b). The psychotherapeutic relationship. In B. Maher (Ed.), *Clinical psychology and personality: The selected papers of George Kelly* (pp. 66–93). New York: Wiley.

Kendall, R. E. (1983). DSM-III: A major advance in psychiatric nosology. In A. L. Spitzer, J. B. W. Williams, & A. E. Skodol (Eds.), *International perspectives on DSM-III* (pp. 55–68). Washington, DC: American Psychiatric Press.

Kennedy, S. H., McVey, G., & Katz, R. (1990). Personality disorders in anorexia nervosa and bulimia nervosa. *Journal of Psychiatric Research, 24,* 259–269.

Kernberg, O. F. (1975). *Borderline conditions and pathological narcissism.* Northvale, NJ: Jason Aronson.

Kernberg, O. F. (1977). The structural diagnosis of borderline personality organization. In P. Hartocoullis (Ed.), *Borderline personality disorder* (pp. 87–121). Madison, CT: International Universities Press.

Kernberg, O. F. (1984). *Treatment of severe personality disorders: Psychotherapeutic strategies.* New Haven, CT: Yale University Press.

Kessel, J. B., & Zimmerman, M. (1993). Reporting errors in studies of the diagnostic performance of self-administered questionnaires: Extent of the problem, recommendations for standardized presentation of results, and implications for the peer review process. *Psychological Assessment, 5,* 395–399.

Kiesler, D. J. (1977). *Communications assessment of interview behavior of the obsessive personality.* Unpublished manuscript.

Kiesler, D. J. (1979). An interpersonal communication analysis of relationship in psychotherapy. *Psychiatry, 42,* 299–311.

Kiesler, D. J. (1982). Interpersonal theory for personality and psychotherapy. In J. Anchin & D. Kiesler (Eds.), *Handbook of interpersonal psychotherapy* (pp. 3–24). New York: Pergamon Press.

Kiesler, D. J. (1983). The interpersonal circle: A taxonomy for complementarity in human transactions. *Psychological Review, 90,* 184–214.

Kiesler, D. J. (1985). *The maladaptive transaction cycle.* Unpublished manuscript.

Kiesler, D. J. (1986a). The 1982 interpersonal circle: An analysis of DSM-III personality disorders. In T. Millon & G. Klerman (Eds.), *Contemporary issues in psychopathology* (pp. 1–23). New York: Guilford Press.

Kiesler, D. (1986b). Interpersonal methods of diagnosis and treatment. In R. Michels & J. Cavenar (Eds.), *Psychiatry* (pp. 571–597). Philadelphia: Lippincott.

Kiesler, D., Van Denburg, T., Sikes, V., Larus, J., & Goldston, C. (1990). Interpersonal behavior profiles of eight cases of DSM-III personality disorder. *Journal of Clinical Psychology, 46,* 440–453.

King, R. E. (1994). Assessing aviators for personality pathology with the Millon Clinical Multiaxial Inventory (MCMI). *Aviation, Space, and Environmental Medicine, 65,* 227–231.

Kleiger, J. H., & Kinsman, R. A. (1980). The developoment of an MMPI alexithymia scale. *Psychotherapy and Psychosomatics, 34,* 17–24.

Klein, M. H., Benjamin, L. S., Rosenfeld, R., Treece, C., Husted, J., & Greist, J. H. (1993). The Wisconsin Personality Disorders Inventory: Development, reliability, and validity. *Journal of Personality Disorders, 7,* 285–303.

Klein, M. H., Wonderlich, S., & Shea, M. T. (1993). Models of relationships between personality and depression: Toward a framework for theory and research. In M. H. Klein, D. J. Kupfer, & M. T. Shea (Eds.), *Personality and depression* (pp. 1–54). New York: Guilford Press.

Klerman, G., Weissman, M., Rounsaville, B., & Chevron, E. (1984). *Interpersonal psychotherapy of depression.* New York: Basic Books.

Kohut, H. (1971). *The analysis of the self.* Madison, CT: International Universities Press.

Kohut, H. (1977). *The restoration of the self.* Madison, CT: International Universities Press.

Lachar, D. (1974). *The MMPI: Clinical assessment and automated interpretation.* Los Angeles: Western Psychological Services.

Lambert, N. M. (1981). Psychological evidence in *Larry P. v. Wilson Riles. American Psychologist, 36,* 937–952.

Langevin, R., Lang, R., Reynolds, R., Wright, P., Garrels, D., Marchese, V., Handy, L., Pugh, G., & Frenzel, R. (1988). Personality and sexual anomalies: An examination of the Millon Clinical Multiaxial Inventory. *Annals of Sex Research, 1,* 13–32.

Langs, R. (1973). *The technique of psychoanalytic psychotherapy* (Vol. 1). Northvale, NJ: Jason Aronson.

Lanyon, R. I. (1984). Personality assessment. *Annual Review of Psychology, 35,* 667–701.

Lanyon, R. I. (1993). Partly scientific. *Contemporary Psychology, 38,* 403–404.

Leaf, R. C., Alington, D. E., Ellis, A., DiGiuseppe, R., & Mass, R. (1992). Personality disorders, underlying traits, social problems, and clinical syndromes. *Journal of Personality Disorders, 6,* 134–152.

Leaf, R., Alington, D., Mass, R., DiGiuseppe, R., & Ellis, A. (1991). Personality disorders, life events, and clinical syndromes. *Journal of Personality Disorders, 5,* 264–280.

Leaf, R. C., DiGiuseppe, R., Ellis, A., Mass, R., Backx, W., Wolfe, J., & Alington, D. E. (1990). "Healthy" correlates of MCMI Scales 4, 5, 6, and 7. *Journal of Personality Disorders, 4,* 312–328.

Leaf, R. C., Ellis, A, DiGiuseppe, R., Mass, R., & Alington, D. E. (1991). Rationality, self-regard and the "healthiness" of personality disorders. *Journal of Rational–Emotive and Cognitive–Behavior Therapy, 9,* 3–37.

Leaf, R. C., Ellis, A., Mass, R., DiGiuseppe, R., & Alington, D. E. (1990). Countering perfectionism in research on clinical practice: II. Retrospective analysis of treatment progress. *Journal of Rational–Emotive and Cognitive–Behavior Therapy, 8,* 203–220.

Leary, T. (1957). *Interpersonal diagnosis of personality.* New York: Ronald Press.

Leary, T., & Coffey, H. (1955). Interpersonal diagnosis: Some problems of methodology and validation. *Journal of Abnormal and Social Psychology, 50,* 110–124.

Lees-Haley, P. R. (1992). Efficacy of MMPI-2 validity scales and MCMI-II modifier scales for detecting spurious PTSD claims: F, F K, Fake Bad scale, Ego Strength, Subtle Obvious subscales, DIS, and DEB. *Journal of Clinical Psychology, 48,* 681–689.

Lemkau, J. P., Purdy, R. R., Rafferty, J. P., & Rudisill, J. R. (1988). Correlates of burnout among family practice residents. *Journal of Medical Education, 63,* 682—691.

Leroux, M. D., Vincent, K. R., McPherson, R. H., & Williams, W. (1990). Construct validity of the Diagnostic Inventory of Personality and Symptoms: External correlates. *Journal of Clinical Psychology, 46,* 285–291.

Levine, J., Tischer, P., Antoni, M., Green, C., & Millon, T. (1985). Refining personality assessments by combining MCMI high-point profiles and MMPI codes, Part II: MMPI 27/72. *Journal of Personality Assessment, 49,* 501–507.

Levinson, D. J. (1978). *The seasons of a man's life.* New York: Knopf.

Levinson, D. J. (1980). Toward a conception of the adult life course. In N. J. Smelser & E. H. Erikson (Eds.), *Themes of work and love in adulthood* (pp. 265–290). Cambridge, MA: Harvard University Press.

Levy, S. (1987). Therapeutic strategy and psychoanalytic technique. *Journal of the American Psychoanalytic Association, 35,* 447–466.

Lewis, S., & Harder, D. (1990). Factor structure of the MCMI among personality disordered outpatients and in other populations. *Journal of Clinical Psychology, 46,* 613–617.

Lewis, S. J., & Harder, D. W. (1991). A comparison of four measures to diagnose DSM-III-R borderline personality disorder in outpatients. *Journal of Nervous and Mental Disease, 179,* 329–337.

Libb, J. W., Murray, J., Thurstin, H., & Alarcon, R. D. (1992). Concordance of the MCMI-II, the MMPI, and Axis I discharge diagnosis in psychiatric inpatients. *Journal of Personality Assessment, 58,* 580–590.

Libb, J. W., Stankovic, S., Freeman, A., Sokol, R., Switzer, P., & Houck, C. (1990). Personality disorders among depressed outpatients as identified by the MCMI. *Journal of Clinical Psychology, 46,* 277–284.

Libb, J. W., Stankovic, S., Sokol, R., Freeman, A., Houck, C., & Switzer, P. (1990). Stability of the MCMI among depressed psychiatric outpatients. *Journal of Personality Assessment, 55,* 209–218.

Lindsay, K. A., & Widiger, T. A. (1995). Sex and gender bias in self-report personality disorder inventories: Item analyses of the MCMI-II, MMPI, and PDQ-R. *Journal of Personality Assessment, 65*, 1–20.

Litman, L. C., & Cernovsky, Z. Z. (1993). An MCMI-II taxonomy of substance abusers. *Research Communications in Psychology, Psychiatry and Behavior, 18*, 67–72.

Llorente, M. D., Currier, M. B., Norman, S. E., & Mellman, T. A. (1992). Night terrors in adults: Phenomenology and relationship to psychopathology. *Journal of Clinical Psychiatry, 53*, 392–394.

Lohr, J. M., Hamberger, L. K., & Bonge, D. (1988). The nature of irrational beliefs in different personality clusters of spouse abusers. *Journal of Rational–Emotive and Cognitive–Behavior Therapy, 6*, 273–285.

Lorr, M., Katz, M., & Rubinstein, E. (1958). The prediction of length of stay in psychotherapy. *Journal of Consulting Psychology, 22*, 321–327.

Lorr, M., Retzlaff, P. D., & Tarr, H. C. (1989). An analysis of the MCMI-I at the item level. *Journal of Clinical Psychology, 45*, 884–890.

Lorr, M., & Strack, S. (1990). Profile clusters of the MCMI-II personality disorder scales. *Journal of Clinical Psychology, 46*, 606–612.

Lorr, M., Strack, S., Campbell, L., & Lamnin, A. (1990). Personality and symptom dimensions of the MCMI-II: An item factor analysis. *Journal of Clinical Psychology, 46*, 749–754.

Lovitt, R. (1988). Current practice of psychological assessment: Response to Sweeney, Clarkin, and Fitzgibbon. *Professional Psychology: Research and Practice, 19*, 516–521.

Lumsden, E. A. (1986, March). *Internal structure validation of the MCMI: Correlations among unshared scale items.* Paper presented at the Conference of the Millon Clinical Inventories, Miami, FL.

Lumsden, E. A. (1988). The impact of shared items on the internal structure validity of the MCMI. *Educational and Psychological Measurement, 49*, 669–678.

Lundholm, J. K. (1989). Alcohol use among university females: Relationship to eating disordered behavior. *Addictive Behaviors, 14*, 181–185.

Lundholm, J. K., Pellegreno, D. D., Wolins, L., & Graham, S. L. (1989). Predicting eating disorders in women: A preliminary measurement study. *Measurement and Evaluation in Counseling and Development, 22*, 23–30.

Luteijn, F. (1990). The MCMI in the Netherlands: First findings. *Journal of Personality Disorders, 4*, 297–302.

Machiavelli, N. (1931). *The prince* (W. Marriott, Trans.). London: J. M. Dent. (Original work published 1532)

Malan, D. (1976). *Frontiers of brief psychotherapy.* New York: Plenum.

Malec, J., Wolberg, W., Romsaas, E., Trump, D., & Tanner, M. (1988). Millon Clinical Multiaxial Inventory (MCMI) findings among breast clinic patients after initial evaluation and at 4- or 8-month follow-up. *Journal of Clinical Psychology, 44*, 175–180.

Mann, J. (1973). *Time limited psychotherapy.* Cambridge, MA: Harvard University Press.

Marlowe, D. B., & Wetzler, S. (1994). Contributions of discriminant analysis to differential diagnosis by self-report. *Journal of Personality Assessment, 62*, 320–331.

Marsella, A. J., Sanaborn, K. O., Kameoka, V., Shizuru, L., & Brennan, J. (1975). Cross-validation of self-report measures of depression among normal populations of Japanese, Chinese, and Caucasian ancestry. *Journal of Clinical Psychology, 31*, 281–287.

Marsh, D. T., Stile, S. A., Stoughton, N. L., & Trout-Landen, B. L. (1988). Psychopathology of opiate addiction: Comparative data from the MMPI and MCMI. *American Journal of Drug and Alcohol Abuse, 14*, 17–27.

Martin, P., Langone, M., Dole, A., & Wiltrout, J. (1992). Post-cult symptoms as measured by the MCMI before and after residential treatment. *Cultic Studies Journal, 9*, 219–251.

Maruish, M. (Ed.). (1994). *The use of psychological testing for treatment and planning and outcome.* Hillsdale, NJ: Erlbaum.

Matano, R. A., & Locke, K. D. (1995). Personality disorder scales as predictors of interpersonal problems of alcoholics. *Journal of Personality Disorders, 9*, 62–67.

Matano, R. A., Locke, K. D., & Schwartz, K. (1994). MCMI personality subtypes for male and female alcoholics. *Journal of Personality Assessment, 63*, 250–264.

Matarazzo, J. D. (1986). Computerized clinical psychological test interpretations: Unvalidated plus all mean and no sigma. *American Psychologist, 41*, 14–24.

Mayer, G. S., & Scott, K. J. (1988). An exploration of heterogeneity in an inpatient male alcoholic population. *Journal of Personality Disorders, 2*, 243–255.

McCann, J. T. (1989). MMPI personality disorder scales and the MCMI: Concurrent validity. *Journal of Clinical Psychology, 45*, 365–369.

McCann, J. T. (1990a). Bias and Millon Clinical Multiaxial Inventory (MCMI-II) diagnosis. *Journal of Psychopathology and Behavioral Assessment, 12*, 17–26.

McCann, J. T. (1990b). A multitrait–multimethod analysis of the MCMI-II clinical syndrome scales. *Journal of Personality Assessment, 55*, 465–476.

McCann, J. T. (1991). Convergent and discriminant validity of the MCMI-II and MMPI personality disorder scales. *Psychological Assessment, 3*, 9–18.

McCann, J. T. (1992). A comparison of two measures for obsessive–compulsive personality disorder. *Journal of Personality Disorders, 6*, 18–23.

McCann, J. T., & Dyer, F. J. (1996). *Forensic assessment with the Millon Inventories.* New York: Guilford Press.

McCann, J. T., Flynn, P. M., & Gersh, D. M. (1992). MCMI-II diagnosis of borderline personality disorder: Base rates versus prototypic items. *Journal of Personality Assessment, 58*, 105–114.

McCann, J., & Gergelis, R. (1990). Utility of the MCMI-II in assessing suicide risk. *Journal of Clinical Psychology, 46*, 764–770.

McCann, J., & Suess, J. (1988). Clinical applications of the MCMI: The 1-2-3-8 codetype. *Journal of Clinical Psychology, 44*, 181–186.

McCrae, R. (1991). The five factor model and its assessment in clinical settings. *Journal of Personality Assessment, 57*, 399–414.

McCrae, R., & Costa, P. (1985). Updating Norman's "adequate taxonomy": Intelligence and personality dimensions in natural language and in questionnaires. *Journal of Personality and Social Psychology, 49*, 710–721.

McCrae, R., & Costa, P. (1986). Clinical assessment can benefit from recent advances in personality psychology. *American Psychologist, 41*, 1001–1003.

McCrae, R. R., & Costa, P. T. (1990). *Personality in adulthood.* New York: Guilford Press.

McCreary, C., & Padilla, E. (1977). MMPI differences among Black, Mexican-American and White male offenders. *Journal of Clinical Psychology, 33*, 171–177.

McCullough, J. (1984). Cognitive–behavioral analysis system of psychotherapy: An interactional treatment approach for dysthymic disorder. *Psychiatry, 47*, 234–250.

McDermott, W. F. (1987). The diagnosis of post-traumatic stress disorder using the Millon Clinical Multiaxial Inventory. In C. Green (Ed.), *Conference of the Millon Clinical Inventories (MCMI, MBHI, MAPI)* (pp. 257–262). Minneapolis, MN: National Computer Systems.

McGill, J. C. (1980). MMPI score differences among Anglo, Black and Mexican American welfare recipients. *Journal of Consulting and Clinical Psychology, 36*, 147–171.

McMahon, R., Applegate, B., Kouzekanani, K., & Davidson, R. (1990, August). *Confir-*

matory factor analysis of the Millon Clinical Multiaxial Inventory. Paper presented at the 98th Annual Convention of the American Psychological Association, Boston.

McMahon, R., & Davidson, R. (1985a). An examination of the relationship between personality patterns and symptom/mood patterns. *Journal of Personality Assessment, 49,* 552–556.

McMahon, R., & Davidson, R. (1985b). Transient versus enduring depression among alcoholics in inpatient treatment. *Journal of Psychopathology and Behavioral Assessment, 7,* 317–328.

McMahon, R., & Davidson, R. (1986a). Concurrent validity of the clinical symptom scales of the Millon Multiaxial Inventory. *Journal of Clinical Psychology, 42,* 908–912.

McMahon, R., & Davidson, R. (1986b). An examination of depressed vs. nondepressed alcoholics in inpatient treatment. *Journal of Clinical Psychology, 42,* 177–184.

McMahon, R. C., & Davidson, R. S. (1988, August). *Factor structure of the Millon Clinical Multiaxial Inventory in an alcohol abusing population.* Paper presented at the 96th Annual Convention of the American Psychological Association, Atlanta, GA.

McMahon, R., & Davidson, R. (1989, August). *A comparison of continuous and episodic drinkers using the MCMI, MMPI, and ALCEVAL-R.* Paper presented at the 97th Annual Convention of the American Psychological Association, New Orleans, LA.

McMahon, R. C., Davidson, R. S., & Flynn, P. M. (1986). Psychosocial correlates and treatment outcomes for high and low social functioning alcoholics. *International Journal of Addictions, 21,* 819–835.

McMahon, R. C., Davidson, R. S., Gersh, D., & Flynn, P. (1991). A comparison of continuous and episodic drinkers using the MCMI, MMPI, and ALCEVAL-R. *Journal of Clinical Psychology, 47,* 148–159.

McMahon, R. C., Flynn, P. M., & Davidson, R. S. (1985a). The personality and symptoms scales of the Millon Clinical Multiaxial Inventory: Sensitivity to posttreatment outcomes. *Journal of Clinical Psychology, 41,* 862–866.

McMahon, R. C., Flynn, P. M., & Davidson, R. S. (1985b). Stability of the personality and symptom scales of the Millon Clinical Multiaxial Inventory. *Journal of Personality Assessment, 49,* 231–234.

McMahon, R. C., Gersh, D. M., & Davidson, R. S. (1989a, August). *Factor structure and correlates of the Millon Clinical Multiaxial Inventory.* Paper presented at the 97th Annual Convention of the American Psychological Association, New Orleans, LA.

McMahon, R. C., Gersh, D., & Davidson, R. S. (1989b). Personality and symptom characteristics of continuous vs. episodic drinkers. *Journal of Clinical Psychology, 45,* 161–168.

McMahon, R. C., Kelley, A., & Kouzekanani, K. (1993). Personality and coping styles in the prediction of dropout from treatment for cocaine abuse. *Journal of Personality Assessment, 61,* 147–155.

McMahon, R., Kouzekanani, K., & Bustillo, S. (1991, August). *Factor structure of the Millon Clinical Multiaxial Inventory—II.* Paper presented at the 99th Annual Convention of the American Psychological Association, San Francisco, CA.

McMahon, R., Schram, L., & Davidson, R. (1993). Negative life events, social support, and depression in three personality types. *Journal of Personality Disorders, 7,* 241–254.

McMahon, R., & Tyson, D. (1989). *Transient versus enduring depression among alcoholic women.* Paper presented at the 97th Annual Convention of the American Psychological Association, New Orleans, LA.

McMahon, R., & Tyson, D. (1990). Personality factors in transient versus enduring depression among inpatient alcoholic women: A preliminary analysis. *Journal of Personality Disorders, 4,* 150–160.

McNiel, K., & Meyer, R. (1990). Detection of deception on the Millon Clinical Multiaxial Inventory (MCMI). *Journal of Clinical Psychology, 46,* 755–764.

Meehl, P. (1960). The cognitive activity of the clinician. *American Psychologist, 15,* 19–27.

Meehl, P. (1973). *Psychodiagnosis: Selected papers.* New York: Norton.

Meehl, P. E., & Rosen, A. (1955). Antecedent probability and the efficiency of psychometric signs, patterns, or cutting scores. *Psychological Bulletin, 52,* 194–216.

Merbaum, M., & Butcher, J. (1982). Therapists' liking of their psychotherapy patients: Some issues related to severity of disorder and treatability. *Psychotherapy: Theory, Research, and Practice, 19,* 69–76.

Miller, C., Knapp, S., & Daniels, C. (1968). MMPI study of Negro mental hygiene clinic patients. *Journal of Abnormal Psychology, 73,* 168–173.

Miller, C., Wertz, C., & Counts, S. (1961). Racial differences on the MMPI. *Journal of Clinical Psychology, 17,* 159–160.

Miller, H. R., Goldberg, J. O., & Streiner, D. L. (1993). The effects of the modifier and correction indices on MCMI-II profiles. *Journal of Personality Assessment, 60,* 477–485.

Miller, H. R., & Streiner, D. L. (1990). Using the Millon Clinical Multiaxial Inventory's Scale B and the MacAndrew Alcoholism Scale to identify alcoholics with concurrent psychiatric diagnoses. *Journal of Personality Assessment, 54,* 736–746.

Miller, H. R., Streiner, D. L., & Parkinson, A. (1992). Maximum likelihood estimates of the ability of the MMPI and MCMI personality disorder scales and the SIDP to identify personality disorders. *Journal of Personality Assessment, 59,* 1–13.

Millon, C., Salvato, F., Blaney, N., Morgan, R., Montero-Atienza, E., Klimas, N., & Fletcher, M. A. (1989). A psychological assessment of chronic fatigue syndrome/ chronic Epstein-Barr virus patients. *Psychology and Health, 3,* 131–141.

Millon, T. (1969). *Modern psychopathology: A biosocial approach to maladaptive learning and functioning.* Philadelphia: W. B. Saunders.

Millon, T. (1973). A biosocial-learning approach. In T. Millon (Ed.), *Theories of psychopathology and personality* (pp. 492–502). Philadelphia: W. B. Saunders.

Millon, T. (1977). *Millon Clinical Multiaxial Inventory.* Minneapolis, MN: National Computer Systems.

Millon, T. (1981). *Disorders of personality: DSM-III Axis II.* New York: Wiley.

Millon, T. (1982). *Millon Clinical Multiaxial Inventory manual* (2nd ed.). Minneapolis, MN: National Computer Systems.

Millon, T. (1983). *Millon Clinical Multiaxial Inventory manual* (3rd ed.). Minneapolis, MN: National Computer Systems.

Millon, T. (1985). The MCMI provides a good assessment of DSM-III disorders: The MCMI-II will prove even better. *Journal of Personality Assessment, 49,* 379–391.

Millon, T. (1986). The MCMI and DSM-III: Further commentaries. *Journal of Personality Assessment, 50,* 205–207.

Millon, T. (1987). *Manual for the MCMI-II* (2nd ed.). Minneapolis, MN: National Computer Systems.

Millon, T. (1988). Personologic psychotherapy: Ten commandments for a posteclectic approach to integrative treatment. *Psychotherapy, 25,* 209–219.

Millon, T. (1990). *Toward a new personology: An evolutionary model.* New York: Wiley.

Millon, T. (1994). *Manual for the MCMI-III.* Minneapolis, MN: National Computer Systems.

Millon, T. (1995). *Disorders of personality: DSM-IV and beyond.* New York: Wiley.

Millon, T., & Davis, R. (1995). Putting Humpty Dumpty together again: Using the MCMI in psychological assessment. In M. Beutler & M. Berren (Eds.), *Integrative assessment of adult personality* (pp. 240–279). New York: Guilford Press.

Millon, T., & Millon, R. (1974). *Abnormal behavior and personality*. Philadelphia: W. B. Saunders.

Mischel, W. (1968). *Personality assessment*. New York: Wiley.

Mischei, W. (1973). Toward a cognitive social learning reconceptualization of personality. *Psychological Review, 80,* 252–283.

Montag, I., & Comrey, A. L. (1987). Millon MCMI scales analyzed and correlated with MMPI and CPS scales. *Multivariate Behavioral Research, 22,* 401–413.

Moreland, K. (1992). If it's personality patterns you're interested in. . . . *Journal of Personality Assessment, 58,* 438–440.

Moreland, K. L., & Onstad, J. A. (1987). Validity of Millon's computerized interpretation system for the MCMI: A controlled study. *Journal of Consulting and Clinical Psychology, 55,* 113–114.

Moreland, K. L., & Onstad, J. A. (1989). Yes, our study could have been better: Reply to Cash, Mikulka, and Brown. *Journal of Consulting and Clinical Psychology, 57,* 313–314.

Morey, L. C. (1985). An empirical comparison of interpersonal and DSM-III approaches to classification of personality disorders. *Psychiatry, 48,* 358–364.

Morey, L. C. (1986). A comparison of three personality disorder assessment approaches. *Journal of Psychopathology and Behavioral Assessment, 8,* 25–30.

Morey, L. C., Blashfield, R. K., Webb, W. W., & Jewell, J. (1988). MMPI scales for the DSM-III personality disorders: A preliminary validation study. *Journal of Clinical Psychology, 44,* 47–50.

Morey, L. C., & Le Vine, D. J. (1988). A multitrait–multimethod examination of Minnesota Multiphasic Personality Inventory (MMPI) and Millon Clinical Multiaxial Inventory (MCMI). *Journal of Psychopathology and Behavioral Assessment, 10,* 333–344.

Morey, L. C., Waugh, M. H., & Blashfield, R. K. (1985). MMPI scales for the DSM-III personality disorders: Their derivation and correlates. *Journal of Personality Assessment, 49,* 245–251.

Mortensen, E. L., & Simonsen, E. (1990). Psychometric properties of the Danish MCMI-I translation. *Scandinavian Journal of Psychology, 31,* 149–153.

Mortimer, R., & Smith, W. (1983). The use of the psychological test report in setting the focus of psychotherapy. *Journal of Personality Assessment, 47,* 134–138.

Munley, P. H., Bains, D. S., Frazee, J., & Schwartz, L. T. (1994). Inpatient PTSD treatment: A study of pretreatment measures, treatment dropout, and therapist ratings of response to treatment. *Journal of Traumatic Stress, 7,* 319–325.

Muran, J., Segal, Z., Samstag, L., & Crawford, C. (1994). Patient pretreatment interpersonal problems and therapeutic alliance in short-term cognitive therapy. *Journal of Consulting and Clinical Psychology, 62,* 185–190.

Murphy, C. M., Meyer, S. L., & O'Leary, K. D. (1993). Family of origin violence and MCMI-II psychopathology among partner assaultive men. *Violence and Victims, 8,* 165–176.

Murphy, T. J., Greenblatt, R. L., Mozdzierz, G. J., & Trimakas, K. A. (1990). Stability of the Millon Clinical Multiaxial Inventory among psychiatric inpatients. *Journal of Psychopathology and Behavioral Assessment, 12,* 143–150.

Nakao, K., Gunderson, J., Phillips, K., Tanaka, N., Yorifuji, K., Takaishi, J., & Nishimura, T. (1992). Functional impairment in personality disorders. *Journal of Personality Disorders, 6,* 24–33.

Nazikian, H., Rudd, R. P., Edwards, J., & Jackson, H. J. (1990). Personality disorder assessment for psychiatric inpatients. *Australian and New Zealand Journal of Psychiatry, 24,* 37–46.

Neimeyer, G. (1987). Personal construct assessment, strategy, and technique. In R. Neimeyer & G. Neimeyer (Eds.), *Personal construct therapy casebook* (pp. 20–36). New York: Springer.

Nerviano, V., & Gross, W. (1983). Personality types of alcoholics in objective inventories. *Journal of Studies on Alcohol, 44,* 837–851.

Neugarten, B. L. (1975). The awareness of middle age. In B. L. Neugarten (Ed.), *Middle age and aging* (pp. 93–98). Chicago: University of Chicago Press.

Norcross, J. (1993). Tailoring relationship stances to client needs: An introduction. *Psychotherapy, 30,* 402–403.

Norcross, J., & Prochaska, J. (1982). A national survey of clinical psychologists: Characteristics and activities. *Clinical Psychologist, 35,* 1–8.

Norman, D., Blais, M., & Herzog, D. (1993). Personality characteristics of eating-disordered patients as identified by the Millon Clinical Multiaxial Inventory. *Journal of Personality Disorders, 7,* 1–9.

O'Callaghan, T., Bates, G. W., Jackson, H. J., Rudd, R. P., & Edwards, J. (1990). The clinical utility of the Millon Clinical Multiaxial Inventory Depression subscales. *Australian Psychologist, 25,* 45–61.

Oldham, J., Clarkin, J., Appelbaum, A., Carr, A., Kernberg, P., Lotterman, A., & Haas, G. (1985). A self-report instrument for borderline personality organization. In T. H. McGlashan (Ed.), *The borderline: Current empirical research* (pp. 1–18). Washington, DC: American Psychiatric Press.

Overholser, J. C. (August, 1989). *Temporal stability of the MCMI personality disorder scales.* Paper presented at the 97th Annual Convention of the American Psychological Association, New Orleans, LA.

Overholser, J. C. (1990). Retest reliability of the Millon Clinical Multiaxial Inventory. *Journal of Personality Assessment, 55,* 202–208.

Overholser, J. C. (1991). Categorical assessment of the dependent personality disorder in depressed inpatients. *Journal of Personality Disorders, 5,* 243–255.

Overholser, J. C., Kabakoff, R., & Norman, W. H. (1989). The assessment of personality characteristics in depressed and dependent psychiatric inpatients. *Journal of Personality Assessment, 53,* 40–50.

Ownby, R. L., Wallbrown, F., Carmin, C., & Barnett, R. W. (1990). A combined factor analysis of the Millon Clinical Multiaxial Inventory and the MMPI in an offender population. *Journal of Clinical Psychology, 46,* 89–96.

Ownby, R. L., Wallbrown, F. H., Carmin, C., & Barnett, R. (1991). A canonical analysis of the Millon Clinical Multiaxial Inventory and the MMPI for an offender population. *Journal of Personality Disorders, 5,* 15–24.

Page, R. D., & Bozlee, S. (1982). A cross-cultural MMPI comparison of alcoholics. *Psychological Reports, 50,* 639–646.

Palmer, C. (1975). Characteristics of effective counselor-trainees. *Dissertation Abstracts International, 36,* A2031.

Pancoast, D. L., Archer, R. P., & Gordon, R. A. (1988). The MMPI and clinical diagnosis: A comparison of classification system outcomes with discharge diagnoses. *Journal of Personality Assessment, 52,* 81–90.

Papciak, A. S., & Feuerstein, M. (1991). Psychological factors affecting isokinetic trunk strength testing in patients with work related chronic low back pain. *Journal of Occupational Rehabilitation, 1,* 95–104.

Patrick, J. (1988). Concordance of the MCMI and the MMPI in the diagnosis of three DSM-III Axis I disorders. *Journal of Clinical Psychology, 44,* 186–191.

Patrick, J. (1990). Assessment of narcissistic psychopathology in the clergy. *Pastoral Psychology, 38,* 173–180.

Patrick, J. (1993). Validation of the MCMI-I Borderline Personality Disorder scale with a well-defined criterion sample. *Journal of Clinical Psychology, 49,* 28–32.

Pendleton, L., Tisdale, M., & Marler, M. (1991). Personality pathology in bulimics versus controls. *Comprehensive Psychiatry, 32,* 516–520.

Peniston, E. G., & Kulkosky, P. J. (1990). Alcoholic personality and alpha–theta brainwave training. *Medical Psychotherapy, 3,* 37–45.

Peterson, G., Clark, A., & Bennet, B. (1989). The utility of the MMPI subtle, obvious scales for detecting fake good and fake bad response sets. *Journal of Clinical Psychology, 45,* 575–582.

Pettem, O., West, M., Mahoney, A., & Keller, A. (1993). Depression and attachment problems. *Journal of Psychiatry and Neuroscience, 18,* 78–81.

Piekarski, A. M., Sherwood, R., & Funari, D. J. (1993). Personality subgroups in an inpatient Vietnam veteran treatment program. *Psychological Reports, 72,* 667–674.

Piersma, H. L. (1986a, August). *Computer-generated diagnoses: How do they compare to clinical judgment?* Paper presented at the 94th Annual Convention of the American Psychological Association, Washington, DC.

Piersma, H. L. (1986b). The factor structure of the Millon Clinical Multiaxial Inventory (MCMI) for psychiatric inpatients. *Journal of Personality Assessment, 50,* 578–584.

Piersma, H. L. (1986c). The Millon Clinical Multiaxial Inventory (MCMI) as a treatment outcome measure for psychiatric inpatients. *Journal of Clinical Psychology, 42,* 493–499.

Piersma, H. L. (1986d). The stability of the Millon Clinical Multiaxial Inventory for psychiatric inpatients. *Journal of Personality Assessment, 50,* 193–197.

Piersma, H. L. (1987a). The MCMI as a measure of DSM-III Axis II diagnoses: An empirical comparison. *Journal of Clinical Psychology, 43,* 478–483.

Piersma, H. L. (1987b). Millon Clinical Multiaxial Inventory (MCMI) computer-generated diagnoses: How do they compare to clinical judgment? *Journal of Psychopathology and Behavioral Assessment, 9,* 305–312.

Piersma, H. L. (1987c). The use of the Millon Clinical Multiaxial Inventory in the evaluation of seminary students. *Journal of Psychology and Theology, 15,* 227–233.

Piersma, H. L. (1989a). The MCMI-II as a treatment outcome measure for psychiatric inpatients. *Journal of Clinical Psychology, 45,* 87–93.

Piersma, H. L. (1989b). The stability of the MCMI-II for psychiatric inpatients. *Journal of Clinical Psychology, 45,* 781–785.

Piersma, H. L. (1991). The MCMI-II depression scales: Do they assist in the differential prediction of depressive disorders? *Journal of Personality Assessment, 56,* 478–486.

Piersma, H. L., & Smith, A. Y. (1991). Individual variability in self-reported improvement for depressed psychiatric inpatients on the MCMI-II. *Journal of Clinical Psychology, 47,* 227–232.

Pincus, A. L., & Wiggins, J. S. (1990). Interpersonal problems and conceptions of personality disorders. *Journal of Personality Disorders, 4,* 342–352.

Piotrowski, C., & Keller, J. W. (1989). Psychological testing in outpatient mental health facilities: A national study. *Professional Psychology: Research and Practice, 20,* 423–425.

Piotrowski, C., & Lubin, B. (1989). Assessment practices of Division 38 practitioners. *Health Psychologist, 11,* 1.

Piotrowski, C., & Lubin, B. (1990). Assessment practices of health psychologists: Survey of APA Division 38 clinicians. *Professional Psychology: Research and Practice, 21,* 99–106.

Plemons, G. (1977). A comparison of the MMPI scores of Anglo and Mexican-American psychiatry patients. *Journal of Consulting and Clinical Psychology, 45,* 149–150.

Pochyly, J. M., Greenblatt, R. L., & Davis, W. E. (1989, August). *The effect of race on MCMI clinical scales.* Paper presented at the 97th Annual Convention of the American Psychological Association, New Orleans, LA.

Pollack, D., & Shore, J. H. (1980). Validity of the MMPI with Native Americans. *American Journal of Psychiatry, 137,* 946–950.

Prifitera, A., & Ryan, J. J. (1984). Validity of the Narcissistic Personality Inventory (NPI) in a psychiatric sample. *Journal of Clinical Psychology, 40,* 140–142.

Pritchard, D. A., & Rosenblatt, A. (1980). Racial bias in the MMPI: A methodological review. *Journal of Consulting and Clinical Psychology, 48,* 263–267.

Raskin, R. N., & Hall, C. S. (1979). A narcissistic personality inventory. *Psychological Reports, 45,* 590.

Reich, J. (1985). Measurement of DSM-III Axis II. *Comprehensive Psychiatry, 26,* 352–363.

Reich, J. (1989). Update on instruments to measure DSM-III and DSM-III-R personality disorders. *Journal of Nervous and Mental Disease, 177,* 366–370.

Reich, J. (1990). The effect of personality on placebo response in panic patients. *Journal of Nervous and Mental Disease, 178,* 699–702.

Reich, J., Noyes, R., & Troughton, E. (1987). Dependent personality disorder associated with phobic avoidance in patients with panic disorder. *American Journal of Psychiatry, 144,* 323–326.

Reich, J., & Troughton, E. (1988). Comparison of DSM-III personality disorders in recovered depressed and panic disorder patients. *Journal of Nervous and Mental Disease, 176,* 300–304.

Reich, W. (1949). *Character analysis.* New York: Noonday Press.

Renneberg, B., Chambless, D. L., Dowdall, D. J., Fauerbach, J. A., & Gracely, E. J. (1992). The Structured Clinical Interview for the DSM-III-R and the Millon Clinical Multiaxial Inventory: A concurrent validity study of personality disorders among anxious outpatients. *Journal of Personality Disorders, 6,* 117–124.

Repko, G. R., & Cooper, R. (1985). The diagnosis of personality disorder: A comparison of MMPI profile, Millon inventory, and clinical judgment in a workers' compensation population. *Journal of Clinical Psychology, 41,* 867–881.

Retzlaff, P. D. (1991, August). *MCMI-II scoring challenges: Multi-weight items and site specific algorithms.* Paper presented at the 99th Annual Convention of the American Psychological Association, San Francisco, CA.

Retzlaff, P. (1995a). *The relationship between reliability and validity in a Bayesian world.* Paper presented at the 103rd Annual Convention of the American Psychological Association, New York.

Retzlaff, P. (Ed.). (1995b). *Tactical psychotherapy of the personality disorders.* Boston: Allyn & Bacon.

Retzlaff, P. (1996). MCMI-III validity: Bad test or bad validity study. *Journal of Personality Assessment, 66,* 431–437.

Retzlaff, P. D., & Bromley, S. (1991). A multi-test alcoholic-taxonomy: Canonical coefficient clusters. *Journal of Clinical Psychology, 47,* 299–309.

Retzlaff, P., & Deatherage, T. (1993). Air Force mental health consultation: A six-year retention follow-up. *Military Medicine, 158,* 338–340.

Retzlaff, P., & Gibertini, M. (1987a). Air Force pilot personality: Hard data on "the right stuff." *Multivariate Behavioral Research, 22,* 383–399.

Retzlaff, P., & Gibertini, M. (1987b). Factor structure of the MCMI basic personality scales and common item artifact. *Journal of Personality Assessment, 51,* 588–594.

Retzlaff, P. D., & Gibertini, M. (1988). Objective psychological testing of U.S. Air Force officers in pilot training. *Aviation, Space, and Environmental Medicine, 59,* 661–663.

Retzlaff, P. D., & Gibertini, M. (1990). Factor based special scales for the MCMI. *Journal of Clinical Psychology, 46,* 47–52.

Retzlaff, P., Lorr, M., Hyer, L., & Ofman, P. (1991). An MCMI-II item-level component analysis: Personality and clinical factors. *Journal of Personality Assessment, 57,* 323–334.

Retzlaff, P., Ofman, P., Hyer, L., & Matheson, S. (1994). MCMI-II high-point codes: Severe personality disorder and clinical syndrome extensions. *Journal of Clinical Psychology, 50,* 228–234.

Retzlaff, P. D., Sheehan, E. P., & Fiel, A. (1991). MCMI-II report style and bias: Profile and validity scales analyses. *Journal of Personality Assessment, 56,* 466–477.

Retzlaff, P. D., Sheehan, E. P., & Lorr, M. (1990). MCMI-II scoring: Weighted and unweighted algorithms. *Journal of Personality Assessment, 55,* 219–223.

Reynolds, C. R. (1982). The problem of bias in psychological assessment. In C. R. Reynolds & T. B. Gutkin (Eds.), *The handbook of school psychology* (pp. 178–208). New York: Wiley.

Reynolds, C. R. (1983). Test bias: In God we trust; all others must have data. *Journal of Special Education, 17,* 241–260.

Ritzler, B. (1996, Spring/Summer). Personality assessment and research: The state of the Union. *SPA Exchange, 6,* 15.

Robbins, S. B., & Patton, M. J. (1986). Procedures for construction of scales for rating counselor outcomes. *Measurement and Evaluation in Counseling and Development, 19,* 131–140.

Robert, J. A., Ryan, J. J., McEntyre, W. L., McFarland, R. S., Lips, O. J., & Rosenberg, S. (1985). MCMI characteristics of DSM-III: Posttraumatic stress disorder in Vietnam veterans. *Journal of Personality Assessment, 49,* 226–230.

Rogers, C. (1951). *Client centered therapy.* Cambridge, MA: Riverside Press.

Rorer, L. G., & Dawes, R. M. (1982). A base-rate bootstrap. *Journal of Consulting and Clinical Psychology, 50,* 419–425.

Ross, C., Ryan, L., Voigt, H., & Eide, L. (1991). High and low dissociators in a college student population. *Dissociation, 4,* 147–151.

Rouff, L., Van Denburg, E., Newman, A., & Choca, J. (1995, August). *Prediction of dropout in an outpatient VA psychiatric clinic.* Paper presented at the 103rd Annual Convention of the American Psychological Association, New York.

Rubino, I., Saya, A., & Pezzarossa, B. (1992). Percept-genetic signs of repression in histrionic disorder. *Perceptual and Motor Skills, 74,* 451–464.

Sabshin, M. (1989). Normality and the boundaries of psychopathology. *Journal of Personality Disorders, 3,* 259–273.

Safran, J. D., Segal, Z. V., Vallis, T. M., Shaw, B. F., & Wallner Samstag, L. (1993). Assessing patient suitability for short-term cognitive therapy with an interpersonal focus. *Cognitive Therapy and Research, 17,* 23–38.

Sansone, R. A., & Fine, M. A. (1992). Borderline personality as a predictor of outcome in women with eating disorders. *Journal of Personality Disorders, 6,* 176–186.

Schectman, F. (1989). Countertransference dilemmas with borderline patients. *Bulletin of the Menninger Clinic, 53,* 310–318.

Schinka, J. A., & Borum, R. (1993). Readability of adult psychopathology inventories. *Psychological Assessment, 5,* 384–386.

Schmidt, J. P., Sanders, A. U., Burdick, T. H., & Lohr, J. M. (1991, August). *Bulimia symptoms and personality characteristics: A cluster analysis comparison.* Paper presented at the 99th Annual Convention of the American Psychological Association, San Francisco, CA.

Schuler, C. E., Snibbe, J. R., & Buckwalter, J. G. (1994). Validity of the MMPI Personality Disorder scales (MMPI-PD). *Journal of Clinical Psychology, 50,* 220–227.

Schuller, D. R., Bagby, R. M., Levitt, A. J., & Joffe, R. T. (1993). A comparison of personality characteristics of seasonal and nonseasonal major depression. *Comprehensive Psychiatry, 34,* 360–362.

Schwartz, M. A., Wiggins, O. P., & Norko, M. A. (1989). Prototypes, ideal types and personality disorders: The return to classical psychiatry. *Journal of Personality Disorders, 3,* 1–9.

Serkownek, K. (1975). *Subscales for scales 5 and 0 of the Minnesota Multiphasic Personality Inventory.* Unpublished material.

Sexton, D. L., McIlwraith, R., Barnes, G., & Dunn, R. (1987). Comparison of the MCMI and the MMPI-168 as psychiatric inpatient screening inventories. *Journal of Personality Assessment, 51,* 388–398.

Shapiro, D. (1989). *Psychotherapy of neurotic character.* New York: Basic Books.

Shapiro, T. (1988). *Structure and psychoanalysis.* Madison, CT: International Universities Press.

Shapiro, T. (1989). Psychoanalytic classification and empiricism with borderline personality disorder as a model. *Journal of Consulting and Clinical Psychology, 57,* 187–194.

Shaughnessy, R., Dorus, E., Pandey, G. N., & Davis, J. M. (1980). Personality correlates of platelet monoamine oxidase activity and red blood cell lithium transport. *Psychiatric Research, 2,* 63–74.

Sherwood, R. J., Funari, D. J., & Piekarski, A. M. (1990). Adapted character styles of Vietnam veterans with posttraumatic stress disorder. *Psychological Reports, 66,* 623–631.

Shure, G. H., & Rogers, M. S. (1965). Note of caution on the factor analysis of the MMPI. *Psychological Bulletin, 63,* 14–18.

Siddall, J. W., & Keogh, N. J. (1993). Utility of computer interpretive reports based on counselors' ratings of the Diagnostic Inventory of Personality and Symptoms. *Psychological Reports, 72,* 347–350.

Sifneos, P. (1972). *Short-term psychotherapy and emotional crisis.* Cambridge, MA: Harvard University Press.

Silverman, J. S., & Loychik, S. (1990). Brain-mapping abnormalities in a family with three obsessive compulsive children. *Journal of Neuropsychiatry, 2,* 319–322.

Silverman, J. T. (1979). *The effect of personality variables on the patient–therapist relationship in psychotherapy.* Unpublished doctoral dissertation, Boston College, Boston.

Sim, J. P., & Romney, D. M. (1990). The relationship between a circumplex model of interpersonal behaviors and personality disorders. *Journal of Personality Disorders, 4,* 329–341.

Simonsen, E., Haslund, J., Larsen, A., & Borup, C. (1992). Personality pattern in first time admitted alcoholics. *Nordic Journal of Psychiatry, 46,* 175–179.

Simonsen, E., & Mortensen, E. L. (1990). Difficulties in translation of personality scales. *Journal of Personality Disorders, 4,* 290–296.

Smith, D., Carroll, J., & Fuller, G. (1988). The Millon Clinical Multiaxial Inventory and the MMPI in a private outpatient mental health clinic population. *Journal of Clinical Psychology, 44,* 165–174.

Snibbe, J. R., Peterson, P. J., & Sosner, B. (1980). Study of psychological characteristics of a worker's compensation sample using the MMPI and the Millon Clinical Multiaxial Inventory. *Psychological Reports, 47*, 959–966.

Soldz, S., Budman, S., Demby, A., & Merry, J. (1993a). Diagnostic agreement between the Personality Disorder Examination and the MCMI-II. *Journal of Personality Assessment, 60*, 486–499.

Soldz, S., Budman, S., Demby, A., & Merry, J. (1993b). Representation of personality disorders in circumplex and five factor space: Explorations with a clinical sample. *Psychological Assessment, 5*, 41–52.

Sperling, M. B., Sharp, J. L., & Fishler, P. H. (1991). On the nature of attachment in a borderline population: A preliminary investigation. *Psychological Reports, 68*, 543–546.

Stankovic, S., Libb, J. W., Freeman, A., & Roseman, J. (1992). Post-treatment stability of the MCMI-II personality scales in depressed outpatients. *Journal of Personality Disorders, 6*, 82–89.

Stark, M. J., & Campbell, B. K. (1988). Personality, drug use, and early attrition from substance abuse treatment. *American Journal of Drug and Alcohol Abuse, 14*, 475–485.

Stewart, A. E., Hyer, L., Retzlaff, P., & Ofman, P. (1995, August). *MCMI-II personality scales: Factors and latent traits*. Paper presented at the 103rd Annual Convention of the American Psychological Association, New York.

Stone, M. H. (1980). *The borderline syndromes*. New York: McGraw-Hill.

Strack, S. (1987). Development and validation of an adjective check list to assess the Millon personality types in a normal population. *Journal of Personality Assessment, 51*, 588–594.

Strack, S. (1990). *Manual for the Personality Adjective Check List (PACL)*. Richland, WA: Pacific Psychological.

Strack, S. (1991a). Factor analysis of the MCMI-II and the PACL basic personality scales in a college sample. *Journal of Personality Assessment, 57*, 345–355.

Strack, S. (1991b, August). *Response bias and the MCMI-II: Clinical and research issues*. Paper presented at the 99th Annual Convention of the American Psychological Association, San Francisco, CA.

Strack, S., Lorr, M., & Campbell, L. (1989, August). *Similarities in Millon personality styles among normals and psychiatric patients*. Paper presented at the 97th Annual Convention of the American Psychological Association, New Orleans, LA.

Strack, S., Lorr, M., & Campbell, L. (1990). An evaluation of Millon's circular model of personality disorders. *Journal of Personality Disorders, 4*, 353–361.

Strack, S., Lorr, M., Campbell, L., & Lamnin, A. (1992). Personality disorder and clinical syndrome factors of MCMI-II scales. *Journal of Personality Disorders, 6*, 40–52.

Strassberg, D., Cooper, L., & Marks, P. (1987). *The Marks Adult MMPI Report Version 2.1: The MMPI Scoring Program II*. Wakefield, RI: Applied Innovations.

Strauman, T. J., & Wetzler, S. (1992). The factor structure of SCL-90 and MCMI scale scores: Within measure and interbattery analyses. *Multivariate Behavioral Research, 27*, 1–20.

Streiner, D. L., Goldberg, J. O., & Miller, H. R. (1993). MCMI-II item weights: Their lack of effectiveness. *Journal of Personality Assessment, 60*, 471–476.

Streiner, D. L., & Miller, H. R. (1989). The MCMI-II: How much better than the MCMI? *Journal of Personality Assessment, 53*, 81–84.

Streiner, D., & Miller, H. (1990). Maximum likelihood estimates of the accuracy of four diagnostic techniques. *Educational and Psychological Measurement, 50*, 653–662.

Strupp, H., & Binder, J. (1984). *Psychotherapy in a new key*. New York: Basic Books.

Sullivan, H. S. (1953). *The interpersonal theory of psychiatry*. New York: Norton.

Sweeney, J. A., Clarkin, J. F., & Fitzgibbon, M. L. (1987). Current practice of psychological assessment. *Professional Psychology: Research and Practice, 18*, 377–380.

Swirsky-Sacchetti, T., Gorton, G., Samuel, S., Sobel, R., Genetta-Wadley, A., & Burleigh, B. (1993). Neuropsychological function in borderline personality disorder. *Journal of Clinical Psychology, 49*, 385–396.

Tamkin, A. S., Carson, M. F., Nixon, D. H., & Hyer, L. A. (1987). A comparison among some measures of depression in male alcoholics. *Journal of Studies on Alcohol, 48*, 176–178.

Tango, R. A., & Dziuban, C. D. (1984). The use of personality components in the interpretation of career indecision. *Journal of Student Personnel, 25*, 509–512.

Terpylak, O., & Schuerger, J. M. (1994). Broad factor scales of the 16 PF Fifth Edition and Millon personality disorder scales: A replication. *Psychological Reports, 74*, 124–126.

Terry, C. (1990, December 30). Vaclav Havel's new role. *Chicago Tribune*, Section 13, p. 3.

Tisdale, M. J., Pendleton, L., & Marler, M. (1990). MCMI characteristics of DSM-III-R bulimics. *Journal of Personality Assessment, 55*, 477–483.

Tolman, R. M. (1989). The development of a measure of psychological maltreatment of women by their male partners. *Violence and Victims, 4*, 159–177.

Torgersen, S., & Alnæs, R. (1990). The relationship between the MCMI personality scales and the DSM-III Axis II. *Journal of Personality Assessment, 55*, 698–707.

Trimboli, F. (1979). *MMPI interpretation and treatment implications*. Unpublished manuscript.

Trimboli, F., & Kilgore, R. (1983). A psychodynamic approach to MMPI interpretation. *Journal of Personality Assessment, 47*, 614–626.

Turkat, I. (1988). Issues in the relationship between assessment and treatment. *Journal of Psychopathology and Behavioral Assessment, 10*, 185–197.

Turkat, I. (1990). *The personality disorders: A psychosocial approach to clinical management*. Elmsford, NY: Pergamon Press.

Turkat, I., & Maisto, S. (1985). Application of the experimental method to the formulation and modification of personality disorders. In D. H. Barlow (Ed.), *Clinical handbook of psychological disorders* (pp. 503–570). New York: Guilford Press.

Turley, B., Bates, G. W., Edwards, J., & Jackson, H. J. (1992). MCMI-II personality disorders in recent onset bipolar disorders. *Journal of Clinical Psychology, 48*, 320–329.

Tyrer, P. (1988). What's wrong with the DSM-III personality disorders? *Journal of Personality Disorders, 2*, 281–291.

Uomoto, J. M., Turner, J. A., & Herron, L. D. (1988). Use of the MMPI and the MCMI in predicting outcome of lumbar laminectomy. *Journal of Clinical Psychology, 44*, 191–197.

Vaglum, P., Friis, S., Irion, T., Johns, S., Karterud, S., Larsen, F., & Vaglum, S. (1990). Treatment response of severe and nonsevere personality disorders in a therapeutic community day unit. *Journal of Personality Disorders, 4*, 161–172.

Van Denburg, E., & Choca, J. P. (in press). Interpretation of the MCMI-III. In T. Millon (Ed.), *The Millon inventories*. New York: Guilford Press.

Van Denburg, T. (1987). *Stage process model of psychotherapy: Passive–dependent personality disorder*. Unpublished manuscript.

Van Gorp, W. G., & Meyer, R. G. (1986). The detection of faking on the Millon Clinical Multiaxial Inventory (MCMI). *Journal of Clinical Psychology, 42*, 742–747.

van Reken, M. (1981). Psychological assessment and report writing. In C. E. Walker (Ed.), *Clinical practice of psychology* (pp. 129–160). Elmsford, NY: Pergamon Press.

Vollrath, M., Alnæs, R., & Torgersen, S. (1994). Coping and MCMI-II personality disorders. *Journal of Personality Disorders, 8*, 53–63.

Vollrath, M., Alnæs, R., & Torgersen, S. (1995). Coping styles predict change in personality disorders. *Journal of Personality Disorders, 9*, 371–385.

Vorce, D. E., Jones, K. A., Helder, L. M., Pettibon, W. H., & Reiter, W. M. (1995, August). *Correcting MCMI-II subscale Base Rate scores for chronic fatigue syndrome (CFS) patients.* Paper presented at the 103rd Annual Convention of the American Psychological Association, New York.

Wade, T., & Baker, T. (1977). Opinions and use of psychological tests: A survey of clinical psychologists. *American Psychologist, 31*, 874–888.

Wakefield, H., & Underwager, R. (1993). Misuse of psychological tests in forensic settings: Some horrible examples. *American Journal of Forensic Psychology, 11*, 55–75.

Walker, J. (1974). The word association sentence method as a predictor of psychotherapeutic outcome. *British Journal of Social and Clinical Psychology, 77*, 219–221.

Wall, T. L., Schuckit, M. A., Mungas, D., & Ehlers, C. L. (1990). EEG alpha activity and personality traits. *Alcohol, 7*, 461–464.

Ward, L. C. (1994). Correspondence of the MMPI-2 and MCMI-II in male substance abusers. *Journal of Personality Assessment, 64*, 390–393.

Webb, J. T., Miller, M. L., & Fowler, R. D. (1970). Extending professional time: A computerized MMPI interpretation service. *Journal of Clinical Psychology, 26*, 210–214.

Weekes, J. R., & Morrison, S. J. (1993). Offender typologies: Identifying treatment-relevant personality characteristics. *Forum on Corrections Research, 5*, 10–12.

Weiner, I. (1972). Does psychodiagnosis have a future? *Journal of Personality Assessment, 36*, 534–546.

Werman, D. (1984). *The practice of supportive psychotherapy.* New York: Brunner/Mazel.

Wetzler, S. (1990). The Millon Clinical Multiaxial Inventory (MCMI): A review. *Journal of Personality Assessment, 55*, 445–464.

Wetzler, S., & Dubro, A. (1990). Diagnosis of personality disorders by the Millon Clinical Multiaxial Inventory. *Journal of Nervous and Mental Disease, 178*, 261–263.

Wetzler, S., Kahn, R. S., Cahn, W., van Praag, H. M., & Asnis, G. M. (1990). Psychological test characteristics of depressed and panic patients. *Psychiatry Research, 31*, 179–192.

Wetzler, S., Kahn, R., Strauman, T., & Dubro, A. (1989). Diagnosis of major depression by self-report. *Journal of Personality Assessment, 53*, 22–30.

Wetzler, S., Khadivi, A., & Oppenheim, S. (1995). The psychological assessment of depression: Unipolars versus bipolars. *Journal of Personality Assessment, 65*, 557–566.

Wetzler, S., & Marlowe, D. (1990). "Faking bad" on the MMPI, MMPI-2 and Millon-II. *Psychological Reports, 67*, 1117–1118.

Wetzler, S., & Marlowe, D. (1993). The diagnosis and assessment of depression, mania, and psychosis by self-report. *Journal of Personality Assessment, 60*, 1–31.

Wheeler, D. S., & Schwarz, J. C. (1989). Millon Clinical Multiaxial Inventory (MCMI) scores with a collegiate sample: Long-term stability and self–other agreement. *Journal of Psychopathology and Behavioral Assessment, 11*, 339–352.

Whyne-Berman, S. M., & McCann, J. T. (1995). Defense mechanisms and personality disorders: An empirical test of Millon's theory. *Journal of Personality Assessment, 64*, 132–144.

Widiger, T. A. (1985). Review of Millon Clinical Multiaxial Inventory. In J. V. Mitchell, Jr. (Ed.), *Ninth mental measurement yearbook* (pp. 986–988). Lincoln, NE: Buros Institute.

Widiger, T. A. (1989). The categorical distinction between personality and affective disorders. *Journal of Personality Disorders, 3,* 77–91.

Widiger, T. A. (1992). Categorical versus dimensional classification: Implications from and for research. *Journal of Personality Disorders, 6,* 287–300.

Widiger, T. A., & Frances, A. (1987). Interviews and inventories for the measurement of personality disorders. *Clinical Psychology Review, 7,* 49–74.

Widiger, T. A., Frances, A., Spitzer, R. L., & Williams, J. B. (1988). The DSM-III-R personality disorders: An overview. *American Journal of Psychiatry, 145,* 786–795.

Widiger, T. A., Hurt, S. W., Frances, A., Clarkin, J. F., & Gilmore, M. (1984). Diagnostic efficiency and the DSM-III. *Archives of General Psychiatry, 41,* 1005–1012.

Widiger, T. A., & Kelso, K. (1983). Psychodiagnosis of Axis II. *Clinical Psychology Review, 3,* 491–510.

Widiger, T. A., & Sanderson, C. (1987). The convergent and discriminant validity of the MCMI as a measure of the DSM-III personality disorders. *Journal of Personality Assessment, 51,* 228–242.

Widiger, T. A., Williams, J. B. W., Spitzer, R. L., & Frances, A. (1985). The MCMI as a measure of DSM-III. *Journal of Personality Assessment, 49,* 366–378.

Widiger, T. A., Williams, J. B. W., Spitzer, R. L., & Frances, A. (1986). The MCMI and DSM-III: A brief rejoinder to Millon. *Journal of Personality Assessment, 50,* 198–204.

Wierzbicki, M. (1993a). The relationship between MCMI subtlety and severity. *Journal of Personality Assessment, 61,* 259–263.

Wierzbicki, M. (1993b). Use of MCMI subtle and obvious scales to detect faking. *Journal of Clinical Psychology, 49,* 809–814.

Wierzbicki, M., & Daleiden, E. L. (1993). The differential responding of college students to subtle and obvious MCMI subscales. *Journal of Clinical Psychology, 49,* 204–208.

Wierzbicki, M., & Goldade, P. (1993). Sex typing of the Millon Clinical Multiaxial Inventory. *Psychological Reports, 72,* 1115–1121.

Wierzbicki, M., & Howard, B. J. (1992). The differential responding of male prisoners to subtle and obvious MCMI subscales. *Journal of Personality Assessment, 58,* 115–126.

Wiggins, J. S. (1969). Content dimensions in the MMPI. In J. N. Butcher (Ed.), *MMPI: Research developments and clinical applications* (pp. 127–180). New York: McGraw-Hill.

Wiggins, J. S. (1982). Circumplex models of interpersonal behavior in clinical psychology. In P. C. Kendall & J. N. Butcher (Eds.), *Handbook of research methods in clinical psychology* (pp. 183–222). New York: Wiley.

Wiggins, J., & Pincus, A. (1989). Conceptions of personality disorders and dimensions of personality. *Psychological Assessment, 4,* 305–316.

Winston, A., Pinsker, H., & McCullough, L. (1986). A review of supportive psychotherapy. *Hospital and Community Psychiatry, 37,* 1105–1114.

Wise, E. A. (1994a). Managed care and the psychometric validity of the MMPI and MCMI personality disorder scales. *Psychotherapy in Private Practice, 13,* 81–97.

Wise, E. A. (1994b). Personality style codetype concordance between the MCMI and the MBHI. *Journal of Clinical Psychology, 50,* 367–380.

Wise, E. A. (1996). Comparative validity of the MMPI-2 and MCMI-II personality disorder classifications. *Journal of Personality Assessment, 66,* 569–582.

Wolberg, W. H., Tanner, M. A., Romsaas, E. P., Trump, D. L., & Malec, J. F. (1987). Factors influencing options in primary breast cancer treatment. *Journal of Clinical Oncology, 5,* 68–74.

Wright, W. (1975). Counselor dogmatism: Willingness to disclose and client's empathy ratings. *Journal of Counseling Psychology, 22*, 390–394.

Yeager, R. J., DiGiuseppe, R., Resweber, P. J., & Leaf, R. (1992). Comparison of Millon personality profiles of chronic residential substance abusers and a general outpatient population. *Psychological Reports, 71*, 71–79.

Young, D., & Beier, E. (1982). Being asocial in social places: Giving the client a new experience. In J. Anchin & D. Kiesler (Eds.), *Handbook of interpersonal psychotherapy* (pp. 262–273). Elmsford, NY: Pergamon Press.

Zarrella, K. L., Schuerger, J. M., & Ritz, G. H. (1990). Estimation of MCMI DSM-III Axis II constructs from MMPI scales and subscales. *Journal of Personality Assessment, 55*, 195–201.

Author and Subject Index

About the Authors

James P. Choca, PhD, is chief of the Psychology Service at Lakeside Medical Center, Department of Veterans Affairs. He is an associate professor in the Psychology Division, Department of Psychiatry and Behavioral Sciences, Northwestern University Medical School. Dr. Choca serves as a diagnostic consultant in several school districts in the Chicago metropolitan area and as an attending psychologist in three private hospitals. He is the author of numerous articles and book chapters and has given presentations on different aspects of the MCMI. His interest in the use of computers in psychology also has led to articles and presentations, as well as to the development of two commercially available programs: one to administer the Category Test of the Halstead Reitan Battery and one to assist with the administration and scoring of the Rorschach Inkblot Test.

Eric Van Denburg, PhD, is director of Psychology Training at Lakeside VA and is also responsible for directing the Mental Health Clinic at that facility. In addition, he is an assistant professor in the Psychology Division, Department of Psychiatry and Behavioral Sciences, Northwestern University Medical School. Dr. Van Denburg has a private practice in psychotherapy and psychological testing in Chicago. He received his doctorate in clinical psychology from Washington University in 1984, did a postdoctoral fellowship at Harbor-UCLA Medical Center from 1984 to 1985, and completed a 2-year fellowship in psychodynamic psychotherapy at Northwestern Memorial Hospital from 1985 to 1987. Published articles and book chapters span topics such as psychological assessment, hypnosis, and psychotherapy. His articles have appeared in the *International Journal of Clinical and Experimental Hypnosis; American Journal of Psychotherapy; Imagination, Cognition and Personality; American Journal of Clinical Hypnosis;* and *Psychotherapy.* He is married and the proud father of a 7-year-old girl and a 4-year-old boy.